RETHINKING MIGRATION

RETHINKING MIGRATION

New Theoretical and Empirical Perspectives

Edited by

Alejandro Portes

and

Josh DeWind

Berghahn Books

New York • Oxford

Published in 2007 by
Berghahn Books
www.berghahnbooks.com

©2007, 2008 Center for Migration Studies of New York
First paperback edition published in 2008

Library of Congress Cataloging-in-Publication Data

Rethinking migration : new theoretical and emperical perspectives / edited by
Alejandro Portes and Josh DeWind.
      p. cm.
   Includes bibliographical references and index.
   ISBN 978-1-84545-347-3 (hardback : alk. paper) ISBN 978-1-84545-543-9
(paperback : alk. paper)
   1. Emigration and immigration--Political aspects. 2. Emigration and
immigration—Social aspects. 3. Transnationalism. I. Portes, Alejandro, 1944-
II. DeWind, Josh.

   JV6011.R48 2007
   304.8--dc22   2007010522

British Library Cataloguing in Publication Data
A catalogue record for this book is available from the British Library

Printed in the United States on acid-free paper

ISBN 978-1-84545-347-3 (hbk)
ISBN 978-1-84545-543-9 (pbk)

CONTENTS

Part I

Conceptual and Methodological Developments in the Study of International Migration

Chapter 1

A CROSS-ATLANTIC DIALOGUE
The Progress of Research and Theory in the Study of
International Migration

Alejandro Portes and Josh DeWind

The articles included in this volume were originally presented at a conference on "Conceptual and Methodological Developments in the Study of International Migration" held at Princeton University in May 2003. The conference was jointly sponsored by the Committee on International Migration of the Social Science Research Council (SSRC), the Center for Migration and Development (CMD) at Princeton University, and the International Migration Review (IMR). Its purpose was to review recent innovations in this field, both in theory and empirical research, across both sides of the Atlantic. The conference was deliberately organized as a sequel to an earlier, similar event convened by the SSRC on Sanibel Island, Florida, in January 1996 in order to assess the state of international migration studies within the United States from an interdisciplinary perspective. Articles from the first conference were published as *The Handbook of International Migration: The American Experience* (eds., Charles Hirschman, Philip Kasinitz, and Josh DeWind, New York: Russell Sage Foundation, 1999).

The Princeton conference sought to review and update the principal concepts, lines of research, and methodological problems discussed in the *Handbook* and, in this manner gauge what progress the field has been making and in what directions. In contrast to the earlier and more encompassing event, the Princeton conference was thematically selective, targeting only a few strategic topics. It was the first major event of its kind that deliberately sought equal representation of immigration scholars from both sides of the Atlantic. The organizers tried to extend, in this fashion, the scope of the earlier SSRC conference and subsequent publications that had focused primarily on U.S.-bound immigration and patterns of adaptation.

Consequently, this Issue presents, and deliberately contrasts, the approaches taken to the same specific topics in the field of immigration studies by European and North American scholars and the lessons to be learned from one another. By and large, this dialogue occurred among anthropologists, political scientists, and sociologists. Economists were not included in the event for several reasons, such as the significant gap in theorizing and research styles between economics and other social sciences; the major challenge in organizing a meaningful dialogue between economists and other scholars of migration; and the relative abundance of volumes written by economists on the origins and "cost/benefit" ratios of immigration. While convening a future meeting on the economics of migration would be a worthwhile task, the Princeton conference sought instead to bring together specialists from other disciplines in Europe and North America, increasing their mutual knowledge and learning from their different orientations.

For various reasons, the paired symmetry featured in the conference between European and North American contributions could not be preserved in all instances in this final collection. Nevertheless, it presents a wealth of novel ideas and contrasting ways of understanding migration so as to give readers a clearer sense of where the field is moving on both sides of the Atlantic.

THEMATIC LINES

The editors of the *Handbook* grouped the articles from the 1996 Sanibel conference around three basic questions:

1. What motivates people to migrate across international boundaries, often at great financial and psychological costs?
2. How are immigrants changed after arrival? (Responses to this question address such issues as adaptation, assimilation, pluralism, and return migration.)
3. What impacts do immigrants have on American life and its economic, sociocultural, and political institutions? (Hirschman *et al.*, 1999:6).

These three questions aptly synthesize the main goals of the field and the bulk of the existing literature. They are, as it were, the basic pillars supporting the study of immigration. Going beyond them, the first chapter of the *Handbook* outlined a series of thematic priorities for future research grounded on the author's perception of the state of the field back then (Portes, 1999). The chapter argued that there is no such thing as a grand theory of migration encompassing all its aspects and that seeking such a synthesis would be misguided. To encompass the very heterogeneous questions addressed in this field, a comprehensive theory would have to be pitched at such a high level of abstraction as to be useless for the explanation and prediction of concrete processes. Instead, the chapter advocated the development of mid-range concepts and theories and presented a research agenda where this task could be fruitfully attempted. Areas included were:

- Transnationalism and Transnational Communities
- The New Second Generation
- Households and Gender
- States and State Systems
- Cross-national Comparisons

The latter area represents less a substantive field than a call to develop and test concepts and theories comparatively. A first step in this direction is to see how specific topics are approached by scholars in different social and historical contexts, which is one of the goals of the present collection. The remaining four areas above were included and extended in the topical agenda for the Princeton conference which thus offers the opportunity to examine how their analysis evolved in recent years. These topics are:

- States and supra-state entities in the governance of migration and refugee movements
- Modes of immigrant political incorporation in the United States and Europe
- New developments in the study of immigrant transnationalism
- The role of religion in the origins and adaptations of immigrant groups
- The continuing debate on immigrant entrepreneurship and ethnic enclaves
- Methodological problems in the study of the immigrant second generation
- Methodological problems in the study of undocumented migration

This substantive agenda, developed in collaboration by the SSRC Committee, the CMD at Princeton, and the *IMR* editors, attempted to identify areas at the frontier of immigration research that have garnered the attention of theorists and researchers on both sides of the Atlantic in recent years. The different approaches to each of these topics are presented in the following articles and summarized in their respective abstracts. They need not be repeated here. Instead we call attention in this introduction to what we envision as significant developments in one or more of these subfields referring, when appropriate, to articles in this collection.

STATES AND MODES OF POLITICAL INCORPORATION

The first four articles in this issue have to do, in one form or another, with the problematic relationship between national states and international migration. By definition, states seek to regulate what takes place within their borders and what comes from the outside. International migrants are one of the most potent and most problematic of these flows because, unlike commodities or other inanimate exchanges, they are composed of people who can, by their sustained presence, alter the very character of the receiving society. For this reason, as Hollifield (2004) and Castles (2004) contend, all modern states have sought to carefully monitor and regulate such entries in order to balance demands for greater openness and restriction, although their record of performance at this task has been mixed.

As Zolberg (1999) and Castles (2004) have pointed out, the economic distance between the global North and South has become so vast as to create a virtually inexhaustible supply of potential migrants. The gap is aggravated by the forces of capitalist globalization that expose and entice Third World populations to the benefits of modern consumption, while denying them the means to acquire them. In the developed world, meanwhile, a growing thirst for labor willing to perform the harsh and low-paid menial work that citizen workers increasingly avoid creates a powerful magnet for migrants from less developed lands. The fit between such labor needs and the motivations of citizens of the global South to improve their life chances is so powerful as to defy state efforts at controlling it (Hollifield, 2004).

Once international labor flows start, networks emerge between migrants and their places of origin that make the movement self-sustaining over time. Networks tend to develop such strength and momentum as to support continuing migration even after the original economic motives have declined or disappeared (Massey *et al.*, 2002; Massey, 2004; Portes and Bach 1985). The rapid exchange of information and flexibility of these networks can easily bypass official efforts to channel or suppress migrant flows. Governments of sending nations cannot be counted on to cooperate in such efforts either. Almost without exception, Third World countries have come to understand the significant advantages of out-migration, both as a safety valve to alleviate the pressure of domestic scarcities and as a future source of important financial contributions (Guarnizo *et al.*, 2003). There is no logical incentive for these governments to try to repress emigration and every incentive to maintain ties with large expatriate communities functioning as an increasingly important economic resource.

Ambivalently arraigned against these powerful forces are the governments and policies of receiving nations. While the native population of receiving countries tends to be hostile toward large-scale immigration, this sentiment is generally diffuse, it is far from universal, and it seldom coalesces in organized or militant opposition. In contrast, as several authors have noted, the interests of those favoring the continuation of immigrant flows, including the migrants themselves and their employers, are often highly focused and determined (Freeman, 1995, 2004; Cornelius, 1998; Massey *et al.*, 2002). Governments of countries in the developed world are not impotent in the face of those pressures. Indeed, these states represent the key institutional actor enforcing the North/South divide and keeping the vast majority of would-be migrants in their respective countries (Zolberg, 1999). However, the social forces at play inevitably create a gap between regulatory intent and results, frequently leading to paradoxical outcomes. For instance, redoubling border enforcement compels migrant laborers to abandon their previous pattern of circular migration, encouraging them instead to settle in the host country and bring their families. Instead of stopping migration, these "get tough" policies end up consolidating migrants' presence and further entrenching their support networks (Castles, 2004; Portes and Rumbaut, 1996:Ch. 8).

Students of the politics of migration have been preoccupied by a second set of forces hampering official control efforts. By and large, the wealthy receiving nations are also democracies where human rights legislation applies to all those within their borders, not just citizens, preventing state attempts to deal summarily with unwelcome newcomers. Religious groups, philanthropic organizations, and associations of settled migrants stand ready to mobilize the judiciary against the executive branch in the name of migrants' human rights. This gives rise to the "liberal paradox" in which the most powerful nations in the world are prevented by their own laws from effectively controlling or suppressing unwanted immigration (Hollifield, 2004; Freeman, 2004). Figure I summarizes the interplay of forces giving rise to these unexpected consequences.

The complex interplay of political forces supporting international migration is no better reflected than in the rise and growing recognition of dual nationality and dual citizenship. Promoted originally by the governments of sending nations as a means to sustain the loyalty of their expatriates and keep their investments and remittances flowing, dual citizenship has become accepted as well by host countries in the developed world, either explicitly or tacitly. Contradicting the previously enshrined principle in international law that every person must have one and only one nationality, dual citizenship laws are currently accepted and defended as a novel form of political incorporation that reconciles immigrants' competing loyalties and actually facili-

Figure I.   **States and Immigration**

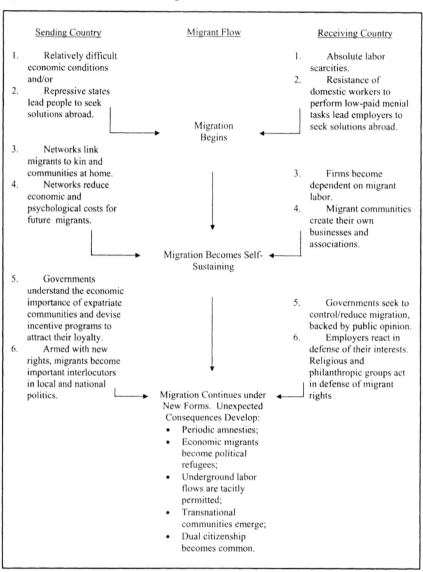

tates their long-term integration to host societies. Though opponents point to the patent injustice of migrants being able to play off one set of national laws against another, something that native citizens cannot do, supporters point to the equally patent justice of giving common people the same transnational reach and rights as those granted to multinational corporations and the wealthy. These dynamics (analyzed in detail by Faist, 2004) show, above all, how the interplay of competing forces outlined in Figure I can lead to unanticipated effects, startlingly at variance with the original expectations of actors involved in the process. The effect of regulatory regimes in state, market, welfare, and cultural domains of Western democracies in promoting the incorporation of immigrants, as described by Freeman (2004), can be offset not only by dual citizenship, but also by other ties that migrants sustain with their homeland societies.

TRANSNATIONAL COMMUNITIES AND IMMIGRANT ENTERPRISE

A second area of increasing theoretical and research interest has been the rise and consolidation of transnational ties between immigrant diasporas and their respective sending countries. Dual citizenship represents the most visible political aspect of this process, but its social, economic, and cultural manifestations are equally important. Transnationalism represents, in this sense, the obverse of the canonical notion of assimilation, sustained as the image of a gradual but irreversible process of acculturation and integration of migrants to the host society. Instead, transnationalism evokes the alternative image of a ceaseless back-and-forth movement, enabling migrants to sustain a presence in two societies and cultures and to exploit the economic and political opportunities created by such dual lives.

The early literature on the topic conveyed the sense that transnationalism was becoming the normative pattern of adaptation among contemporary migrants. "Everyone was doing it," and, hence, old-style assimilation was a thing of the past. Indeed, the call for attention to this field in the first chapter of the *Handbook* argued that:

> Communication facilities, added to the economic, social, and psychological benefits that transnational enterprise can bring, may turn these activities into the normative adaptation path for certain immigrant groups. . . .That path is, of course, at variance with those envisioned by the assimilation perspective. (Portes, 1999:29).

Another question at that time was whether transnational practices existed only among immigrants to the United States or were present elsewhere. The subsequent literature has answered this question affirmatively, while correcting some of the earlier excessive expectations. Indeed, though transnational practices may be as common among immigrants in Europe as among those in the United States, in neither case are they necessarily normative. An empirical, statistically representative survey of Latin American immigrants in the United States discovered that involvement in transnational activities was exceptional, with less than 15 percent of immigrant family heads taking part in them on a regular basis. Even occasional participation was not generalized and involved only a minority of the relevant populations (Portes *et al.*, 2002; Guarnizo *et al.*, 2003; Itzigsohn and Saucedo, 2002).

Despite this numerical limitation, the same study discovered that participants were not generally the most recent or least integrated immigrants, but those who had managed to establish a more solid foothold in the receiving country. Transnational practices were found to increase with time since immigration, a result that leads to the expectation that they would continue to expand in the future. Other studies in the countries of origin demonstrated the enormous impact that remittances, regular visits, and the philanthropic activities organized by expatriates can have on the communities of origin (Smith, 1998; Landolt, 2001; Levitt, 2001). As a Salvadoran sociologist put it trenchantly: "Migration and remittances are the true economic adjustment program of the poor in our country" (Ramos, 2002).

Two of the articles in this issue review the recent literature in this subfield and highlight the potential significance of transnational activities for the identities and social lives of participants, for the political order of sending and receiving states, and for economic development (Vertovec, 2004; Levitt and Glick Schiller, 2004). In their contribution to this issue, Levitt and Glick Schiller trace the development of knowledge in this field and distinguish between "modes of being" and "modes of belonging" as an analytic lens to clarify the organization, meaning, and implications of immigrant transnationalism.

A controversy that began prior to the publication of the *Handbook* was whether there was "anything new" in this concept since practices labeled today as "transnational" could also be found in abundance among earlier immigrant groups, such as those coming to the United States in the nineteenth and early twentieth centuries. That controversy was resolved by a growing consensus that transnationalism represents a new analytic perspective, not a novel phenomenon (Glick Schiller, 1999). Through this analytic lens, it becomes possible to reconceptualize a set of disparate experiences described in the early historical literature, to highlight their common features, and to compare them fruitfully to contemporary events (Smith, 2003).

In addition, there is growing recognition that developments in transportation and communication technologies have qualitatively transformed the character of immigrant transnationalism, turning it into a far more dense and dynamic cross-border exchange than anything that would have been possible in earlier times. No matter how committed and mindful of their native villages Italian or Polish immigrants of an earlier era were, they could not possibly send remittances, make investments, visit, or communicate with kin and friends with the ease and speed made possible by air travel and the internet. Figure II portrays, in synthetic form, the cumulative character of this phenomenon.

A parallel literature on immigrant self-employment and entrepreneurship developed in the past with an almost exclusive domestic focus. Publications on the topic, including those in the *Handbook*, concentrated, almost exclusively, on determinants of entrepreneurship and their economic consequences for those involved (Raijman and Tienda, 1999; Light, 1984; Light and Rosenstein, 1995; Aldrich and Waldinger, 1990). In her contribution to this issue, Zhou makes the important point that immigrant entrepreneurship is frequently tied to the countries of origin and it is thus transnational. This assertion is backed by empirical evidence from the survey of Latin American migrants cited earlier which shows that the majority of self-employed family heads in these communities are actually transnational entrepreneurs (Portes *et al.*, 2002). By linking together previously separate literatures, Zhou's article opens a new perspective on the topic of immigrant entrepreneurship, pointing toward possibilities for its expansion and development beyond what an exclusively domestic perspective would allow.

The same article makes a second theoretical contribution by highlighting the noneconomic consequences of immigrant enclaves (one of the three forms of entrepreneurship distinguished in the literature), especially with regard to the adaptation process of the second generation. Zhou points out that these tightly-knit communities, with a high diversity of institutional resources, promote selective acculturation and, hence, high self-esteem and a strong achievement orientation among second-generation youths. They also furnish them with the resources and information necessary to succeed, which are absent or less abundant among less entrepreneurial migrant groups. The various ways in which these resources are made available to children of immigrants are described in detail in the article.

UNAUTHORIZED IMMIGRATION AND THE SECOND GENERATION

From a methodological standpoint, one of the most persistently difficult problems in this field is the measurement and analysis of determinants of

Figure II.   **The Process of Immigrant Transnationalism**

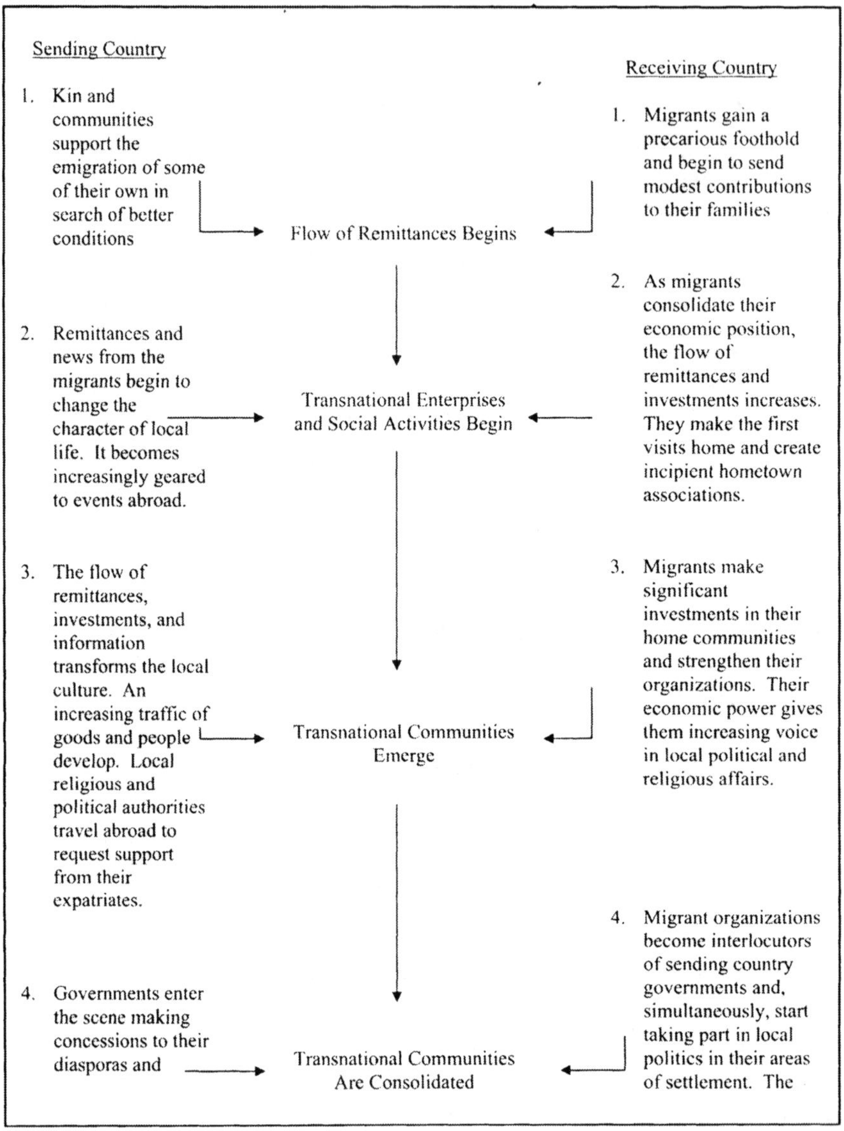

Sending Country

Receiving Country

1. Kin and
    communities
    support the
    emigration of some
    of their own in
    search of better
    conditions

1. Migrants gain a
    precarious foothold
    and begin to send
    modest contributions
    to their families

Flow of Remittances Begins

2. As migrants
    consolidate their
    economic position,
    the flow of
    remittances and
    investments increases.
    They make the first
    visits home and create
    incipient hometown
    associations.

2. Remittances and
    news from the
    migrants begin to
    change the
    character of local
    life. It becomes
    increasingly geared
    to events abroad.

Transnational Enterprises
and Social Activities Begin

3. The flow of
    remittances,
    investments, and
    information
    transforms the local
    culture. An
    increasing traffic of
    goods and people
    develop. Local
    religious and
    political authorities
    travel abroad to
    request support
    from their
    expatriates.

Transnational Communities
Emerge

3. Migrants make
    significant
    investments in their
    home communities
    and strengthen their
    organizations. Their
    economic power gives
    them increasing voice
    in local political and
    religious affairs.

4. Migrant organizations
    become interlocutors
    of sending country
    governments and,
    simultaneously, start
    taking part in local
    politics in their areas
    of settlement. The

4. Governments enter
    the scene making
    concessions to their
    diasporas and

Transnational Communities
Are Consolidated

unauthorized immigration. The illegal flow of persons across national borders wreaks havoc with national population statistics as well as with attempts
to establish a measure of order and regulation in labor markets. In their
contributions to this issue, Douglas Massey and Friedrich Heckmann ad-

dress the problem from different perspectives. Massey examines in detail reasons why census data, surveys, or deportation statistics provide very imperfect coverage of the phenomenon, given its elusive nature. He proposes instead the methodology of "ethnosurveys" based on detailed interviews of individuals and families in communities of origin and extensive data gathering of the characteristics of these communities themselves.

The data generated by Massey's Mexican Migration Project (MMP) and Latin American Migration Project (LMP) provide ample evidence that labor-intensive ethnosurveys can provide reliable information on the extent of unauthorized migration, its determinants, and its relationships to parallel legal flows (Massey, 1987, 2004; Massey and Espinosa, 1997). But, when financial or time constraints prevent the implementation of this measurement approach, other approximations may be necessary. Heckmann discusses several of these for the German case, including interviews with apprehended aliens, statistics regarding asylum applicants already living in Germany, and in-depth ethnographic studies of networks of people smugglers. This last approach appears uniquely suitable for the analysis of long-distance clandestine flows, such as those originating in China and the Asian successor states of the former Soviet Union that ferry people into Western Europe and the United States (Heckmann, 2004; Kyle and Koslowski, 2001).

From a theoretical standpoint, enough empirical information exists to arrive at a general understanding of the determinants of unauthorized flows. They emerge out of the clash between attempts to enforce borders by receiving states and the mutually supportive forces of migrant motivations, their networks, and employer demand for low wage labor in host societies. The networks constructed by migrants across national borders and the "migration industry" of travel agents, lawyers, people smugglers, document forgers, and the like have proven extraordinarily resilient over time. The length to which people are willing to go in order to reach the developed world is palpable proof of the wide and growing economic gap between the global North and South (Zolberg, 1989, 1999; Castles, 1986, 2004).

At the same time, however, stagnant or declining populations, growing economies, and an increasing reluctance by educated workers to engage in menial, low-wage labor creates a structural demand in the labor market of wealthy nations that migrants are more than happy to fill (Bach and Brill, 1991; Cornelius, 1998; Ballard, 2000). Common depictions of "alien invasions" in the popular literature neglect the fact that migrants in general, and unauthorized ones in particular, come not only because they want to but because they are wanted. While the general population may oppose their presence, firms and employers in a number of sectors need and rely heavily upon this labor supply (Portes and Rumbaut, 1996:Ch. 3; Massey *et al.*, 2002).

Faced with the combined forces of migrant networks, the migration industry, and structural labor demand, receiving states have not been able to consistently and effectively control their borders. As we have seen above, a series of unexpected consequences emerge instead out of this clash. One of the most important and least noticed is the link between unauthorized migration and the fate of the second generation. The issue of illegality is generally studied as a first-generation phenomenon, in terms of the migrants' origins, their ways of overcoming legal barriers, and their impact on host labor markets. Forgotten is the fact that illegals, like other migrants, can spawn a second generation that grows up under conditions of unique disadvantage despite their legal citizenship.

The concept of segmented assimilation was coined to highlight the point that, under present circumstances, children of immigrants growing up in the United States confront a series of challenges to their successful adaptation that will define the long-term position in American society of themselves and their descendants – the ethnic groups spawned by today's immigration. Facing barriers of widespread racism, a bifurcated labor market, the ready presence of countercultural models in street gangs and the drug culture, immigrants' success depends on the economic and social resources that they, their families, and their communities can muster (Portes and Zhou, 1993; Rumbaut, 1994). Immigrant professionals and entrepreneurs commonly possess the necessary human capital and economic means to protect their children. They can face the challenges posed by the host society with a measure of equanimity.

Immigrants of more modest backgrounds but who are part of strong, solidary communities can create the necessary social capital to support parental expectations and steer youths away from the lures of consumerism, drugs, and the culture of the street. In such cases, immigrant families are able to create a measure of "closure," supporting one another's expectations and steering children to success in the educational system (Coleman, 1988; Zhou and Bankston, 1996). On the other hand, poorly educated migrants who come to fill menial positions at the bottom of the labor market and who lack strong community bonds have greater difficulty supporting their youths. Because of poverty, these migrants often move into central city areas where their children are served by poor schools and are daily exposed to countercultural models and deviant lifestyles.

The trajectory followed by a number of children of immigrants trapped in this situation has been labeled downward assimilation to denote the fact that, in their case, acculturation to the norms and values of the host society is not a ticket for material success and status advancement, but exactly the opposite. Dropping out of school, adolescent pregnancies, incidents of arrest and incarceration, injuries or death in gang fights, and increasing conflict and estrangement from parents are all consequences and indicators of this situation. Because of their situation of unique vulnerability, children of unauthorized immigrants are among the most likely to confront challenges posed by the host society unaided and, hence, to be at risk of downward assimilation (Fernandez-Kelly and Curran, 2001; Lopez and Stanton-Salazar, 2001).

In the past, it made sense to study unauthorized immigration as a one-generation phenomenon because the flow was comprised of young adults who came to the United States for cyclical work periods, such as those marked by agricultural harvests, and then returned home. As seen previously, vigorous border enforcement has encouraged unauthorized migrants and others in tenuous legal positions to bring their families along, as cyclical returns home become too costly or dangerous. This pattern appears to be common to receiving countries on both sides of the Atlantic (Cornelius, 1998; Massey et al., 2002; Castles, 1984, 2004; Heckmann, 2004). A settled unauthorized population in these countries establishes the demographic basis for the emergence of a handicapped second generation and, hence, for the theoretical link between determinants of these flows and the process of segmented assimilation. Figure III graphically portrays the process, as it has taken place in the United States.

It is not clear whether this model is entirely applicable to the second generation in Western Europe. It is possible that in urban cores lacking entrenched deviant subcultures and in very different contexts of reception, immigrants follow alternative paths not contemplated in the segmented assimilation model. One such possibility, adumbrated by one of the articles discussed next, is the perpetuation across generations of institutionally diverse ethnic communities that maintain their own language and customs and create parallel hierarchies of prestige and power.

In their contributions to this issue, Rubén Rumbaut and Hartmut Esser approach the topic of the second generation from very different perspectives. Rumbaut's article is an inductive effort to disaggregate the concept of second generation by demonstrating the empirical variations in important adaptation outcomes among immigrant children arriving in the United

Figure III.   **Immigration Border Control and its Unexpected Consequences**

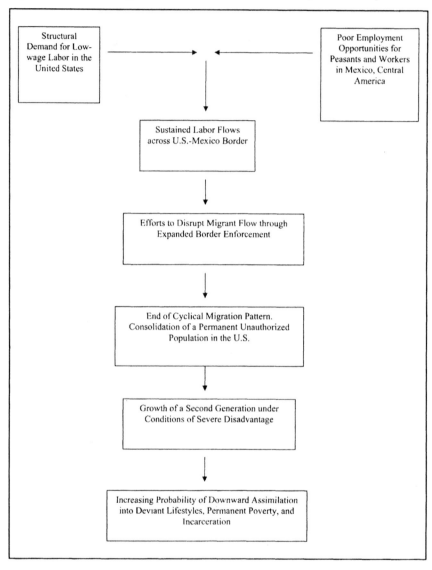

States at different points of their life cycle. In distinguishing between the 1.25, 1.5, 1.75, 2.00 (U.S. born, two immigrant parents), and even 2.5 (U.S. born, one immigrant parent) generations, he finds significant differences with regard to language acquisition, education, and occupational attainments. Hartmut Esser takes the opposite tack, offering us a broad deductive theory presumably applicable to all immigrant groups. Inspired by rational action theory, the model focuses on the utility functions that immigrants and their offspring have for investing in "host country capital" (*i.e.*, language instruction and education in the receiving country) as opposed to "ethnic community capital" (preserving the culture, language, and social networks grounded in their home nations).

Despite its proposed generality, this original effort at theory building has the historical experience of West Germany and other European countries as tacit background insofar as it takes as its main *explanandum* the possible perpetuation of cohesive and more or less institutionally complete ethnic communities across generations, which may even mobilize politically to impose their views on the host society. This possibility is difficult to conceive in the United States where immigrant communities, including the most institutionally diverse ethnic enclaves, tend to weaken and eventually disappear in the course of two or three generations. In the North American context, the question is not whether assimilation will take place, but to what segment of American society will migrants assimilate. Americans all, the descendants of today's immigrants may find themselves in very different positions in the society's hierarchies of prestige and power, depending on the resources that they, their families, and their communities were able to bring to the fray.

By reframing the European experience in theoretical terms, Esser's analysis raises the possibility of revising the concept of segmented assimilation to include refusal to assimilate and the perpetuation of autonomous ethnic social systems over generations. Overall, Rumbaut's and Esser's contributions highlight the contrasting perspectives that can be brought to bear on the same topic by scholars coming from different intellectual traditions and, hence, the fruitfulness of a cross-Atlantic dialogue. The same lesson is apparent in the last substantive issue covered in this chapter.

THE ROLE OF RELIGION IN MIGRANT INCORPORATION

Until recently, the theoretical literature on immigration imitated, unwittingly, the French state emphasis on *laïcité* by focusing on the economic, political, linguistic, and identificational parameters of immigrant incorporation, while ignoring the presence and effects of religion. This has been changing as a result of several factors that include: 1) empirical evidence pointing to the strong and growing presence of religion in the general American population (Hout and Greeley, 1998); 2) additional studies pointing to the importance of religious beliefs and communities in the emergence of transnational communities and the successful integration of the second generation (Ebaugh and Chafetz, 2002; Levitt, 2003; Zhou and Bankston, 1996, 1998); and 3) the rise of Islam as an organized religious presence in Western Europe and the United States and the subsequent series of confrontations and negotiations with national states.

The articles by Charles Hirschman and Riva Kastoryano on religion and immigrant incorporation point, once again, to the wide differences in perspectives arising from diverse national contexts and intellectual traditions. Hirschman takes a historical, ground-up perspective in highlighting the vital significance of religious identity and the material resources of religious institutions in the early incorporation and subsequent integration of immigrant groups in the United States. The focus is resolutely on the migrants themselves and on the religious institutions which, like the Catholic Church, protected them from mainstream Protestant hostility, helped them preserve their language and customs, educated their children, and launched their second generation into successful careers and lives. The American state is, at best, a distant presence, processing and often renaming migrants at Ellis Island, but otherwise letting them fend for themselves in the new land.

By contrast, Kastoryano resolutely focuses on contemporary trends and on the role of West European states as they attempt to absorb the Muslim population in their midst and incorporate it into the national body politic. Hers is a top-down perspective with the state-religion dynamics at the core of the narrative. Those dynamics vary significantly from one case (France), where official efforts center on weakening past loyalties and incorporating migrants and their descendants into a common civic culture, to another (Germany), where the predominant orientation is toward recognition and institutionalization of distinct religious/ethnic minorities. In contrast to the American experience, where ethnicity – heavily backed by religious institutions – was allowed to play itself over the years in the private sphere, the European cases show the heavy hand of the state as it intervenes to mold and shape the course of ethnic identities and religious loyalties. Not surprisingly, such an interventionist stance has often resulted in unexpected consequences, including some that were the reverse of those intended. Kastoryano insightfully analyzes these outcomes.

Religious beliefs and the institutions that support them can play significant roles in each of the substantive areas discussed previously: state attempts to regulate migration and the "liberal paradox"; immigrant transnationalism and entrepreneurship; illegal immigration and the rise of a new second generation. By and large, religion has been less a main determinant of migration and incorporation than one that led to a series of "interaction effects" with other factors: it seldom creates immigrant flows by itself, but accompanies them and cushions their roughest transitions; it does not dictate state policy, but helps implement it or, alternatively, resists it when seen as inimical to the interests of its members; it seldom initiates transnational activities, but strengthens them through the activities and connections of churches, mosques, and temples from "here" and "there"; it does not create the social context confronted by the second generation, but can become a vital force in guiding youths and helping integrate them successfully. Figure IV graphically portrays these relationships.

Figure IV. **Religion and Immigrant Incorporation: Interaction Effects**

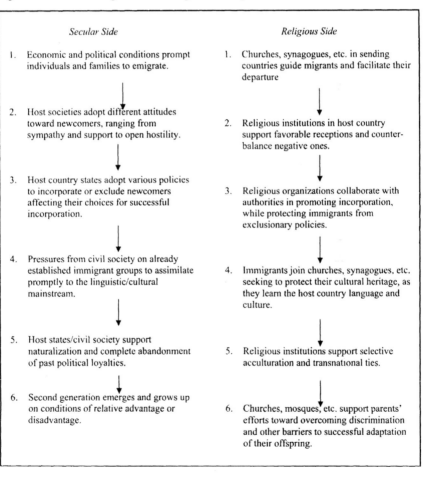

Secular Side

1. Economic and political conditions prompt individuals and families to emigrate.

2. Host societies adopt different attitudes toward newcomers, ranging from sympathy and support to open hostility.

3. Host country states adopt various policies to incorporate or exclude newcomers affecting their choices for successful incorporation.

4. Pressures from civil society on already established immigrant groups to assimilate promptly to the linguistic/cultural mainstream.

5. Host states/civil society support naturalization and complete abandonment of past political loyalties.

6. Second generation emerges and grows up on conditions of relative advantage or disadvantage.

Religious Side

1. Churches, synagogues, etc. in sending countries guide migrants and facilitate their departure

2. Religious institutions in host country support favorable receptions and counterbalance negative ones.

3. Religious organizations collaborate with authorities in promoting incorporation, while protecting immigrants from exclusionary policies.

4. Immigrants join churches, synagogues, etc. seeking to protect their cultural heritage, as they learn the host country language and culture.

5. Religious institutions support selective acculturation and transnational ties.

6. Churches, mosques, etc. support parents' efforts toward overcoming discrimination and other barriers to successful adaptation of their offspring.

On the whole, religious interactions and interventions have been guided by a logic entirely at variance with the core beliefs underlying state policy and the dominant stereotypes held by the native population. That logic is well captured in Hirschman's observation that "immigrants become Americans by joining a church and participating in its religious and community life" (Hirschman, this issue). In other words, the road to successful integration passes through the creation of ethnic communities and the re-assertion of a common cultural background, with strong religious under-tones. By contrast, the predominant orientation among the native-born population and often among state authorities is that immigrants' vigorous assertion of distinct ethnic identities and foreign cultures somehow under-mines the unity of the nation and the preservation of its integrity.

In their time, Irish Catholics and Russian Jews were targets of such accusations and their "Popish" loyalties and Semitic clannishness denounced as un-American and contrary to national values. In 1917, Madison Grant deplored "The Passing of the Great Race" and blamed the Russian Jews, Italians, and others for the "mongrelization of America" (Grant, 1916). Riots, lynchings, exclusionary quotas and widespread discrimination fol-lowed (Handlin, 1973; Vecoli, 1977; Howe, 1976; Greeley, 1971). Merci-fully, the American state was either too weak or too indifferent to take a heavy interventionist stance, letting immigrant groups develop their own social and cultural institutions, including their parishes, school, and syna-gogues. The long-term results of such developments are celebrated today as the success stories of European immigrant groups in the United States and of the American ability to integrate them. That "ability" was grounded precisely in the state doing rather little and religious institutions doing a great deal. The lesson can provide a salutary point of reference as Western European states and societies ponder today ways to cope with the growing Islamic population in their midst.

CONCLUSION: ADVANCING A CROSS-ATLANTIC DIALOGUE

One reason that the SSRC's Committee on International Migration began its work, including the 1996 Sanibel conference and the resulting *Handbook*, by focusing on "the American experience" was that consolidating a national and interdisciplinary perspective seemed to be a necessary preliminary step toward being able to structure meaningful comparisons. The development of post-World War II migration studies in the United States, Europe, and other countries has laid a foundation for a variety of cross-national comparisons and collaborations. The inclusion in this issue of chapters by European and North American scholars illustrates various types and benefits of such comparisons and suggests other forms of international scholarly collaborations. While this volume does not provide the basis for elaborating a full agenda for the internationalization of migration studies, we believe that a number of issues merit notice and consideration in subsequent efforts to organize international exchanges.

As objects of research, nations provide useful comparative contexts for assessing the significance of similarities and differences in migration processes and outcomes. The articles in this issue illustrate advantages that can be derived from the comparative methods of agreement and difference (Mill, 1846). Like Mill's method of comparative agreement, the approaches of Hollified, Castles, and Faist assume the basic similarity of liberal democracies as a context and then provide unified models or frameworks for identifying and explaining cross-national differences in immigrant incorporation. Consistent with Mill's method of comparative difference, the articles of Hirschman and Kastoryano, by focusing on the distinctive roles of religion in the incorporation of immigrants in the United States and in France and Germany, respectively, highlight important dissimilarities between each state's involvement in constructing national identities and cultures.

The depth and significance of insights that can be gained from such cross-national comparisons of research findings depends in large measure, of course, on the methods upon which the research is based. The article by Rumbaut makes clear the importance of precision in defining, distinguishing, and employing analytical concepts. Similarly the article by Heckmann highlights the importance of employing a variety of methods – ranging from the qualitative to the quantitative – in adapting to the topical focus of the research and variable access to reliable information. Though scholars from different countries and disciplines might have preferences for various methodological approaches to research and analysis, there is no reason to closely identify such approaches with the nationality of scholars themselves.

Despite the existing facility and significance of cross-national comparisons in the field of migration studies, the articles by Levitt and Glick Schiller and by Vertovec on transnational aspects of migration and other global processes remind us that nation-states and national societies are not the only units or contexts for migration that ought to be the focus of internationally comparative scholarship. In defining the concept of "social fields" in order to identify the boundaries of migrants' transnational networks, Levitt and

Glick Schiller assume such cross-border relations will connect migrants on various levels – local, regional, and global, as well as national. No matter how transnational communities are bounded, their networks or social fields are also useful units for comparisons of agreement and difference. Vertovec's article goes further in suggesting how the "bi-focality" of transnational migration affects other global processes, such as economic development. Thus migration flows can not only be compared with regard to their relations with other global processes, but those relationships themselves are proper subjects for comparative research and analysis.

In this examination of only a few of the ways in which international scholarship on migration can be fruitfully linked, it becomes clear that doing so requires concepts, frameworks, and methodologies designed for this purpose. But, like the original orientation of the SSRC International Migration Program, most scholars' disciplinary training is focused on examining migration within single national contexts. This tendency suggests that internationalizing the field of migration studies so that scholars can collaborate more fully in refining concepts or advancing theoretical explanations will in the future require a different kind of training and a more explicitly comparative intellectual stance. The insights that have resulted from bringing together scholars from Europe and the United States in this issue are an indication of the potential value that promoting such international efforts can bring to the field of migration studies.

REFERENCES

Aldrich, H. and R. Waldinger
1990　"Ethnicity and Entrepreneurship," *Annual Review of Sociology,* 16:111–135.

Bach, R. L. and H. Brill
1991　*Impact of IRCA on the U.S. Labor Market and Economy.* Report to the U.S. Department of Labor, Institute for Research on International Labor. Binghamton: State University of New York.

Ballard, R.
2000　"The South Asian Presence in Britain and Its Transnational Connections." Article Presented at the International Workshop on Transnational Research, Sponsored by the Social Science Research Council and the Economic and Social Research Council (U.K.), Oxford University, July.

Castles, S.
2004　"The Factors that Make and Unmake Migration Policies," *International Migration Review,* 38(3):852–885.

———
1986　"The Guest-Worker in Western Europe: An Obituary," *International Migration Review,* 20(4):761–778.

1984 *Here for Good: Western Europe's New Ethnic Minorities.* London: Pluto Press.

Coleman, J. S.
1988 "Social Capital in the Creation of Human Capital," *American Journal of Sociology,* 94:S95–121. Supplement.

Cornelius, W. A.
1998 "The Structural Embeddedness of Demand for Mexican Immigrant Labor: New Evidence from California." In *Crossings, Mexican Immigration in Interdisciplinary Perspective.* Ed. M. Suarez-Orozco. Cambridge: Center for Latin American Studies, Harvard University. Pp. 115–155.

Ebaugh, H. R. and J. Saltzman Chafetz, eds.
2002 *Religion across Borders: Transnational Immigrant Networks.* Altamira Press.

Fernandez-Kelly, P. and S. Curran
2001 "Nicaraguans: Voices Lost, Voices Found." In *Ethnicities: Children of Immigrants in America.* Ed. R. G. Rumbaut and A. Portes. Berkeley: University of California Press and Russell Sage Foundation.

Freeman, G. P.
2004 "Immigrant Incorporation in Western Democracies," *International Migration Review,* 38(3):945–970.

1995 "Modes of Immigration Politics in Liberal Democratic States," *International Migration Review,* 29(4):881–902.

Glick Schiller, N.
1999 "Transmigrants and Nation-States: Something Old and Something New in the U.S. Immigrant Experience." In *Handbook of International Migration: The American Experience.* Ed. C. Hirschman, P. Kasinitz and J. DeWind. New York: Russell Sage Foundation. Pp. 94–119.

Grant, M.
1916 *The Passing of the Great Race, Or, the Racial Basis of European History.* Scribner's.

Greeley, A. M.
1971 *Why Can't They Be Like Us? America's White Ethnic Groups.* New York: E. P. Dutton.

Greeley, A. and M. Hout
1999 "Americans Increasing Belief in Life after Death," *American Sociological Review,* 64: 813–835.

Guarnizo, L. E., A. Portes and W. J. Haller
2003 "Assimilation and Transnationalism: Determinants of Transnational Political Action among Contemporary Immigrants," *American Journal of Sociology,* 108:1211–1248. May.

Handlin, O.
1973 *The Uprooted: The Epic Story of the Great Migrations That Made the American People. Second Edition.* Boston, MA: Little, Brown.

Heckmann, F.
2004 "Illegal Migration: What Can We Know and What Can We Explain? The Case of Germany," *International Migration Review,* 38(3):1103–1126.

Hirschman, C., P. Kasinitz and J. DeWind
1999 *Handbook of International Migration: The American Experience.* New York: Russell Sage Foundation.

Hollifield, J.
2004 "The Emerging Migration State," *International Migration Review*, 38(3):885–913.

Hout, M. and A. M. Greeley
1998 "What Church Officials' Reports Don't Show: Another Look at Church Attendance Data," *American Sociological Review*, 63:113–119.

Howe, I.
1976 *World of Our Fathers.* New York: Harcort, Brace, and Jovanovich.

Itzigsohn, J. and S. G. Saucedo
2002 "Immigrant Incorporation and Sociocultural Transnationalism," *International Migration Review*, 36(3):766–799.

Kyle, D. and R. Koslowski
2001 *Global Human Smuggling: Comparative Perspectives.* Baltimore, MD: Johns Hopkins University Press.

Landolt, P.
2001 "Salvadoran Economic Transnationalism: Embedded Strategies for Household Maintenance, Immigrant Incorporation, and Entrepreneurial Expansion," *Global Networks*, 1:217–242.

Levitt, P.
2003 "'You Know, Abraham Was Really the First Immigrant': Religion and Transnational Migration," *International Migration Review*, 37(3):847–873.

———
2001 *The Transnational Villagers.* Berkeley: University of California Press.

Levitt, P. and N. Glick Schiller
2004 "Conceptualizing Simultaneity: A Transnational Social Field Perspective on Society," *International Migration Review*, 38(3):1002–1040.

Light, I.
1984 "Immigrant and Ethnic Enterprise in North America," *Ethnic and Racial Studies*, 7:195–216.

Light, I. and C. Rosenstein
1995 "Expanding the Interaction Theory of Entrepreneurship." In *The Economic Sociology of Immigration.* Ed. A. Portes. New York: Russell Sage. Pp. 166–212.

Lopez, D. E. and R. D. Stanton-Salazar
2001 "Mexican-Americans: A Second Generation at Risk." In *Ethnicities: Children of Immigrants in America.* Ed. R. G. Rumbaut and A. Portes. Berkeley: University of California Press and Russell Sage Foundation. Pp. 57–90.

Massey, D. S.
2004 "Measuring Undocumented Migration," *International Migration Review*, 38(3):1075–1103.

———
1987 "Understanding Mexican Migration to the United States," *American Journal of Sociology*, 92:1372–1403.

Massey, D. S. and K. E. Espinosa
1997 "What's Driving Mexico-U.S. Migration? A Theoretical, Empirical, and Policy Analysis," *American Journal of Sociology*, 102:939–999.

Massey, D. S., J. Durand and N. J. Malone
2002 *Beyond Smoke and Mirrors: Mexican Immigration in an Era of Economic Integration.* New York: Russell Sage Foundation.

Mill, J. S.
1846   *A System of Logic: Ratiocinative and Inductive: Being a Connected View of The Principles of Evidence and the Methods of Scientific Investigation.* New York: Harper and Brothers.

Portes, A.
1999   "Immigration Theory for a New Century: Some Problems and Opportunities." In *Handbook of International Migration: The American Experience.* Ed. C. Hirschman, P. Kasinitz, and J. DeWind. New York: Russell Sage Foundation. Pp. 21–33.

Portes, A. and R. L. Bach
1985   *Latin Journey: Cuban and Mexican Immigrants in the United States.* Berkeley, CA: University of California Press.

Portes, A., W. Haller and L. E. Guarnizo
2002   "Transnational Entrepreneurs: An Alternative Form of Immigrant Adaptation," *American Sociological Review,* 67:278–298. April.

Portes, A. and R. G. Rumbaut
1996   *Immigrant America: A Portrait.* Berkeley, CA: University of California Press.

Portes, A. and M. Zhou
1993   "The New Second Generation: Segmented Assimilation and Its Variants among Post-1965 Immigrant Youth," *The Annals of the American Academy of Political and Social Sciences,* 530:74–96.

Raijman, R. and M. Tienda
1999   "Immigrants' Socioeconomic Progress Post-1965: Forging Mobility or Survival." In *Handbook of International Migration: The American Experience.* Ed. C. Hirschman, P. Kasinitz and J. DeWind. New York: Russell Sage Foundation. Pp. 239–256.

Ramos, C. G.
2002   "Rapporteurs' Comments." Delivered at the Conference on Immigrant Transnationalism and its Impact on Sending Nations. Sponsored by the Center for Migration and Development, Princeton University and Latin American School of Social Science (FLASCO), Santo Domingo, D.R. January.

Rumbaut, R.
1994   "The Crucible Within: Ethnic Identity, Self-Esteem, and Segmented Assimilation among Children of Immigrants," *International Migration Review,* 28(4):748–794.

Smith, R. C.
2003   "Diasporic Memberships in Historical Perspective," *International Migration Review,* 37(3):724–759.

1998   "Mexican Immigrants, the Mexican State, and the Transnational Practice of Mexican Politics and Membership," *LASA Forum,* 24:19–24.

Vecoli, R.
1977   "The Italian Americans." In *Uncertain Americans: Readings in Ethnic History.* Ed. L. Dinnerstein and F. C. Jaher. New York: Oxford University Press. Pp. 201–215.

Vertovec, S.
2004   "Migrant Transnationalism and Modes of Transformation," *International Migration Review,* 38(3):970–1001.

Zhou, M. and C. Bankston
1998   *Growing Up American: How Vietnamese Immigrants Adapt to Life in the United States.* New York: Russell Sage Foundation.

1996 "Social Capital and the Adaptation of the Second Generation: The Case of Vietnamese Youth in New Orleans." In *The New Second Generation*. Ed. A. Portes. New York: Russell Sage Foundation. Pp. 197–220.

Zolberg, A.
1999 "Matters of State: Theorizing Immigration Policy." In *Handbook of International Migration: The American Experience*. Ed. C. Hirschman, P. Kasinitz, and J. DeWind. New York: Russell Sage Foundation. Pp. 71–93.

1989 "The Next Waves: Migration Theory for a Changing World," *International Migration Review*, 23(3):403–431.

Part II

STATES AND MODES OF POLITICAL INCORPORATION

Chapter 2

THE FACTORS THAT MAKE AND UNMAKE MIGRATION POLICIES[1]

Stephen Castles

Observers of international migration are often struck by the failure of states to effectively manage migration and its effects on society. In particular, undocumented migration keeps growing despite control efforts by states and supranational bodies. "Paradoxically, the ability to control migration has shrunk as the desire to do so has increased" (Bhagwati, 2003). This is not to say that states always, or even mostly, fail to influence migration through their policies. As Mark Miller has written: "what governments do matters a great deal" (Castles and Miller, 2003:94). But there are many cases in which governments fail to achieve their declared objectives. Here are two examples.

Australia defined itself historically as a white outpost of Europe. Ever since British settlement in 1788, Australians have felt threatened by 'Asia's teeming millions.' When the Australian federal state was founded in 1901, one of its first legislative acts was to establish the White Australia Policy. After World War II, Australia set up a large-scale immigration program. The government believed that the small population (7.5 million in a continent as

[1]This article is based on a paper presented at the Conference on Conceptual and Methodological Developments in the Study of International Migration, Princeton University, May 23–24, 2003. I thank the discussant, Mark J. Miller and the other participants for their comments. I also thank Alejandro Portes and Josh DeWind for their suggestions. An earlier version of some parts of the argument is to be found in Castles (2004).

big as the United States) made the country vulnerable to invasion and that a larger labor force was vital to industrial growth. The government persuaded a skeptical public to accept the policy by declaring that the great majority of immigrants would be British and the rest white and European. As non-British entries grew, the public was assured that a policy of assimilation would prevent cultural change. However, by the 1970s, the White Australia Policy was unsustainable in the face of increasing trade with Asia. Increasing numbers of immigrants were non-European. Similarly, assimilation failed due to processes of labor market segmentation, residential segregation and ethnic community formation. Australia became one of the world's most ethnically diverse societies, and a policy of multiculturalism was introduced. Despite a backlash in the mid-1990s, the policy has been retained by successive governments (Castles and Vasta, 2004; Jupp, 2002).

A second example is Germany, which recruited migrant workers from 1955 to 1973. The guestworkers were to come for a few years only and were not supposed to bring in dependents or settle permanently. Germany's model of national identity was based on ideas of common descent and culture, and it had no place for ethnic minorities – as recent history had shown so dramatically. After labor recruitment was stopped in 1973, the newcomers started to settle and form distinct communities. Yet German leaders continued to recite the mantra that "the German Federal Republic is not a country of immigration." It was not until the late 1990s that German politicians were forced to recognize the permanent nature of immigration. The 1999 citizenship law represented a historic shift from *ius sanguinis* (citizenship by descent) to *ius soli* (citizenship by birth on the territory). In 2001, an official commission finally recognized that Germany is and indeed has always been a country of immigration (Süssmuth, 2001).

These cases both concern strong, efficient states with long traditions of active migration policy. Clearly, it is not just weak states that experience policy failures. Moreover, both governments initially saw their policies as successful – policy failure only became obvious after many years. Thus, migration policies may fail because they are based on short-term and narrow views of the migratory process. It is important to look at the entire migratory process, starting from the initial movement right through to settlement, community formation and emergence of new generations in the immigration country. Third, it appears that there were factors inherent in the experience of migration which led to outcomes that were not necessarily expected or wanted by the participants. It is therefore necessary to analyze the migratory process as a long-term social process with its own inherent dynamics.

What constitutes 'policy failure'? This is not used here as a normative term. Some people might say that both Germany and Australia are better places because of immigration and the emergence of multicultural societies. Rather, policy failure can be said to occur when a policy does not achieve its stated objectives – in the case of Australia, to remain white and monocultural; in the case of Germany, to import labor and not people. This leads to an analytical problem: it premises judgments about the success of policies on the existence of explicit and honest policy objectives. But policymakers may be reluctant to declare their true objectives for fear of arousing opposition. This makes it necessary to deconstruct official goals and look for hidden agendas. One yardstick could be the failure to use effective measures to achieve declared objectives – even when such measures are obvious and available. An example is the failure to enforce employer sanctions to prevent illegal employment in the United States, Japan and many other countries. In any case, policy success or failure depends on the eye of the beholder. Few policies fail completely. Rather they tend to achieve some of their objectives, but not all, or to have unintended consequences.

This article focuses mainly on migration from less-developed countries to industrial countries. It starts by looking briefly at the history of state migration management. Then it examines a range of factors which shape migratory processes and discusses the interaction of these factors in shaping state policies – and in undermining them. The central argument is that the various factors are so complex that states tend towards compromises and contradictory policies. This is partly because of conflicts between competing social interests and partly because of the way the policy process works. An important underlying reason is the contradiction between the national logic of migration control and the transnational logic of international migration in an epoch of globalization. Finally, the article suggests some elements of a conceptual framework for more effective policy formation and discusses elements of policies at the national, regional and global levels.

MIGRATION POLICY IN HISTORY

Until recently, many migration theorists (especially in the United States) accepted a long-standing orthodoxy that migration was mainly determined by market forces. Neoclassical economists, who often had the ear of policymakers, argued that this should be so and that state action merely distorted the "migration market," often with negative consequences (Borjas, 1989). However, migration control by the state actually has a long history. The market factors posited as crucial in economic theory often did not shape migration, because "border control usually intervenes as a determinative factor." Potential receiving countries restrict entry, by erecting "protective walls" with "small doors that allow for specific flows" (Zolberg, 1989:405–406). If we look back in history, we find a variety of state roles, some of which go far beyond mere border control.

Potential emigration countries have often tried to prohibit departures. Mercantilist European monarchs saw their wealth as consisting mainly of people and forbade departure (Fahrmeir, Faron and Weil, 2003:3). In the 1820s, industrializing Britain banned emigration of skilled workers, who were being enticed away by employers from France, Russia, Germany and America (Thompson, 1968:272). More recently, European fascist regimes refused to let people depart. That is why many Portuguese and Spanish migrants to France in the 1960s had to cross the Pyrenees with the help of smugglers. When they arrived they were regularized as workers – not refugees (Castles and Kosack, 1973:34–35). The Soviet Bloc prohibited departure, which made it easy for Western countries to have generous asylum policies towards those few who did get out. This was to change in the early 1990s: once the nondeparture regime collapsed, Western countries hastened to establish a nonarrival regime (Chimni, 1998; Keeley, 2001).

Labor recruitment also goes back a long way. In the ancient world, conquest was often motivated by the aim of taking slaves as cheap labor power. Capitalism has always needed "unfree labor" (Cohen, 1987). In early modernity, the slave trade was part of the colonial political economy. When slavery was abolished it was succeeded by indentured labor systems, in which colonial states played a central role. Colonial states also played a big part in attracting free immigrants for settler colonies. Australian colonial administrations carried out publicity campaigns in Britain, organized and subsidized travel, and provided assistance to migrants upon arrival. European industrialization also used migrant labor, but much of the migration was spontaneous or organized by employers, rather than by states. In World War I, the main combatant states recruited workers from their colonies (Britain and France) or from European sources (Germany). The Nazi war economy relied heavily on migrant labor – many of them recruited by force (Homze, 1967).

The idea of a past era of nonintervention by the state is based on the U.S. experience between 1820 and 1914. Here the role of the state was to encourage immigration and to screen entrants for disease and criminal records. Openness to migration was limited by the discriminatory rules against Asians in the 1880s and was finally stopped by the national origins system after World War I. Britain, Canada and Australia all introduced rules excluding specific groups in the late nineteenth century – Britain against East European Jews; Australia and Canada against Asians. In France, where demographic decline was already an issue, we can observe the early use of immigrant incorporation for strategic purposes: the Nationality Code of 1889 was explicitly designed to obtain soldiers for future conflicts with Germany (Schnapper, 1994:66). German officials, by contrast, feared that Polish immigration into the Eastern provinces of the Reich would dilute the German population and threaten their hold on the region. They therefore devised a policing system designed to keep migrants mobile and prevent settlement. This is an early example of a nonincorporation (or exclusion) regime, which was deliberately used to keep wages low and to create a split labor market (Dohse, 1981:33–83).

Thus the picture of an era of *laissez-faire* in migration that ended with World War I is misleading. "States took an active interest in 'their' emigrants and in the immigrants who crossed their borders, and used various means of classifying international migrants as 'desirable' or 'undesirable'" (Fahrmeir *et al.*, 2003:2). The nineteenth century was an age of experimentation in migration control. Democratic revolutions and industrialization led to greater freedom of movement than ever, but also to the need to register national belonging and personal identity. The emergence of the welfare state reinforced the distinction between citizens and foreigners, and the (re)birth of the passport was an inevitable consequence (Torpey, 2003).

In retrospect, it is easy to see a logical historical progression towards the present, yet one could also interpret past migration experiences in terms of 'unintended consequences.' Did British colonial authorities seek to create multiracial societies in Fiji, Malaya or the Caribbean? Did European labor importers consider long-term effects on the demographic and ethnic composition of their populations? Did U.S. governments foresee an ethnically diverse society? The answer to these and many similar questions is "obviously not." Does this mean that today's policymakers should be equally oblivious to the consequences of their decisions? Again, obviously not. That, in turn, leads to the questions whether democratic states possess: 1) the capacity to analyze and forecast the long-term consequences of migration policy decisions; 2) the political ability to reach consensus on long-term goals in this field; and 3) the policy tools to achieve these goals in a manner consistent with democracy and the rule of law.

I have my doubts on all these counts.

FACTORS SHAPING MIGRATION AND MIGRATION POLICY

Political concern about 'unwanted' migration increased in the 1960s in Britain, the 1970s in Western Europe and Australia, and a little later in North America. By the 1990s, migration control had shifted from a merely domestic issue to become part of 'high politics' – that is, an aspect of "problems affecting relations between states, including questions of war and peace" (Cornelius, Martin and Hollifield, 1994:7). Following September 11, 2001, there was much talk of the 'securitization' of migration. The terrorist attacks may have focused public attention on the issue, but the perception of migration as a security issue goes back much further.

Through the 1980s and 1990s, efforts at migration control became more intense in developed countries. In addition to a range of measures by individual states, attempts were made to create multilateral or supranational regulation systems. The most important were the 1985 Schengen Agreement (implemented in 1995) and the European Union's (EU) decision on common migration and asylum policies through the 1997 Amsterdam Treaty (Castles, Loughna and Crawley, 2003; Geddes, 2003). Regional initiatives in North America, Latin America, Africa and Asia are less developed, but may point to significant future developments (Castles and Miller, 2003:Ch. 5).

Despite these intensive efforts, there is a public perception that migration is out of control. The fall in the number of asylum seeker entries to Europe in the mid-1990s appeared at first to show the success of migration control. But the main reason was that large East-West flows were a passing phenomenon following the collapse of the Soviet Bloc. The subsequent increase in asylum flows to Western Europe and Australia was widely seen as demonstrating the inefficacy of control. Similarly, the recent U.S. Census suggested that some 9 million aliens live illegally in the United States. Do such figures really indicate a 'migration crisis,' as has been claimed not only by media and politicians but also by some academics (Weiner, 1995; Zolberg, 2001), or are they more a result of changed perceptions?

To understand these issues, it is necessary to examine the factors that drive migratory processes. It is impossible to include all possible factors here, so the choice is based on a judgment about their relative importance. Three types will be discussed:

- Factors arising from the social dynamics of the migratory process;
- Factors linked to globalization, transnationalism and North-South relationships; and
- Factors within political systems

Factors Arising from the Social Dynamics of the Migratory Process

Two types of belief have been particularly influential in migration policy formation. One is the economic belief in market behavior based on neo-classical theory, according to which people move to maximize their individual utility (usually through higher income), and cease to move, or return home, if the cost-benefit equation changes. The second is the bureaucratic belief that regulations designed to categorize migrants and to regulate their admission and residence effectively shape aggregate behavior. Together these two beliefs add up to the idea that migration can be turned on and off like a tap by appropriate policy settings.

An example is the belief of German policymakers after 1973 that unwanted guestworkers would go away because of the temporary residence principle built into the labor recruitment system and because employment opportunities had declined due to the Oil Crisis. These predictions proved false. Migrants took a long-term view and changed their behavior, becoming permanent settlers. Should German policymakers really have been surprised? After all, the same thing had happened with regard to Polish workers in the Ruhr industrial region before World War I. France had had a similar experience with Polish and Italian workers in the interwar period. Emigration countries also often failed to understand such tendencies: Turkey and Algeria remained wedded to an official view of emigration as temporary long after trends towards permanent settlement in Germany and France had become clear.[2] In all these cases, historical memories were overridden by the belief that modern administrative systems were more effective than in the past. However, the main reason was probably a failure to see migration as a social process. This can be summarized in the following factors.

Chain migration and networks. Chain migration was a term used in older literature to describe the way an initial migration – usually of young workers – would be followed by others from the same family or community, sometimes leading to a partial recreation of the home community in the new country (Price, 1963). More recently, the focus has been on the role of migrant networks in easing the move to a new country and providing help with work, housing and other needs on arrival (Boyd, 1989). Such links provide vital resources for individuals and groups and may be referred to as 'social capital' (Bourdieu and Wacquant, 1992:119). The importance of

---

[2] I am indebted to Mark Miller for this point.

networks applies not only to economic migrants, but also to refugees and asylum seekers, whose choice of route and destination is strongly influenced by existing connections (Koser, 1997). Networks also provide the basis for processes of adaptation and community formation. Migrant groups develop their own social and economic infrastructure such as places of worship, associations, shops, cafés, lawyers and doctors.

Family and Community. The family and community are crucial in migration. Research on Asian migration has shown that migration decisions are usually made not by individuals but by families. In situations of rapid change, a family may decide to send one or more members to work in another region or country in order to maximize income and survival chances (Hugo, 1994). Family linkages often provide both the financial and the cultural capital (that is, the knowledge of opportunities and means of mobility), which make migration possible. The 'new economics of labor migration' approach, which emerged in the 1980s, emphasized the importance of family strategies designed to obtain secure employment and investment capital and to manage risk over long periods (Stark, 1991; Taylor, 1987).

Position within the Lifecycle. In economic migration, the primary migrant is usually a young man or woman in search of temporary work and often intending to return home once certain savings targets have been reached. The difficulty in achieving such targets leads to prolonged stay. This, in turn, encourages family reunion. People start to see their life perspectives in the new country. This process is especially linked to the situation of migrants' children: once they go to school in the new country, learn the language, form peer group relationships and develop bicultural or transcultural identities, it becomes more and more difficult for the parents to return to their homelands.

The Migration Industry. The migration industry develops out of migration networks. Once a migration gets underway, needs arise for a variety of special services. The migration industry includes travel agents, lawyers, bankers, labor recruiters, brokers, interpreters, and housing agents. The agents have an interest in the continuation of migration and may go on organizing it even when governments try to restrict movements, though the form may change (for example, from legal worker recruitment to asylum migration or undocumented entry). Facilitating migration is a major and largely legal international business (Salt and Clarke, 2000:327). Recently, governments have drawn attention to the illegal side of the migration industry – human smuggling and trafficking – and have attempted to control it through international legal and police measures.

Policies as Opportunity Structures. People lucky enough to enjoy a middle-class position in developed countries tend to have fairly positive views of the state and the law. This does not necessarily apply to the majority of the world's population, who live in inefficient, corrupt and violent states. Most people have to learn to cope despite the state, not because of it. From this perspective, migration rules become just another barrier to be overcome in order to survive. Potential migrants do not cancel migration just because the receiving state says they are not welcome – especially if the labor market tells a different story. Policies become opportunity structures to be compared and negotiated.

Migrant Agency. All of the factors mentioned can be summed up in the notion of migrant agency: migrants are not isolated individuals who react to market stimuli and bureaucratic rules, but social beings who seek to achieve better outcomes for themselves, their families and their communities by actively shaping the migratory process. Migratory movements, once started, become self-sustaining social processes. It is vital to add this sociological and anthropological insight to the structural or institutional models provided by economists, political scientists and legal specialists.

However, structural factors are also part of the migratory process. Both emigration and immigration countries can become structurally dependent on migration.

Structural Dependence on Emigration. Many less-developed countries have identified labor export as important in reducing unemployment, improving the balance of payments, securing skills and investment capital, and stimulating development. In some cases, the export of discontent and reduction of political tension also become goals. Migration can become a substitute for development rather than a contribution to it (Castles, 2000). Where governments encourage emigration, as in the Philippines under Marcos, it can become a long-term structural feature of the economy (Abella, 1993; Saith, 1997). This, in turn, can lead to a culture of emigration, in which people may migrate 'because everyone else does so,' rather than on the basis of very precise goals. This happened in Italy between 1861 and about 1970 and occurs today in certain regions of Mexico, the Philippines, China and other countries.

Structural Dependence on Immigrant Labor. Structural dependence on immigrant labor has been significant in many countries. In the 1970s, Western European countries found they could not dispense with migrants despite the existence of high unemployment, because migrant workers were concentrated in jobs which locals were unable or unwilling to do. The U.S. agricultural sector needs undocumented Mexican workers in order to keep production costs low. When Malaysia tried to repatriate large numbers of Indonesian and Filipino workers during the 1997–99 Asian financial crisis, plantation employers requested the government to admit thousands of new workers, arguing that U.S.$500 million had been lost in 1997 due to labor shortages (Pillai, 1999). Western European governments claim they do not need low-skilled workers, yet carry out privatization and deregulation measures which have led to a burgeoning informal sector (Reyneri, 2001).

Factors Linked to Globalization, Transnationalism and North-South Relationships

International migration has always been linked to trends towards cross-border activity and was especially marked in the early phase of accelerated globalization prior to 1914. However, the rapid economic, political, technological and cultural changes associated with the current phase of globalization have had important effects on the volume, directions and characteristics of migration.

Until recently, United Nations statisticians argued that international migrants only made up about 2 percent of the world's population and that most migration was intraregional – that is, within Africa, Asia or Europe, rather than from South to North (Zlotnik, 1999). Recent data from the U.N. Population Division makes it necessary to revise this view. In 2000, there were 175 million international migrants worldwide (defined as people who had lived outside their country of birth for at least 12 months). The global total has doubled since 1970. Sixty percent of migrants now live in developed countries, where one in ten persons is a migrant, compared with one in 70 in developing countries. Migrants make up about 3 percent of global population. From 1990 to 2000, the number of migrants increased by 21 million persons or 14 percent. The total net growth took place in developed countries: Europe, North America, Australia, New Zealand and Japan registered an increase in migrant stock of 23 million, while the migrant population of less-developed regions fell by 2 million. Thus, the trend is towards an acceleration of South-North Migration (United Nations Population Division, 2002).

The North-South Divide Generates Migration. International borders help maintain inequality (Zolberg, 1989:406). However, the most crucial borders are no longer between nation-states, but those between North and South – that is, between the powerful industrial nations (North America, Western Europe, Japan, Australia and New Zealand), and the poorer countries of Africa, Asia and Latin America.[3] In recent years, the disparities in income, social conditions, human rights and security have increased. Despite some areas of rapid growth, other parts of the South have become disconnected from the global economy, leading to stagnation and conflict (Castells, 1998). Since weak economies and weak states generally go together, people move both to escape impoverishment and human rights abuse (Duffield, 2001). Such 'multiple motivations' lead to a 'migration-asylum nexus,' which makes it hard to distinguish clearly between economic migrants and refugees. Thus the perceived migration crisis is really a crisis in North-South relations, caused by uneven development and gross inequality. Migration control is essentially about regulating North-South relations. Because northern countries are doing their best to stop migration – with the exception of the highly skilled – movement can often only take place through means classified as illegal by receiving countries.

Globalization Creates the Cultural Capital and Technical Means Needed for Migration. Globalization essentially means flows across borders – flows of capital, commodities, ideas and people. States welcome the first two types, but are suspicious of the others. Especially the mobility of people is regulated and differentiated. Bauman argues that, in the globalized world, "mobility has become the most powerful and most coveted stratifying factor." The new global economic and political elites are able to cross borders at will, while the poor are meant to stay at home: "the riches are global, the misery is local" (Bauman, 1998:9, 74). However, globalization also creates strong pressures to move. Global media beam idealized images of First World lifestyles into the poorest villages. Electronic communications facilitate the dissemination

---

[3]The North-South divide expresses not a geographical configuration, but a political and social one. The North also includes areas and groups subject to social exclusion, while the South has elite groups and enclaves which enjoy considerable prosperity. There are also important regions and groups in intermediate or transitional positions.

of knowledge of migration routes and work opportunities. Long-distance travel has become far cheaper and more accessible than in the past.

Globalization Transforms the Character of Migration. The cultural and technological factors that drive migration also change its forms. People move farther, leading to greater ethnocultural diversity in receiving countries. In the past, migrants moved either with the intention of permanent settlement or of a temporary sojourn in one receiving country. Now it is possible to go back and forth or to move on to other countries. For example, recent research on trans-Mediterranean migration has revealed migrant careers which lead neither to permanent settlement nor permanent return, but rather to repeated sojourns of varying duration, punctuated by returns to the country of origin (Peraldi, 2001). Similarly, even classical migration countries like Australia now find that temporary entry for work and study exceeds permanent settler entry (DIMIA, 2001). At the same time, many young Australians discover that a period of work abroad is important for professional advancement. There is, however, no guarantee that the temporary migrants will not become settlers. Indeed, recent legal changes are designed to turn Asian students of information technology or business studies into permanent settlers (Birrell, 2001).

Transnational Communities. Globalization leads to changes in the ways immigrants are incorporated into society (*see also* Faist, 2004). In the past, most migrants were treated either as permanent settlers, who were to be assimilated, or as temporary sojourners, who were to be kept separate from the host population through special (and often discriminatory) legal regimes. The experience of community formation and ethnic mobilization led to the rise of a third approach – multiculturalism – in the 1970s. But all these approaches were premised on the idea that people would focus their social existence on just one society at a time and would therefore owe their allegiance to just one nation-state. The new ease of movement and communication has made it possible for many people to live their lives across borders. Transnational communities may be defined as groups based in two or more countries, which engage in recurrent, enduring and significant cross-border activities, which may be economic, political, social or cultural (Portes, Guarnizo and Landolt, 1999). If mobility across borders is a part of a group's economic, social, cultural and political life, this provides a powerful motivation to overcome barriers imposed by states.

National versus Transnational Logic. All the above factors connected with globalization and transnationalism can be summarized in the statement that state migration control efforts still follow a national logic, while many of the forces driving migration follow a transnational logic (*see also* Levitt and Glick Schiller, 2004 and Vertovec, 2004). It would be misleading to claim that the logic of globalization or transnationalism has fully superseded national logic. As already noted, only about 3 percent of the world's population are migrants, and most of these probably still see themselves either as settlers or sojourners. But there is a clear trend towards growth in transnational behavior and consciousness. Castells has written that globalization means a change in the spatial organization of the world from 'a space of places' to a 'space of flows' (Castells, 1996:Ch. 6). The new forms of mobility and transnational behavior fit this logic much better than do state migration rules.

Nonmigration Policies. Nonmigration policies may be more powerful in shaping South-North movements than explicit migration policies. Economists argue that the most effective way of encouraging development is through policies designed to bring about free trade and encourage foreign direct investment (FDI), thereby including less developed countries in global economic relationships (Martin and Straubhaar, 2002). This is likely to lead to increased migration in the short run (the 'migration hump') but should, in the long run, lead to greater equality and reduced pressure for South-North migration (Martin and Taylor, 2001:106). Similarly, when authoritarian regimes collapse, there may be a 'refugee hump' as people seize the opportunity to flee, but, in the long run, democratization and improved governance are likely to lead to reduced outflows and return of exiles (Schmeidl, 2001). The implication is that developed-country policies on trade, human rights and conflict prevention may be crucial in reducing migration – especially flows of undocumented workers and asylum seekers.

However, the record of developed countries and international financial institutions in this area is far from positive. Former World Bank Vice-President Stiglitz argues that free market ideologies and narrow financial interests have prevailed in the International Monetary Fund (IMF), leading to policies which exacerbated the crises in East Asia, Latin America and Russia in the 1990s (Stiglitz, 2002). Similarly, the World Trade Organization (WTO) is designed to free-up world trade by creating a system of fair and universal rules. Yet the developed countries continue to subsidize their own producers. U.S. subsidies to cotton farmers so depress world prices that peasant farmers in Africa lose over $350 million a year – more than the entire U.S. aid budget for these areas (Stiglitz, 2002:269). Some West African farmers are likely to abandon cotton production and emigrate to Europe, due to historical links between countries like Mali and France.

Oxfam estimates that trade restrictions by rich countries cost developing countries around $100 billion a year – twice as much as they receive in aid. The EU's Common Agricultural Policy remains a major barrier to trade. EU agricultural products are exported at subsidized prices one third lower than production costs, causing considerable damage to producers in less developed countries (Oxfam, 2002:11). On a more positive note, the EU has built human rights clauses into its trade and cooperation agreements since the early 1990s (Castles *et al.*, 2003:34–35). Yet trade in oil, diamonds, timber and other commodities continues to fuel conflicts in Africa and Asia. ". . . Stopping arms exports to regimes that persecute their citizens and to countries engulfed in violent internal conflicts or wars of aggression against other countries could be the biggest single step towards reducing the number of asylum seekers" (UNHCR, 2000:22). The United States along with EU countries like the United Kingdom, France and Germany are among the world's largest arms exporters.

Overall, it could be argued that Northern policies in the areas of trade, international cooperation and foreign affairs are major causes of the very migratory flows that Northern migration policies seek to control.

Factors within Political Systems

The problems of migration policies arise largely from the interactions between the factors already mentioned and the political systems of the states concerned. However, political systems are complex and contradictory in themselves. This applies particularly to liberal-democratic receiving states, but countries of emigration also face contradictions, and even less-democratic receiving states find that migration control comes up against competing interests.

Political Conflicts in Emigration Countries. Structural dependence on labor export was referred to above. Some governments have encouraged labor migration, while others concluded that, since they could not prevent it, at least some form of regulation was desirable (Abella, 1995). Several sending countries have set up special departments to manage recruitment and to protect workers, such as Bangladesh's Bureau of Manpower, Employment and Training (BMET) and India's Office of the Protector of Emigrants. The

Philippine government takes an active role in migration management. Prospective migrants have to register with the Philippine Overseas Employment Administration (POEA), while the Overseas Workers' Welfare Administration (OWWA) has the tasks of assisting and protecting workers abroad. But, as economies become dependent on remittances, it becomes increasingly difficult for governments to effectively regulate migration or protect their citizens. The result can be political mobilization around the idea that the inability to provide a decent livelihood at home is a major failure of the state (Aguilar, 1996). This was shown vividly in the Philippines in 1995 in the case of Flor Contemplacion, a Filipina domestic worker hanged for murder in Singapore, which became a major focus of political conflict (Gonzalez, 1998:6–7).

Interest Conflicts in Immigration Countries. Interest conflicts in immigration countries are also linked to the issue of structural dependence. Lobbying by plantation owners in Malaysia during the 1997–99 economic crisis was mentioned above. This was part of a trend to politicization of migration involving many interest groups (Pillai, 1999:182–186). By 1999, the government was under pressure from the Malaysian Agricultural Producers Association, the construction industry and some state governments to bring in more workers. The Malaysian Trade Unions Congress opposed labor recruitment due to its effects on jobs and wages for local workers, while Chinese political groups feared that Indonesian immigration would alter the ethnic balance to their disadvantage. The government party, UMNO, and the main Islamic opposition party, PAS, both supported Indonesian entries as a potential boost to Malay and Islamic interests (Jones, 2000).

Interest Conflicts and Hidden Agendas in Migration Policies. Interest group politics are all the more important in Western democracies, where such groups are seen as legitimate actors in policy formation. Typically, employers (at least in certain sectors) favor recruitment of migrant workers, while competing local workers may be opposed. Unions are often ambivalent: they may wish to oppose immigration in the interests of local workers, but are reluctant to do so, because they see the need to organize the newcomers. At the social level, some people may oppose settlement of immigrants in their neighborhoods because they feel it will worsen their housing conditions and amenities, while others may see immigration as a source of urban renewal and a more vibrant cultural mix. Politicians, social movements and the media all have roles in shaping and directing people's reactions to migration (*see* Freeman, 2004). This topic cannot be explored further here because it requires detailed analysis of varying institutional structures and political cultures (Baldwin-Edwards and Schain, 1994; Hollifield, 2000; Koopmans and Statham, 2000).

The main point is that the state cannot easily decide to favor the interests of one group and ignore others. There are examples, such as German guestworker policy that was overwhelmingly driven by employer interests. But more often, the state tries to balance competing interests, or at least to convince certain groups that their wishes are being considered (*see* Hollifield, 2004). The strength of nationalist and ethnocentric ideologies in immigration countries has made it easy to mobilize public opinion against immigration. The mass media have done much to create hostility to immigrants and asylum seekers. In response, politicians sometimes give lip service to anti-immigration rhetoric while actually pursuing policies that lead to more immigration, because it is important for labor market and economic objectives. This helps explain the frequent hidden agendas in migration policies – that is, policies which purport to follow certain objectives while actually doing the opposite. The tacit acceptance of undocumented labor migration in many countries despite strong control rhetoric is an example.

The Political Ability to Control Migration. The notion of hidden agendas could be cast differently as whether the state (or the political class) really has the ability and the will to control migration. Official rhetoric stresses the desire to manage flows, but the reality seems to contradict this. Why, for instance, did the 1986 U.S. Immigration Reform and Control Act (IRCA) lead to new streams of undocumented workers (Martin and Miller, 2000)? Was it because the authorities were unable to conceive of effective control measures, especially employer sanctions? Or was it because they lacked the political strength in the face of strong lobbying by employer groups? Similarly, one could ask why the 2002 U.K. Immigration and Asylum Act failed to set up a legal entry system for low-skilled workers, even though the need for them in such sectors as catering and the National Health Service was widely recognized? The reason surely lay in the heated polemics of Britain's tabloid press against immigration. In a wider sense, the growth of undocumented migration throughout Europe can be seen as a response to neoliberal trends towards labor market deregulation, which have led to a weakening of inspection systems and the decline of the trade unions. Growth of casual employment and subcontracting has led to a rapid growth in the informal sector, even in Northern European countries. This is a major source of attraction for migrant workers. Thus, undocumented migration is an indirect effect of state policies which have quite different motivations (Reyneri, 1999).

Contradictions within the Policy Formation Process. Much of the above underlines the importance of economic and social interests and the way the state tries to balance these, or at least to convince the public that it is doing so. This leads to such ideas as 'clientelist politics,' according to which migration policymaking can be dominated by powerful organized interests, such as agricultural employers or the construction industry (Freeman, 1995). In a similar way, some Australian scholars believe that there is a 'new class,' consisting apparently of a mixture of employers and left-wing intellectuals, which has succeeded in imposing large-scale immigration on an unwilling public (Betts, 1993). Such critiques often take on a normative tone, with the implication that the state is somehow being captured or manipulated, yet surely this is how the liberal state is meant to function – as a mechanism for aggregating and negotiating group interests. Of course, in countries where immigrants can easily become citizens, they, too, can play a part in such politics.

In any case, as Hollifield has pointed out, such approaches tend to portray the state as a mere reflection of powerful economic interests (Hollifield, 2000:144–146) He argues instead for the need to take the state itself as the unit of analysis in explaining policy formation processes and policy outcomes. This approach is also advocated by Sciortino. He seeks to explain the "low rationality of immigration policy in relation to its declared goals," by focusing on the "social structure of policymaking" rather than on group interests. Using Luhmann's model of the sociology of the political system, he argues that immigration policy is actually close to the 'unstable/unable pole' of policy, but is generally misunderstood as being close to the 'stable/able pole' represented by labor market or economic policy. This explains how migration policy could shift from being seen as an economic issue to a national identity issue in Europe over the last two decades (Sciortino, 2000). However, it is important to understand that investigating the political economy of interests and studying the political sociology of the state are not mutually exclusive (as Sciortino seems to imply). Both clearly influence policy outputs and outcomes. The interaction between the two is yet another factor which makes migration policy so complex and contradictory.

The Importance of Rights. In his 'liberal state thesis,' Hollifield draws attention to the importance of rights as a factor limiting the ability of the state to manage migration (Hollifield, 2000). Similarly, Hammar has shown how the acquisition of rights within receiving states led to a form of quasi-citizenship which he called 'denizenship' (Hammar, 1990). Soysal (1994) has emphasized the role of international legal norms in improving migrant rights. Constitutional norms concerning protection of the family and role of the courts in enforcing these helped to frustrate government attempts to send guestworkers home in 1970s Europe. Today, the European Convention on Human Rights is regularly invoked by migrants, often through appeals to the European Court of Justice. In Japan, constitutional rights and the strong legal system have been important in improving migrant rights (Kondo, 2001). As long-term immigrants acquire rights to employment and welfare in liberal states, it becomes harder to see them as temporary outsiders in society. This generates strong pressures for social incorporation and eventually for access to citizenship. It seems that inherent factors in the liberal state lead to settlement, integration and even multiculturalism in the long run (Bauböck, 1996; Castles and Davidson, 2000).

The Importance of Civil Society. Apart from the legal constraints, there has always been an additional factor: civil society or nongovernmental organizations (NGOs). In most immigration countries, movements have emerged to campaign against discrimination and racism and for the rights of migrants. Much of the motivation has been value- rather than interest-based, although as migrants gain rights they have also played an important role through their own associations. Civil society is also important in countries where political systems are very resistant to the granting of rights to immigrants (Castles, 2001). In Malaysia, for instance, a growing number of associations support migrants. The trial of Irene Fernandez, leader of the women's rights organization *Tenaganita,* for exposing bad conditions in migrant detention centers, became a major public issue in the late 1990s (Jones, 2000). However, in October 2003, Ms. Fernandez was sentenced to a year in jail "for publishing false news," showing the limits of civil society action in authoritarian states (Sittamparam, 2003).

The Welfare State. Social rights are an important part of the bundle of citizenship rights in liberal states. Some observers suggest that strong welfare states tend towards closure to newcomers (Bommes and Halfmann, 1998). This is born out by attempts to restrict access to welfare for recent immigrants in Australia and the United States. However, the welfare state has also been a major factor driving incorporation of immigrants. This is because the welfare state follows a logic of inclusion: failure to grant social rights to any group of residents leads to social divisions and can undermine the rights of the majority. The local state was far ahead of the national state in providing integration programs in education and welfare in Germany. A de facto local multiculturalism was evolving in the 1980s, long before it became a policy issue at the national level (Cohn-Bendit and Schmid, 1993). In Japan, public authorities are gradually including foreign residents – even irregular workers – in health, education, employment and welfare services (Mori, 1997: 189–206; OECD, 1998:131).

LEARNING FROM POLICY FAILURE

The central argument of this article is not that all, or even most, migration policies are misguided and unsuccessful. It would be equally possible – and useful – to write an article about well-conceived and successful policies. I have chosen here to focus on policy failures because of the widespread perception that "the gap between the *goals* of national immigration policy . . . and the actual results of policies in this area (policy *outcomes*) is wide and growing wider in all major industrialized democracies" (emphasis in original) (Cornelius *et al.*, 1994). This crisis of national migration policies is exacerbated by the relative absence of global governance with regard to international migration, which contrasts with the development of global rules and institutions in other areas of economic and political relations.

Whether one focuses on policy success or policy failure, the point is to realize that such outcomes are not coincidental, but systemic and potentially changeable. If we possess a conceptual framework, which helps us to understand the basic dynamics of contemporary international migrations, then it becomes easier to understand why certain policy approaches have failed. This, in turn, should assist in working out more successful approaches to policy formation. In this section, I briefly summarize some principles for a conceptual framework. I go on to discuss ideas for possible improvements in policy approaches.

First, contemporary migrations should be analyzed within the context of a broad understanding of migration as a social process, with its own inherent dynamics. This can be summed up in three principles: the importance of migrant agency; the self-sustaining nature of migratory processes; and the trend towards structural dependence of both emigration and immigration countries on continuation of migration processes, once these have become established.

Second, it is important to understand much of contemporary migration (and particularly those flows seen by some as constituting a 'migration crisis') as an integral aspect of North-South relations in the current phase of globalization. Policy in this area is doomed to failure unless it addresses the causes of both economic and forced migration in current patterns of global inequality. Globalization contains the inherent contradiction of producing both a North-South gap and the technological and cultural means of overcoming this gap. Migration networks based on transnational dynamics will undermine migration control as long as this is based on a narrow national logic.

Third, understanding of the migratory process and of transnational factors must be linked to an analysis of the way policy formation takes place in states and supranational bodies. This includes examining interests and the way they are articulated, as well as the way the political system functions. Many policy failures or unintended consequences of policy can be explained in this way. To this must be added the fact that migration processes are of a long-term nature, while the policy cycle is essentially short-term and often determined by the length of electoral periods.

Fourth, it is important to realize that the declared objectives of states are often misleading. Political agenda are shaped both by the need to maintain legitimacy and the unwillingness to face up to past policy failures. An important example is the policies that claim to exclude undocumented workers while often concealing practices that allow them to enter in covert ways, so they can be more readily exploited. This is one aspect of differential policies towards migrants with different levels of human capital, which seem to be generating a new transnational labor force, stratified not only by skill and ethnicity but also by legal status. Such hierarchies are a key element of global economic stratification. Control of mobility reinforces existing global hierarchies and helps maintain inequality between the rich and the poor. Thus migration control is often part of a broader (and often hidden) objective of regulating North-South relationships.

Finally, nonmigration policies may be more powerful in shaping migration than are migration policies. A major cause of both economic and forced migration is the huge gap between North and South in economic prosperity, social conditions, security and human rights. Foreign aid by rich countries can help reduce the gap, but even more important are measures to encourage international trade – especially by removing trade barriers – and to increase investment in developing countries. Conflict resolution and reconstruction measures can also play a part in reducing migration pressures.

This means involving ministries responsible for development aid, trade, finance, foreign affairs and even defense in strategies for addressing migration. It also means exercising patience, since the very policies that lead to long-term improvements may precipitate a short-term 'migration hump' (Martin and Straubhaar, 2002:13).

These elements of a conceptual framework should not be seen as stepping-stones towards some new general theory of international migration. Here it is advisable to remember Portes' warning not to expect a "grand theory" of migration that can explain every aspect in every place. Such a theory would be so general as to be vacuous. Instead, he advocates a set of "mid-range theories" that can help explain specific empirical findings by linking them to appropriate bodies of historical and contemporary research (Portes, 1997). This means replacing narrow and monodisciplinary explanations of migration with a sensitivity for the varied factors discussed above. It also means constantly analyzing the way such factors interact in specific contexts of economic, social and political change.

OPEN BORDERS?

What could such principles mean for a reform of migration policies? Is there some 'magic formula,' which could help us find a way out of the current dilemmas? One such sweeping solution is the idea of open borders – the removal of any form of migration control. Interestingly, this slogan comes from two normally very divergent schools of thought: neoclassical economists and left-wing critics of government migration policies. The former believe that leaving regulation to market forces will optimize the benefits of migration for both sending and receiving countries and help in the long run to equalize wages between them, leading to a new global economic equilibrium (Borjas, 1989; Chiswick, 2000; *see also* Martin and Taylor, 2001). Many people on the left think that freedom of movement will eliminate discriminatory and repressive state measures (especially detention and deportation) and enhance migrants' human rights. They also argue that the economies of both sending and receiving countries will benefit and that migration will not rise to insupportable levels because most people will prefer to stay at home (Harris, 2002; Hayter, 2001).

This belief in the beneficial effects of the 'invisible hand' of markets is understandable for neoclassical economists, but curious for the Left, which normally calls for state regulation and welfare measures to protect vulnerable groups. Open borders is a desirable long-term aim, but there are reasons to think that eliminating all migration control at the present time would be downright harmful:

- Effectively, there is already free movement for the highly skilled. This allows rich countries to plunder the scarce human capital of poor countries. More – not less – regulation of highly-skilled migration is needed, perhaps through use of a taxation mechanism (analogous to the Tobin Tax) to compensate source countries for loss of skills.
- Employers often favor uncontrolled migration precisely because it leads to lower wages for competing local labor (especially for lower-skilled occupations). There is no guarantee of reaching equilibrium levels of wages, but if they are achieved they are likely to be at very low levels, which would significantly worsen conditions of local labor in receiving areas.
- The labor markets of developed countries could absorb only a small proportion of the unemployed or underemployed workers of the South. This is not likely to lead to significant improvements in wages or conditions in countries of origin.
- Labor inflows and pressure on wages in the North could lead to conflict between immigrant and local workers. In view of the existing anti-immigration mobilization by mass media and right-wing politicians, the consequences could be an upsurge in racism and violence, paving the way for extreme-right political gains.
- Open borders would eliminate the distinction between refugees and economic migrants – if there is no control of entry, the asylum determination process would become superfluous. Some people would welcome this, for the current process has many deficiencies. But in a situation of widespread conflict and human rights abuse, especially in less-developed countries, the international refugee regime remains the only means of protection for millions of vulnerable people.
- The elegant simplicity of the open borders slogan is deceptive, as it would create many new problems. In the current global context it could lead to an anarchic situation in which the weakest – in both sending and receiving countries – would be even more disadvantaged.

TOWARDS FAIRER AND MORE EFFECTIVE MIGRATION POLICIES

Reform will have to take the messier course of pursuing a variety of measures at different spatial and political levels and finding better ways of coordinating them. Increasingly, migration analysts and policymakers are using the term 'migration management' to refer to the "range of measures needed to effectively address migration issues at national, regional and global levels" (IOM, 2003:53; *see also* Spencer, 2003). The term is helpful, as long as we exercise caution about its technocratic undertone: a top-down management process is exactly what we have now, and it cannot resolve the crucial issues at stake. Migration management should be understood as a cooperative process in which all participants have a voice, including the governments and civil societies of the sending countries, the receiving populations and above all the migrants themselves. To be effective, policies need to be fair and to be perceived as fair by all the groups involved. This requires changes in legal frameworks, institutional structures and specific policies.

National Measures

It is at the national level that migration policies often seem to be at their most ambiguous. Governments have found it hard to adopt balanced approaches in the face of the electoral threats posed by nationalism and anti-immigration mobilization. There is a need for public debate on the role of migration in open societies embedded in global relationships. This should be linked with regular public consultation to ensure that benefits for some are not at the expense of others. An example is to be found in the German government's commission on migration and integration, which effectively challenged outmoded but dominant ideas, and paved the way for major changes in thinking and policy (Süssmuth, 2001). The Australian government's annual public consultations on the level and composition of immigration are also a good example. Efforts do not always need to be on such a grand scale – sometimes officially commissioned studies on a particular issue (like the economics of migration) can be important for public perceptions and policy formation (Glover *et al.*, 2001; Smith and Edmonston, 1997).

Credible information and widespread consultation could pave the way for transparent policies, based on a balancing out of values (such as protection for refugees) and goals (such as economic growth and the safeguarding of labor standards). Specific measures would vary from country to country. It is important to assess demand for migration in terms of labor market needs, family reunion flows and trends in asylum seeker entries. These should be related to historical migration patterns and to the broader social, economic, cultural and political context. The policy issue is then how best to facilitate necessary movements while avoiding possible negative effects for particular groups.

A basic principle is that undocumented migration can best be avoided by providing mechanisms and incentives for legal entry. Where sanctions are needed they should not target the migrants, but rather those who profit from illegal movements – smugglers, traffickers and exploitative employers. This type of national migration management may require a reversal of trends to deregulation of labor markets, which have opened up the space for illegal employment (especially in Europe) in recent years.

Regional Regulation

Much international migration takes place at the regional level. Cooperation on migration has been discussed within such regional organizations as NAFTA, MERCOSUR and APEC, but only in the European Union have comprehensive common policies been adopted – and even here it has been a long process. Until recently, free movement only applied to citizens moving from one member state to another. Entry and integration of the much larger numbers of migrants from outside the EU was seen as a matter of national sovereignty. The 1997 Treaty of Amsterdam was path-breaking in its objectives for common policies on asylum and migration. The EU planned to introduce joint policies for 25 states (by May 2004), covering management of migration flows, common rules and standards for asylum, partnership with countries of origin and integration of third-country nationals.

There is no space to go into detail on the difficulties of EU policy formation and implementation here (*see* Castles, 2004; Castles *et al.*, 2003; Geddes, 2003). Progress has been slow and it proved impossible to introduce all planned policy components by the target date of May 2004. The question was whether the policies would follow the more open approaches developed within some member states, or adopt the lowest common denominator of the most restrictive approaches to asylum and migration. Over the last few years there has been a struggle between some European governments which have seen the main issue as one of greater control (for instance, through setting up a common border police force), and others which have emphasized integration policies and cooperation with countries of origin. Despite such problems, common European immigration and asylum policies may well offer a useful model for other regions.

Global Governance

Representatives of international organizations argue that international cooperation could help to ensure orderly movements and enhance the contribution of migration to development (Abella, 1995). However, it has not so far proved possible to create effective instruments for global governance of migration. The one significant exception is the 1951 Geneva Refugee Convention, signed by some 146 states. Its implementation is overseen by the Office of the UN High Commissioner for Refugees. Together, the Convention and the UNHCR provide the legal and institutional basis for defining who is a refugee and what this status means in international law.

Economic migrants lack comparable legal and institutional arrangements. Normative elements of an international regulatory framework do already exist in ILO Conventions No. 97 of 1949 and No. 143 of 1975 and in the 1990 United Nations Convention on the Rights of Migrant Workers and Members of their Families. These standards need to be linked together in a comprehensive framework to regulate the rights and conditions of migrant workers. However, relatively few countries have ratified or applied these instruments. The main reasons for this seem to be lack of long-term strategies on migration by both sending and receiving countries and the reluctance of immigration countries to take steps which might increase the cost of migrant labor to employers.

The demand for stronger rules and institutions to protect migrant workers was raised by a number of migrant-sending countries at the 1994 UN Population Conference in Cairo. They called for an international intergovernmental conference to map out basic principles and to discuss modes of regulation. The northern labor-importing countries – which often seem to dominate political agendas in international agencies – were not willing to accept this approach. However, in recent years the pressure for more cooperation on migration has grown. The establishment of a Global Commission on International Migration (GCIM), with the endorsement of UN Secretary General Kofi Annan, in 2004 is an encouraging sign. It remains to be seen whether there is more willingness today to make real changes than there was just a few years ago.

An effective international migration regime would need to include a new instrument of international law – analogous to the Refugee Convention – which would provide a declaration of the rights of migrants, together with definitions of the groups covered and procedural rules for international governance in this field. It could build on the ILO and UN Conventions mentioned above. Another possible analogy would be with the General Agreement on Tariffs and Trade (GATT), which led to the formation of the World Trade Organization (WTO) – Straubhaar has suggested the establishment of a General Agreement on Movements of People (GAMP)

(Straubhaar, 2002). Such a legal instrument would play a crucial role is setting standards for the treatment of migrants and management of migration.

A second crucial element of a global migration regime would be the establishment of an international migration agency – probably within the UN system – to act as an advocate and protector for migrants and to oversee the adoption of the international legal instrument into national law. Bhagwati speaks of a World Migration Organization (Bhagwati, 2003:104). Such an agency could be built by bringing together the migration functions of the International Organization for Migration (IOM), the International Labor Organization (ILO), the United Nations Population Division, UNHCR, UNESCO and similar bodies, but would need greatly enhanced responsibilities, funding and standing. However, the first problem may be that of overcoming interagency rivalries: there is considerable competition between certain existing agencies to take on the role, while others fear loss of their existing functions.

A third element of a global migration regime would be a set of policies designed to make migration into a tool for development of poorer countries. Recruitment of workers to fill vacancies in industrial economies could take place in the framework of bilateral or multilateral agreements, conforming with international law and watched over by the international migration agency. Such agreements would lay down wages and conditions (based on the national standards of the employment country), rules on residence, integration and family reunion. This could be linked to arrangements to support economic and social development of migrant-sending countries, including:

- Measures for cheap, safe and rapid transfer of remittances;
- Inducements for investment of migrants' remittances and savings in productive enterprises or infrastructure;
- Credit mechanisms and subsidies to multiply the effects of migrant transfers (like the Mexican '3 for 1' scheme);
- Compensation to countries of origin for loss of human capital;
- Schemes to provide migrants with education and training relevant to development needs while in receiving countries;
- Schemes to encourage 'return of talents' on a temporary or long-term basis;
- Support for transnational networks which maintain links between migrants and their areas of origin (e.g., through hometown associations);

• Planning and advice mechanisms for migrants to help them develop long-term approaches to migration and return.

However, past experience shows that such measures do not in themselves ensure that migration will support development. If migrants come from impoverished areas with weak and corrupt governments, no amount of support measures will create a climate favorable to development. Moreover, one-sided measures to support migrants and returnees can increase inequality and arouse envy among nonmigrants. Migration policies must therefore always also be linked to measures designed to reduce inequality and improve governance, which address societies as a whole.

Why Should the Rich Cooperate with the Poor?

Finally, it is important to ask why those countries and groups which currently benefit from the inequalities of global migration should agree to change? Of course, there is a normative answer: the current system is unfair, discriminatory and morally wrong. But moral imperatives are rarely crucial in international politics. A more pragmatic, interest-based answer is that the current arrangements are unsustainable. Migration policies are failing because it is not possible to permanently impose the interests of relatively small privileged groups (especially in the North) on the rest of the world. The formal power of governments and bureaucracies is being subverted by the human agency embodied in migration networks and transnational communities. The failure of migration policies has become a major issue in many countries, with potentially high political costs for ruling parties and other powerful groups.

A more equitable system of migration management, which seeks common ground between the interests of all those involved, is more likely to lead to sustainable outcomes. In the long run it is the best way of avoiding exploitation, abuse and conflict. One could argue therefore that reform of migration policies is in everyone's long-term interests. However, it will only come about if there is genuine willingness to reduce global inequality and to work for greater democracy and participation in global governance. At present, the domination of global bodies like WTO and the IMF by northern elites does not augur well for the prospects of more equitable arrangements in the framework of some future global agreement on international migration.

REFERENCES

Abella, M. I.
1995 "Policies and Institutions for the Orderly Movement of Labour Abroad." In *Orderly International Migration of Workers and Incentives to Stay: Options for Emigration Countries.* Ed. M. I. Abella and K. J. Lönnroth. Geneva: International Labor Office.

———
1993 "Labor Mobility, Trade and Structural Change: The Philippine Experience," *Asian and Pacific Migration Journal,* 2(3):249–268.

Aguilar, F. V. J.
1996 "The Dialectics of Transnational Shame and National Identity," *Philippine Sociological Review,* 44(1–4):101–136.

Baldwin-Edwards, M. and M. A. Schain
1994 *The Politics of Immigration in Western Europe.* Ilford, Essex: Frank Cass.

Bauböck, R.
1996 "Social and Cultural Integration in a Civil Society." In *The Challenge of Diversity: Integration and Pluralism in Societies of Immigration.* Ed. R. Bauböck, A. Heller and A. R. Zolberg. Aldershot: Avebury. Pp. 67–131.

Bauman, Z.
1998 *Globalization: The Human Consequences.* Cambridge: Polity.

Betts, K.
1993 "Public Discourse, Immigration and the New Class." In *The Politics of Australian Immigration.* Ed. J. Jupp and M. Kabala. Canberra: AGPS.

Bhagwati, J.
2003 "Borders Beyond Control: 98–104," *Foreign Affairs,* 82(1):98–104.

Birrell, R.
2001 "Immigration on the Rise: The 2001–2002 Immigration Program," *People and Place,* 9(2):21–28.

Bommes, M. and J. Halfmann
1998 *Migration in Nationalen Wohlfahrstaaten: Theoretische und Vegleichende Untersuchungen.* Osnabrück: Universitätsverlag Rasch.

Borjas, G. J.
1989 "Economic Theory and International Migration," *International Migration Review,* 23(3):457–485.

Bourdieu, P. and L. Wacquant
1992 *An Invitation to Reflexive Sociology.* Chicago: University of Chicago Press.

Boyd, M.
1989 "Family and Personal Networks in Migration," *International Migration Review,* 23(3): 638–670.

Castells, M.
1998 *End of Millennium.* Oxford: Blackwell.

———
1996 *The Rise of the Network Society.* Oxford: Blackwell.

Castles, S.
2004 "Why Migration Policies Fail," *Ethnic and Racial Studies,* 27(2):205–227.

2001   "International Migration and the Nation-state in Asia." In *International Migration in the 21st Century*. Ed. M. A. B. Siddique. Cheltenham: Edward Elgar. Pp. 178–201.

2000   "The Impacts of Emigration on Countries of Origin." In *Local Dynamics in an Era of Globalization*. Ed. S. Yusuf, W. Wu and S. Evenett.

Castles, S. and A. Davidson
2000   *Citizenship and Migration: Globalisation and the Politics of Belonging*. London: Macmillan.

Castles, S. and G. Kosack
1973   *Immigrant Workers and Class Structure in Western Europe*. London: Oxford University Press.

Castles, S., S. Loughna and H. Crawley
2003   *States of Conflict: Causes and Patterns of Forced Migration to the EU and Policy Responses*. London: Institute of Public Policy Research.

Castles, S. and M. J. Miller
2003   *The Age of Migration: International Population Movements in the Modern World* (Third edition). Basingstoke: Palgrave-Macmillan.

Castles, S. and E. Vasta
2004   "Australia: New Conflicts around Old Dilemmas." In *Controlling Immigration: A Global Perspective*. Ed. W. Cornelius, P. L. Martin and J. F. Hollifield (Second edition). Stanford, CA: Stanford University Press.

Chimni, B. S.
1998   "The Geo-politics of Refugee Studies: A View from the South," *Journal of Refugee Studies*, 11(4):350–374.

Chiswick, B. R.
2000   "Are Immigrants Favorably Self-selected? An Economic Analysis." In *Migration Theory: Talking across Disciplines*. Ed. C. B. Brettell and J. F. Hollifield. New York and London: Routledge. Pp. 61–76.

Cohen, R.
1987   *The New Helots: Migrants in the International Division of Labour*. Aldershot: Avebury.

Cohn-Bendit, D. and T. Schmid
1993   *Heimat Babylon: Das Wagnis der Multikulturellen Demokratie*. Hamburg: Hoffmann und Campe.

Cornelius, W., P. L. Martin and J. F. Hollifield
1994   "Introduction: The Ambivalent Quest for Control." In *Controlling Immigration: A Global Perspective*. Ed. W. Cornelius, P. L. Martin and J. F. Hollifield (First edition). Stanford, CA: Stanford University Press.

DIMIA
2001   *Key Facts in Immigration*. Canberra: Department of Immigration and Multicultural Affairs and Indigenous Affairs.

Dohse, K.
1981   *Ausländische Arbeiter und bügerliche Staat*. Konistein/Taunus: Hain.

Duffield, M.
2001   *Global Governance and the New Wars: The Merging of Development and Security*. London and New York: Zed Books.

Fahrmeir, A., O. Faron and P. Weil
2003 "Introduction." In *Migration Control in the North Atlantic World*. Ed. A. Fahrmeir, O. Faron and P. Weil. New York and Oxford: Berghahn. Pp. 1–7.

Faist, T.
2004 "Dual Citizenship as a Path-Dependent Process," *International Migration Review*, 38(3):913–944.

Freeman, G. P.
2004 "Immigrant Incorporation in Western Democracies," *International Migration Review*, 38(3):945–969.

1995 "Models of Immigration Politics in Liberal Societies," *International Migration Review*, 24(4):881–902.

Geddes, A.
2003 *The Politics of Migration and Immigration in Europe*. London: Sage.

Glover, S. *et al.*
2001 *Migration: An Economic and Social Analysis*. London: Home Office.

Gonzalez, J. L. I.
1998 *Philippine Labour Migration: Critical Dimensions of Public Policy*. Singapore: Institute of Southeast Asian Studies.

Hammar, T.
1990 *Democracy and the Nation-State: Aliens, Denizens and Citizens in a World of International Migration*. Aldershot: Avebury.

Harris, N.
2002 *Thinking the Unthinkable: The Immigration Myth Exposed*. London: I. B. Tauris.

Hayter, T.
2001 *Open Borders*. London: Pluto Press.

Hollifield, J. F.
2004 "The Emerging Migration State," *International Migration Review*, 38(3):885–912.

2000 "The Politics of International Migration: How Can We 'Bring the State Back In'?" In *Migration Theory: Talking across Disciplines*. Ed. C. B. Brettell and J. F. Hollifield. New York and London: Routledge. Pp. 137–185.

Homze, E. L.
1967 Foreign Labor in Nazi Germany. New Jersey: Princeton University Press.

Hugo, G.
1994 *Migration and the Family*. Vienna: United Nations Occasional Papers Series for the International Year of the Family, No. 12.

IOM
2003 *World Migration 2003: Managing Migration – Challenges and Responses for People on the Move*. Geneva: International Organization for Migration.

Jones, S.
2000 *Making Money Off Migrants: The Indonesian Exodus to Malaysia*. Hong Kong and Wollongong: Asia 2000 and Centre for Asia Pacific Social Transformation Studies.

Jupp, J.
2002 *From White Australia to Woomera: The History of Australian Immigration*. Melbourne: Cambridge University Press.

Keeley, C. B.
2001 "The International Refugee Regimes(s): The End of the Cold War Matters," *International Migration Review,* 35(1):303–314.

Kondo, A.
2001 "Citizenship Rights for Aliens in Japan." In *Citizenship in a Global World.* Ed. A. Kondo. Basingstoke: Palgrave. Pp. 8–30.

Koopmans, R. and P. Statham
2000 "Migration and Ethnic Relations as a Field of Political Contention: An Opportunity Structure Approach." In *Challenging Immigration and Ethnic Relations Politics.* Ed. R. Koopmans and P. Statham. Oxford: Oxford University Press. Pp. 13–56.

Koser, K.
1997 "Social Networks and the Asylum Cycle: The Case of Iranians in the Netherlands," *International Migration Review,* 31(3):591–611.

Levitt, P. and N. Glick Schiller
2004 "Conceptualizing Simultaneity: A Transnational Social Field Perspective on Society," *International Migration Review,* 38(3):1002–1039.

Martin, P. L. and M. J. Miller
2000 *Employer Sanctions: French, German and U.S. Experiences.* Geneva: ILO.

Martin, P. L. and T. Straubhaar
2002 "Best Practices to Reduce Migration Pressures," *International Migration,* 40(3):5–21.

Martin, P. L. and J. E. Taylor
2001 "Managing Migration: The Role of Economic Policies." In *Global Migrants, Global Refugees: Problems and Solution.* Ed. A. R. Zolberg and P. M. Benda. New York and Oxford: Berghahn. Pp. 95–120.

Mori, H.
1997 *Immigration Policy and Foreign Workers in Japan.* London: Macmillan.

OECD
1998 *Trends in International Migration: Annual Report 1998.* Paris: OECD.

Oxfam
2002 *Rigged Rules and Double Standards: Trade, Globalisation, and the Fight against Poverty.* Oxford: Oxfam.

Peraldi, M.
2001 *Cabas et Containers: Activités Marchandes Informelles et Réseaux Transfrontaliers.* Paris: Maisonneuve et Larose.

Pillai, P.
1999 "The Malaysian State's Response to Migration," *Sojourn,* 14(1):178–197.

Portes, A.
1997 "Immigration Theory for a New Century: Some Problems and Opportunities," *International Migration Review,* 31(4):799–825.

Portes, A., L. E. Guarnizo and P. Landolt
1999 "The Study of Transnationalism: Pitfalls and Promise of an Emergent Research Field," *Ethnic and Racial Studies,* 22(2):217–237.

Price, C.
1963 *Southern Europeans in Australia.* Melbourne: Oxford University Press.

Reyneri, E.
2001 *Migrants' Involvement in Irregular Employment in the Mediterranean Countries of the European Union.* Geneva: International Labor Organization.

Saith, A.
1997 *Emigration Pressures and Structural Change: Case Study of the Philippines.* Geneva: International Labor Office.

Salt, J. and J. Clarke
2000 "International Migration in the UNECE Region: Patterns, Trends, Policies," *International Social Science Journal,* (165):313–328.

Schmeidl, S.
2001 "Conflict and Forced Migration: A Quantitative Review, 1964–95." In *Global Migrants, Global Refugees: Problems and Solutions.* Ed. A. R. Zolberg and P. M. Benda. New York and Oxford: Berghahn. Pp. 62–85.

Schnapper, D.
1994 *La Communauté des Citoyens.* Paris: Gallimard.

Sciortino, G.
2000 "Towards a Political Sociology of Entry Policies: Conceptual Problems and Theoretical Proposals," *Journal of Ethnic and Migration Studies,* 26(2):213–228.

Sittamparam, R.
2003 "A Year's Jail for Irene Fernandez for Publishing False News," *New Straits Times.* Kuala Lumpur.

Smith, J. P. and B. Edmonston
1997 *The New Americans: Economic, Demographic and Fiscal Effects of Immigration.* Washington, DC: National Academy Press.

Soysal, Y. N.
1994 *Limits of Citizenship: Migrants and Postnational Membership in Europe.* Chicago and London: University of Chicago Press.

Spencer, S.
2003 *The Politics of Migration: Managing Opportunity, Conflict and Change.* London: Blackwell.

Stark, O.
1991 *The Migration of Labour.* Oxford: Blackwell.

Stiglitz, J. E.
2002 *Globalization and its Discontents.* London: Penguin.

Straubhaar, T.
2002 "Towards a General Agreement on Movements of People (GAMP)," *Journal of International Peace and Organization,* 77(1–2):71–96.

Süssmuth, R.
2001 *Zuwanderung Gestalten, Integration Fördern: Bericht der Unabhängigen Kommission 'Zuwanderung.'* Berlin: Bundesminister des Innern.

Taylor, E. J.
1987 "Undocumented Mexico-U.S. Migration and the Returns to Households in Rural Mexico," *American Journal of Agricultural Economics,* 69:616–638.

Thompson, E. P.
1968 *The Making of the English Working Class.* Harmondsworth: Penguin.

Torpey, J.
2003 "Passports and the Development of Immigration Controls in the North Atlantic during the Long Nineteenth Century." In *Migration Control in the North Atlantic World.* Ed. A. Fahrmeir, O. Faron and P. Weil. New York and Oxford: Berghahn. Pp. 73–91.

UNHCR
2000 *Reconciling Migration Control and Refugee Protection in the European Union: A UNHCR Perspective.* Geneva: UNHCR.

United Nations Population Division
2002 *International Migration Report 2002.* New York: United Nations.

Vertovec, S.
2004 "Migrant Transnationalism and Modes of Transformation," *International Migration Review,* 38(3):970–1001.

Weiner, M.
1995 *The Global Migration Crisis: Challenges to States and Human Rights.* New York: Harper Collins.

Zlotnik, H.
1999 "Trends of International Migration since 1965: What Existing Data Reveal," *International Migration,* 37(1):21–62.

Zolberg, A. R.
1989 "The Next Waves: Migration Theory for a Changing World," *International Migration Review,* 23(3):403–430.

————
2001 "Introduction: Beyond the Crisis." In *Global Migrants, Global Refugees: Problems and Solutions.* Ed. A. R. Zolberg and P. M. Benda. New York and Oxford: Berghahn. Pp. 1–16.

Chapter 3

THE EMERGING MIGRATION STATE[1]

James Hollifield

In response to a plea from high-tech businesses that German industry was at a competitive disadvantage because of its lack of access to foreign computer and software engineers, the German government in May 2000 launched a new "green card" program, designed to recruit up to 20,000 highly skilled workers, from outside the European Union. To garner support for the initiative and to head off criticism from those who cling to the myth that Germany is not a country of immigration (*Deutschland ist kein Einwanderungsland*), Chancellor Gerhard Schröder asserted that "We [Germans] must make sure that in these times of globalization we don't suffer from a lack of cosmopolitanism. . . . There's a huge amount of international com-

[1]I would like to thank Rainer Bauböck, Klaus Bade, Ewald Engelen, Christian Joppke, Douglas Massey, Rainer Münz, Christopher Rudolph, and Dietrich Thränhardt, as well as the editors of this volume, Josh DeWind, Mark Miller, Alejandro Portes, and Lydio Tomasi, for their helpful comments on earlier versions of this article.

petition for the best people, and Germany would be making a big mistake if it didn't take part." This statement reflects a sea-change in Germany's foreigner policy (*Ausländerpolitik*), which is on the verge of becoming a legal immigration policy (*Einwanderungspolitik*). Together with the change in German nationality law – adopted by the Red-Green government in 1999 and which for the first time injected an element of birthplace citizenship (*jus soli*) into German law – the new green card program is pushing Germany in a decidedly liberal direction. Yet, at the same time that the green card policy was announced, the Schröder government declared that foreign high-tech workers would not be allowed to bring their families with them. After criticism from human rights groups and gentle reminders from experts about the difficulty of preventing "guest workers" from settling, the government quickly revised its policy to allow for the possibility of settlement and family reunification.

This recent episode in German immigration history illustrates well the dilemma that modern states must face in dealing with "globalization"[2] and rising levels of international migration. States are trapped in a "liberal paradox" (Hollifield, 1992a). Since the end of World War II, international economic forces (trade, investment, and migration) have been pushing states towards greater openness, while the international state system and powerful (domestic) political forces push states towards greater closure. This is a liberal paradox because it highlights some of the contradictions inherent in liberalism, which is the quintessentially modern political and economic philosophy and a defining feature of globalization.

Since the eighteenth century, when Adam Smith laid down the precepts of economic liberalism in his treatise on *The Wealth of Nations,* the ideology of free trade has come to dominate international relations. With Britain's rise to power – which reached its zenith in the Victorian era of the late nineteenth century – and America's dominance of the post-World War II international system, it has become increasingly difficult to refute Smith's argument that laissez-faire economics and free trade are the best ways to enhance the wealth, power, and security of the nation-state. The debacle of World War I and its aftermath of isolationism, intense nationalism, protectionism, and depression only served to reinforce this lesson. After 1945, the victorious Western democracies, led by Britain and the United States, were determined not to repeat the mistakes of the 1920s and 30s, and they set about constructing a new international order, based on liberal

[2]Here defined simply as increasing levels of international exchange.

principles of free trade and respect for fundamental human rights (Rose-crance, 1986; Jacobson, 1996).

The problem, however, is that the source of power and authority in international relations continues to revolve around the nation-state. Since the Peace of Westphalia in 1648, the international legal system has been based upon the inviolability of the nation-state. In the Grotian tradition of international law, in order for a state to exist, it must have a territory, a population, and the capacity for self-governance. Once a state has fulfilled these criteria, it may be recognized as independent, and it takes on the legal attribute of sovereignty, which Stephen Krasner (1999) wryly describes as "organized hypocrisy." If a state is sovereign, it has a legal personality and the capacity to enter into relations with other states.

Transnationalism, in the form of trade, cross-border investment, and migration, can challenge the sovereignty and authority of the nation-state. Migration in particular represents a challenge, in the sense that the (unauthorized) movement of individuals across national boundaries can violate the principle of sovereignty, which requires a degree of territorial closure (Hollifield, 1994b; Sassen, 1996; Joppke, 1998a). In every region of the globe – with the partial exception of Western Europe – borders are sacrosanct and they represent a fundamental organizational feature of the international system (Andreas and Snyder, 2000). Unlike trade in goods or international financial flows, migration can change the ethnic composition of societies and disrupt what Rey Koslowski (2000) has aptly described as the "demographic maintenance regime." If too many foreigners reside on the national territory, then it may become difficult for a state to identify its population vis-à-vis other states. The national community may feel threatened, and there may be a social or political backlash against immigration. Finally – and this is most important from the standpoint of political liberalism – the citizenry or the *demos* may be transformed in such a way as to violate the social contract and undermine the legitimacy of the government and the sovereignty of the state itself (Walzer, 1983). Thus, migration can be seen as a threat to national security, and it can lead to conflicts within and between states (Weiner, 1993, 1995; Huntington, 1996). Hence the liberal paradox: the economic logic of liberalism is one of openness, but the political and legal logic is one of closure (Hollifield, 1998). How can states escape from this paradox?

In order to answer this question, we need 1) to review the causes and consequences of international migration in historical perspective, and 2) to look at the ways in which states have tried to regulate it in an era of globalization, but 3) with an eye to understanding the evolution of what I shall call the migration state. In international relations theory, states are defined primarily by their security or military function. The Westphalian state is above all else a garrison state. Realists like Hans Morgenthau (1978) and neo-realists like Kenneth Waltz (1979) view the state as a unitary rational actor, with the overweening responsibility to maximize power, protect its territory and people, and pursue its national interest. However, at least since the beginning of the industrial revolution in Europe, the state has increasingly taken on an economic function. Ensuring material wealth and power has required states to risk greater economic openness and to pursue policies of free trade, giving rise to what Richard Rosecrance (1986) has called the trading state. As a result, states have been partially liberated from their dependence on territory and the military as sources of power. International relations theory has moved away from the narrow realist view of the state, recognizing that in an increasingly interdependent world, power is more diffuse (Keohane and Nye, 1977). In this neoliberal view, states are increasingly linked together by international trade and finance, forcing them to alter their grand strategies and seek new ways to cooperate. Here I shall argue that migration and trade are inextricably linked – two sides of the same coin. Hence the rise of the trading state necessarily entails the rise of the migration state, where considerations of power and interest are driven as much by migration (the movement of people) as they are by commerce and finance.

CAUSES AND CONSEQUENCES OF INTERNATIONAL MIGRATION

To go back to the German example, we can see clearly how migration has become a driving feature of the international political economy. In the eighteenth and nineteenth centuries, Germany, which only loosely could be defined as a state until it was unified by Bismarck in 1870, was primarily a country of emigration, with millions of Germans migrating to East Central Europe and to the Americas (Bade, 1992). Not until relatively late in the nineteenth century did the German economy begin to grow at a sufficient rate to absorb its surplus population and excess labor supply. Strong supply-push factors were at work, compelling Germans to go abroad. At the same time there were powerful demand-pull forces, leading German farmers and workers to emigrate to neighboring countries, such as France, Switzerland, and the Low Countries, in search of employment, while many went to Russia or the United States, lured by the promise of cheap land and a new start. In eighteenth century Russia, this migration was organized by the German-born empress, Catherine the Great, who sought to upgrade Russian agriculture and tame the eastern frontier by bringing in skilled German farmers as pioneers who could teach Russian peasants new farming techniques. For centuries, states have been in the business of organizing mass migrations for the purposes of colonization, economic development, and to gain a competitive edge in a globalizing economy. In this respect, Chancellor Schröder's quest for Indian software engineers is but the latest chapter in the long history of globalization and migration.

Once an international market for labor has been created, however, it may be difficult to manage or regulate it. Migration can quickly become self-perpetuating because of chain migration and social networks (Massey, 1987, 1998). Word begins to spread from one family and one village to another about the possibilities for gainful employment – or even striking it rich. At the same time, the individual risks and costs associated with migration are reduced by these kinship networks, which can grow into transnational communities and constitute a form of social capital (Morawska, 1990; Portes, 1996, 1997). As international migration accelerates, states are forced to respond by developing new policies to cope with newcomers and their families (in the host country) or to deal with an exodus and potential return migration (in the sending country). Again, looking at the eighteenth and nineteenth centuries – a period of relatively free migration – many states with open frontiers, like the United States and Russia, were happy to receive immigrants, whereas overpopulated societies, with a growing rural exodus and burgeoning cities, were happy to be rid of masses of unskilled and often illiterate peasants and workers (Thomas, 1973; Bade, 1992; Nugent, 1992).

By the end of the nineteenth and beginning of the twentieth centuries, however, the sending societies in Europe were well into the industrial revolution and entering a demographic transition, with falling birth rates and more stable populations. Nationalism was on the rise (Hobsbawm, 1990), and it was increasingly important, in terms of military security, for states to be able to identify their citizens and to construct new demographic regimes (Koslowski, 2000). The need to regulate national populations, for purposes of taxation and conscription, led to passport and visa systems and the concomitant development of immigration and naturalization policies (Torpey, 1998). Every individual was expected to have one and only one nationality, and nationality, as a legal institution, would provide the individual with a measure of protection in a hostile and anarchic world of nation-states (Shaw, 1997). Countries of emigration, like Germany, tended to opt for nationality laws based upon *jus sanguinis* (blood, kinship or ethnicity), whereas countries of immigration, like the United States and France, developed a more expansive political citizenship based upon *jus soli* (soil or birthplace). The German nationality law of 1913 had a strong ethnic component, and it was designed specifically to accommodate return migration, whereas birthright citizenship in the United States, as codified in the Fourteenth Amendment to the Constitution, was more inclusive (Brubaker, 1989, 1992; Schuck, 1998). It is important to remember, however, that the Fourteenth Amendment was adopted in the aftermath of the Civil War, and its primary purpose was to grant immediate and automatic citizenship to former slaves (Kettner, 1978). Moreover, American immigration policy in the late nineteenth and early twentieth centuries evolved along racial lines, culminating in the Chinese Exclusion Act of 1882 and the National Origins Quota system, enacted in 1924 (Smith, 1997; King, 2000; Hollifield, 2000c).

Until 1914, international migration was driven primarily by the dynamics of colonization and the push and pull of economic and demographic forces (Hatton and Williamson, 1998), even though many receiving states were struggling to put in place national regulatory schemes to manage the growing international market for labor. Illegal or unauthorized immigration was not recognized as a major policy issue, and there were virtually no provisions for political migration, *i.e.,* refugees and asylum seekers. To a large extent, efforts to regulate international migration would be rendered moot by the outbreak in 1914 of war in Europe, which stopped economic migration in its tracks. However, war and decolonization fostered the rise of intense and virulent forms of nationalism – often with a strong ethnic dimension. War sparked irredentism and the redrawing of national boundaries in Europe, which in turn fostered new kinds of migration. Millions of displaced persons, refugees, and asylum seekers would cross national boundaries in the twentieth century to "escape from violence" (Zolberg, Suhrke and Aguayo, 1989). Thus, World War I marked a crucial turning point in the history of migration and international relations. States would never return to the relatively open migration regimes of the eighteenth and nineteenth centuries when market forces (supply-push and demand-pull) were the dominant forces driving international migration (Thomas, 1973). The twentieth-century world became increasingly closed, and travel would require elaborate documentation. World War I also marked the beginning of the end of imperialism, with struggles for independence and decolonization in Asia and Africa, movements that would eventually result in the displacement of more millions of people.

In the interwar years, the Westphalian system of nation-states hardened and became further institutionalized in the core countries of the Euro-Atlantic region, and it continued to spread around the globe with the creation of new states (or the reemergence of old ones) in Asia, Africa and the Middle East. Old and new states guarded their sovereignty jealously, and peoples in every region gained a stronger sense of citizenship and national identity. Because of these developments, international migration took on more of a political character, with diaspora and exile politics coming to the fore (Shain, 1989). Henceforth, crossing borders had the potential of being a political as well as an economic act, and states reasserted their authority with a vengeance. The rise of anti-state revolutionary movements, such as anarchism and communism, provoked harsh crackdowns on immigration and the roll-back of civil rights and liberties, in the name of national security and national identity (Reimers, 1998; Smith, 1997; King, 2000).

The interwar period was marked by intense protectionism and nativism (Eichengreen, 1989; King, 2000). States enacted draconian laws to protect their markets and their populations. The international community was not prepared to deal with new forms of political migration. Under international law, states are not required to admit aliens, but if they do, they are obliged to treat them in a humane and civilized manner. This concern for the rights of aliens was clearly enunciated in Articles 22 and 23 of the Covenant of the League of Nations, which created a kind of rudimentary human rights law, aimed at protecting those in former colonies (Shaw, 1997).

The events of the 1930s and 40s in Europe radically changed legal norms governing international migration. The Holocaust and World War II led to the creation of the United Nations and a new body of refugee and human rights law. Although states retained sovereign control over their territory, and the principle of noninterference in the internal affairs of others still holds, the postwar international order created new legal spaces (*i.e.,* rights) for individuals and groups. The 1951 Geneva Convention Relating to the Status of Refugees established the principle of asylum, whereby an individual with a "well-founded fear of persecution," once admitted to the territory of a safe state, cannot be arbitrarily expelled or sent back to the state of his or her nationality. Under international law, the individual is entitled to a legal hearing, but it is important to remember that no state is compelled to admit an asylum seeker (Goodwin-Gill, 1996). If, however, the state is a signatory of the Convention, it cannot legally send an individual back to his or her country of origin if he or she is threatened with persecution and violence. This is the principle of *nonrefoulement.*

The United Nations Charter as well as the Universal Declaration of Human Rights, which was adopted by the U.N. General Assembly in December 1948, reinforced the principle of the rights of individuals "across borders" (Jacobson, 1996). Likewise, as a direct response to the Holocaust and other crimes against humanity, the international community in 1948 adopted and signed the Convention on the Prevention and Punishment of the Crime of Genocide. Alongside these developments in international law, we can see a growing "rights-based liberalism" in the politics and jurisprudence of the most powerful liberal states in Europe and North America (Cornelius, Martin, and Hollifield, 1994; Joppke, 2001). These liberal developments in international and municipal law feed off of one another, creating new rights (legal spaces) for aliens at both the international and domestic levels.

Why are these legal developments so important, and how can they help states escape from the liberal paradox? Unlike trade and financial flows, which can be promoted and regulated through international institutions like the WTO and the IMF, the movement of individuals across borders requires a qualitatively different set of regulatory regimes – ones based squarely on the notion of civil and human rights. It is almost a truism to point out that individuals, unlike goods, services or capital, have a will of their own and can become subjects of the law and members of the societies in which they reside (Hollifield, 1992a; Weiner, 1995). They also can become citizens of the polity (Koslowski, 2000). The question, of course, is how far states are willing to go in establishing an international regime for the orderly (legal) movement of people (Ghosh, 2000), and to what extent would such a regime rely upon municipal as opposed to international law (Hollifield, 2000a)?

REGULATING MIGRATION IN AN ERA OF GLOBALIZATION

The last half of the twentieth century has marked an important new chapter in the history of globalization. With advances in travel and communications technology, migration has accelerated, reaching levels not seen since the end of the nineteenth century. At the beginning of the twenty-first century, roughly 175 million people are living outside of their countries of birth or citizenship.[3] Even though this figure constitutes a mere 2.5 percent of the world's population, the perception is that international migration is rising at

[3]The trend in international migration has been steadily upward since the end of World War II (IOM, 1996, 2000).

an exponential rate and that it is a permanent feature of the global economy. It seems that economic forces compelling people to move are intensifying. With more than half the world's migrant population in the less-developed countries (LDCs), especially those rich in natural resources, like oil or diamonds, the biggest regulatory challenge confronts states like Nigeria, South Africa or the United States, which share land borders with overpopulated and underdeveloped states. Supply-push forces remain strong, while the ease of communication and travel have reinforced migrant networks, making it easier than ever for potential migrants to gather the information they need to make decisions about whether or not to move.

To some extent supply-push forces are constant or rising and have been for many decades. What is variable, however, are demand-pull forces, both in the OECD world and in the wealthier LDCs, many of which suffer from a shortage of skilled and unskilled labor. The oil sheikdoms of the Persian Gulf are perhaps the best examples, but increasingly we have seen labor shortages in the newly industrialized countries (NICs) of East and Southeast Asia as well (Fields, 1994). Singapore, Malaysia, Hong Kong and Taiwan, for example, have become major importers of cheap labor from other LDCs in Southeast Asia, particularly the Philippines and Thailand. Taiwan also has experienced rising levels of illegal migration from mainland China, which poses a security threat for the island country.

With very few exceptions, however, these LDCs have not evolved elaborate laws or policies for governing migration. Wealthier Third World states have put in place contract or guest worker schemes, negotiated with the sending countries and with no provisions for settlement or family reunification. These types of pure manpower policies leave migrants with few if any rights, making them vulnerable to human rights abuses and arbitrary expulsion. The only protections they have are those afforded by the negotiating power of their home countries, which may choose to protest the treatment of their nationals. But, more often than not, the sending countries are unwilling to provoke a conflict with a receiving state over individual cases of abuse for fear of losing access to remittances, which are one of the largest sources of foreign exchange for many LDCs (Russell, 1986). Hence, economics and demography (forces of supply-push and demand-pull) continue to govern much of international migration in the developing world, and the liberal paradox is less acute because there are fewer legal or institutional constraints on the behavior of states vis-à-vis foreign nationals. Summary deportations and mass expulsions are viable options for controlling immigration in nonliberal states.

In the advanced industrial democracies, immigration has been trending upward for most of the post-World War II period, to the point that well over 40 percent of the world's migrant population resides in Europe and America, where roughly 10 percent of the population is foreign born (IOM, 2000; OECD, 1998). Postwar migration to the core industrial states of Europe and North America has gone through several distinct phases, which make these population movements quite different from the transatlantic migration of the nineteenth century or economic migrations in the Third World today. As pointed out above, the first wave of migration in the aftermath of World War II was intensely political, especially in Europe, where large populations were displaced as a result of the redrawing of national boundaries, irredentism, and ethnic cleansing. Much of the remaining Jewish population in Europe fled to the United States or Israel, whereas the large ethnic German populations in East Central Europe flooded into the newly created Federal Republic of Germany. The partitioning of Germany, the Cold War, and the division of Europe contributed to the exodus of large ethnic populations, seeking refuge in the democratic West. Until the construction of the Berlin Wall in 1961, 12 million German refugees arrived in West Germany.

Once this initial wave of refugee migration had exhausted itself and Europe began to settle into an uneasy peace that split the continent between the superpowers – thus cutting (West) Germany and other industrial states in Western Europe off from their traditional supplies of surplus labor in Central Europe – new economic forms of migration began to emerge. The massive effort to reconstruct the war-ravaged economies of Western Europe in the 1950s exhausted indigenous supplies of labor, especially in Germany and France. Like the United States, which launched a guest worker (*bracero*) program (1942–1964) during World War II to recruit Mexican agricultural workers (Calavita, 1992), the industrial states of Northwest Europe concluded bilateral agreements with labor-rich countries in Southern Europe and Turkey, that allowed them to recruit millions of guest workers during the 1950s and 60s (Miller and Martin, 1982).

However, from the beginning of the guest worker phase, we could see an important distinction between those European states, like France, which had a legal immigration policy that allowed for the settlement of immigrant workers and their families, and those states, like Germany or Switzerland, which attempted to maintain strict rotation policies with a minimum of settlement and family reunification (Rogers, 1985; Hollifield, 1992a; Cornelius, Martin and Hollifield, 1994). Britain was something of a special case in that its economy was growing at a slower pace and it had continuous access to Irish labor to fill any gaps in the British labor market. Moreover, the struggle to regulate post-colonial migrations began earlier in Britain than in the former imperial powers on the continent (*e.g.*, France and Holland), thus injecting a bias towards restriction into British policy (Layton-Henry, 1992; Joppke, 1998c; Hansen, 2000).

The guest worker phase ended in the United States with the winding down of the *bracero* program in the 1950s, whereas in Europe it continued until the first signs of economic slowdown in 1966. However, the big shift in migration policy in Western Europe came in 1973–74, following the first major oil shock and recession, which rapidly spread around the globe. European governments abruptly suspended all foreign/guest worker recruitment and took steps to encourage foreigners to return home. Policies were put in place to discourage or, wherever possible, prevent settlement and family reunification. The prevailing sentiment was that guest worker migrations were primarily economic in nature and that these workers constituted a kind of economic shock absorber (*Konjunkturpuffer*). They were brought into the labor market during periods of high growth and low unemployment, and they should be sent home during periods of recession (Miller and Martin, 1982; Rogers, 1985; *see also* Castles and Kosack, 1973). Moreover, during the recessions of the 1970s, the hardest hit sectors in the West European economies were heavy industry and manufacturing, both big users of cheap, unskilled foreign labor. In these circumstances of recession and rising unemployment, it seemed logical that guest workers should behave, like all commodities, according to the laws of supply and demand.

The governments of Western Europe had succeeded in creating an international labor market, in response to a high demand for unskilled or semi-skilled foreign labor. Yet just when this labor migration was no longer needed, powerful supply-push forces and networks came into play to sustain it at high levels, even after the official suspension of recruitment programs in 1973–74. Turkish migration to Germany and North African migration to France continued well into the 1980s, taking the form of family rather than worker migration. What made the family reunification phase of postwar migration possible was the intervention of courts, extending rights of residence to guest workers and their families (Hollifield, 1992a, 2000b). Executive and administrative authorities were hampered by legal/constitutional constraints in their quest to reverse the migration flows. States with universalistic, republican traditions (like the United States, France, and to a lesser extent Germany), along with elements of separation of powers, including a strong and independent judiciary, had much greater difficulty in cutting immigration flows (Weil, 1991; Hollifield, 1994a, 1999b; Joppke, 1998b, 2001). Again, Britain, with its system of parliamentary supremacy, unitary government, and the absence of a universalistic, republican tradition constitutes something of an exception among the industrial democracies – Gary Freeman refers to Britain as the "deviant case" (Freeman, 1994; see also Messina, 1996; and Hansen, 2000).

The difficulty of using guest workers for managing labor markets in Western Europe is a perfect illustration of the liberal paradox. Importing labor to sustain high levels of noninflationary growth during the 1950s and 60s was a logical move for states and employers. This move was in keeping with the growing trend towards internationalization of markets for capital, goods, services and labor; and it was encouraged by international economic organizations, particularly the OECD (Hollifield, 1992a). But, as the Swiss novelist Max Frisch pointed out at the time, the European governments had "asked for workers, but human beings came." Unlike goods or capital, migrants (human beings) can and do acquire rights, particularly under the aegis of the laws and constitutions of liberal states, which afford migrants a measure of due process and equal protection. When it became clear that the guests had "come to stay" (Rogers, 1985), the initial reaction of most governments was to stop further recruitment of foreign workers, try to induce those residing in the country to return, and prevent family reunification. When this proved not to be possible, these liberal states had to accept the fact that large numbers of guest workers and their family members would become permanent settlers, leading most governments to redouble their efforts to stop any future immigration.

The settlement of large foreign populations transformed the politics of Western Europe, giving rise to new social movements and political parties demanding a halt to immigration (Betz, 1994; Kitschelt, 1995; Messina, 1996). Public opinion was by and large hostile to immigration, and governments were at a loss how to manage ethnic diversity (Freeman, 1979; Ireland, 1994; Fetzer, 2000; Bleich, 2003). Problems of integration began to dominate the public discourse, amid perceptions that Muslim immigrants in particular posed a threat to civil society and to the secular (republican) state. The fear was (and is) that dispossessed and disillusioned youth of the second generation would turn to radical Islam, rather than following the conventional, secular, and republican path to assimilation (Kepel, 1988; Kastoryano, 1997). European societies looked increasingly like the United States where older, linear conceptions of assimilation had given way to multiculturalism and an increasingly uneven or segmented incorporation, whereby large segments of the second generation, particularly among the unskilled and uneducated, experienced significant downward mobility (Hollifield, 1997b; Santel and Hollifield, 1998; Portes and Rumbaut, 1996; Alba and Nee, 2003).

In part because of this (perceived) crisis of integration and the threat it posed, pressures for greater control of immigration intensified, not only in Western Europe, but in the United States and Australia as well. However, in the face of these political pressures, it is important to note the pervasive and equally powerful rights-dynamic in the liberal democracies. Rights for minorities and foreigners were deeply embedded in the jurisprudence and the political culture of these societies, helping to blunt the impact of nativist and xenophobic movements. The more draconian laws, like the 1986 and 1995 Pasqua Laws in France, Proposition 187 in California, or the 1996 Illegal Immigration Reform and Immigrant Responsibility Act in the United States, were either struck down by the courts or substantially modified to conform with liberal, constitutional principles (Hollifield, 1997a, 1999b, 2000b; Schuck, 1998; Tichenor, 2002). Even though all states have the right to expel unauthorized migrants, deportation is not a very attractive policy instrument, and it is used sparingly and largely for its symbolic and deterrent effect (Ellermann, 2003). Mass expulsions (like Operation Wetback in the United States in the 1950s) are not politically or legally viable.

In spite of the enormous pressures on the asylum process that were building in the last two decades of the twentieth century, European democracies maintained a relatively strong commitment to the 1951 Convention and the international refugee and human rights regime. In the 1980s and 90s, asylum seeking became the principal avenue for entry into Western Europe, in the absence of full-fledged legal immigration policies and in the face of growing fears that large numbers of asylum seekers would undermine the refugee regime and destabilize European welfare states.

In this atmosphere of crisis, control policies shifted in the 1990s to stepped up external (border) control – Operations Gatekeeper and Hold the Line on the U.S.-Mexican border and the Schengen system in Western Europe to allow states to turn away asylum seekers if they had transited a "safe third country" – internal regulation of labor markets (through employer sanctions and the like), and integrating large, established foreign populations (Brochmann and Hammar, 1999; Cornelius *et al.*, 2004). Controlling borders in Europe required a renewed emphasis on international cooperation, especially among the member states of the European Community (EC). The EC, soon to become the European Union (EU), was committed to building a border-free Europe, relaxing and eventually eliminating all internal borders in order to complete the internal market. This process of integration was given new impetus by the Single European Act of 1986, which called for the elimination of all barriers to the movement of capital, goods, services and people within the territory of the EC by January 1992, and by the Maastricht Treaty on Economic and Monetary Union (EMU), ratified in 1993, which established a new kind of European citizenship (Caporaso, 2000). Given the desire of member states to stop further immigration, creating a border-free Europe meant reinforcing external borders, building a "ring fence" around the common territory, and moving towards common asylum and visa policies (Hollifield, 1992b; Uçarer, 1997; Guiraudon and Lahav, 2000).

A series of conventions dealing with migration and security issues were drafted to help construct a new European migration regime, including the Schengen Agreement of 1985, whereby EU governments committed themselves to eliminating border checks in exchange for common visa requirements to control the movement of third-country nationals (TCNs). In the same vein, the Dublin Convention of 1990 requires asylum seekers to apply for asylum in the first "safe country" where they arrive. Schengen and Dublin helped to establish buffer states in the formerly communist countries of Central Europe. EU member states could return asylum seekers to these now safe third countries without violating the principle of *nonrefoulement*. The Dublin and Schengen Conventions also were designed to eliminate "asylum shopping" by requiring signatory states to accept the asylum decision of other member states. Thus an asylum seeker is permitted to apply for asylum in only one state, assuming he or she did not transit a safe third country before arriving on the common territory.

Project 1992 together with the Maastricht process launched the most ambitious program of regional integration and economic liberalization in European history. But just as this process was taking off in 1989–90, the strategic situation in Europe was turned upside down, with the end of the Cold War and the collapse of the USSR and its communist satellites in East Central Europe. This change in the international system, which began in the 1980s during the period of *glasnost* under Mikhail Gorbachev, made it easier for individuals wishing to emigrate from the East to leave and seek asylum in the West. The result was a dramatic increase in the number of asylum seekers in Western Europe, not just from Eastern Europe, but from all over the world.

International migration had entered a new phase in the 1980s and 90s, with refugee migration and asylum seeking reaching levels not seen since the period just after World War II. The situation in Europe was further complicated by a resurgence of ethnic nationalism (Brubaker, 1996), by war in the Balkans, and by a dramatic increase in the number of refugees from almost every region of the globe. By the mid-1990s there were more than 16 million refugees in the world, with two thirds of them in Africa and the Middle East. The U.N. system for managing refugee migration, which had been created during the Cold War primarily to accommodate those fleeing persecution under communist rule, suddenly came under enormous pressure (Teitelbaum, 1984). The United Nations High Commission for Refugees (UNHCR) was transformed virtually overnight into one of the most important international institutions. The UNHCR was thrust into the role of managing the new migration crisis, as the Western democracies struggled to contain a wave of asylum seeking. The claims of the vast majority of those seeking asylum in Western Europe and the United States would be rejected, leading Western governments (and their publics) to the conclusion that most asylum seekers are in fact economic refugees (Fetzer, 2000). By the same token, many human rights advocates feared that genuine refugees would be submerged in a tide of false asylum seeking.

Whatever conclusion one draws from the high rate of rejection of asylum claims, the fact is that refugee migration surged in the last two decades of the twentieth century, creating a new set of dilemmas for liberal states (Teitelbaum, 1980, 1984). A large percentage of those whose asylum claims were refused would remain in the host countries either legally, pending appeal of their cases, or illegally, simply going underground. With most of the European democracies attempting to slow or stop all forms of legal immigration, the number of illegal immigrants, many of whom are individuals who entered the country legally and overstayed their visas, has increased steadily. Closing off avenues for legal immigration in Western Europe led to a surge in illegal migration. But with the perception among Western publics that immigration is raging out of control and with the rise of right-wing and xenophobic political parties and movements, especially in Western Europe, governments are extremely reluctant to create new programs for legal immigration or to expand existing quotas.

Instead, the thrust of policy change in Western Europe and the United States has been in the direction of further restriction. To give a few examples, Germany in 1993 amended its constitution in order to eliminate the blanket right of asylum that was enshrined in Article 16 of the old Basic Law. France in 1995–96 enacted a series of laws (the Pasqua and Debré Laws) that were designed to roll back the rights of foreign residents and make it more difficult for immigrants to naturalize (Brochmann and Hammar, 1999). Also in 1996, the Republican-majority Congress enacted the Illegal Immigration Reform and Immigrant Responsibility Act, which curtailed social or welfare rights for all immigrants (legal as well as illegal) and severely limited the due process rights of illegal immigrants and asylum seekers.

Yet, at the same time that the U.S. Congress was acting to limit immigrant rights, it took steps to expand legal immigration, especially for certain categories of highly skilled immigrants. The H-1B program, which gives American businesses the right to recruit foreigners with skills that are in short supply among native workers, was expanded in the 1990s. In France in 1997 and in Germany in 1999, laws were passed by left-wing governments to liberalize naturalization and citizenship policy (Hollifield, 1999b, 2000b,c). Most European governments recognize that they now preside over multicultural/immigrant societies, and attempts to ostracize settled foreign populations only feed the flames of xenophobia and racism. Moreover, with stagnant or declining populations and a shortage of highly skilled workers, European governments are now turning to new recruitment programs, seeking to emulate some aspects of American and Canadian immigration policy, and make their economies more competitive in a rapidly globalizing world. How can we make sense of these seemingly contradictory trends? Have states found ways of escaping from the liberal paradox, or are they still caught between economic forces that propel them toward greater openness (to maximize material wealth and economic security) and political forces that seek a higher degree of closure (to protect the *demos,* maintain the integrity of the community, and preserve the social contract)? This is already a daunting task – for states to find the appropriate "equilibrium" between openness and closure – but they also face the very real threat of terrorism. The attacks of September 11, 2001 on the United States served as a reminder that the first responsibility of the state is to provide for the security of its territory and population.

THE EMERGING "MIGRATION STATE"

International migration is likely to increase in coming decades unless there is some cataclysmic international event, like war or economic depression. Even after the 9/11 terrorist attack on the United States, the liberal democracies have remained relatively open to international migration. Global economic inequalities mean that supply-push forces remain strong, while at the same time demand-pull forces are intensifying (Martin and Widgren, 1996). The growing demand for highly skilled workers, as we have seen in the

German case, and the demographic decline in the industrial democracies create economic opportunities for migrants. Transnational networks have become more dense and efficient, linking the sending and receiving societies. These networks help to lower the costs and the risks of migration, making it easier for people to move across borders and over long distances. Moreover, when legal migration is not an option, migrants have increasingly turned to professional smugglers, and a global industry of migrant smuggling – often with the involvement of organized crime – has sprung up, especially in the last decade of the twentieth century. Hardly a week passes without some news of a tragic loss of life associated with migrant smuggling (Kyle and Koslowski, 2001).

But migration, like any type of transnational economic activity (such as trade and foreign investment), cannot and does not take place in a legal or institutional void. As we have seen, states have been and still are deeply involved in organizing and regulating migration, and the extension of rights to non-nationals has been an extremely important part of the story of international migration in the post-World War II period. For the most part, rights that accrue to migrants come from the legal and constitutional protections guaranteed to all "members" of society (Hollifield 1992a, 1999a). Thus, if an individual migrant is able to establish some claim to residence in the territory of a liberal state, his or her chances of being able to remain and settle will increase. At the same time, developments in international human rights law have helped to solidify the position of individuals vis-à-vis the nation-state, to the point that individuals (and certain groups) have acquired a sort of international legal personality, leading some analysts to speculate that we are entering a post-national era, characterized by "universal personhood" (Soysal, 1994), the expansion of "rights across borders" (Jacobson, 1995), and even "transnational citizenship" (Bauböck, 1994). Others have argued that migrants have become transnational, because so many no longer reside exclusively within the territory of one state (Glick-Schiller, 1999; Levitt, 2001), opting to shuttle between a place of origin and destination. This line of argument gives priority to agency as a defining feature of contemporary migrations; but it ignores the extent to which state policies have shaped the choices that migrants make (Hollifield, 2000d; Waldinger and Fitzgerald, 2004). The migration state is almost by definition a liberal state inasmuch as it creates a legal and regulatory environment in which migrants can pursue individual strategies of accumulation.

But regulating international migration requires liberal states to be attentive to the (human or civil) rights of the individual. If rights are ignored or trampled upon, then the liberal state risks undermining its own legitimacy and *raison d'être* (Hollifield, 1999a). As international migration and transnationalism increase, pressures build upon liberal states to find new and creative ways to cooperate, to manage flows. The definition of the national interest and *raison d'Etat* have to take this reality into account, as rights become more and more a central feature of domestic and foreign policy. New international regimes will be necessary if states are to risk more openness, and rights-based (international) politics will be the order of the day (Hollifield, 1992b, 1994b, 2000b; Cornelius *et al.*, 2004; Ghosh, 2000).

Some politicians and policymakers, as well as international organizations, continue to hope for market-based/economic solutions to the problem of regulating international migration. It is hoped that trade and foreign direct investment – bringing capital and jobs to people, either through private investment or official development assistance – will substitute for migration, alleviating both supply-push and demand-pull factors (Bhagwati, 1983; Martin and Widgren, 1996). Even though trade can lead to factor-price equalization in the long term, as we have seen in the case of the European Union (Stolper and Samuelson, 1941; Mundell, 1957; Straubhaar, 1988), in the short and medium term exposing LDCs to market forces often results in increased (rather than decreased) migration, as is evident with NAFTA and the U.S.-Mexican relationship (Martin, 1993; Massey *et al.*, 2002). Likewise, trade in services can stimulate more "high end" migration because these types of products often cannot be produced or sold without the movement of the individuals who make and market them (Bhagwati, 1998; Ghosh, 1997).

In short, the global integration of markets for goods, services and capital entails higher levels of international migration. Therefore, if states want to promote freer trade and investment, they must be prepared to manage higher levels of migration. Many states (like Canada and Germany) are willing, if not eager, to sponsor high-end migration because the numbers are manageable and there is likely to be less political resistance to the importation of highly skilled individuals. However, mass migration of unskilled and less educated workers is likely to meet with greater political resistance, even in situations and in sectors like construction or health care, where there is high demand for this type of labor. In these instances, the tendency is for governments to go back to the old guest worker models in hopes of bringing in just enough temporary workers to fill gaps in the labor market, but with strict contracts between foreign workers and their employers that limit the length of stay and prohibit settlement or family reunification (Miller and

Martin, 1982; Hönekopp, 1997). The alternative is illegal immigration and a growing black market for labor – a Hobson's choice.

The nineteenth and twentieth centuries saw the rise of what Richard Rosecrance (1986) has labeled the trading state. The latter half of the twentieth century has given rise to the migration state. In fact, from a strategic, economic and demographic standpoint, trade and migration go hand in hand. Because the wealth, power and stability of the state is now more than ever dependent on its willingness to risk both trade and migration (Lusztig, 1996; Hollifield, 1998), as our German example shows. In launching a modest "green card" program, Germany is clearly seeking to emulate the United States and Canada on the premise that global competitiveness, power, and economic security are closely related to a willingness to accept immigrants. Germans in particular and Europeans in general are (reluctantly) following the American and Canadian examples in order to enhance their material power and wealth. But, in one important respect, Germany and Europe have an advantage over the United States, and Canada or Australia for that matter. Germany is part of a regional economic enterprise (the European Union), which is not only creating a free trade zone, but also a free migration area.

Now more than ever, international security and stability are dependent on the capacity of states to manage migration. It is extremely difficult, if not impossible, for states to manage or control migration either unilaterally or bilaterally. Some type of multilateral/regional regime is required, similar to what the EU has constructed for nationals of the member states. The EU model, as it has evolved from Rome to Maastricht to Amsterdam and beyond, points the way to future migration regimes because it is not based purely on *homo economicus,* but incorporates rights for individual migrants and even a rudimentary citizenship, which continues to evolve (Caporaso, 2000). The problem, of course, in this type of regional migration regime is how to deal with third-country nationals (TCNs). As the EU expands and borders are relaxed, the issue of TCNs, immigrants, and ethnic minorities becomes ever more pressing, and new institutions, laws and regulations must be created to deal with them (Geddes, 1994, 2003; Guiraudon, 1998). In the end, the EU, by creating a regional migration regime and a kind of supra-national authority to deal with migration and refugee issues, allows the member states to finesse, if not escape, the liberal paradox (Geddes, 2000, 2003). Playing the good cop/bad cop routine and using symbolic politics and policies to maintain the illusion of border control help governments fend off the forces of closure, at least in the short run (Rudolph, 2003).

In the end, however, it is the nature of the liberal state itself and the degree to which openness is institutionalized and (constitutionally) protected from the "majority of the moment" that will determine whether states will continue to risk trade and migration (Hollifield, 2000d).

Regional integration reinforces the trading state and acts as a midwife for the migration state. In the EU, migrants, including TCNs, are gradually acquiring the rights that they need in order to live and work on the territory of the member states (Groenendijk, Guild and Barzilay, 2000; Geddes, 2003; Hollifield, 2000b). Regional integration blurs the lines of territoriality, lessening problems of integration and national identity. The fact that there is an increasing disjuncture between people and place – which in the past might have provoked a crisis of national identity and undermined the legitimacy of the nation-state – is less of a problem when the state is tied to a regional regime, like the EU. This does not mean, of course, that there will be no resistance to freer trade and migration. Protests against globalization and nativist or xenophobic reactions against immigration have been on the rise throughout the OECD world. Nonetheless, regional integration, especially when it has a long history and is deeply institutionalized as it is in Europe, makes it easier for states to risk trade and migration and for governments to construct the kinds of political coalitions that will be necessary to support and institutionalize greater openness.

Not surprisingly, Mexican President Vicente Fox, like his predecessors, is looking to Europe as a model for how to solve problems of regional integration, especially the very delicate political issue of illegal Mexican immigration to the United States. His argument is that freer migration and a more open (normalized) border are logical extensions of the North American Free Trade Agreement (NAFTA). The previous Mexican government, under Ernesto Zedillo, by moving to grant dual nationality to Mexican nationals living north of the border, took a big step towards consolidating and extending the rights of this, the largest migrant population in North America. But the U.S. government is reluctant to move so fast with economic and political integration, especially after the attack of September 11, 2001, preferring instead to create new guest worker programs or to continue with the current system, which tolerates high levels of unauthorized migration from Mexico (Massey, 2002). Clearly, however, North America is the region that is closest to taking steps towards an EU-style regional migration regime, and the United States is facing the prospect of another legalization. In the long run, it is difficult for liberal states, like the United States, to sustain a large, illegal population. For this reason, amnesties, legalizations, or regularizations have become a common feature of the migration state.

Even though there are large numbers of economic migrants in Asia, this region remains divided into relatively closed and often authoritarian societies, with little prospect of granting rights to migrants and guest workers. The more liberal and democratic states, like Japan, Taiwan and South Korea, are the exceptions; but they have only just begun to grapple with the problem of immigration, on a relatively small scale (Cornelius *et al.,* 2004). In Africa and the Middle East, which have high numbers of migrants and refugees, there is a great deal of instability, and states are fluid with little institutional or legal capacity for dealing with international migration.

In conclusion, we can see that migration is both a cause and a consequence of political and economic change. International migration, like trade, is a fundamental feature of the postwar liberal order. But, as states and societies become more liberal and more open, migration has increased. Will this increase in migration be a virtuous or a vicious cycle? Will it be destabilizing, leading the international system into greater anarchy, disorder and war, or will it lead to greater openness, wealth and human development? Much will depend on how migration is managed by the more powerful liberal states, because they will set the trend for the rest of the globe. To avoid a domestic political backlash against immigration, the rights of migrants must be respected and states must cooperate in building an international migration regime. In this article, I have argued that the first, halting steps towards such a regime have been taken in Europe and that North America is likely to follow. As liberal states come together to manage this extraordinarily complex phenomenon, it may be possible to construct a truly international regime, under the auspices of the United Nations. But I am not sanguine about this possibility because the asymmetry of interests, particularly between the developed and the developing world, is too great to permit states to overcome problems of coordination and cooperation. Even as states become more dependent on trade and migration, they are likely to remain trapped in a liberal paradox for decades to come.

REFERENCES

Alba, R. and V. Nee
2003 *Remaking the American Mainstream: Assimilation and Contemporary Immigration.* Cambridge, MA: Harvard University Press.
Andreas, P. and T. Snyder, eds.
2000 *The Wall around the West: State Borders and Immigration Controls in Europe and North America.* Boulder, CO: Rowman & Littlefield.

Bade, K. J., ed.
1992 *Deutsche im Ausland – Fremde in Deutschland: Migration in Geschichte und Gegenwart.* Munich.

Bauböck, R.
1994 *Transnational Citizenship: Membership and Rights in International Migration.* Aldershot: Edward Elgar.

Betz, H. G.
1994 *Radical Right-wing Populism in Western Europe.* New York: St. Martin's Press.

Bhagwati, J.
1998 *A Stream of Windows: Unsettling Reflections on Trade, Immigration, and Democracy.* Cambridge, MA: MIT Press.

1983 *International Factor Mobility.* Cambridge, MA: MIT Press.

Bleich, E.
2003 *Race Politics in Britain and France.* New York: Cambridge University Press.

Brochmann, G. and T. Hammar, eds.
1999 *Mechanisms of Immigration Control: A Comparative Analysis of European Regulation Policies.* Oxford: Berg.

Brubaker, R., ed.
1996 *Nationalism Reframed. Nationhood and the National Question in the New Europe.* Cambridge: Cambridge University Press.

1992 *Citizenship and Nationhood in France and Germany.* Cambridge, MA: Harvard University Press.

1989 *Immigration and the Politics of Citizenship in Europe and North America.* Lanham, MD: University Press of America.

Calavita, K.
1992 *Inside the State: The Bracero Program, Immigration and the INS.* New York: Routledge.

Caporaso, J. A.
2000 "Transnational Markets, Thin Citizenship, and Democratic Rights in the European Union: From Cradle to Grave or From Job to Job?" Unpublished paper presented at the Annual Meeting of the International Studies Association, Los Angeles, CA.

Carens, J. H.
1989 "Membership and Morality: Admission to Citizenship in Liberal Democratic States." In *Immigration and the Politics of Citizenship in Europe and North America.* Ed. R. Brubaker. Lanham, MD: University Press of America.

Castles, S. and G. Kosack
1973 *Immigrant Workers and Class Structure in Western Europe.* London: Oxford University Press.

Cornelius, W. A.
1998 "The Role of Immigrant Labor in the U.S. and Japanese Economies." San Diego: Center for U.S.-Mexican Studies.

Cornelius, W. A., P. L. Martin and J. F. Hollifield, eds.
2004 *Controlling Immigration: A Global Perspective.* 2nd Edition. Stanford, CA: Stanford University Press.

Eichengreen, B.
1989 "The Political Economy of the Smoot-Hawley Tariff," *Research in Economic History,* 12:1–43.

Ellermann, A.

2003 "Limiting the Scope of Conflict: Deportation and Damage Control in Germany and the United States." Paper presented at the 2003 Annual Meeting of the European Union Studies Association, Nashville, Tennessee.

Espenshade, T. J. and C. A. Calhoun

1993 "An Analysis of Public Opinion toward Undocumented Immigration," *Population Research and Policy Review,* 12:189–224.

Fetzer, J. S.

2000 *Public Attitudes toward Immigration in the United States, France, and Germany.* Cambridge: Cambridge University Press.

Fields, G.

1994 "The Migration Transition in Asia," *Asian and Pacific Migration Journal,* 3(1):7–30.

Freeman, G. P.

1994 "Britain, the Deviant Case." In *Controlling Immigration: A Global Perspective.* Ed. W. A. Cornelius, P. L. Martin and J. F. Hollifield. Stanford, CA: Stanford University Press.

1986 "Migration and the Political Economy of the Welfare State," *The Annals,* 485:51–63.

1979 *Immigrant Labor and Racial Conflict in Industrial Societies: The French and British Experiences.* Princeton, NJ: Princeton University Press.

Geddes, A.

2003 *The Politics of Migration and Immigration in Europe.* London: Sage.

2000 *Immigration and European Integration: Towards Fortress Europe?* Manchester: Manchester University Press.

1995 "Immigrant and Ethnic Minorities and the EC's Democratic Deficit," *Journal of Common Market Studies,* 33(2):197–217.

Ghosh, B.

2000 *Managing Migration: Time for a New International Regime.* Oxford: Oxford University Press.

1997 *Gains from Global Linkages: Trade in Services and Movement of Persons.* London: Macmillan.

Glick Schiller, N.

1999 "Transmigrants and Nation-States: Something Old and Something New in the U.S. Immigrant Experience." In *The Handbook of International Migration.* Ed. C. Hirschman, P. Kasinitz and J. DeWind. New York: Russell Sage.

Goodwin-Gill, G. S.

1996 *The Refugee in International Law.* Oxford: Clarendon.

Groenendijk, K., E. Guild and R. Barzilay

2000 "The Legal Status of Third Country Nationals Who Are Long-Term Residents in a Member State of the European Union." Nijmegen: University of Mijmegen Centre for Migration Law.

Guiraudon, V.

1998 "Third Country Nationals and European Law: Obstacles to Rights' Expansion," *Journal of Ethnic and Migration Studies,* 24(4):657–674.

Guiraudon, V. and G. Lahav
2000 "A Reappraisal of the State Sovereignty Debate: The Case of Migration Control," *Comparative Political Studies,* 33(2):163–195.

Hammar, T., ed.
1990 *Democracy and the Nation-State: Aliens, Denizens and Citizens in a World of International Migration.* Aldershot: Avebury.

———
1985 *European Immigration Policy: A Comparative Study.* New York: Cambridge University Press.

Hansen, R.
2000 *Immigration and Citizenship in Postwar Britain.* Oxford: Oxford University Press.

Hatton, T. J. and J. G. Williamson
1998 *The Age of Mass Migration: Causes and Economic Impact.* New York: Oxford University Press.

Hobsbawm, E.
1990 *Nations and Nationalism since 1780.* Cambridge: Cambridge University Press.

Hollifield, J. F.
2000a "Migration and the 'New' International Order: The Missing Regime." In *Managing Migration: Time for a New International Regime.* Ed. B. Ghosh. Oxford: Oxford University Press.

———
2000b "Immigration and the Politics of Rights." In *Migration and the Welfare State in Contemporary Europe.* Ed. M. Bommes and A. Geddes. London: Routledge.

———
2000c "Immigration in Two Liberal Republics," *German Politics and Society,* 18(1):76–104.

———
2000d "The Politics of International Migration: How Can We Bring the State Back In?" In *Migration Theory: Talking Across Disciplines.* Ed. C. Brettell and J. Hollifield. New York: Routledge.

———
1999a "Ideas, Institutions and Civil Society: On the Limits of Immigration Control in Liberal Democracies," *IMIS-Beiträge,* 10:57–90. January.

———
1999b "On the Limits of Immigration Control in France." In *Mechanisms of Immigration Control.* Ed. G. Brochmann and T. Hammar. Oxford: Berg.

———
1998 "Migration, Trade and the Nation-State. The Myth of Globalization," *UCLA Journal of International Law and Foreign Affairs,* 3(2):595–636.

———
1997a *L'Immigraiton et L'Etat-Nation à La Recherche d'un Modèl National.* Paris: L'Harmattan.

———
1997b "Immigration and Integration in Western Europe: A Comparative Analysis." In *Immigration Into Western Societies: Problems and Policies.* Ed. E. M. Uçarer and D. J. Puchala. London: Pinter.

1994a "Immigration and Republicanism in France: the Hidden Consensus." In *Controlling Immigration: A Global Perspective.* Ed. W. A. Cornelius, P. L. Martin and J. F. Hollifield. Stanford, CA: Stanford University Press.

1994b "Entre Droit et Marché." In *Le défi migratoire: Questions de relations internationales.* Ed. B. Badie and C. W. de Wenden. Paris: Presses de la Fondation Nationale des Sciences Politiques.

1992a *Immigrants, Markets and States: The Political Economy of Postwar Europe.* Cambridge, MA: Harvard University Press.

1992b "Migration and International Relations: Cooperation and Control in the European Community," *International Migration Review,* 26(2):568–595.

Hönekopp, E.
1997 "Labour Migration to Germany from Central and Eastern Europe – Old and New Trends," *Labour Market Research Topics,* No. 23. Nuremberg: Institut für Arbeitsmarkt- und Berufsforschung der Bundesanstalt für Arbeit.

Huntington, S. P.
1996 "The West: Unique, Not Universal," *Foreign Affairs,* 75(6):28–46.

IOM
2000 *World Migration Report 2000.* Geneva: International Organization for Migration.

1996 *Foreign Direct Investment, Trade, Aid and Migration.* Geneva: International Organization for Migration.

Ireland, P.
1994 *The Policy Challenge of Ethnic Diversity: Immigrant Politics in France and Switzerland.* Cambridge, MA: Harvard University Press.

Jacobson, D.
1996 *Rights across Borders: Immigration and the Decline of Citizenship.* Baltimore, MD: Johns Hopkins University Press.

Joppke, C.
2001 "The Legal-Domestic Sources of Immigrant Rights: The United States, Germany and the European Union," *Comparative Political Studies,* 34(4):339–366.

———, ed.
1998a *Challenge to the Nation-State: Immigration in Western Europe and the United States.* Oxford: Oxford University Press.

1998b "Why Liberal States Accept Unwanted Migration," *World Politics,* 50(2):266–293.

1998c *Immigration and the Nation-State.* Oxford: Oxford University Press.

Kastoryano, R.
1997 *La France, l'Allemagne et Leurs Immigrés: Négocier l'Identité.* Paris: Armand Colin.

Kepel, G.
1988 *Les Banlieus de l'Islam.* Paris: Seuil.

Keohane, R. O. and J. S. Nye
1977 *Power and Interdependence: World Politics in Transition.* Boston: Little Brown.

Kettner, J.
1978 *The Development of American Citizenship, 1608–1870.* Chapel Hill, NC: University of North Carolina Press.

King, D.
2000 *Making Americans: Immigration, Race and the Diverse Democracy.* Cambridge, MA: Harvard University Press.

Kitschelt, H.
1995 *The Radical Right in Western Europe.* Ann Arbor, MI: University of Michigan Press.

Koslowski, R.
2000 *Migrants and Citizens: Demographic Change in the European System.* Ithaca, NY: Cornell University Press.

Kyle, D. and R. Koslowski
2001 *Global Human Smuggling: Comparative Perspectives.* Baltimore, MD: Johns Hopkins University Press.

Krasner, S. D.
1999 *Sovereignty: Organized Hypocrisy.* Princeton: Princeton University Press.

Layton-Henry, Z.
1992 *The Politics of Race: Immigration, 'Race' and 'Race' Relations in Post-war Britain.* Oxford: Blackwell.

Levitt, P.
2001 *The Transnational Villagers.* Berkeley, CA: University of California Press.

Lusztig, M.
1996 *Risking Free Trade: The Politics of Trade in Britain, Canada, Mexico and the United States.* Pittsburgh: University of Pittsburgh Press.

Martin, P. L.
1993 *Trade and Migration: NAFTA and Agriculture.* Washington: Institute for International Economics.

Martin, P. L. and J. Widgren
1996 "International Migration: A Global Challenge," *Population Bulletin,* 51(1):1–48.

Massey, D. S.
1998 *Worlds in Motion: Understanding International Migration as the End of the Millennium.* Oxford: Oxford University Press.

1987 *Return to Aztlan: The Social Processes of International Migration from Western Mexico.* Berkeley: University of California Press.

Massey, D. *et al.*
2002 *Beyond Smoke and Mirrors: Mexican Immigration in an Era of Economic Integration.* New York: Russell Sage Foundation.

Messina, A. M.
1996 "The Not So Silent Revolution: Postwar Migration to Western Europe," *World Politics,* 49(1):130–154.

Miller, M. J. and P. L. Martin
1982 *Administering Foreign Worker Programs.* Lexington, MA: D.C. Heath.

Morawska, E.
1990 "The Sociology and Historiography of Immigration." In *Immigration Reconsidered. History, Sociology, and Politics.* Ed. V. Yans-McLaughlin. New York: Oxford University Press.

Morgenthau, H. J.
1978 *Politics among Nations: The Struggle for Power and Peace.* New York: Alfred A. Knopf.

Mundell, R. A.
1957 "International Trade and Factor Mobility," *American Economic Review*, 47:321–335.

Nugent, W.
1992 *Crossings: The Great Transatlantic Migrations, 1870–1914.* Bloomington, IN: Indiana University Press.

OECD
1998 *Trends in International Migration.* Paris: SOPEMI/Organization for Economic Cooperation and Development.

Portes, A.
1997 "Immigration Theory for a New Century," *International Migration Review*, 31(4): 799–825.

1996 "Transnational Communities: Their Emergence and Significance in the Contemporary World-System." In *Latin America in the World Economy.* Ed. R. P. Korzeniewidcz and W. C. Smith. Westport, CT: Greenwood.

Portes, A. and R. Rumbaut
1996 *Immigrant America: A Portrait.* Berkeley: University of California Press.

Reimers, D. M.
1998 *Unwelcome Strangers: American Identity and the Turn against Immigration.* New York: Columbia University Press.

Rogers, R., ed.
1985 *Guests Come to Stay: The Effects of European Labor Migration on Sending and Receiving Countries.* Boulder, CO: Westview.

Rogowski, R.
1989 *Commerce and Coalitions: How Trade Affects Domestic Political Alignments.* Princeton, NJ: Princeton University Press.

Rosecrance, R.
1986 *The Rise of the Trading State.* New York: Basic Books.

Rudolph, C.
2003 "Security and the Political Economy of International Migration," *American Political Science Review*, 97(4):603–620.

Russell, S. S.
1986 "Remittances from International Migration. A Review in Perspective," *World Development*, 41(6):677–696.

Santel, B. and J. F. Hollifield
1998 "Erfolgreich Integrationsmodelle? Zur Wirtschaftlichen Situation von Einwanderen in Deutschland und den USA." In *Migration in nationalen Wohlfahrtsstaaten.* Ed. M. Bommes and J. Halfmen. Osnabrück: Universitätsverlag Rasch.

Sassen, S.
1996 *Losing Control? Sovereignty in an Age of Globalization.* New York: Columbia University Press.

Schuck, P. H.
1998 *Citizens, Strangers and In-Betweens: Essays on Immigration and Citizenship.* Boulder, CO: Westview.

Shain, Y.
1989 *The Frontier of Loyalty: Political Exiles in the Age of the Nation-State.* Middletown, CT: Wesleyan University Press.

Shaw, M. N.
1997 *International Law.* Cambridge: Cambridge University Press.

Smith, R.
1997   *Civic Ideals: Conflicting Visions of Citizenship in U.S. History.* New Haven: Yale University Press.

Soysal, Y. N.
1994   *Limits of Citizenship: Migrants and Postnational Membership in Europe.* Chicago: University of Chicago Press.

Stolper, W. F. and P. A. Samuelson
1941   "Protection and Real Wages," *Review of Economic Studies,* 9:58–73.

Straubhaar, T.
1988   *On the Economics of International Law Migration.* Bern: Haupt.

Tapinos, G.
1974   *L'Economie des Migraitons Internationales.* Paris: Colin.

Teitelbaum, M. S.
1984   "Immigration, Refugees and Foreign Policy," *International Organization,* 38(3):429–450.

1980   "Right Versus Right: Immigration and Refugee Policy in the United States," *Foreign Affairs,* 59(1):21–59.

Thomas, B.
1973   *Migration and Economic Growth.* Cambridge: Cambridge University Press.

Tichenor, D. J.
2002   *Dividing Lines: The Politics of Immigration Control in America.* Princeton, NJ: Princeton University Press.

Torpey, J.
1998   "Coming and Going: On the State's Monopolization of the Legitimate 'Means of Movement,'" *Sociological Theory,* 16(3):239–259.

Uçarer, E. M.
1997   "Europe's Search for Policy: The Harmonization of Asylum Policy and European Integration." In *Immigration into Western Societies: Problems and Policies.* Ed. E. M. U. Harer and D. J. Puchala. London: Pinter.

Waldinger, R. and D. Fitzgerald
2004   "Transnationalism in Question," *American Journal of Sociology,* 109(5):1177–1195.

Waltz, K. N.
1979   *Theory of International Politics.* Reading, MA: Addison-Wesley.

Walzer, M.
1983   *Spheres of Justice: A Defense of Pluralism and Equality.* New York: Basic Books.

Weil, P.
1991   *La France et Ses Étrangers: L'Aventure d'une Politique de l'Immigration 1938–1991.* Paris: Calmann-Lévy.

Weiner, M.
1995   *The Global Migration Crisis: Challenge to States and to Human Rights.* New York: HarperCollins.

———, ed.
1993   *International Migration and Security.* Boulder, CO: Westview.

Zolberg, A. R., A. Suhrke and S. Aguayo
1989   *Escape from Violence: Conflict and the Refugee Crisis in the Developing World.* New York: Oxford University Press.

Chapter 4

Dual Citizenship as a Path-Dependent Process[1]

Thomas Faist, Jürgen Gerdes and Beate Rieple

Over the last few decades, the number of cases of multiple nationalities worldwide has increased rapidly, and for various reasons is being tolerated by a growing number of sovereign states. This is astonishing when one considers that a few decades ago citizenship and political loyalty to a specific national political community were considered inseparable. Dual citizenship is thus a particularly interesting case for studying the prerequisites and contexts for policies directed at immigrants and politics around immigration issues. Nonetheless, the degree to which dual nationality is tolerated by states differs widely. The questions then are: What are the factors encouraging the increasing tolerance towards multiple nationalities? How can national differ-

[1] The editors of this volume and Aristide R. Zolberg provided helpful criticism. Thomas Faist also wishes to thank the School of International Migration and Ethnic Relations (IMER) at Malmö University, where he spent the Spring of 2003 as the Willy-Brandt-Guestprofessor.

ences regarding *de jure* and *de facto* tolerance towards dual nationality be explained?

Generally speaking, the proponents of dual nationality in immigration states argue that state authorities need to create favorable conditions for the political integration of newcomers. They emphasize the individual rights necessary for successful incorporation. In a nutshell, the proponents of dual nationality insist, first, on the importance of social integration. This claim hinges on the observation that those states tolerating dual nationality have had, *ceteris paribus,* proportionally more immigrants naturalizing. In political debates, dual nationality and thus citizenship – understood as the set of institutionalized ties between the governed and the governing which are based upon social and symbolic ties among citizens – is also justified as a mechanism to enhance political participation of immigrants or to motivate political representatives to take into account immigrants' interests, along with other tools such as political rights for resident noncitizens, *viz.* denizens (*e.g.,* Jones-Correa, 1998).

Second, those in favor of tolerating dual citizenship point to the requirement of congruence between the people and the resident population. Thinking on citizenship has traditionally assumed some kind of congruence between the people (*demos*), state territory and state authority (*cf.* Jellinek, 1964:406–427). Ideally, citizens are the basic law-givers in a democratic society. Those subject to a law should see themselves as its authors (*cf.* Rousseau, 1966; Habermas, 1992). Third, according to a multicultural perspective, border-crossing ties of persons should or could be tolerated as constituting specific cultural resources held by citizens with immigrant backgrounds (Gerdes, 2000). Such transnational resources form part of the cultural repertoire which immigrants may need to act successfully in public life (*cf.* Kymlicka, 1995). This argument is found less often in public debates and academic discourse, probably because it is arguable whether cultural rights as such could also form the basis for new divisions among citizens, contradicting the notion of equal democratic citizenship (*cf.* Offe, 1998).

In contrast to the proponents of dual nationality who uphold the enabling function of states for immigrant incorporation, critics first emphasize that the individual migrants themselves need to adjust to the new political environment. They focus on the obligations of naturalizing immigrants who have to give proof of their readiness to adapt and to be loyal to the new state by renunciation of their previous nationality. Second, on the duty side of citizenship, dual nationality involves multiple loyalties and links of citizens across state borders or even within a world society. This has a direct bearing on issues such as dual military service and double taxation and thus pertains to state sovereignty. Third, and more importantly, dual citizenship raises the fundamental question of whether political membership across borders in democratically legitimated states can be designed in a way that it upholds the feedback loops between the governed and the governing. It is thus a question of democratic legitimacy and equal political rights. Empirically, we observe that national citizenship has developed over time in territorially enclosed, relatively socially coherent and intergenerationally viable political communities with effective state authorities (*cf.* Rokkan and Urwin, 1983).

Ties of citizens reaching into multiple states seem to question the supposed congruence of the *demos,* the state territory and the state authority and, in particular, violate basic principles such as 'one person, one vote.' It could lead to a certain degree of incongruence between *demos* and state authority because dual citizens could exert voice but still exit at will when the political outputs and outcomes do not suit them. One might ask whether loyalty and trust among citizens (*cf.* Putnam, 1993:Ch. 6) are divisible. Multiple loyalties are often seen to damage the public spirit. Fourth, dual nationality may also create problems of output legitimacy (Easton, 1967) if dual citizens withdraw from certain obligations or are seen to endanger national security. In those cases, dual nationality could give further incentives to populist politics.

Nonetheless, tolerance towards dual nationality is still increasing. In order to capture this truly seminal development, we need to expand our conceptual horizon and go beyond nationally-bound political systems to include a postnational perspective.[2] This is one way to counter "methodological nationalism" (Hermenius Martin, 1974, quoted by Smith, 1979: 191) in comparative political studies which has unduly privileged politics in national states, as if these systems could be thought of as tightly bounded political containers. In short, national and postnational perspectives are necessary to give a satisfactory account of the development and consequences

---

[2]The ongoing project "Multiple Citizenship in a Globalizing World: Germany in Comparative Perspective" aims towards a more comprehensive analysis of the politics of dual citizenship in Europe. This project, which is housed at the University of Applied Sciences Bremen, is funded by the Volkswagen Foundation (2002–2005). The research compares the politics of three immigration countries – Germany, Sweden and the Netherlands – and two emigration countries – Turkey and Poland. The analysis in this article draws on results from the immigration countries.

of dual citizenship in the context of immigrant policies and political incorporation. It means that each perspective is useful for explaining different parts of the puzzle. The postnational perspective on the extension of personhood rights vis-à-vis states highlights either the devaluation of national citizenship or the gradual extension of nationality as a human right, and the national perspective on political incorporation is helpful in accounting for variations in tolerance across national states. The results from both perspectives point in the same direction: in legal cases and legislation the rights of citizens and persons have gained in importance vis-à-vis considerations of state sovereignty.

Methodologically, we propose to use the notion of path-dependency to trace the seminal trend towards an uneven yet clearly increasing tolerance of dual nationality in liberal democracies. The concept basically means that once political actors have started to move along a certain path – tolerating dual nationality under certain circumstances such as children out of binational marriages – there is every incentive to continue along the same way, and serious disincentives exist to reverse course. The original incentives for starting down the path may arise out of different contexts, *e.g.*, dual nationality as a tool for social and political integration in immigration countries, or dual nationality as a means used by emigration country governments to maintain the loyalty of expatriates (*cf.* Glick-Schiller and Levitt, 2004).[3]

The first part of this article defines the key term nationality as a normative-legal notion, and the term citizenship as a normative-political concept. The second outlines the methodological tools of path-dependency. The third part sketches the two conceptual perspectives for analyzing dual citizenship: postnational and national. The fourth lists the factors that have led to a growing tolerance of dual nationality worldwide over the past decades and thus deals with state sovereignty. This includes an analysis of nationality as a human right, in this case the implications of international conventions for national law. The fifth part describes national variations in the *de facto* and *de jure* tolerance or even acceptance of dual nationality, ranging on a continuum from restrictive to liberal cases. The main purpose

---

[3]It is certainly no coincidence that many emigration states have also changed their laws to permit dual nationality even upon naturalization in an immigration country. Other measures include the renaturalization of former citizens and eased access to property and heritage for former citizens. Such countries include Mexico, Turkey, Tunisia, El Salvador, Colombia and the Dominican Republic (Freeman and Ögelman, 1998).

is to discern factors that account for nationally-specific modes of dealing with multiple nationality in Germany, the Netherlands, and Sweden. The concluding section then identifies some of the crucial mechanisms of path-dependency that have driven both tolerance and resistance towards dual nationality in particular and citizenship in general over the past decades.

NATIONALITY AND CITIZENSHIP

Contested dual nationality implies the importance of citizenship as full membership in a political community. Nationality means full membership in a state and the corresponding tie to state law and subjection to state power. The interstate function of nationality is to clearly define a people within a relatively clearly delineated territory and to protect the citizens of a state against the outside, at times hostile, world. The intrastate function of nationality is to define the rights and duties of members. According to the principle of *domaine reservée* – exclusive competence – each state decides within the limits of sovereign self-determination on the criteria required for access to its nationality. One general condition for membership is that nationals have some kind of close ties to the respective state, a genuine link (Rittstieg, 1990:1402).

Citizenship, in contrast, essentially comprises three mutually qualifying dimensions: first and foremost, the notion of collective self-determination and democracy; second, the legally guaranteed status of equal political freedom and other rights; and third, membership in a political community. Citizenship means, above all, the principle of unity of both governing and being governed, whatever form the democratic procedures of each state take in detail. Citizens endowed with equal political liberty obey the laws, the creation of which they participated in and to whose validity they thus consent (Walzer, 1989). Without democratic procedures guiding citizens' political self-determination, citizenship would only amount to members of political communities being subjects of a sovereign. Second, the constitutions of modern states enshrine human and fundamental rights of liberty belonging to citizenship as a legal status. In general, citizens' rights fall into various realms, for example, civil or negative rights to liberty, political rights to participation such as the right to vote and to associate, and social rights – which in the Anglo-Saxon context not only means the right to social benefits in case of sickness, unemployment and old age, but in particular also the right to education (Marshall, 1964). It is highly contested whether, to which degree, and for which category of citizens cultural or even group-differentiated rights should be a constitutive part of citizenship. The duties corresponding to citizens' entitlements are the duty to serve in the armed forces in order to protect state sovereignty toward the exterior, while the duty to pay taxes, to acknowledge the rights and liberties of other citizens, and to accept democratically legitimated decisions of majorities structure the internal sphere (*cf.* Habermas, 1992:371).

Third, citizenship rests on an affinity of citizens to certain political communities, the partial identification with and thus loyalty to a self-governing collective. The qualifications required of citizens of modern national states is an affinity to their political community – often a nation (*cf.* Weber, 1972:242–244) or a multi-nation – that is, identification with a self-governing collective that is able to establish a balance between the individual and common interests, on the one hand, and rights and responsibilities within the political community, on the other. Affiliation to a collective, expressed as a set of relatively continuous social and symbolic ties of citizens otherwise anonymous to each other, is linked to the status dimension because citizenship means the formalization of reciprocal obligations of members in a political community, akin to a social treaty (Dahrendorf, 1992:116). By means of laws and official norms, government institutions hold in trust networks of reciprocity and collectives of solidarity, which cannot be produced by the state itself.

Nationality and citizenship are intricately related. The underlying argument here is that changing state-citizen relations and also state-denizen ties (*cf.* Motomura, 1998) have implications for the growing tolerance towards dual nationality. In international law, for example, nationality is increasingly seen as a human right. And on the national level, rights of noncitizens, in particular permanent residents *viz.* denizens in social science parlance (Hammar, 1990), have increased and changed the discourse on citizenship. One result has been that in countries such as the Netherlands and Sweden, dual nationality was discussed as an alternative to extending local voting rights for permanent residents from the local to the national level.

TOWARDS A DESCRIPTION OF DUAL NATIONALITY AS A PATH-DEPENDENT PROCESS

Globally, the tolerance towards dual nationality has increased steadily over the past few decades, albeit at a very uneven pace. The factors driving this growing tolerance point towards changes in basic factors enabling and structuring immigrant political incorporation in many immigration countries. To draw on a metaphor used for immigrant assimilation, this 'bumpy-line' (Gans, 1992) trend towards increasing tolerance constitutes a path-dependent development. There is no reason to suppose that the development of dual citizenship has to unravel as if ushered along by some historical teleology, a charge often advanced against T.H. Marshall's triadic stages of the subsequent development of civil, political and social rights. Nonetheless, there is evidence to surmise that citizenship has been shaped by significant developmental pressures.   \

To describe the growth of tolerance towards dual nationality as a path-dependent development means to specify the 'positive' feedback effects – what economists call "increasing returns" – driving this development (Pierson, 2000). The basic idea here is that once collective actors such as states and state organizations have started down a track, the costs of reversal are very high. There will be other choice points, however, at which decisions have to be taken. A path-dependent effect occurs when a previous decision, norm or rule reinforces itself, when it determines in part the subsequent development of events. Decisions taken by national states and international organizations, over time, limit the range of available options at subsequent points. In so doing, they may encourage continuity in the form of retention of the original choice. In this analysis, the concept of path dependency is used to both uncover the main factors contributing to the overall global trend towards growing tolerance of dual nationality in the postnational perspective and to identity the factors that explain the divergent paths se-lected immigration states have taken in this respect in a national perspective.

TWO PERSPECTIVES ON DUAL NATIONALITY – POSTNATIONAL AND NATIONAL

The growing interest in citizenship beyond the traditional understanding of territorial and exclusive liberal democratic states has been accompanied by the discussion of two noteworthy aspects. First, political issues and decisions migrate beyond national borders, and second, persons are perceived to be crossing state borders on a new scale (*cf.* Castles, 2004). In the national and more traditional perspective, however, the question of dual citizenship is predominantly defined as a problem pertaining to individual states and immigrant integration, while from the postnational perspective, dual citi-zenship is characterized as a result of international cooperation of national states. From a postnational point of view, it is related to rights and democ-racy beyond the national state.

The Postnational Perspective: Dual Citizenship as a Transitory Phenomenon

The postnational concept comes in at least two variants: postnational membership and supranational citizenship. Postnational membership focuses on the impact of interstate norms upon citizenship in sovereign states. Supranational citizenship asks about the rights of citizens in multilevel governance systems such as the European Union (EU).

Postnational Membership. The main idea is that two of the three main components of citizenship – in the postnational membership concept, simply rights and collective identity – have increasingly decoupled over the past decades. Thus, for example, human rights, formerly tightly connected to nationality, nowadays also apply to noncitizen residents. In other words, settled noncitizens also have access to significant human, civil and social rights. Therefore, nationality as the 'right to have rights' is no longer the fundamental basis for membership in political communities. Instead, discourses tied to international norms, such as the various charters on fundamental rights by the United Nations and the EU, are supposed to contribute to postnational citizenship or membership (Soysal, 1994). However, some postnational concepts primarily emphasize the devaluation of nationality and national citizenship and its replacement by a set of rights pertaining to personhood.

It does not identify the international and supranational developments which underpin the emergence of nationality as a human right, overlooking the fact that rights accorded to noncitizens have repercussions for access to nationality. Also, this perspective cannot comprehend the democratically legitimated part of citizenship status and the importance of affective ties to and within states, *i.e.,* the first dimension of citizenship discussed before. It is thus no coincidence that analysts often speak of postnational membership instead of citizenship. The popular legitimation of membership in political communities, of utmost importance for any democratic regime, gets lost. Instead, the focus is on courts who uphold interstate norms – "rights across borders" (Jacobson, 1995). The very basis of equal political liberty is neglected by the postnational membership concept. For example, the tension of political rights attached to both denizenship and citizenship is not considered.

Supranational Citizenship. This concept primarily concerns citizenship in political multilevel systems such as the EU. At first sight, supranational citizenship appears as the logical next step in the centuries-old evolution of citizenship in what nowadays are liberal democracies. It is a current process much like the one by which sovereign states have gradually centralized and assimilated local and regional citizenships over the past centuries. Over the past decades, this has occurred under propitious political-economic conditions, such as continued prosperity and the absence of war, and under the umbrella of a sort of proto-federal system, the EU. The formidable obstacles on the road to substantive EU citizenship include the acceptance of democratic majority decisions and supranational social policies and the resources necessary for the integration of political communities, such as trust and solidarity (*cf.* Delanty, 1996:6). European Union citizenship, as it has developed since the Treaty of Maastricht (1991), is not coterminous with dual citizenship, overlapping several sovereign states. Rather, it is multiple citizenships nested on several governance levels – regional, member state and supranational. Only citizens of a member state are citizens of the Union (Faist, 2001). Yet in such a supranational perspective, dual citizenship is ultimately of secondary importance. It is only a transitory step to European citizenship.

The National Perspective: Dual Nationality as a Mechanism of Immigrant Integration

Citizens living abroad belong to territorially and intergenerationally bounded political communities. It is no coincidence that many countries are usually more tolerant towards multiple nationalities of their own citizens living abroad compared to immigrant newcomers in their territories. Nevertheless, in a national perspective there may be plausible reasons for tolerating or even accepting dual citizenship. The most persuasive is that dual citizenship increases the propensity among newcomers, *viz.* immigrants, to naturalize in the country of settlement. Some empirical surveys suggest that immigrants prefer maintaining their old citizenship when naturalizing in another country (*cf.* Chavez, 1997:131).

The Postnational Perspective – Nationality as a Human Right

When viewed from a postnational perspective, nationality has gradually emerged as a human right over the past decades. Supranational integration within the EU has furthered this trend. This meant, for example, that dual nationality has become one of the means to combat statelessness for categories such as refugees. Also, the legal norm of gender equity has ensured that dual nationality has spread. More specifically, the right of independent nationality for married women and the opportunity of either parent to pass on nationality to their children have left their marks. Supranational developments further show how postnational and national levels are interlinked, such as mutual recognition of nationalities within member states of the European Union. Such measures make it increasingly harder to exclude immigrants from so-called third countries from dual nationality within national states. As several cases suggest, such as Sweden, Switzerland and the Netherlands, granting dual nationality to nationals abroad makes it more difficult to exclude immigrants from the same benefits.

The postnational perspective is most useful in outlining crucial inter- and supranational background factors conducive to the tolerance towards dual nationality. While the conventional postnational membership perspective suggests a decoupling of rights and identities linked to the citizenship status and asserts the increasing salience of rights attached to personhood, the empirical study of dual nationality adds an additional interpretation. Retaining the focus on personhood, one may usefully trace the emergence of the right to nationality as a human right, instead of emphasizing the importance of human rights discourses on denizenship rights. This has gone hand in hand with a growing change in legal perspectives concerning states and citizens. Whereas half a century ago the judiciary prioritized the state's perspective when passing judgment on the genuine link persons entertain toward states (*e.g.* the famous *Nottebohm* case in 1955), international courts have increasingly begun to shift attention to the rights of persons.

Nationality as a human right at first sight challenges the traditional notion of state sovereignty, as expressed in the notion of *domaine reservée*. According to this principle, every state has the sovereign right to determine the criteria for acquiring the nationality of that state. Traditionally, there are few matters more symbolic of state sovereignty than the internationally recognized right of states to determine nationality. A few decades ago, most states on earth agreed that multiple nationalities should be avoided as best as possible. The preamble to the Hague Convention reads: "All persons are entitled to possess one nationality, but one nationality only." (League of Nations, 1930). State laws, bilateral treaties – such as the famous Bancroft Treaties the United States concluded with European countries around the middle of the nineteenth century – and international conventions such as *The*

Hague Convention of 1930 and the *European Convention on the Reduction of Multiple Nationality* (Council of Europe, 1963), all bear testimony to this dominant belief.

The rights and duties of states versus citizens were built on the assumption of the congruence of an almost holy trinity of territory, people and political regime (*Montevideo Convention of 1933*). The only conditions attached to the international recognition of a nationality have been that 1) it is related in a certain way to the legal system of the state in question, 2) a so-called genuine link exists between the state citizen and the respective state, and 3) the self-determination of other states is likewise respected. Further restrictions may only arise out of international agreements. While these conventions did not carry the more binding character of international regimes, such as the fledgling human rights regime, they guided sovereign states' declared policies.

In concrete terms, two rules dominated law and state practice from the late nineteenth century until the Cold War. First, acquiring a new nationality meant losing the previous one. Most states automatically excluded a citizen from membership when this person acquired the nationality of another state, or when other signs suggested that a citizen expressed loyalty to a foreign potentate – for example, serving in its army or voting in elections (Spiro, 1997). Political commentators used to connect dual citizenship to treason, espionage and a whole range of subversive activities. In many cases, countries of immigration required release from the original nationality upon naturalization. Second, since dual citizenship could never be avoided completely, some states dealt with the actual increase in multiple nationalities by providing for an optional rule. Upon reaching majority age, a person had to choose one of the two nationalities, otherwise, he or she risked being expatriated (*cf.* Bar-Yaacov, 1961).

However, there has been a gradual and lengthy but fundamental shift from exclusive state sovereignty to the increasing recognition of the legitimate claims and rights of individuals. In particular, the post-World War II human rights norms in international law significantly constrained the states "sovereign prerogative paradigm" in nationality law (*cf.* Kimminich and Hobe, 2000). A significant expression of this change is Art. 15 of the *Universal Declaration of Human Rights* (1948), according to which "[e]veryone has the right to nationality." This article recognizes nationality as the precondition for effective individual rights. This provision, at least initially, only meant a minimal constraint of state sovereignty, because no particular state is required thereby to grant the right to citizenship. Like the right to emigration, the individual right to change one's nationality is essentially of a negative kind. Furthermore, nationality as a human right has found its way only into one of the major human rights treaties adopted in the era after World War II, namely the *American Convention on Human Rights* (1969); upheld by the Inter-American Court of Human Rights (1988). Because states were reluctant to relinquish their right to determine the conditions of their nationality, in the *International Covenant on Civil and Political Rights* (1966) in Art. 24, para. 3, only children were given the right to acquire a nationality.

Nevertheless, there are meaningful international conventions and treaties, judgments of international courts and evaluations of nationality laws through intergovernmental organizations that have strengthened the individual right to citizenship in several respects against the claims of states to define exclusively the rules of their nationality laws. Especially relating to the issues of avoidance of statelessness and securing of gender equality, there have been more far-reaching conclusions with respect to the individual right to nationality. Examples include the Convention on the Reduction of Statelessness in 1961; the Conventions on Dual Nationality by the Council of Europe in 1963, 1977 and 1997; the Convention on the Nationality of Married Women in 1957; and the Convention on the Elimination of All Forms of Discrimination against Women in 1979. In sum, states' regulations bearing on nationality can no longer be deemed within their sole jurisdiction but are circumscribed by their obligations to ensure the full protection of human rights (Chan, 1991).

Also, supranational political integration has slowly increased tolerance towards dual nationality. Dual citizenship could be said to have an auxiliary function of smoothing the road to European citizenship. For example, European integration has fostered the mutual recognition of multiple citizenships in the member states. For example, Germany does not require citizens of other member states to ask for release from their former citizenship when acquiring German nationality. Dual citizenship could thus be envisioned as a bridge between national and supranational citizenship.

In sum, the evidence suggests that dual citizenship is not simply a foreboding of cosmopolitan citizenship. The main trend has been the spread of dual nationality and the tolerance towards dual citizenship as a result of an emerging trend of nationality as a human right. Importantly, the very principles national states have enshrined in their constitutions and agreed upon in international conventions, regimes and institutions have found their way back to shape legislation on nationality and the practices of citizenship.

NATIONAL VARIATIONS IN INTEGRATING NATIONS AND IMMIGRANTS

The extension of denizenship status and cultural pluralism in many Western European countries since the 1970s has also brought the question of political rights and the franchise to the fore. This has been helped by developments identified through the postnational perspective, the emergence of nationality as a human right, and rights for denizens. Dual nationality has become one of the legitimate means to achieve the congruence between the resident population and the *demos*. In those countries where dual nationality became a matter of political debate and legal regulation, efforts to advance social integration and to thus extend the franchise to noncitizens on the local and national levels preceded those on multiple nationalities. Mostly, social integration policies favorable to dual citizenship were of a multicultural kind. These culturally pluralist policies have, at least discursively, expanded the range of legitimate ties immigrants may hold.

This comparative sketch probes into the question of why we observe different degrees of *de jure* tolerance towards dual nationality across European states. Over the past years, a great many immigration states have made naturalization less and less dependent upon release from the former nationality. This trend clearly pervades nationality laws and regulations. Examples include France in 1973, Portugal in 1981 and Italy in 1992. Others have only made minor concessions, such as Germany. Yet, even those national states that, in principle, strive to avoid dual nationality usually have some exempting rules. In general, such regulations apply when the former state refuses to release the citizen from nationality or makes the release dependent upon unreasonable conditions – for example, the rule that young men need to serve in the army before being discharged from nationality. The analysis suggests that nationally-specific modes have shaped the politics surrounding the varying degrees of tolerance of dual citizenship found in the respective countries.

As to the cases selected, there are two ways of classifying tolerance and restriction towards dual nationality. The first is to look at states' *de jure* tolerance versus restriction towards dual nationality. The second is to analyze the *de facto* behavior of states. Fundamentally, dual nationality arises when children are born in countries where the *ius soli* principle holds, while the countries of their parents' origin apply the *ius sanguinis* principle. Also relevant for *de facto* tolerance is when states are indifferent to dual nationality for various reasons. For example, despite the 'oath of allegiance,' the United States does not require written evidence that immigrants have actually renounced a previous nationality. Other countries, such as the United Kingdom, do not even regulate dual nationality (Hansen, 2002). Here, the analysis focuses on the *de jure* dimension. The comparative analysis includes Germany, the Netherlands and Sweden. These three countries have varying policies on the acceptance of dual citizenship and can be classified accordingly on a continuous scale ranging from restrictive to tolerant and, finally, open. The most restrictive cases are characterized by the following criteria:

1) Assignment by birth: only one nationality possible;
2) Obligation to choose a nationality on reaching maturity;
3) Renunciation requirement (in some cases, proof also required) upon naturalization in another country; and
4) Forced expatriation upon naturalization in another country.

The more stringently the acquisition of a nationality corresponds to the above principles, the more restrictive the regime – and conversely, the more lenient the procedure. The more exemptions there are from these requirements, the more open the regime in question is to dual citizenship. The most important form of *de jure* tolerance in this respect is the abolishment of the renunciation requirement.

Of the three immigration countries, Germany is the most restrictive *de jure,* the Netherlands more tolerant, and Sweden has followed in 2001, now being the most liberal. Although the recent extension of the *ius soli* clause in Germany's nationality legislation is extremely generous in comparison to that of other European states, the principle of avoiding dual nationality is adhered to rather strictly. The individuals in question must, by the end of their 23rd year, opt for one or the other nationality and may otherwise be deprived of their German nationality. As before, in the case of naturalization – apart from the special case of late repatriates of German origin (so-called ethnic Germans or Spätaussiedler) – the relinquishment of the previous citizenship is generally required. Nevertheless, several exceptions apply, for example, when there are overriding constitutional grounds, or if there are no provisions for the relinquishment of the nationality of the other country in question, or if it is refused or obstructed.[4] During the early 1990s in the Netherlands, dual nationality was tolerated but the relinquishment of the prior nationality is now generally required again. Compared to Germany, however, there are much more extensive exemption clauses. In Sweden, by comparison, dual citizenship is now accepted in general. Sweden previously belonged to the restrictive category and demanded the relinquishment of the previous nationality.

The propositions guiding the cross-national analysis[5] are the following:

1)   The respective understandings of nationhood and explicit culturally pluralist policies directed at immigrants are decisive factors. A republican understanding of nationhood[6] tends, at a minimum, to foster indifference towards dual nationality. However, it is questionable to what extent the ethnocultural versus republican distinction is appli-

---

[4]In general, the reality of law has been more tolerant than the letter. For example, there are crude estimates that more than a quarter and up to one third of all those naturalized in Germany in the 1970s and 1980s – apart from ethnic Germans – kept their former citizenship and thus were dual citizens. In 2000, more than 40 percent of all naturalizations in Germany occurred under maintenance of the original citizenship. In the Netherlands, the tightening of the rules in 1997 did not significantly affect the share of persons who kept their original citizenship. In 1996, 80 percent of those persons who naturalized retained the original citizenship. In 2000, after the reinstallation of the reunification demand, the proportion still amounted to 77 percent (de Hart, 2003).

[5]The summary of the German case is based on the studies of Faist *et al.* (2003b, c); the Swedish case draws on the work by Spång (2003); and the analysis of the Dutch case rests on de Hart's (2003) analysis.

[6]A republican understanding of nationhood is based on the premise that government in a republic is in principle the common business (*res publica*) of the citizens, conducted by them for the common good. The concept of nation is focused on a state (*Staatsnation*), in which citizens run their own affairs. Inclusion of all permanent residents into the nation and thus nationality is seen as a basis for public-mindedness. Access to nationality is based on the subjective avowal of loyalty of individuals to the nation. In this sense republicanism strives to ensure an optimum of equal opportunities regarding political participation for all those (permanently) residing in the territory of a state. According to this definition, republicanism does not necessarily mean that public affairs should take precedence over the citizens' private life. An ethnic understanding of nationhood also holds that government is based on popular consent and participation. Yet, in contrast to a republican understanding, the nation is focused on the idea of a common culture (*Kulturnation*), historically preceding even statehood. Inclusion into the nation is traced to common descent, cultural traditions or lineage. There is less scope for persons for making their own decisions on the issue of nationality. Political participation and opportunities are seen and interpreted as issues of intergenerational continuity.

Figure I.   Access to Nationality in Germany, Sweden and the Netherlands
                   (after 2000)

	Germany	Sweden	The Netherlands
As-of-right naturalization	After 8 years of residence; conditions attached: no welfare dependency; language test: evidence of sufficient knowledge of German	As-of-right after 5 years of residence (5 years for citizens from non-Nordic countries; 2 years for citizens from Nordic countries)	As-of-right after 5 years of lawful residence; conditions attached: ability to conduct a simple conversation in Dutch was deemed sufficient (until recently); criterion of "being incorporated" did not play any role in practice; now: language proficiency and citizenship courses required
Second and subsequent generations	*Jus sanguinis, jus soli*, provided that one parent has lived for eight years in Germany or holds a permanent residence permit for at least three years (since 2000); also: educated in Germany for 8 years for second generation (since 1991)	*Jus sanguinis*, coupled with socialization principle for those born or raised in Sweden	*Jus sanguinis* and limited form of *jus soli* option right (since 1984); foreign children born in the Netherlands have an 'option right'; they can acquire Dutch nationality by unilateral declaration between the ages of 18 and 25
Dual nationality	Accepted for ethnic Germans and, in specific circumstances, such as economic loss or when country of origin does not allow expatriation; 'optional principle' if the child obtains the parents' nationalit(ies), he or she must give up the non-German or German nationality before reaching the age of 23	Dual citizenship explicitly allowed since 2001; no requirement to renounce former nationality; before 2001, the rules were as restrictive as in Germany	Dual citizenship allowed as a rule (1991-97), since then a wide range of exceptions; further restrictions are now (2003) widely discussed

cable to the countries concerned. Second, for *de jure* tolerance of dual
nationality to take hold, culturally pluralist, *viz.* 'multicultural,'[7] policies and discourses are also supportive, especially if connected with
republican elements. Culturally pluralist policies towards immigrants
have steadily gained in importance in European countries of settlement
over the past decades (*cf.* Brubaker, 2001). The tolerance towards dual
nationality is coupled tightly with the enfranchisement of immigrants
in their roles as denizens or citizens. The two factors overlap in cases

[7]Multicultural policies are based on the assumption that a person's possibility to uphold his
or her own cultural traditions, language and religion is crucial to personal identity and
self-confidence and therefore a precondition for successful economic, social, cultural and
political integration. Multicultural policies include various forms of public support for immigrant organizations and their cultural practices, the provision of the immigrant languages
in schools and rights concerning their religious freedom and practices. Assimilationist policies,
by contrast, aim towards the melting of immigrants into the majority core of an immigrant
state, *viz.* society. No special provisions for immigrants are desirable in the political or cultural
realm in order to foster their integration into the mainstream.

such as the Netherlands and Sweden, where local voting rights and dual nationality have been seen, at times, as part of minority or multicultural policies, inspired by an integrative understanding of nationhood.

2)   The eventual legislative output is decisively mediated by nationally-specific modes of politics which form part of broader institutional – legal and political – opportunity structures and prevail in the field of immigrant integration, such as competitive party politics in Germany, corporatist consensus politics in Sweden, and a slowly eroding elite consensus in the Netherlands.

Germany: Competitive Party Politics and Mainstream Populism

The most recent changes in German nationality law, which went into effect in 2000, facilitated the naturalization of foreign citizens who have lived in Germany for a certain length of time, and the automatic acquisition of German nationality by birth for the second and third generations – *i.e.*, the extension of the principle of descent (*ius sanguinis*) and the principle of naturalization based upon socialization of young persons by the application of the principle of territoriality (*ius soli*). Another major issue of the debate was whether, as a rule, naturalization required the relinquishment of an individual's previous nationality or whether multiple nationalities should be tolerated to a greater degree than before. The chancellor of the new Red-Green governing coalition announced that new nationality legislation would make Germany 'compatible with Europe.' Interestingly, after a short and highly politicized public debate in early 1999, the rules for including the second generation were more liberal than demanded by the government, while dual nationality was not allowed as a rule. However, by adding the *ius soli* rule, the German government added impetus to the *de facto* growth of multiple nationalities.

The run-of-the-mill explanation for Germany's lag in adopting a more liberal nationality law has been that the so-called ethnocultural concept of nationhood presented a formidable obstacle (*cf.* Brubaker 1992). This argument not only neglects changes in German political culture since 1945, it disregards the division of Germany until 1989 and the subsequent speedy reforms of nationality law, such as the introduction of as-of-right naturalization in 1993. It is also not supported by an analysis of parliamentary and public discourses on nationality legislation during the 1990s. There is not much evidence for explicit references to an ethnic or cultural understanding of citizenship among the opponents of dual nationality. Quite to the contrary, the opponents have consistently called for strengthening the renunciation rule for German citizens living abroad – at odds with an ethnocultural understanding of nationhood. Moreover and ironically, tolerance towards dual nationality has been higher under the old nationality law dating back to 1913 (RuStAG) than in the subsequent reforms in 1977, 1991 and 2000.

A factor directly impinging on the prospects for increasing *de jure* tolerance towards dual nationality has been the discursive use of 'multiculturalism.' While Germany would score somewhat lower than the Netherlands or Sweden regarding actually existing culturally pluralist policies towards immigrants (*e.g.,* Rath and Groenendijk, 2000), it is also crucial that in political debates 'multiculturalism' has been elevated to become the polar and negatively loaded opposite to Germany not being a 'country of immigration' position in academic and political debates during the 1980s and 1990s. Indirectly, multiculturalism entered the citizenship debate only as a dystopic vision, when the opposition Christian Democrats (CDU/CSU), who opposed increasing tolerance for dual nationality, succeeded in tying nationality to allegedly mounting immigration.

Connecting dual nationality to issues of immigration, crime and security and thus treat it as a meta-issue, *i.e.,* far remote from the political issue at hand, has been aided by extremely contentious party politics. This type of politics has largely determined the political opportunity structures regarding immigrant insertion. Since the 1970s, immigration and nationality issues have – intermittently – served as rallying posts for center right parties. Thus, mainstream parties have selectively used populist strategies in party competition. In the debate on dual nationality, the CDU instigated a signature campaign against dual citizenship. It proved very successful, with more than 5 million signatures against the proposed new citizenship law. Ultimately, it was one of the main reasons for the defeat of the Social Democratic and the Green parties in the state elections in Hesse in early 1999.

The Netherlands: Slowly Eroding Elite Consensus

Debates on dual nationality partly developed out of earlier efforts to enfranchise non-nationals in the 1970s and 1980s. During the 1970s, self-appointed advocates of immigrants started to push for local voting rights for noncitizens. In the 1980s, a majority of political parties hoped that enfranchisement could serve as a symbolic means to show that the government was responding to the need to improve the social position of non-nationals, responding to events such as the Moluccan train hijacking in 1974 and subsequent violent incidents. Local voting rights, instituted in 1985, were considered part of 'minority policies' meant to advance social integration of immigrants. Policymakers justified both local voting rights and dual nationality (1991–97) with the claim that they would ease social integration and serve as tools for immigrant incorporation. Individual rights were meant to accompany incorporation policies aimed at immigrant groups along established institutional structures of representation and consultation in the political, social and religious spheres. This approach was helped by the tradition of pillarization (*verzuiling*), which could be applied to immigrants as well. In the late 1980s, it became clear that a Left-Right coalition for an extension of the franchise for denizens to the national level was impossible because liberal and right-wing parties blocked it. Subsequently, the discussion on political insertion turned to dual nationality. Dual nationality also entered debates as a result of the realities of gender equity which were to be accepted. Since the 1960s, women have not followed the status of their husbands automatically. And since the mid-1980s, Dutch fathers and mothers could pass on nationality to their children, both in the Netherlands and abroad. In effect, this led to a *de facto* increase in dual nationality. Finally, the renunciation requirement was abolished and dual nationality practically accepted in 1991. However, the policy changed back again in 1997, now demanding renunciation of the former nationality of naturalizing immigrants. Accordingly, formal citizenship law was changed in 2000 and came into effect in 2003. Nonetheless, when compared to more restrictive cases, such as Germany, more exceptions still persist. The current law still accepts formal ties to more than one country for categories such as spouses in mixed marriages, children born of mixed marriages, and second generation immigrants.

The Dutch case suggests that conceptions of the nation and nationhood have been changing constantly and in tandem with understandings of immigrant integration. In the *Minderhedennota* of 1983 – the government report initiating 'minority policies' – the Dutch nation was portrayed as a territorially bounded multiform, *viz.* multicultural society. The *Nota Integratiebeleid* of 1994 reflected the policy shift away from cultural to socioeconomic and from collective to individual concerns. This report used the dominant image of a Dutch nation built around an autochthone core, open to the rest of the world. This latter document and the *Allochtonenbeleid* of 1989 manifest a change in immigrant insertion policy, a move from 'minority policy' of the 1980s to 'integration' or 'allochtonen' policy, also called *inburgerungsi*-policy. Interestingly, the concept of citizenship emerged as the leading principle of the 'new version of the persons of different cultures in the Netherlands' (Groenendijk and Heijs, 1999). The focus shifted from cultural pluralism to individual responsibility as a means to advance integration of the immigrant categories considered problematic, *i.e.*, Surinamese, Moroccans and Turks. Language and civics courses for immigrants have since become dominant integration schemes.

Unlike Germany, politicians and political parties in the Netherlands agreed to keep immigration out of political campaigns until the late 1990s. This was possible because of a consensus among the political elite of keeping contentious issues out of public debates. One of the most visible outcomes was the 1991 law. It emerged as a political compromise between the main political parties. How much immigrant integration policy dominated the reasoning on nationality rules can be seen in the fact that the legislators did not discuss or consider the issue of multiple bonds to several states. Instead, not surprisingly, the formula was to improve the legal position of immigrants in order to foster social integration. However, as it became apparent that social problems among certain immigrant categories persisted, politics became more contentious and the elite consensus began to erode. As in the German case, the main political parties fell into two blocks. The Social Democratic PdVA and the left-liberal D66 continued to favor tolerance, while the conservative-liberal VVD and the Christian CDA demanded to uphold or reinstall the renunciation demand. The main ideological fault line was the use of naturalization as a way to stimulate the social integration of immigrants. Since the mid-1990s, other issues have also been brought into the public arena, such as dual loyalties and immigrants as calculating citizens who collect passports. Thus, the issue of dual nationality has increasingly become part of a politicized discussion on immigrant insertion.

Sweden: Sociopolitical Nationhood and Political Equality - Consensus Politics

Like in the Netherlands, the Swedish debate emerged out of discussions on social integration policies. More specifically, the discussion on dual nationality started as a continuation of voting rights for resident noncitizens. After the government granted local voting rights in 1975, advocates of immigrant rights demanded to extend enfranchisement to the national level. While this proposal encountered strong opposition, dual nationality entered political debates as an alternative to voting rights for noncitizens. This discursive window widened in the mid-1980s, when the government instituted a parliamentary commission to explore opportunities for dual nationality. Yet most parties rejected the proposal. In 1990, the Social Democrats explicitly proposed allowing multiple nationality. The governing Center-Right government blocked and withdrew the proposition. Their stance shifted when yet another government commission on citizenship began to deal with nationality and citizenship in broad terms in 1997.

This time it was the commission that asked the government for permission to propose changes in dual citizenship. While the multicultural rhetoric of the mid-1970s had been discarded by that time, the principles of political equality and, above all 'freedom of choice' (*valfrihet*) for immigrants, were very much alive and enjoyed widespread majority support among politicians and the populace. Freedom of choice concerned the right of immigrants to choose whether to retain their cultural traditions, hence forming the linchpin of multiculturalism in its 1970s version. By the late 1990s, freedom of choice had become part of so-called 'integration policies.' Moreover, one of the most widely discussed arguments in favor of accepting dual nationality was the principle of gender equity. Gradually, from the 1950s onwards – in accord with international law – the principle of gender equity became more important than avoiding multiple nationalities. Also, fair treatment of Swedish citizens naturalizing abroad and immigrants naturalizing in Sweden played a role in the discourse. In 1979, the Swedish government took steps to allow Swedish citizens to acquire other nationalities without renouncing Swedish citizenship. However, that was not fully recognized and put into practice until 2001.

In terms of the understanding of nationhood and its importance for nationality and citizenship, Sweden is a clear example of how restrictive and misleading the republican versus ethnocultural dichotomy can be. For the Swedish case, a sociopolitical understanding of citizenship, usually referred to by the shorthand of the 'people's home,' is important for understanding both immigrant policies in general and citizenship politics and policies in particular. In the past, the people's home was a way to envision and mobilize support for the social democratic welfare state project. It also has often been taken as a shorthand description of the welfare state program in Sweden more generally. There are various interpretations of its meaning. The first implies a scheme of social cooperation between citizen-workers, built around accommodations between capital and labor and other interest organizations and parties.

Although the people's home may be seen to carry elements of an ethnocultural understanding of nationhood – cultural cohesiveness enabling strong social solidarity and reciprocity on a national level – it also can be interpreted as a break with ethnocultural forms of nationalism and geared towards social inclusion on the basis of political equality and freedom. A second interpretation hinges on the articulation of Swedishness on the one hand, and the differentiation between the normal and the pathological on the other hand. This form of the people's home nationalism was especially prevalent during the latter part of the nineteenth and the turn of the twentieth centuries, as evidenced by policies towards the Saami and the Roma. These latter groups, along with immigrants, became the targets of multicultural policies in their first phase during the late 1970s. The sociopolitical connotations of the people's home, especially those regarding the first interpretation, may have made it easier to introduce dual nationality. Regarding policies of cultural pluralism, dual nationality could be cast as an extension of the freedom of choice principle stemming from the 1970s. In 2000, it was beneficial to apply this principle to citizenship because dual nationality does not involve contentious group rights but rather pure and simple individual rights.

As to the institutional opportunity structure, Swedish politics in general and immigrant accommodation politics in particular have occurred between consensus politics with a focus on seeking broad societal and political majorities on the one hand and block politics of the left and the center right parties on the other. Although, as in the German case, no right-wing populist party of national importance existed, mainstream parties, unlike the German case, refrained from exploiting the citizenship issue in a populist fashion. In addition to consensus politics, this characteristic further contributed to the fact that the dual nationality issue never sparked heated public debates and strong media attention. As to the discursive opportunity structure, it is remarkable how strong the argument of political equality was in the discussions of the 1980s and 1990s. It was applied to equal treatment of Swedish citizens acquiring nationality abroad and denizens naturalizing in Sweden – but also to more arcane and indirect arguments about the minimal difference in rights between denizens and citizens: since this difference was already so small, it would make little sense not to tolerate dual nationality.

Preliminary Lessons from the Comparative Analysis

The comparative analysis has profound implications for our understanding of nationality and citizenship politics. In general, there is convergence in the *de facto* tolerance (*ius soli* principle) and *de jure* tolerance (*e.g.*, arising out of international law such as gender equity) towards dual nationality. However, the incorporation processes in all three countries analyzed differ substantially. This is obvious in rules relating to the relaxation of the renunciation requirement. This observation confirms the conclusion that immigrant incorporation policies in European countries have both converged and remained distinct along particular national patterns (*cf.* Freeman, 2004).

Overall, the evidence presented suggests that politically inclusive understandings of nationhood coupled with explicit multicultural or minority policies and political rights for permanent residents have established a favorable context for increasing tolerance towards dual nationality. Yet, there are three more specific findings. First, the classical dichotomy of republican versus ethnocultural concepts of nationhood and its significance for naturalization rules have to be reexamined and specified. Not only are such understandings subject to historical change, as the German case would suggest, more important, this distinction does not capture the specific mix of republican and ethnic understandings of nationhood that are relevant for understanding citizenship. As the Dutch and Swedish cases make clear, for example, sociopolitical interpretations of nationhood connected to welfare statehood have been decisive for legislation on nationality. Also, classical republican understandings of nationhood, such as the ones found in France and the United States, may foster indifference towards dual nationality (de la Pradelle, 2002 on France and Renshon, 2001 on the United States). Yet more explicit forms of recognition of dual nationality can be found in countries not typically associated with classical republicanism, such as Sweden. In general, politically inclusive understandings of nationhood in the liberal democracies analyzed are path-dependent factors which have changed over time but are not easily reversed. The choices that flow into the construction of such understandings have usually taken decades to crystallize.

Second, this finding indicates that other sets of factors, such as culturally pluralist policies, may play a role. This means that understandings of national integration, *viz.* nationhood, usually have to be examined in conjunction with political rights for permanent residents and the prevailing modes of immigrant policies, ranging from multicultural to assimilationist policies. In two of the cases considered – Sweden and the Netherlands – debates and conflicts around dual nationality arose out of efforts to further enfranchise denizens, *i.e.,* to extend the franchise for certain categories of noncitizens from the local to the national level. Even in Germany, the first legislative efforts to deal with multiple nationalities (1993) came in the aftermath of a failed attempt by two northern German Länder to introduce local voting rights for permanent residents. This finding indicates that dual nationality has to be interpreted as part of the broader question of which political rights should be granted to immigrants and in what sequence. The general trend towards an extension of rights to noncitizen immigrants, which can be observed in Western Europe and North America since the 1960s, has led to a renewed discussion of political rights for noncitizens and citizenship as a tool towards integration or a result of integration. Also, it has opened the question of whether political citizenship rights such as the franchise on the national level should also be accessible to denizens (cf. Aleinikoff and Klusmeyer, 2002:Ch.3).

While the jury is still out on this question, it seems evident that rights for permanent residents have gradually strengthened and contributed to discussions on the extension of political rights for immigrants. This is another example of a gradual shift from a state-centric perspective on citizenship to a person-centered view; not engendered simply by international law but primarily arising out of constitutional principles in liberal democracies. This development is also part of discourses and actual policies surrounding explicitly multicultural policies directed at immigrants. Both political rights for denizens and dual nationality have been conceived as part of minority policies in the Netherlands during the 1980s and multicultural policies in Sweden during the second half of the 1970s and during the 1980s. While the labels for such policies may have changed, the substance has remained intact.

Third, however, the Netherlands and Sweden accepted dual nationality *de jure* at a time when multicultural rhetoric was on the wane and was gradually replaced by discourses on individual responsibility and citizenship. Dual nationality thus seems to be a substitute for explicit minorities or multicultural policies. This is not surprising because nationality and citizenship are concepts predicated on individual and not on collective rights. The latter are often seen in public and academic debates – rightly or wrongly – as main ingredients of multicultural policies. Arguments in favor of tolerating dual citizenship in reform debates, which emphasized the legal recognition of border-crossing social and symbolic ties of persons, have often taken recourse to multicultural ideas.

The shift from multicultural to nationality and citizenship policy also suggests that citizenship has emerged as a common denominator for immigrant political insertion. This is true for countries such as Sweden and the Netherlands and for more classical republican countries such as France and the United States. Also, in Germany, the draft for a new immigration law provided for education in civics as one of the central instruments for integrating newcomers. In sum, dual citizenship has become part of the trend towards a revalorization of full political membership in many immigration countries and the resurgence of the 'good citizen,' who is nowadays often conceived in a communitarian way.

Outlook: Dual Nationality and Master-Mechanisms of Political Change

In the case of dual nationality, we can identify two mechanisms engendering path-dependent effects. In particular, lock-in and disincentive mechanisms and their effects have resulted in the 'stickiness' of the policy path. First, the lock-in mechanism means that certain options are rendered almost wholly unattainable by the original choices made. Examples are norms such as gender equity or *jus soli*. In 1974, the German Constitutional Court considered dual nationality as an "evil" in principle. Nevertheless, in terms of gender equity, it maintained that nationality can be transferred to children by the father and the mother. The *jus soli* rule in the United States has traditionally been interpreted as emanating from the Fourteenth Amendment to the Constitution. Therefore, a change of qualification of the principle would require either another Constitutional Amendment or a far-reaching reinterpretation of the clause (*cf.* Aleinikoff and Klusmeyer, 2002: 12).

Taken together, these two principles of gender equity and *ius soli* have resulted in a pervasive growth of dual nationality in the attribution of political membership by marriage, birth and family formation. It is hard to imagine that such principles will be reversed because they are partly enshrined in national constitutions and international conventions. Second, a disincentive effect means that original choices make future options not impossible but deeply unattractive to policymakers. For example, while efforts aimed at multicultural policies towards immigrants are prone to reversal, policymakers often have not done so. Instead, they have relabeled 'multicultural' into 'integration' policies without a change in substance in Sweden, or refocused efforts from politicocultural 'minority' policies to socioeconomic 'integration' policies in the Netherlands. Moreover, the pervasive growth of rights of permanent residents, *viz.* denizens, has put the issue of political rights for noncitizens as a means of incorporation on the table.

However, path-dependent developments are not immune to reversal. In general, this means that choice points and alternatives exist (North, 1990:98–99). In principle, there are two mechanisms that could lead to a reversal – exogenous shocks and learning. First, it is easy to imagine that factors exogenous to the law and politics of nationality and citizenship impinge on their development. The most obvious are armed conflicts between national states which form international migration systems. Although historical comparisons need to be handled with utmost care, it is suggestive that during World War I the public loyalties of immigrants became a matter of concern. More recent wars between immigration and emigration countries and the events of September 11th have renewed public debates about the loyalty of immigrants (Faist, 2003). For instance, dual nationality has been discussed in the Netherlands as a means to expel undesired citizens of immigrant background. After all, they still have nationality of at least one other country (*cf.* de Hart, 2003).

The second mechanism – 'learning' – can be easily observed. The Dutch case is particularly instructive in this regard. For some years during the 1980s, the franchise for denizens and dual nationality were seen as instruments of overall immigrant integration, even beyond the political realm. Later, however, some parties declared the focus on cultural minority policies a failure and, in essence, the emphasis of public policies shifted to socioeconomic integration into labor and housing markets. Concomitantly, during the 1990s, goals such as the congruence of the resident population and the people and instruments such as dual nationality became more contested, as criteria such as the alleged effectiveness of incorporation policies – output legitimacy – gained in importance. Learning in this case reflected a growing skepticism towards minority policies which, among other things, implied collective rights for immigrant groups. Ironically, dual nationality – the relaxation of the renunciation requirement – served as a tool to continue cultural pluralist policies in the publicly more acceptable frame of individual rights.

The spread of dual nationality as a path-dependent process may very well continue. This is especially likely under the propitious circumstances of supranational integration in regional governance structures such as the EU. Seen in this way, the increasing tolerance towards dual nationality may well be interpreted as part of a centuries-long expansion of rights for citizens and denizens in states characterized by some form of rule of law. On the international level, this is signaled by a growing tendency to interpret nationality as a human right and to apply provisions favoring gender equity. On the national level, rights for permanent residents that approach those of citizens also point towards an increasing emphasis of individual rights vis-à-vis state sovereignty. The driving forces enabling lock-ins to emerge have to be sought in group conflicts (*cf.* Tilly, 1996).

These conflicts are, as in the case of social rights, not simply found in working class strength but also in preventive elite counterstrategies, the most well-known outcome of which is the Bismarckian welfare state. Given the absence of formidable immigrant political strength in virtually all European immigration countries, the increasing tolerance towards dual nationality is clearly a symbolic effort by ruling elites to accommodate immigrants and to live up to international norms. The political conflicts and discourses sur-rounding dual citizenship have been shaped by reference to established yet changing understandings of nationhood and immigrant incorporation, po-litical cultures and constitutional principles.

The path-dependent view describes convergent processes of increasing toleration reaching across the national states described. The master mecha-nism could be called a democratic proliferation. Liberal democracies tend to face this dilemma when adhering to the principle of avoiding dual nation-ality as far as possible. Because of the importance of individual rights, liberal democracies are compelled to accept dual nationality upon naturalization if the respective other state makes renouncing nationality impossible or im-poses unreasonable demands. Also, liberal democracies tend to accept dual nationality in the name of gender equity when nationality is acquired by birth. Furthermore, such states may be inclined to grant dual citizenship within regional governance systems such as the EU.

But once some exceptions have been granted, new interpretations of individual rights and new claims of other categories of persons combined with court cases could easily lead to a further increase of exceptions. This could result in a proliferation of 'exception groups.' The more exceptions and thus potential claimant groups, the greater the likelihood that questions of legitimating different treatment arise because each exemption has to be justified on reasonable grounds. Problems of justification and rising costs of administrative procedures may well lead to a general tolerance of dual citi-zenship in the long run. In the rather restrictive German case, for example, it is not unlikely that unequal treatment as a consequence of the so-called 'option model' (*cf.* Figure I) could result in increased tolerance. Most prob-ably, the Federal Constitutional Court will have to decide whether this clause can be upheld.

In a sanguine view, one possible long-term outcome is that dual na-tionality could serve as a bridging construct for supranational and multilayered forms of political membership. Immanuel Kant once drew attention to the alternative of a "federation of free republics" on the level of states to avoid the twin dangers of global tyranny and the anarchy of sovereign states (Kant, 1970). Applied to the case at hand, dual nationality would interface the world of states and the world of societies by institutionalizing the border-crossing, overlapping social and symbolic ties among citizens and between citizens and states. Seen in this way, dual citizenship as overlapping political membership does not constitute a break with the Westphalian system of state sovereignty (*cf.* Ruggie, 1993) – but may be a mechanism in post-Westphalian systems such as the European Union to advance the integration of national and supranational forms of membership in political communities. Indirectly, the nationally distinct modes of immigrant political incorporation would then continue to be shaped by varying yet increasing degrees of tolerance towards and even acceptance of dual nationality.

It is by no means clear, however, that such an optimistic perspective is warranted. The key assumption behind such an optimistic scenario, namely a rather peaceful state system, is historically contingent, applicable to certain regions of the world only, and continuously changing. The postnational perspective has only focused on international law and transnational discourses, forgetting much of the 'hard' factors of the international state system. Much of the future course of border-crossing citizenship would depend on the development of national states and the international system of states. In other words, social integration of immigrants on the national level also depends on the interactions among the system of states, an aspect of international system integration (*cf.* Hollifield, 2004). Outside the OECD world, statehood has by no means developed along the successful Western model of governance in territorially bounded, rule-of-law, democratic and interventionist entities. And it is an open question whether statehood in the OECD world continues along the path taken after World War II. At the very least, a comprehensive analysis of the course of (dual) citizenship needs to take into account the international system and the states within migration systems, thus moving beyond the myopic concern with major Western immigration countries.

REFERENCES

Aleinikoff, A. and D. Klusmeyer
2002 *Citizenship Policies for an Age of Migration.* Washington, DC: Carnegie Endowment for International Peace.

Bar-Yaacov, N.
1961   *Dual Nationality.* New York: Praeger.

Brubaker, W. R.
2001   "The Return of Assimilation? Changing Perspectives on Immigration and Its Sequels in France, Germany, and the United States," *Ethnic and Racial Studies,* 24(1):531–548.

———
1992   *Citizenship and Nationhood in France and Germany.* Cambridge, MA: Harvard University Press.

Castles, S.
2004   "The Factors that Make and Unmake Migration Policies," *International Migration Review,* 38(3):852–884.

Chan, J. M. M.
1991   "The Right to a Nationality as a Human Right. The Current Trend towards Recognition," *Human Rights Law Journal,* 12(1–2):1–14.

Chavez, P. L.
1997   "Creating a United States-Mexico Political Double Helix: The Mexican Government's Proposed Dual Nationality Amendment," *Stanford Journal of International Law,* 33: 119–151.

Council of Europe
1997   *European Convention on Nationality and Explanatory Report.* ETS No. 166. Strasbourg: Council of Europe Publishing. November 6.

Dahrendorf, R.
1992   "Citizenship and the Modern Social Conflict," In *1688–1988. Time for a New Constitution.* Ed. R. Holme and M. Elliot. Basingstoke: Macmillan. Pp. 112–125.

Delanty, G.
1996   *Inventing Europe: Idea, Identity, Reality.* Houndmills: Macmillan Press.

Easton, D.
1967   *A Systems Analysis of Political Life.* New York: Wiley.

Faist, T.
2003   *The Migration-Security Nexus. International Migration and Security before and after 9/11.* Malmö University. School of International Migration and Ethnic Relations (IMER), Willy-Brandt-Working Paper Series, No. 3/2003.

———
2001   "Social Citizenship in the European Union: Nested Membership," *Journal of Common Market Studies,* 39(1):39–60, 2001.

———
2000   *The Volume and Dynamics of International Migration and Transnational Social Spaces.* New York: Oxford University Press.

Faist, T., J. Gerdes and B. Rieple
2003a *Global Conditions Favoring Tolerance towards Multiple Citizenship.* Working Paper No. 1, University of Applied Sciences Bremen, International Studies in Political Management (ISPM).

———
2003b *Concepts of Nationhood and Multiculturalism in Immigrant Integration: The Case of*

Germany. Working Paper No. 2, University of Applied Sciences Bremen, International Studies in Political Management (ISPM).

2003c *Arguments and Belief Systems on Integration and Dual Citizenship: The Case of Germany.* Working Paper No. 3, University of Applied Sciences Bremen, International Studies in Political Management (ISPM).

Freeman, G. P.
2004 "Immigrant Incorporation in Liberal Democracies," *International Migration Review,* 38(3):913–944.

Freeman, G. P. and N. Ögelmann
1998 "Homeland Citizenship Policies and the Status of Third Country Nationals in the European Union," *Journal of Ethnic and Migration Studies,* 24:769–788.

Gans, H. J.
1992 "Second-Generation Decline: Scenarios for the Economic and Ethnic Futures of the Post-1965 American Immigrants," *Ethnic and Racial Studies,* 15(2):173–192.

Gerdes, J.
2000 "Der Doppelte Doppelpass – Transstaatlichkeit, Multikulturalismus und Doppelte Staatsbürgerschaft." In *Transstaatliche Räume. Politik, Wirtschaft und Kultur in und Zwischen Deutschland und der Türkei.* Ed. T. Faist. Bielefeld: transcript. Pp. 235–298.

Groenendijk, K. And E. Heijs
1999 "Einwanderung, Einwanderer und Staatsangehörigkeitsrecht in den Niederlanden von 1945 bis 1998." In *Politische Integration der Ausländischen Wohnbevölkerung.* Ed. U. Davy. Baden-Baden: Nomos. Pp. 105–145.

Habermas, J.
1992 *Faktizität und Geltung.* Frankfurt/M.: Suhrkamp.

Hammar, T.
1990 *Democracy and the Nation-State. Aliens, Denizens and Citizens in a World of International Migration.* Aldershot: Gower.

Hansen, R.
2002 "The Dog That Didn't Bark: Dual Nationality in the United Kingdom." In *Dual Nationality, Social Rights and Federal Citizenship in the U.S. and Europe.* Ed. R. Hansen and P. Weil. New York: Berghahn Books. Pp. 179–190.

de Hart, B.
2003 *Dual Nationality in the Netherlands.* Unpublished Manuscript. University of Nijmegen, Centre of Migration Law.

Jacobson, D.
1995 *Rights across Borders: Immigration and the Decline of Citizenship.* Baltimore, MD: Johns Hopkins University Press.

Jellinek, G.
1964 [1905] *System der Subjektiven Öffentlichen Rechte.* Reprint of the 2nd edition (1919).

Jones-Correa, M.
1998 *Between Two Nations. The Political Predicament of Latinos in New York City.* Ithaca, NY: Cornell University Press.

Kant, I.
1970 [1781] "Perpetual Peace. A Philosophical Sketch." In *Kant's Political Writings.* Ed. H. Reiss. Cambridge, MA: Cambridge University Press. Pp. 93–130.

Kimminich, O. And S. Hobe
2000 *Einführung in das Völkerrecht.* 7th edition. Tübingen: Francke.

Kymlicka, W.
1995 *Multicultural Citizenship. A Liberal Theory of Minority Rights.* Oxford: Oxford University Press.

League of Nations
1930 Treaty Series, *Convention on Certain Questions Relating to the Conflict of Nationality Laws,* April 12, 1930. Treaties and International Engagements Registered with the Secretariat of the League of Nations. Vol. 179, No. 4137 (1937–1938).

Marshall, T. H.
1964 *Class, Citizenship and Social Development. Essays by T. H. Marshall.* New York: Anchor Books.

Maruyama, M.
1963 "The Second Cybernetics: Deviation-Amplifying Mutual Causal Processes," *American Scientist,* 51(2):164–179.

Motomura, H.
1998 "Alienage Classifications in a Nation of Immigrants: Three Models of 'Permanent Residence.'" In *Immigration and Citizenship in the 21st Century.* Ed. N. J. Pickus. Lanham, MD: Rowman & Littlefield. Pp. 199–222.

North, D. C.
1990 *Institutions, Institutional Change and Economic Performance.* Cambridge: Cambridge University Press.

Offe, C.
1998 " 'Homogeneity' and Constitution Democracy: Coping with Identity Conflicts through Group Rights," *The Journal of Political Philosophy,* 6(2):113–141.

Pierson, P.
2000 "Increasing Returns, Path Dependence, and the Study of Politics," *American Political Science Review,* 94(2):251–267.

de la Pradelle, G.
2002 "Dual Nationality and the French Citizenship Tradition." In *Dual Nationality, Social Rights and Federal Citizenship in the U.S. and Europe.* Ed. R. Hansen and P. Weil. New York/Oxford: Berghahn Books. Pp. 191–214.

Putnam, R. D.
1993 *Making Democracy Work: Civic Traditions in Modern Italy.* Princeton, NJ: Princeton University Press.

Rath, J. and K. Groenendijk
2000 *Western Europe and Its Islam.* Leiden: Brill.

Renshon, S. A.
2001 *Dual Citizenship and American National Identity.* Washington, DC: Center for Immigration Studies.

Rittstieg, H.
1990 "Doppelte Staatsangehörigkeit im Völkerrecht," *Neue Juristische Wochenschrift,* 43: 1401–1405.

Rokkan, S. and D. W. Urwin
1983 *Economy, Territory, Identity: Politics of West European Peripheries.* London: Sage.

Rousseau, J.-J.
1966 [1762] *Du Contrat Social: Ou Principes du Droit Politique.* Paris: Garnier.

Ruggie, J. G.
1993 "Territoriality and Beyond: Problematizing Modernity in International Relations," *International Organization,* 47(2):139–174.

Smith, A.
1979 *Nationalism in the 20th Century.* New York: New York University Press.

Soysal, Y. N.
1994 *The Limits of Citizenship.* Chicago: University of Chicago Press.

Spång, M.
2003 *Citizenship in Sweden: Reasons for Changing Citizenship Legislation.* Unpublished Manuscript. Malmö University, School of International Migration and Ethnic Relations (IMER).

Spiro, P. J.
1997 "Dual Nationality and the Meaning of Citizenship," *Emory Law Review,* 46:1411–1485.

Tilly, C., ed.
1996 "Citizenship, Identity and Social History," *International Review of Social History,* 40 (Supplement).

Walzer, M.
1989 "Citizenship." In *Political Innovation and Conceptual Change.* Ed. T. Ball, J. Farr and R. L. Hanson. Cambridge: Cambridge University Press. Pp. 211–219.

Weber, M.
1972 [1922] *Wirtschaft und Gesellschaft.* 5th Edition. Tübingen: J.C.B. Mohr.

Chapter 5

IMMIGRANT INCORPORATION IN WESTERN DEMOCRACIES[1]

Gary Freeman

The Western democracies exhibit strong tendencies to accept the permanent presence of ethnically and religiously diverse immigrants and their descendants and are groping toward mutually agreeable modes of accommodation. This represents a surprising turn of events, especially for those Western European countries that resisted coming to terms with permanent settlement that was transforming them into multiethnic societies. Efforts at accommodation have run the gamut from apparent willingness to see immigrant minorities permanently excluded from full membership in the host society, insistence on more or less complete assimilation into a presumed national cultural norm, to more or less enthusiastic capitulation to multiculturalism. None of these impulses appears to be sustainable, and there is now a clear trend toward a middling form of incorporation – call it integration – that rejects permanent exclusion but neither demands assimilation nor embraces formal multiculturalism.

The emerging pattern of convergence on broad goals among the democracies implies but does not ensure common incorporation outcomes. For one thing, the immigrant populations in various countries differ significantly along national origin, religion, and other dimensions. More pertinent for my

[1] I would like to acknowledge financial support from the Public Policy Institute, University of Texas at Austin and research assistance from Jennifer Richmond and Dave Hill.

purposes, states still vary markedly in the policies, programs, and institutions that shape incorporation outcomes. No state possesses a truly coherent incorporation regime. Instead, one finds ramshackle, multifaceted, loosely connected sets of regulatory rules, institutions, and practices in various domains of society that together make up the frameworks within which migrants and natives work out their differences. Divergent outcomes are likely if some of these institutional patterns are more effective, influential, or durable than others.

The partly deliberate, partly accidental character of incorporation frameworks defeats efforts to identify national models or to construct abstract typologies of incorporation regimes. Although one may find idiosyncratic incorporation mechanisms in particular countries, these cannot be labeled national models because they do not represent self-conscious, deliberate choices so much as the unintended consequences of subsystem frameworks that are weakly, if at all, coordinated. Attempts to stipulate more general and abstract typologies of incorporation regimes that produce cells into which particular states may more or less easily fit oversimplify an extremely messy reality. Instead, I will argue, particular states possess a patchwork of multidimensional frameworks that hardly merit the appellation 'regime' or 'type.' Some elements of these frameworks are similar across states, some are not; some are consistent with stated government goals with respect to immigrant incorporation, others are not. The best we might hope for is that collectively some or all of these elements may fit together in what Engelen (2003) has called "syndromes" that may characterize clusters of countries.

Incorporation and cognate terms used to discuss it are unavoidably value-laden. They imply direction and intentionality, that immigrants should be incorporated into the societies to which they move, that this is a one-way process, and that the host society remains relatively unchanged if incorporation is successful (DeWind and Kasinitz, 1997; Schmitter Heisler, 2000). Post-1960s scholarship delegitimated assimilation as either a policy goal or analytical concept (Rumbaut, 1997; Zolberg, 1997:150), but there is growing concern this critique went too far. Alba and Nee (1997) have bravely called for the resurrection of the assimilation model, properly modified. Others detect evidence of a return to assimilationist policies in Western democracies (Brubaker, 2003). This contentious intellectual history demonstrates that discussions of incorporation are never neutral, and the line between description and prescription is exceptionally thin.

Work on incorporation often assumes an integrated and bounded host society to which immigrants can or must adapt. Joppke and Morawska (2003) observe that integration "assumes a society composed of domestic individuals and groups (as the antipode to 'immigrants') which are integrated normatively by a consensus and organizationally by a state" (p. 3). Such a society does not exist in their view. A better way of thinking about modern society is as multiple autonomous and interdependent fields or systems, which engage actors only partially, never completely. Because politics and the state are only one such field or system, from this perspective the idea of integration, or of the immigrant who is to be integrated, "disappears" (p. 3). Rather, immigrants "are conceptually assimilated to other individuals and groupings with similar positions on some critical indices or indicators..." (p. 3). The nonintegrated immigrant also becomes an impossibility as all immigrants are necessarily integrated in certain fields or systems. If the 'society' into which migrants are incorporated is itself fragmented and decentered, then the incorporation process must also be fragmented. The editors of a recent collection report, "Most of the authors in this volume start with the assumption that the economic, social, political and cultural processes of 'incorporation' are fundamentally interactive" (DeWind and Kasinitz, 1997:1098). Interactive, yes, but not necessarily highly correlated as part of a more cohesive process.

THINKING ABOUT INCORPORATION REGIMES

Numerous scholars have tried to identify national and crossnational patterns of incorporation regimes. One approach tries to build typologies from the ground up. Categories of states based on the mix of policies and practices they pursue vis à vis the integration of foreigners are analytically meaningful, this perspective suggests, even if the fit between category and state is often rough (Hammar, 1985; Hein, 1993; Hoskins, 1991; Reitz, 1998, 2003). Castles and Miller (2003:249–252) exploit an extensive review of policies across the democracies to identify three broad approaches to ethnic diversity: differential exclusion (Germany, Austria, and Switzerland), assimilation (France, Britain, and the Netherlands), and multiculturalism (the United States, Canada, Australia, and Sweden). Their scheme is problematic because some countries fit into more than one category, the classification of particular countries is open for debate and they are unable to place a few key cases, and no theoretical basis for establishing the criteria for inclusion is advanced. Nor do the authors provide a convincing account of the origins of the different approaches to the challenges posed by immigration.

A related approach focuses on national models, idioms, or traditions of citizenship and nationhood. The most influential effort of this sort is Brubaker's study of France and Germany (1992). Certainly Brubaker's methods were inductive, based, as they were, on close readings of the histories of his two cases. Nonetheless, his description of two models – the 'ethno-cultural' and the 'civic territorial' – provided a template for the study of additional countries and in this sense constituted an incorporation typology (cf. Favell, 1998a). Brubaker's path-breaking research convinced many readers that the preferences of states for particular modes of incorporation were not easily modified; indeed, they were deeply rooted in cultural and historical traditions highly resistant to change. Although he dealt more or less exclusively with immigration and citizenship law, his perspective implied that ethnocultural nations would differ from those with civic-territorial traditions across a range of policies and sociopolitical sectors. As Germany moves, albeit slowly, toward embracing immigration and liberalizing citizenship law and France convenes national commissions to think-through the meaning of French citizenship, the staying power of these national models looks more and more dubious.

A few typologies draw on more abstract concepts, although they are not usually derived deductively (Portes and Borocz, 1989; Portes and Rumbaut, 1990). They search for critical dimensions of incorporation alternatives and, by cross-referencing them, produce distinctive types of incorporation frameworks. According to Soysal (1994), "incorporation regime" refers to "the patterns of policy discourse and organization around which a system of incorporation is constructed" (p. 32). In her view, each European host country has a complex state system for the management of the membership of the native population that has been adapted and extended to deal with immigrants (pp. 3–4). This is an appealing framework because it recognizes that immigrants are mostly managed via institutions created for other purposes, but insists that the pertinent institutions are those concerned with the terms of membership. If correct, Soysal's approach implies a good deal more coherence within a given national approach and more divergence among them than I am postulating.

Koopmans and Statham (2000) wed Brubaker's ethnocultural and civic-territorial distinction to a conception of the cultural obligations of citizenship that can be based on cultural monism or pluralism. They drop the effort to stipulate types or regimes, opting instead for identifying a two-dimensional space bounded by ethnic assimilationism and ethnic segregation on one dimension and civic republicanism and civic pluralism on the other. This model captures variations in stances towards the integration of minority groups. For my purposes, however, it places too great an emphasis on citizenship proper: Nonetheless, the stress on the institutional features of the opportunity structures in which migrants operate is well-considered (pp. 29–39; *cf.* Ireland, 1994).

Entzinger (2000) identifies three domains of integration policies: legal-political (state), cultural (nation), and socioeconomic (market). The first includes primarily citizenship rules, especially distinguishing between *jus sanguinis* and *jus soli*. The cultural dimension refers to whether a society expects assimilation or accepts the formation of ethnic minorities. Finally, socioeconomic variation is depicted as the difference in the market rights of temporary versus permanent immigrants. Within each domain, expectations may be directed at individuals or groups (pp.101–106), yielding a six-cell typology including equal rights or group rights, liberal pluralism or multi-culturalism, and equal opportunity or equity. This model is consistent with the idea that an integrated host society is a fiction. It also focuses on "publicly stated objectives of integration policies, and the existing options for the implementation of these policies. . . .The basic assumption . . . is that integration is actively pursued at the level of policy-making, even though the actual outcome of the integration process may not always be a fuller integration" (p. 105). Entzinger places more emphasis than I would on official policy goals. Where they can be identified, researchers should ask whether goals are realized. My presumption is that explicit integration policies are typically absent in some domains.

A MULTISECTORAL FRAMEWORK

I present a multisectoral framework for understanding incorporation processes and outcomes in Western democracies that builds on the efforts of the scholars just reviewed and extends work I initially did with Ögelman (Freeman and Ögelman, 2000). Following Soysal, I focus on the terms by which membership is accessed not just in the political system, but across the various domains of society stressed by Entzinger. Following Entzinger and Favell (1998a), I concentrate on policies and regulations and the ideas that underlie them and that constitute the main elements of the political opportunity structures highlighted by Koopmans and Statham.

This approach is inspired by the new institutional economics that gives to institutions an independent role in shaping economic behavior by establishing and protecting rights, allocating privileges, and creating penalty structures that encourage adherence to the rules (North, 1990). Incorpora-tion is conceived as the result of the intersection of institutional incentive structures and the strategic decisions of migrants themselves. This article deals almost exclusively with incentive structures, the specification of which is logically prior to analyzing migrant strategic choices in specific contexts. Which of the multiple sets of institutions in societies are most likely to affect the incorporation process? I argue that the four key sets of regulatory insti-tutions are the state, market, welfare, and cultural sectors. Generally, only the policies discussed under the state and cultural sectors are directed spe-cifically at immigrants.

States

Hardly anything can be more important for the eventual status of immi-grants than the legal circumstances of their first entry. As a result of prox-imity, salience, and directness, immigration and citizenship policies should be important sources of the incorporative experience of migrants. Immigra-tion laws, observed or violated, necessarily precede and often constrain the migrant's interaction with market, welfare, and cultural regulations (*see* Hol-lifield, 2000, 1994; *see also* Castles, 1988; Zolberg, 1999). Among the as-pects of a country's immigration policy that bear on incorporation are the methods and purposes in recruiting, accepting, and deterring immigrants, enforcement of immigration rules regarding illegal entry and unauthorized work, and rules regulating acquisition and rights of citizenship.

Castles and Miller (2003) argue that there is a strong but imperfect relation between a country's historical experience of immigration and the kinds of policies they develop towards migrants at home. The traditional countries of immigration (the United States, Canada, Australia) operate annual immigration quotas and support family reunion, permanent settle-ment, and ready acquisition of citizenship. Guestworker countries (Ger-many, Switzerland, Austria) have tried to prevent family reunion, were re-luctant to grant secure residence status, and adopted restrictive naturalization rules. On the other hand, former colonial migrants to countries like France, the Netherlands, and Britain often enjoyed citizenship at entry and were generally allowed to bring in close family members, whereas immigrants from countries with no colonial ties were usually treated less favorably.

Immigrants of different legal origin are treated substantially differently. Permanent residence visas create a class of immigrants with rights and privi-leges distinct from those holding temporary work visas. Skilled migrants may be better positioned than the unskilled to control the terms of their integration. Refugees selected from abroad enter under terms highly distinct from on-shore asylum seekers. Countries that go to the trouble of recruiting immigrants may presume that they would be able to get on by themselves and need fewer direct government services and guidance in the settlement process. Perhaps the most fundamental consideration is that some immigrants are wanted and others are not. As Joppke (1999) argues in the cases of Germany and Britain, migrants who are formally recruited may enjoy advantages because policymakers feel moral obligations to them that they lack toward the uninvited.

While differences in immigration programs across the liberal democracies are substantial, they appear to be declining. All are now countries of destination and have developed immigration control apparatuses and moved toward formalizing policies towards resident aliens. Forgoing the immigration halt of 25 years ago, they are now engaged in fierce competition for highly-skilled temporary workers. Within the European Union, considerable energy has been devoted to the harmonization of immigration and asylum policies, a key force behind convergence. The Amsterdam Treaty (1997) put immigration, asylum, and visa policy into the 'community' pillar and initiated a five-year period for giving the Commission exclusive right of initiative in these areas. In 1999, the Tampere Council mandated the development of a framework for a common asylum policy, and the Commission has issued communications on common policies on asylum and legal and illegal immigration (Commission, 2000a, b; 2001a, b). Despite all this effort, however, the Council has approved few of the Commission's proposals in the immigration area. The traditional countries of immigration, on the other hand, continue to promote substantial annual admissions for permanent settlement. Only Australia shows signs of going its own way on issues of family reunion and asylum policy, but has followed her peers in opening her doors to highly-skilled temporary entrants (Freeman, 1999; Freeman and Birrell, 2001).

Citizenship policy directly shapes the ability of migrants to acquire full legal and constitutional rights. The extension of many of the rights of citizens to denizens is a notable development in the liberal democracies (Soysal, 1994; Plascencia *et al.*, 2003). Nonetheless, in the ubiquitous locution of social science "citizenship still matters," as a growing comparative literature attests (Bauböck, 1994; Hansen, 2003; Hansen and Weil, 2000, 2001; Feldblum, 1998, 2000; Guiraudon, 1998; Feldblum and Klusmeyer, 1999).

How much variation is there across countries, and is it sufficient to contribute to distinctive national citizenship models? Is there a trend toward liberalization of naturalization requirements among the liberal democracies? Our ability to answer these questions is limited by the complexity of national citizenship regimes and the absence of readily comparable indicators, but a number of scholars have begun to tackle this problem (Bauböck and Çinar, 1994; Çinar, 1999). Çinar *et al.* (1999) develop indicators of seven dimensions of legal integration of noncitizens in eight European countries: security of residence, labor market access, family reunification, social security rights and welfare benefits, civil rights, political rights, and conditions of the acquisition and loss of citizenship. Money (2002) collected data on citizenship policies for 62–84 countries in the period from 1929 to 1954. She focuses on acquisition of citizenship for three categories: children, adults, and women. Between 1929 and 1954, rules for children remained relatively stable, access of adults to citizenship grew more difficult, but treatment of women became more equal to that of men. In other words, trends differ among the three dimensions of citizenship policy. Furthermore, the various dimensions of citizenship policy are only weakly correlated so that "we need to dis-aggregate the dimensions of citizenship into the component parts and move away from understanding citizenship as a dichotomous variable or an ordinal variable on a single scale" (p. 12).

Howard (2003) creates an index out of four components of citizenship laws in fifteen EU States – 1) *jus soli* or *jus sanguinis;* 2) difficulty of naturalization; 3) availability of dual nationality for naturalized immigrants; and 4) rates of naturalization. He finds considerable variation along all four dimensions and few differences in the index scores of countries in the 1980s and twenty years later. Arguing that "it is still too early to speak of a convergence process within the countries of the EU" (p. 22), he sees a pattern of durable divergence.

Hansen's (1998) review of citizenship in EU member states provides a slightly different take on these questions. He concludes, "there is no clear direction to policy change in Europe, and that one can at most speak confidently of a liberal harmonization of naturalization in North-Western Europe" (p. 760). He places a good deal more stress, however, on another development – the fact that "with the exception of Austria, Luxembourg, and Greece, all second-generation migrants have a right to acquire citizenship either at birth or by the age of 21" (p. 760). Hansen also explores the effects of the creation of an EU citizenship (CEU). Considering the obstacles to extending CEU to third-country nationals, he concludes that their best avenue for achieving a more liberal citizenship status is through national-level decisions to accept dual nationality that would remove one major obstacle to naturalization (p. 761).

These preliminary studies suggest significant residual variation across the Western democracies in the content of citizenship rules. Weak correlations among the various dimensions of these rules, and the clear need to disaggregate putative types into their components, imply that the identification of national models of citizenship policy may do violence to reality. The creation of a CEU does not appear to be leading to a common EU citizenship policy (citizenship and nationality remain intergovernmental prerogatives). Despite the absence of consistent patterns of liberalization, however, one prototypical case – Germany – has made decisive strides in opening up naturalization. There is general movement toward entitlement for the second-generation, and greater, if grudging, acceptance of dual nationality.

Market

Markets and the welfare sector form integral parts of national political economies. Migrant participation in labor markets and business and the characteristics of political economies that impinge on their success are central to incorporation. I argued above that immigration and citizenship formats were among the most pertinent characteristics of receiving societies from the point of view of immigrant incorporation. Nevertheless, research designs that pay attention to political economy may yield more results than those that proceed from case selection based on immigration experiences or cultural traditions. This would require the combination of the two research enterprises that have, to date, had little intercourse.

The identification of changing patterns of political economy in capitalist countries has preoccupied scholars in recent years. Hardly any of this work explicitly addresses the pertinence of these models for migrant fortunes (for a notable exception, *see* Engelen, 2003). Hall and Soskice (2001) do not broach the subject in their agenda-setting essay on varieties of capitalism, nor do any of the contributors to their volume. Nonetheless, it may be possible to build on their and other frameworks (Shonfield, 1965; Lehmbruch, 1984; Katzenstein, 1985; Piore and Sabel, 1984) to identify linkages between particular forms of political economy and the fate of migrants in markets and welfare systems.

Hall and Soskice focus on how firms coordinate their activities. In the liberal market economies (LMEs) that include such countries as the United

States, Britain, Australia, Canada, New Zealand, and Ireland, coordination takes place through competitive market arrangements. In the coordinated market economies (CMEs), such as Germany, Japan, Switzerland, the Netherlands, Belgium, Sweden, Norway, Denmark, Finland, and Austria, coordination is achieved through nonmarket relationships. They cannot classify six countries (France, Italy, Spain, Portugal, Greece, and Turkey). Rueda and Pontusson (2000), referring to CMEs as 'social market economies,' argue they are distinguished from LMEs to the extent that they have comprehensive, publicly-funded social welfare systems; regulations that standardize employment security, increasing costs for employers who shed labor and achieving greater parity of employment conditions across sectors and categories of labor; and institutionalization of collective bargaining and coordination of wage formation (pp. 364–365). There is a close but imperfect fit between CMEs and what Esping-Andersen (1990) calls social democratic and corporatist welfare states.

As Engelen (2003) has argued, these typologies suffer from "methodological nationalism" and probably overstate the degree of fit even for those countries that can be placed in one or the other category (for an alternative schema that admits intranational variations, *see* Whitley, 1992, 1999). These models may provide a starting point for seeking out linkages between structures of political economy and incorporation. They should be pertinent to answering such questions as 1) how effectively states and their firms adapt to changing labor market trajectories, especially to shifts in skill requirements, and how migrants figure into these plans; 2) whether migrants are primarily located in the formal or informal sectors; 3) whether they are protected by the same rules that protect national workers; 4) the extent to which migrants are self-employed and whether this represents entrepreneurial initiative or failure in the labor market; 5) how effectively states combat unauthorized work; and 6) how seriously states attempt to prevent ethnic and racial discrimination in the marketplace (on the latter, *see* Bleich, 2002; Chopin and Neissen, 2002; MacEwan, 1995).

CMEs, for example, can be expected to pursue stricter enforcement of labor market regulations and the development of ambitious and activist labor market policies. These, in turn, should reduce the likelihood of the development of dual labor markets and large informal sectors with significant immigrant participation. LMEs, on the other hand, would be expected to tolerate higher levels of illegal immigration, more unauthorized labor, and more pervasive business activity on the borders of legality.

There is no space to canvass the available evidence on these propositions. I have argued elsewhere that there is an observable but imperfect relationship between modes of political economy and the estimated size of informal economies (Freeman and Ögelman, 2000:119–120). Rath (2002) and his colleagues' study of the clothing industry in cities in France, Britain, the United States, and the Netherlands found that only Amsterdam belatedly took steps to repress sweatshops and illegal work, suggesting a link between corporatist institutions and efforts to combat informality.

Welfare

Social benefit programs affect the marginal utility of work for those who are eligible. For employers, on the other hand, they are a chief element of the cost of doing business while at the same time they may increase the productivity of active workers through training, education, and improved healthcare. Social benefits, the taxes that support them, and the regulations associated with them constitute a major incentive structure for the economic behavior of migrants, their employers, and those who formulate state immigration policies. One of the most striking peculiarities of contemporary migration to the rich democracies is that they are all welfare states, possessing social protection schemes that were absent during mass migrations at the turn of the century and that are absent in the Third World cities to which millions have migrated in recent decades.

What difference does the existence of welfare institutions and the incentive structures they produce make for migration and incorporation patterns? The welfare state, I argue, has been a force for the inclusion of migrants, providing surprisingly open access for them to participate in benefits programs. While this may be desirable from humanitarian and economic perspectives, it has, nonetheless, heightened tensions over welfare politics. Backlash fueled by perceptions of migrant welfare abuse threatens to erode both consensus over welfare provision and tolerance of continued mass immigration.

That most types of welfare state benefits have been made available to immigrants, regardless of their citizenship, is puzzling in a number of respects. The territorial character of the nation-state suggests that welfare systems would be closed to nonmembers. Persons who belong to other states are foreigners and, therefore, ineligible in theory to enjoy the benefits of membership (Ryner, 2003). Migrants receiving benefits, therefore, pose a threat to the logic of the welfare state (Halfmann, 2002:35; Freeman, 1986). Yet territoriality turns out to be a double-edged sword and becomes a mechanism by which migrants acquire welfare rights.

The constitutions and laws of the democracies typically accord protections to persons, not citizens, and even if citizenship is required, courts and administrators have stretched the terms of eligibility. Presence in the territory – residency and simple participation – have emerged as legally enforceable bases for claiming benefits. Welfare benefits have been distributed to denizens on terms not unlike those for citizens (Hammar, 1985, 1990). Welfare bureaucrats and independent courts foiled the plans of immigration policymakers to deny benefits to guestworkers in order to encourage return. Access to social protection schemes for workers, in turn, made family migration more feasible and, again, courts intervened to derail government efforts to prevent it.

Why bureaucrats and judges chose to interpret residence as implying rights is subject to debate. Inclusive social policies for migrants, as Joppke (1999) notes in the case of Germany, could be the correlate and compensation for an externally exclusive immigration policy (*cf.* Geddes, 2000b) as well as a morally-driven sense of obligation to workers who had been actively recruited. Guiraudon's close studies of Germany, the Netherlands, and France (1998, 2000) find evidence that popular opposition to welfare benefits for migrants was sidestepped in bureaucratic and judicial venues where there was a bias toward equal rights before the law and decisionmakers were insulated from public opinion and electoral pressures. Political rights, on the other hand, could only be extended through constitutional changes that required open debate and political support. Hence social rights were extended, *contra* Marshall, before political rights. This was not simply idealism or generosity on the part of bureaucrats and judges: "What transpires from policy documents in the three countries studied, however, is that equality in law is important because it replaces special services and is thus less costly" (2000:82–83).

If the territorial logic of the welfare state worked mostly in favor of immigrants, is it, nevertheless, eroding general support for the welfare state precisely because its guarantee of access to migrants is seen as illegitimate by sections of the national community? To answer these questions, one needs evidence on 1) rates of migrant welfare participation across the democracies; 2) public perceptions of these rates; and 3) the role of immigration in stimulating backlash against welfare programs. With respect to the first issue, the most comprehensive study is Brücker *et al.* (2002). Although their presentation is inconsistent (p. 122), they conclude that some generous welfare states do act as magnets attracting migrants, the existence of benefit programs distorts the composition of migrant streams, migrant dependency on welfare is more extensive than their socioeconomic characteristics predict, and there are strong residual dependency effects in countries with generous programs (pp. 89–90; *cf.* Borjas, 2003; Reitz, 1998). Comparative data on the perception of electorates in Western states about the nexus between migrants and welfare usage is scarce. Brücker *et al.* (2002), reviewing Euro-barometer polls, conclude, "the claims that migrants are a burden on the welfare state and a threat to the labor market show up in the measured opinions" (p. 122). Fetzer (2000), on the other hand, fails to find statistically significant effects of worries over immigrant use of services and anti-immigrant attitudes in the United States, Germany, or France.

There is contention over the role of immigration in stimulating welfare backlash. Bommes and Geddes (2000) and Banting (2000) make spirited cases against the proposition. Banting concludes that only the liberal welfare states of the United States, Canada, and Switzerland display any ill effects of cultural, ethnic, and linguistic diversity and that the tension between ethnic heterogeneity and welfare state development is potential but not inevitable (p. 21). Banting admits, of course, that "incorporation is not uncontested," and European countries show signs of welfare chauvinism in trying to deny foreigners entry into the country and to deny access to benefits. These efforts, he concludes, have not normally been successful and never decisive (p. 23; *cf.* Freeman, 2001).

The discussion to this point has dealt with national welfare state arrangements and the rules regulating immigrant participation in them. Ireland (1994; 2004) makes a strong case that it is necessary to get much closer to the terrain of local governments in different national settings in order to uncover the real impacts of welfare policies on immigrants (*cf.* Body-Gendrot and Martiniello, 2000; Garbaye, 2000). Guiraudon (2000), as noted above, argues that universalism was a policy designed to avoid expensive and contentious targeted programs for migrants. Nevertheless, such policies have proliferated and might be labeled as settlement programs. Bach (1992) shows that although the United States has few formal settlement programs there is a vast, quasi-public enterprise devoted to settling immigrants. Jupp (1992) contrasts this arrangement with the centrally-directed and highly interventionist settlement tradition in Australia (*cf.* Lanphier and Lukomskyj, 1994, on Canada and Australia).

In Europe, settlement policy has been deeply affected by the anticipation that many of the postwar migration flows would be temporary. It has taken some time for governments to grasp the nettle of deliberately intervening into the settlement and incorporation process. Soysal (1994) remains one of the most useful comparisons of state policies in this regard. Ireland is the most detailed study, focusing on Germany, the Netherlands, and Belgium. Ireland's thesis is that restructuring of the welfare state through retrenchment, decentralization, and delegation to nonprofits has had a greater influence on the incorporation of immigrants and their families into European host societies than ethnic background, social class, high unemployment, or budget cuts (p. 5). These changes have "generally encouraged ethnic-based mobilization" (p. 7). Ireland attacks the broad typologies that scholars employ to describe national immigrant policies. In effect, countries, cities, groups, and even neighborhoods have distinctive "caring strategies" (p. 24) that emphasize either individuals or groups and are either inclusive or exclusive.

Culture

State policies that stipulate the conditions of cultural recognition and expression produce critical incentive structures for the retention or loss of immigrant cultural characteristics and can seek to protect or transform the cultures of the receiving societies. These matters are at the heart of many of the leading conflicts involving immigration in Western states. The depth of feeling can be seen in the explosion of writing by Western intellectual elites seeking agreement on what is normatively acceptable for host societies to ask in the way of cultural concessions by migrants and natives (Kymlicka and Norman, 2000). In addition, the practice of religion and the display of religious symbols, use of native languages, and treatment of women and children have all generated serious conflicts. Empirical studies of state policies toward cultural practice have focused on two broad topics: 1) the location of particular countries along a continuum that includes efforts at marginalization and exclusion, expectations of assimilation, and endorsement of official multiculturalism; and 2) the extent to which states direct their policies at migrants as individuals or as members of ethnic or national-origin groups.

The United States before 1965 is said to have pursued a particularly harsh form of assimilationism (Schmitter Heisler, 2000; Tichenor, 2002; King, 2000; Gerstle and Mollenkopf, 2001). The Germanic countries set themselves apart by their ethnonational bases of statehood (Brubaker, 1992; Joppke, 1999; Klopp, 2002; Schmitter Heisler, 2002). France is depicted as having a civic territorial conception of citizenship but a strongly assimilationist attitude toward cultural practices (Noiriel, 1996; Feldblum,1999;

Hollifield, 1994). Canada, Australia, Sweden, and the Netherlands, on the other hand, have attracted a good deal of favorable comment from scholars impressed with their more enthusiastic embrace of official multiculturalism (Banting, 2000; Coulombe, 2000; Castles *et al.*, 1988; Hammar, 1999; Entzinger, 1994, 2003).

These patterns are not especially stable, however. There can be little doubt that hard-line assimilationism is both out of favor with commentators and losing ground in its few national redoubts. In recent years, the United States has moved sharply away from assimilation towards multiculturalism, but not always in a formal, state-sanctioned manner (de la Garza and De-Sipio, 1992; Salins, 1997). France has made numerous practical concessions to multiculturalism despite its strong republican tradition (Schain, 1999; Feldblum, 1999). Germany has finally yielded to the weight of reality and admitted that it is a country of immigration and its citizenship reforms noted above depart significantly from assimilationist requirements (Brubaker, 2003; Hansen, 1998, 2003).

But a more recent and telling development could be in the making. Joppke and Morawska (2003:10) argue that the infatuation with official multiculturalism is on the wane. Noting that *"de facto* multiculturalism has become a pervasive reality in liberal, immigrant-receiving states," they nonetheless claim that official multiculturalism, the deliberate and explicit recognition and protection of immigrants as distinct ethnic groups, is in decline, notably in Sweden (Hammar, 1999), the Netherlands (Entzinger, 1994, 2003), and Australia (Freeman and Birrell, 2001).

Broad trends at the national level both reflect and camouflage a myriad of small-scale, localized, and diverse outcomes below and ignore the impact of developments at supranational venues above (Lahav, 1998). Recent scholarship has begun to address both of these issues. An example of work on the big issues of immigrant integration through highly detailed, ethnographic research in specific locales is Ireland's important book on Germany and the Low Countries. His painstaking review traces the interaction between large-scale structural changes in the welfare state and migrant trends as they are played on local terrain. At the supranational level, the European Union is playing a growing, if not decisive, role in shaping the social policy of member states towards immigrants. As one observer puts it (Geddes, 2000a, b), EU social policy is creating a "thin Europeanization" that entails a migrant inclusion agenda of free movement rights, transferable social entitlements, and anti-discrimination (Brochmann, 1996, 2002; Favell, 1998b; Favell and Geddes, 2000).

The central issue related to the integration of immigrants in Western Europe is Islam. One reason is sheer novelty. As Bernard Lewis (1994) puts it, the voluntary migration of large numbers of Muslims to non-Muslim countries has "no precedent in Islamic history, no previous discussion in Islamic legal literature . . . . A mass migration, a reverse *hijra* of ordinary people seeking a new life among the unbelievers, is an entirely new phenomenon . . ." (p. 14). This leaves both Muslims and their hosts unprepared as to which rules and practices will be acceptable. Exponents of extreme-right ideologies have declared the incompatibility between communities of devout Muslims and secular/Christian Western societies, while advocates of liberal multiculturalism have been loathe to admit that serious problems exist. Even without the current context of fears of terrorism and pressures to view Muslim inhabitants through the lens of security questions, working out a suitable *modus vivendi* between these different cultural communities will require great patience and ingenuity. Various national and local efforts to date should be viewed as tentative experiments the outcomes of which cannot be known for some time (Nonneman *et al.*, 1996; Lewis and Schnapper, 1994.

CONCLUSION

Social scientists engaging in comparative research must manage the tension between the impulse and call to generalize and to identify unifying trends and the equally compelling need to pay attention to specificity and idiosyncrasy. This article errs on the side of complexity at the expense of general propositions. Against the most ambitious attempts to develop general models of incorporation, it has argued that the idea of incorporation itself is problematic and that the insertion of migrants into the Western democracies takes place in a number of interrelated but distinct domains.

State regulations play a central role in each domain but only occasionally deal with migrants directly. Most countries have only a loosely integrated set of regulatory frameworks that do no more than create incentive (opportunity) structures for both migrants and natives. Taken together, these frameworks constitute the incorporation schemes of Western democracies. Rather than anticipating a small number of distinct 'modes of immigrant incorporation' that might characterize the policies of particular countries, we should expect different modes in particular domains – state, market, welfare, culture – within individual states; the overall outcome being a mixed bag not fully assimilationist, pluralist, or multicultural.

One might describe these as "syndromes" (Engelen, 2003) that involve less than perfectly cohesive approaches across the four domains. It is easier to specify the institutional framework in place in the market and welfare sectors than the others, largely because more comparative work is available upon which to build. Even so, as I have noted, reigning typologies of varieties of capitalism and welfare states accommodate some but not all Western nations. Making sense of immigration and citizenship policy is a more trying task. Most European states are relatively closed to immigration in the sense that they eschew the annual quota systems of the settler societies. Yet they either recruit or accept labor migration, especially but not exclusively high-skilled entrants. Repeated amnesties (Italy) and easy regularization (Spain) also muddy the waters. Cultural policies, where they exist, defy generalization. Except in Canada, Australia, the Netherlands, and Sweden, multiculturalism is less a choice than an unintended and often most unwelcome outcome.

With these reservations, it is possible to perceive the outlines of four syndromes pertinent to immigrant incorporation. One consists of open immigration and citizenship practices, liberal political economies and welfare states, and *laissez-faire* or formal multiculturalism (United States, Canada, and Australia). A second syndrome is exhibited by Sweden and the Netherlands and entails a moderately open immigration and citizenship regime, coordinated market economies, social democratic or corporatist welfare states, and formal settlement policies uneasily embracing multiculturalism. Third, there is a group of countries that are open to labor migration and have coordinated market economies and corporatist welfare systems. However, these same countries discourage access to citizenship and are reluctant to accept permanent settlement. They have at times resisted both multiculturalism and assimilation. The key examples are Germany, Austria, and Switzerland. Finally, a few countries have lacked until recently any formal immigration programs but have alternately condoned irregular migration or have recruited foreign labor. These states have had restrictive citizenship policies, liberal political economies and welfare states, and no policy on assimilation or multiculturalism, although they are perilously close to a *de facto* policy of differential exclusion (Spain, Portugal, and Greece).

The identification of these syndromes begs many questions and requires a number of highly contestable classificatory decisions. Except for the strong linkages between the market and welfare sectors, developments in one domain appear to be largely independent of those in others. Cultural policies seem especially autonomous. Immigration and citizenship frameworks have changed a good deal since the mid-1970s, as have cultural policies. Market and welfare arrangements are more stable. As states gain more experience with different approaches, and as immigrant-origin populations become more settled and entrenched, incorporation practices may eventually display more coherence and order than is currently perceptible.

REFERENCES

Alba, R. and V. Nee
1997 "Rethinking Assimilation Theory for a New Era of Immigration," *International Migration Review*, 31(4):826–874.

Bach, R.
1992 "Settlement Policies in the United States." In *Nations of Immigrants: Australia, the United States, and International Migration*. Ed. G. Freeman and J. Jupp. Melbourne and New York: Oxford University Press. Pp. 145–164.

Banting, K.
2000 "Looking in Three Directions: Migration and the European Welfare State in Comparative Perspective." In *Immigration and Welfare: Challenging the Borders of the Welfare State*. Ed. M. Bommes and A. Geddes. London: Routledge. Pp. 13–33.

Bauböck, R.
1994 *Transnational Citizenship: Membership and Rights in International Migration*. Aldershot, UK: Edward Elgar.

Bauböck, R. and D. Çinar
1994 "Briefing Paper: Naturalization Policies in Western Europe." In *The Politics of Immigration in Western Europe*. Ed. M. Baldwin-Edwards and M. Schain. London: Frank Cass. Pp. 192–196.

Bleich, E.
2002 "Integrating Ideas into Policy-making Analysis: Frames and Race Policies in Britain and France," *Comparative Political Studies*, 35(9):1054–1076.

Body-Gendrot, S. and M. Martiniello, eds.
2000 *Minorities in European Cities: The Dynamics of Social Integration and Social Exclusion at the Neighbourhood Level*. Houndmills: MacMillan.

Bommes, M. and A. Geddes, eds.
2000 *Immigration and Welfare: Challenging the Borders of the Welfare State*. London and New York: Routledge.

Borjas, G.
2002 "Welfare Reform and Immigrant Participation in Welfare Programs," *International Migration Review*, 36(4):1093–1123.

Brochmann, G.
2002 "Citizenship and Inclusion in European Welfare States: The EU Dimension." In *Migration and the Externalities of European Integration*. Ed. S. Lavenex and E. M. Ucarer. Lanham, MD: Lexington Books. Pp. 179–194.

1996 *European Integration and Immigration from Third Countries*. Oslo: Scandinavian University Press.

Brubaker, W. R., ed.
2003 "The Return of Assimilation? Changing Perspectives on Immigration and Its Sequels in France, Germany, and the United States." In *Toward Assimilation and Citizenship: Immigrants in Liberal Nation-States.* Ed. C. Joppke and E. Morawska. Houndmills: Palgrave. Pp. 39–58.

1992 *Citizenship and Nationhood in France and Germany.* Cambridge, MA: Harvard University Press.

1989 *Immigration and the Politics of Citizenship in Europe and North America.* Lanham, MD: University Press of America.

Brücker, H. *et al.*
2002 "Managing Migration in the European Welfare State." In *Immigration Policy and the Welfare System: A Report for the Fondazione Rodolfo Debenedetti.* Ed. T. Boeri, G. Hansen, and B. McCormick. Oxford: Oxford University Press. Pp. 1–168.

Castles, S. *et al.*
1988 *Mistaken Identity: Multiculturalism and the Demise of Nationalism in Australia.* Sydney: Pluto Press.

Castles, S. and M. Miller
2003 *The Age of Migration.* 3rd ed. New York: Guilford.

Chopin, I. and J. Niessen, eds.
2002 *Combating Racial and Ethnic Discrimination: Taking the European Legislative Agenda Further.* Brussels: Migration Policy Group.

Çinar, D.
1994 "From Aliens to Citizens: A Comparative Analysis of Rules of Transition." In *From Aliens to Citizens: Redefining the Status of Immigrants in Europe.* Ed. R. Bauböck. Aldershot, UK: Avebury. Pp. 49–72.

Çinar, D. *et al.*
1999 "Comparing the Rights of Non-Citizens in Western Europe," *Research Perspectives on Migration,* 2(1):8–11.

Commission of the European Communities
2001a *Communication on an Open Method of Coordination for the Community Immigration Policy.* Brussels: Commission of the European Communities.

2001b *On a Common Policy on Illegal Immigration.* Brussels: Commission of the European Communities.

2000a *On the Common Asylum Policy, Introducing an Open Coordination Method.* Brussels: Commission of the European Communities.

2000b *On a Community Immigration Policy.* Brussels: Commission of the European Communities.

Coulombe, P.
2000 "Citizenship and Official Bilingualism in Canada." In *Citizenship in Diverse Societies.* Ed. W. Kymlicka and W. Norman. Oxford: Oxford University Press. Pp. 273–296.

de la Garza, R. and L. DiSipio
1992 "Making Them Us." In *Nations of Immigrants: Australia, the United States, and International Migration.* Ed. G. Freeman and J. Jupp. Melbourne and New York: Oxford University Press. Pp. 202–216.

DeWind, J. and P. Kasinitz
1997 "Everything Old is New Again? Processes and Theories of Immigrant Incorporation," *International Migration Review,* 31(4):1096–1111.

Engelen, E.
2003 "Conceptualizing Economic Incorporation: 'From Institutional Linkages' to 'Institutional Hybrids.'" Paper presented at the Conference on Conceptual and Methodological Developments in the Study of International Migration, Princeton University. May 23–25.

Entzinger, H.
2003 "The Rise and Fall of Multiculturalism: The Case of the Netherlands." In *Toward Assimilation and Citizenship: Immigrants in Liberal Nation-States.* Ed. C. Joppke and E. Morawska. Houndmills: Palgrave. Pp. 59–86.

2000 "The Dynamics of Integration Policies: A Multidimensional Model." In *Challenging Immigration and Ethnic Relations Politics.* Ed. R. Koopmans and P. Statham. Oxford: Oxford University Press. Pp. 97–118.

1994 "A Future for the Dutch Ethnic Minorities Model? In *Muslims in Europe.* Ed. B. Lewis and D. Schnapper. London: Pinter Publishers.

Esping-Andersen, G.
1990 *The Three Worlds of Capitalism.* Princeton: Princeton University Press.

Favell, A.
1998a *Philosophies of Integration: Immigration and the Idea of Citizenship in France and Britain.* London: MacMillan.

1998b "The Europeanisation of Immigration Politics," *European Integration Online Papers,* 2(10).

Favell, A. and A. Geddes
2000 "Immigration and European Integration: New Opportunities for Transnational Mobilization?" In *Challenging Immigration and Ethnic Relations Politics.* Ed. R. Koopmans and P. Statham. Oxford: Oxford University Press. Pp. 407–428.

Feldblum, M.
2000 "Managing Membership: New Trends in Citizenship and Nationality Policy." In *From Migrants to Citizens: Membership in a Changing World.* Ed. T. A. Aleinikoff and D. Klusmeyer. Washington, DC: Carnegie Endowment for International Peace. Pp. 475–499.

1999 *Reconstructing Citizenship: The Politics of Nationality Reform and Immigration in Contemporary France.* Albany: SUNY Press.

1998 "Reconfiguring Citizenship in Western Europe." In *Challenge to the Nation State.* Ed. C. Joppke. Oxford: Oxford University Press. Pp. 231–271.

Feldblum, M. and D. Klusmeyer, eds.
1999 "Immigrants and Citizenship Today: A Comparative Perspective," *Research Perspectives on Migration,* 2(2).

Fetzer, J.
2000 *Public Attitudes toward Immigration in the United States, France, and Germany.* Cambridge: Cambridge University Press.

Freeman, G.
2001 "Client Politics or Populism? Immigration Reform in the United States." In *Controlling a New Migration World.* Ed. V. Guiraudon and C. Joppke. London: Routledge. Pp. 65–95.

———
1999 "The Quest for Skill: A Comparative Analysis." In *Migration and Refugee Policies: An Overview.* Ed. A. Bernstein and M. Weiner. London: Pinter. Pp. 84–118.

———
1997 "Immigration as a Source of Political Discontent and Frustration in Western Democracies," *Studies in Comparative International Development,* 32(3):42–64.

———
1986 "Migration and the Political Economy of the Welfare State," *The Annals,* 485:51–63.

Freeman, G. and B. Birrell
2001 "Diverging Paths of Immigration Policy in Australia and the United States," *Population and Development Review,* 27(3):525–551.

Freeman, G. and N. Ögelman
2000 "State Regulatory Regimes and Immigrants' Informal Economic Activity." In *Immigrant Businesses: The Economic, Political and Social Environment.* Ed. J. Rath. Houndmills: MacMillan. Pp. 107–123.

Garbaye, R.
2000 "Ethnic Minorities, Cities, and Institutions." In *Challenging Immigration and Ethnic Relations Politics.* Ed. R. Koopmans and P. Statham. Oxford: Oxford University Press. Pp. 283–311.

Geddes, A.
2000a "Thin Europeanisation: The Social Rights of Migrants in an Integrating Europe." In *Immigration and Welfare: Challenging the Borders of the Welfare State.* Ed. M. Bommes and A. Geddes. London: Routledge. Pp. 209–226.

———
2000b *Immigration and European Integration: Towards Fortress Europe?* Manchester: Manchester University Press.

Gerstle, G. and J. Mollenkopf, eds.
2001 *E Pluribus Unum? Contemporary and Historical Perspectives on Immigrant Political Incorporation.* New York: Russell Sage Foundation.

Guiraudon, V.
2000 "The Marshallian Tryptich Reordered: The Role of Courts and Bureaucracies in Furthering Migrants' Social Rights." In *Immigration and Welfare: Challenging the Borders of the Welfare State.* Ed. M. Bommes and A. Geddes. London: Routledge. Pp. 72–89.

———
1998 "Citizenship Rights for Non-Citizens: France, Germany, and the Netherlands." In *Challenge to the Nation State.* Ed. C. Joppke. Oxford: Oxford University Press. Pp. 272–318.

Halfmann, J.
2000 "Welfare State and Territory." In *Immigration and Welfare: Challenging the Borders of the Welfare State*. Ed. M. Bommes and A. Geddes. London: Routledge. Pp. 34–50.

Hall, P. and D. Soskice
2001 "An Introduction to Varieties of Capitalism." In *Varieties of Capitalism: The Institutional Foundations of Comparative Advantage*. Ed. P. Hall and D. Soskice. Oxford: Oxford University Press. Pp. 1–67.

Hammar, T. *et al.*, eds.
1999 "Closing the Doors to the Swedish Welfare State." In *Mechanisms of Immigration Control: A Comparative Analysis of European Regulation Policies*. Ed. G. Brochmann and T. Hammar. Oxford: Berg. Pp. 169–201.

Hammar, T.
1990 *Democracy and the Nation State: Aliens, Denizens and Citizens in a World of International Migration*. Aldershot, UK: Avebury.

Hammar, T., ed.
1985 *European Immigration Policy*. Cambridge: Cambridge University Press.

Hansen, R.
2003 "Citizenship and Integration in Europe." In *Toward Assimilation and Citizenship: Immigrants in Liberal Nation-States*. Ed. C. Joppke and E. Morawska. Houndmills: Palgrave. Pp. 87–109.

1998 "A European Citizenship or a Europe of Citizens? Third Country Nationals in the EU," *Journal of Ethnic and Migration Studies*, 24(4):751–768.

Hansen, R. and P. Weil, eds.
2001 *Towards a European Nationality: Citizenship, Immigration and Nationality Law in the EU*. New York: Palgrave.

2000 *Dual Nationality, Social Rights and Federal Citizenship in the U.S. and Europe*. New York: Berghahn Books.

Hein, J.
1993 *States and International Migration: The Incorporation of Indochinese Refugees in the United States and France*. Boulder: Westview Press.

Hollifield, J.
2000 "The Politics of International Migration: Can We 'Bring the State Back In'?" In *Migration Theory: Talking across Disciplines*. Ed. C. Brettell and J. Hollifield. Pp. 137–185.

1994 "Immigration and Republicanism in France: The Hidden Consensus." In *Controlling Immigration: A Global Perspective*. Ed. W. Cornelius *et al.* Stanford: Stanford University Press. Pp. 143–175.

Hoskins, M.
1991 *New Immigrants and Democratic Society: Minority Integration in Western Democracies*. New York: Praeger.

Howard, M.
2003 "Foreigners or Citizens? Citizenship Policies in the Countries of the EU." Paper

presented at the European Union Studies Association Conference, Nashville. March 27–29.

Ireland, P.
2004 *Becoming Europe: Immigration, Integration, and the Welfare State.* Pittsburgh, PA: University of Pittsburgh Press.

————
1994 *The Policy Challenge of Ethnic Diversity.* Cambridge: Harvard University Press.

Joppke, C.
1999 *Immigration and the Nation State.* Oxford: Oxford University Press.

Joppke, C. and E. Morawska
2003 "Integrating Immigrants in Liberal Nation-States: Policies and Practices." In *Toward Assimilation and Citizenship: Immigrants in Liberal Nation-States.* Ed. C. Joppke and E. Morawska. Houndmills: Palgrave. Pp. 1–36.

Jupp, J.
1992 "Settlement Policy in Australia." In *Nations of Immigrants: Australia, the United States, and International Migration.* Ed. G. Freeman and J. Jupp. Melbourne and New York: Oxford University Press. Pp. 130–144.

Katzenstein, P.
1985 *Small States in World Markets.* Ithaca: Cornell University Press.

King, D.
2000 *Making Americans: Immigration, Race, and the Origins of the Diverse Democracy.* Cambridge: Harvard University Press.

Klopp, B.
2002 *German Multiculturalism: Immigrant Integration and the Transformation of Citizenship.* Westport: Praeger.

Koopmans, R. and P. Statham
2000 "Migration and Ethnic Relations as a Field of Political Contention: An Opportunity Structure Approach." In *Challenging Immigration and Ethnic Relations Politics.* Ed. R. Koopmans and P. Statham. Oxford: Oxford University Press. Pp. 13–56.

Kymlicka, W. and W. Norman, eds.
2000 *Citizenship in Diverse Societies.* Oxford: Oxford University Press.

Lahav, G.
1998 "Immigration and the State: The Devolution and Privatisation of Immigration Control in the EU," *Journal of Ethnic and Migration Studies,* 24(4):675–694.

Lanphier, M. and O. Lukomskyj
1994 "Settlement Policy in Australia and Canada." In *Immigration and Refugee Policy: Australia and Canada Compared.* Ed. H. Adelman *et al.* Vol. 2. Toronto: University of Toronto Press. Pp. 337–371.

Lehmbruch, G.
1984 "Concertation and the Structure of Corporatist Networks." In *Order and Conflict in Contemporary Capitalism: Studies in the Political Economy of Western European Nations.* Ed. J. Goldthorpe. Oxford: Clarendon Press.

Lewis, B.
1994 "Legal and Historical Reflections on the Position of Muslim Populations under Non-Muslim Rule." In *Muslims in Europe.* Ed. B. Lewis and D. Schnapper. London: Pinter Publishers. Pp. 1–18.

Lewis, B. and D. Schnapper, eds.
1994 *Muslims in Europe*. London: Pinter Publishers.

MacEwen, M.
1995 *Tackling Racism in Europe: An Examination of Anti-Discrimination Law in Practice*. Oxford: Berg.

Money, J.
2002 "Open or Closed? Citizenship Rules in the Contemporary Era." Paper presented at the 43rd Annual Convention of the International Studies Association, New Orleans. March 24–27.

Nonneman, G. *et al.*
1996 *Muslim Communities in the New Europe*. Reading: Ithaca Press.

Noriel, G.
1996 *The French Melting Pot*. Minneapolis: University of Minnesota Press.

North, D.
1990 *Institutions, Institutional Change and Economic Performance*. Cambridge: Cambridge University Press.

Piore, M. and C. Sabel
1984 *The Second Industrial Divide*. New York: Basic Books.

Plascencia, L. *et al.*
2003 "The Decline of Barriers to Immigrant Economic and Political Rights in the American States: 1977–2001," *International Migration Review*, 37(1):5–23.

Portes, A. and J. Borocz
1989 "Contemporary Immigration: Theoretical Perspectives on Its Determinants and Modes of Incorporation," *International Migration Review*, 23(3):606–630.

Portes, A. and R. Rumbaut
1990 *Immigrant America: A Portrait*. Berkeley: University of California Press.

Rath, J., ed.
2002 *Unraveling the Rag Trade: Immigrant Entrepreneurship in Seven World Cities*. Oxford: Berg.

Reitz, J.
2003 *Host Societies and the Reception of Immigrants*. LaJolla, CA: Center for Comparative Immigration Studies.

––––––––
1998 *Warmth of the Welcome: The Social Causes of Economic Success for Immigrants in Different Nations and Cities*. Boulder, CO: Westview Press.

Rueda, D. and J. Pontusson
2000 "Wage Inequality and Varieties of Capitalism," *World Politics*, 52:350–383.

Rumbaut, R.
1997 "Assimilation and Its Discontents: Between Rhetoric and Reality," *International Migration Review*, 31(4):923–960.

Ryner, M.
2000 "European Welfare State Transformation and Migration." In *Immigration and Welfare: Challenging the Borders of the Welfare State*. Ed. M. Bommes and A. Geddes. Pp. 51–71.

Salins, P.
1997 *Assimilation American Style.* New York: Basic Books.

Schain, M.
1999 "Minorities and Immigrant Incorporation in France." In *Multicultural Questions.* Ed.
       C. Joppke and S. Lukes. Oxford: Oxford University Press. Pp. 199–223.

Schmitter Heisler, B.
2002 "New and Old Immigrant Minorities in Germany: The Challenge of Incorporation."
       In *West European Immigration and Immigrant Policy in the New Century.* Ed. A.
       Messina. Westport, CT: Praeger. Pp. 123–140.

––––––
2000 "The Sociology of Immigration." In *Migration Theory: Talking across Disciplines.* Ed.
       C. Brettel and J. Hollifield. New York: Routledge. Pp. 77–96.

––––––
1992 "The Future of Immigrant Incorporation: Which Models? Which Concepts?" *Inter-
       national Migration Review,* 26(2):623–645.

Shonfield, A.
1965 *Modern Capitalism.* New York: Oxford University Press.

Soysal, Y.
1994 *Limits to Citizenship.* Chicago: University of Chicago Press.

Tichenor, D.
2002 *Dividing Lines: The Politics of Immigration Control in America.* Princeton: Princeton
       University Press.

Whitley, R., ed.
1999 *Divergent Capitalism: The Social Structuring and Change of Business Systems.* Oxford:
       Oxford University Press.

––––––
1992 *European Business Systems: Firms and Markets in Their National Contexts.* London:
       Sage.

Zolberg, A.
1999 "Matters of State: Theorizing Immigration Policy." In *Becoming American, America
       Becoming.* Ed. D. Massey. New York: Russell Sage Foundation.

––––––
1997 "Modes of Incorporation: Towards a Comparative Framework." In *Citizenship and
       Exclusion.* Ed. V. Bader. Aldershot, UK: MacMillan.

Part III

Transnational Communities and Immigrant Enterprise

Chapter 6

MIGRANT TRANSNATIONALISM AND MODES OF TRANSFORMATION[1]

Steven Vertovec

The transnational lens on migrant activities allows social scientists to view the ways some significant things are changing. Notwithstanding certain criticisms of how this research perspective should be fashioned, a look through the lens shows clearly that many migrants today intensively conduct activities and maintain substantial commitments that link them with significant others (such as kin, co-villagers, political comrades, fellow members of religious groups) who dwell in nation-states other than those in which the

[1] I wish to thank the Wissenschaftskolleg zu Berlin/Institute for Advanced Study, Berlin for providing splendid resources and a stimulating intellectual environment where this piece was written. I am also very grateful to the following colleagues who have offered helpful comments on earlier drafts: Ayse Caglar, Josh DeWind, John Eade, Nina Glick Schiller, Felicitas Hillman, Ruud Koopmans, Khalid Koser, Eva Østergaard-Nielsen, Alejandro Portes, Ludger Pries, Alisdair Rogers, Werner Schiffauer, Mario Small, Ninna Nyberg Sørensen and Andreas Wimmer.

migrants themselves reside. Migrants now maintain such connections through uses of technology, travel and financial mechanisms more intensely than ever before possible. What kinds of societal changes are stimulated by these connections? What are their 'knock-on' effects, and in what spheres of life? How deep are the changes and how long-lasting? These are high among the questions begged by transnational takes on migrant dynamics.

In this article, I suggest that current transnational practices among some groups of migrants involve fundamental modes of transformation discernable in at least three basic domains. These include: 1) perceptual transformation affecting what can be described as migrants' orientational 'bifocality' in the sociocultural domain; 2) conceptual transformation of meanings within a notional triad of 'identities-borders-orders' in the political domain; and 3) institutional transformation affecting forms of financial transfer, public-private relationships and local development in the economic domain. Each set of transformations involves multiple causes, linked processes and observable outcomes. It is stressed throughout the article that patterns of migrant transnationalism do not themselves solely cause such modes of transformation, but in each case migrant practices draw upon and contribute significantly to ongoing processes of transformation, largely associated with facets of globalization, already underway.

FROM TRANSNATIONALISM TO TRANSFORMATION

Most studies of migrant transnationalism describe facets of social organization. That is, social scientists in this field of migration studies tend to research the nature and function of border-crossing social networks, families and households, ethnic communities and associations, power relations surrounding gender and status, religious institutions and practices, patterns of economic exchange, and political structures. Social change, in migrant transnationalism studies, tends to be gauged by the ways in which conditions in more than one location impact upon such forms of social organization and the values, activities and relational frameworks that sustain them. In other fields of study concerning global interconnections, though, some theorists attempt to understand broader or deeper shifts in social, political and economic organization. Such shifts are often referred to as forms of deep-seated 'transformation' rather than mere (localized) change.

For instance, in contrast to notions of social change pertaining to specific institutions, Kenneth Wiltshire (2001:8) suggests that 'transformation . . . describes a more radical change, a particularly deep and far-reaching one which within a relatively limited time span modifies the configuration of societies.' Neil Smelser (1998) importantly points to profound social transformations that develop out of both individual and collective short-term actions within immediate environments: these accumulate in often unexpected ways to constitute fundamental changes in societies. Ulf Hannerz (1996) and Stephen Castles (2001) directly link the contemporary study of processes of social transformation to the analysis of emergent transnational connections among a variety of social groups. And in their impressive volume, *Global Transformations,* David Held and his colleagues (1999) advocate the 'transformationalist' thesis or view of the long-term changes wrought by the intensification of interconnections known as globalization.

It is inherent to the theories of Held *et al.* (1999) that large-scale patterns of transformation come about through a constellation of mutually conditioning factors and parallel processes. Such an approach to transnationalism and cumulative societal transformation is exemplified by the work of Manuel Castells (especially 1996, 1997) as he describes the joint impacts of various kinds of enhanced computer-mediated communication on work patterns, collective identities, family life, social movements and states. This is a point to be emphasized in analyzing the impacts of migrant transnationalism: while not bringing about substantial societal transformations by themselves, patterns of cross-border exchange and relationship among migrants may contribute significantly to broadening, deepening or intensifying conjoined processes of transformation that are already ongoing. This is what I argue in each of the three domains discussed below.

What is not transformative in migrant transnationalism? The widening of networks, more activities across distances, and speedier communications reflect important forms of transnationalism in themselves. However, they do not necessarily lead to long-lasting, structural changes in global or local societies. Migrants have historically maintained long-distance social networks, and the fact that messages or visits take shorter time does not always lead to significant alterations in structure, purpose or practice within the network.

But sometimes the matter of degree really counts. The extensiveness, intensity and velocity of networked flows of information and resources may indeed combine to fundamentally alter the way people do things. As Patricia Landolt (2001:220) suggests with regard to migrant transnational activities, there are times when "a quantitative change results in a qualitative difference in the order of things." In this field of study, we can sometimes observe –

following Smelser – how transformation is brought about by numerous individual and collective short-term actions within social environments that span distant locales. As portrayed by Portes (2003:877–878):

> Despite its limited numerical character, the combination of a cadre of regular transnational activists with the occasional activities of other migrants adds up to a social process of significant economic and social impact for communities and even nations. While from an individual perspective, the act of sending a remittance, buying a house in the migrant's hometown, or traveling there on occasion have purely personal consequences, in the aggregate they can modify the fortunes and the culture of these towns and even of the countries of which they are part.

In this cumulative way, migrant transnational practices can modify the value systems and everyday social life of people across entire regions (*see*, for instance, Shain, 1999; Kyle, 2000; Levitt, 2001b).

Processes and practices of migrant transnationalism that can lead to broader transformations take place on different analytical scales in at least three domains of human activity. Of course, as Luis Guarnizo (2003:669) reminds us, "Everyday transnational practices are not neatly compartmentalized, and nor are their consequences." Dividing up the discussion in this way is simply for heuristic purposes. That said, in this article it is suggested that such scales and domains of transformation fostered by migrant transnationalism include basic structures of individual orientation, fundamental political frameworks, and integral processes of economic development.

SOCIOCULTURAL TRANSFORMATION: FASHIONING BIFOCALITY

As mentioned previously, most work on migrant transnationalism has examined social organization or the configuration of social groups as they adapt to cross-border contexts. There has been a considerable amount of research that has detailed "the emergence of transnational social practices and institutions that create a field of sociability and identification among immigrants and people in the country of origin" (Itzigsohn and Saucido, 2002:788). While this approach has certainly been significant and instructive – and there is still much to do – perhaps there has been an overemphasis on the social institutions of transnationalism.

To balance the picture, we also need to observe transnationalism as it occurs within, and has impact upon, the daily lives of individuals (Voigt-Graf, 2002). While actor-centered approaches carry the danger of overlooking larger structural conditions, they have the advantage of emphasizing motivations, meanings and the place of people as their own agents in processes of change. The following subsection suggests just a few ways through which transnationalism has transformed the everyday social worlds of individuals and families in both migrant sending and receiving contexts.

Bifocality

A number of authors have importantly described the ways that transnational practices of exchange, communication and frequent travel impact upon the outlooks and daily experiences of migrants. Such authors do so through invoking a variety of terms and concepts. Robert Smith (2001), for example, describes the practices and relationships linking home and abroad as a 'life world' among immigrants and their descendents. Guarnizo (1997) draws directly upon Bourdieu's ideas of *habitus*. He suggests we might think of a transnational *habitus* as entailing:

> ... a particular set of dualistic dispositions that inclines migrants to act and react to specific situations in a manner that can be, but is not always, calculated, and that is not simply a question of conscious acceptance of specific behavioral or sociocultural rules. . . . The transnational habitus incorporates the social position of the migrant and the context in which transmigration occurs. This accounts for the similarity in the transnational habitus of migrants from the same social grouping (class, gender, generation) and the generation of transnational practices adjusted to specific situations (Guarnizo, 1997:311).

Guarnizo (1997:311) further describes how Dominicans retain 'a dual frame of reference' through which they constantly compare their situation in their 'home' society to their situation in the 'host' society abroad. Roger Rouse (1992), too, has described the 'bifocality' of people's daily rhythms and routines of life joining localities in Michoacán and California. "Their bifocalism," suggests Rouse (1992:46), "stemmed not from transitional adjustments to a new locale, but from a chronic, contradictory transnationalism." Sarah Mahler (1998) takes up Rouse's notion, emphasizing ways in which researchers need to look at the nature of transnational migrants' 'lived reality' to determine whether or how they might be bifocal with regard to their social ties and personal outlooks.

The complex *habitus* of migrant transnationalism has been described in other, related ways. In a transnational community spanning 'OP' – Oaxaca and Poughkeepsie, New York – Alison Mountz and Richard Wright (1996: 404) illustrate how members "act daily in pursuit of shared objectives and with an acute awareness of events occurring in other parts of [OP]." Aspects of life 'here' and life 'there' – whether perceived from the migrant's starting

or destination point – are constantly monitored and perceived as complementary aspects of a single space of experience:

Such a simultaneous and inextricable relationship between here and
there is also conveyed in Katy Gardner's (1993, 1995) accounts of the
interplay between notions of *desh* (home) and *bidesh* (foreign contexts)
among Sylhetis in Britain and Bangladesh. In everyday discourse among
Sylhetis, *desh* is associated with the locus of personal and social identity and
religiosity, while *bidesh* conveys material bounty and economic opportunity.
Gardner (1993:1–2) describes a kind of cognitive tension that arises from
Sylheti bifocality that likely characterizes the predicament of a great many
migrants around the world:

> The economic dominance of families with migrant members has meant that *bidesh*
> is associated with success and power, which *desh* is unable to provide. Statements
> concerning *bidesh* are therefore part of a discourse about the insecurity of life in
> Bangladesh and the continual economic struggle which villagers face. . . . Indi-
> vidual opportunism and enterprise are therefore channeled towards attempting to
> go abroad, leading to dependency on something which for many is no more than
> a fantasy, a dream-land, which few villagers will ever see.
>
> Co-existing, sometimes uneasily, with this set of images and ideals is the centrality
> of *desh* to group identity, and the spiritual powers with which it is linked. There
> is therefore a constant balancing of the two views, between the economic and
> political power of *bidesh,* and the fertility and spirituality of *desh.* This continual
> ambivalence, and negotiation of what might appear to be oppositional presenta-
> tions of the world, is an integral part of migration and the contradictions which it
> involves.

The effects of transnationalism for changing meanings, attitudes and experiences both 'here' and 'there' are relevant to recent studies concerning
migrants and transformations of the meaning of 'home' (Rapport and Dawson, 1998; Al-Ali and Koser, 2002). An illustration of this is provided by
Ruba Salih (2003), who details how Moroccan women in Italy engage in
material practices representing the two countries. Whether in Italy or Mo-
rocco, the women buy, consume, display and exchange commodities from
their 'other home' in order to symbolize their ongoing sense of double
belonging.

Once such a dual orientation is constructed and reproduced by migrants, it might have further impacts. For one, it is hard to dismantle. David
Kyle (2000:2) discusses at least one informant who foresees "no clear exit
strategy from the binational life he had built over eleven years of shuttling
back and forth" between New York City and his village in Ecuador. Another
consequence concerns the transformation of outlook and practice among

those closely associated with the transnational migrant. Here, through the experiences of his informants, Kyle came to think of the links between these distinct places "as more of an emergent transnational social reality, involving migrants and nonmigrants alike, than simply an international movement of labor" (2000:9). The point about nonmigrants is significant: such a transnational social reality incorporates and infuses what we can call the bifocality of many people 'left behind' but whose lives are still transformed by the transnational activities and ideologies among those who actually move.

Relatedly, Rebecca Golbert (2001) documents the case of young Ukrainian Jews who have developed 'transnational orientations from home' towards the Ukraine, Israel and other Jewish communities in the United States, Germany and elsewhere. She describes how young Ukrainian Jews undertake the evaluation of everyday experiences, the past, and the future with 'a double consciousness' garnered from transnational links and a transnational conception of self. "Their daily reality," Golbert (2001:725) observes, "is embedded in a transnational frontier of intersecting ideas, relationships, histories and identities; at the same time, transnational practices are localized through intimate and shared experiences." Recounting narratives and the sharing of experiences – particularly regarding Israel – Golbert shows how returnees have had a powerful impact even on the transnational orientations of those who have never left the Ukraine. They, too, have a life world oriented to, or grounded in, more than one locality.

The transformation of everyday orientations concurrently toward both here and there is a mode of change that accompanies the transnationalization of distinct social practices and institutions among migrants. These significantly include the activities of transnational families and long-distance parenthood (*see,* for instance, Hondagneu-Sotelo and Avila, 1997; Fouron and Glick Schiller, 2001; Herrera 2001; Bryceson and Vuorela, 2002; Gardner and Grillo, 2002), experiences of transnational childhood (Zhou, 1997; Orellana *et al.*, 2001; Menjivar, 2002), the maintenance of moral economies of reciprocity and obligation among extended kin networks (Landolt, 2001; Voigt-Graf, 2002; Ballard, 2003), and the social fields within which members of the so-called second generation grow up (Levitt and Waters, 2002; Smith, 2002; Maira, 2002; *see also* Levitt and Glick Schiller, 2004.

Summary

Stephen Castles (2002:1158) suggests, "It is possible that transnational affiliations and consciousness will become the predominant form of migrant belonging in the future. This would have far-reaching consequences." If this is true, such developments underline the importance of understanding processes of perceptual transformation. Among individual migrants living transnational lives, this entails the emergence of a dual orientation or 'bifocality' in everyday life.

How such bifocality is structured and how it functions depends on a number of variables and contextual conditions. Bifocality is certainly hard to 'measure,' but its workings are clearly discernable in social practices and conveyed in individual narratives. The dispositions and practices generated by a transnational orientation are not, moreover, evenly spread within a group or family. Yet these are not to be underestimated because such dispositions and practices have substantial impact on individual and family life course and strategies, individuals' sense of self and collective belonging, the ordering of personal and group memories, patterns of consumption, collective sociocultural practices, approaches to child-rearing, and other modes of cultural reproduction. These latter functions particularly concern ways in which the re-orienting of first generation perceptions and points of reference condition or influence that of second and subsequent generations.

The emergence of a kind of dual orientation to here and there can be said to occur in the course of any person's relocation. Migrants adapt themselves while maintaining strong ties of sentiment, if not material exchange, with their places of origin. Sustained real time and intensive practices of transnational communication, affiliation and exchange, however, can profoundly affect manners of migrant adaptation. Now as never before, migrants can maintain and act upon particularly strong senses of connection to people, places and senses of belonging associated with their places of origin. Although outside the scope of this article, such change should be seen as both part of and contributing to wider, convergent modes of social and cultural transformation associated with the globalizing of cultural forms, the pluralizing of the public sphere, the multiplying of identities, and the cosmopolitanizing of attitudes (*see, e.g.,* Held *et al.,* 1999; Tomlinson, 1999; Vertovec and Cohen, 2002; Beck *et al.,* 2003). Such large-scale processes are not surprisingly having considerable impacts in the political domain as well.

POLITICAL TRANSFORMATION: RECONFIGURING 'IDENTITIES-BORDERS-ORDERS'

A conventional model of the nation-state puts forward a notion of borders that are presumed to 'contain' a people (usually characterized by some constructed idea of common linguistic, social, and presumed cultural/ethnic identity); in turn, within the 'container' people are organized by an ideology represented in a constitution and a state comprised of legal institutions. There is now a very large body of literature in which scholars debate whether, or how, processes of globalization have affected the conventional nation-state model (*see, inter alia,* Strange, 1996; Sassen, 1996; Albrow, 1997; Guillén, 2001; Carnoy and Castells, 2001; Vertovec and Cohen, 2002). Whether they are skeptics, hyper-globalists or transformationalists (Held *et al.*, 1999), most observers agree that nation-states have been radically challenged, if not changed, by processes and phenomena surrounding the emergence of complex new global economic patterns, regional pacts, multilateral agreements, and coalition military interventions.

Similarly, there has been considerable discussion regarding the challenges to the conventional nation-state specifically posed by immigration (including Soysal, 1994; Bauböck, 1994; Joppke, 1998, 1999). Given that there are preexisting and continuing debates over globalization, immigration and the nation-state, we can see that migrant transnationalism itself does not bring about transformations of the nation-state. Such transformations are happening anyway due to a variety of concomitant processes within the global political economy. But forms of migrant transnationalism do importantly contribute to significant shifts affecting the nation-state model. In what ways is this happening? Some answers become clearer through adopting a particular formulation of concepts surrounding the nation-state model.

Identities – Borders – Orders

Currently within the field of international relations, one attempt to comprehend broad contemporary political challenges is through the 'analytical triad' or 'dynamic nexus' between the three concepts of 'identities-borders-orders' (Albert *et al.*, 2001). The idea here is that developments in each of the three conceptual domains must be assessed in light of the others. Yosef Lapid (2001:7) explains:

> Processes of collective identity formation invariably involve complex bordering issues. Likewise, acts of bordering (*i.e.*, the inscription, crossing, removal, transformation, multiplication and/or diversification of borders) invariably carry momentous ramifications for political ordering at all levels of analysis. Processes of identity, border and order construction are therefore mutually self-constituting. Borders, for instance, are in many ways inseparable from the identities they help demarcate or individuate. Likewise, they are also inseparable from orders constituted to a large extent via such acts of individuation and segmentation. Thus, in

any specific case, if we want to study problems associated with any one of our three concepts, we can richly benefit from also considering the other two.

In other words, as with the conventional model of the nation-state, some sense of identity is presumed to characterize a people; this identity/people is believed to be contiguous with a territory, demarcated by a border; within the border, laws underpin a specific social and political order or system; this social order – which is conceived to be different from orders outside the border – both draws upon and reinforces the sense of collective identity. Identities-borders-orders are legitimated and reproduced through a system of narratives, public rituals and institutions, educational materials, formal state bureaucracies and informal social relationships, written and unwritten regulations, sets of assumptions, and expectations of civility and public behavior (Schiffauer *et al.*, 2003).

Various processes of globalization and the rise of regional, global or 'cosmopolitan' structures of governance assail essential components of national identities-borders-orders by compounding identities, ignoring borders and overruling orders. Migration itself confronts identities-borders-orders. "One reason migration enters political agendas with greater frequency and salience now," suggests Martin Heisler (2001:229), "is that, at least in some host societies, it *disturbs the sense of boundedness*" (emphasis in original).

> The ability to change countries of residence with relative ease and the possibility of reversing the move can vitiate the need to make lasting identitive commitments. Identities can thus be partial, intermittent, and reversible in the modern Western democratic state. Order no longer depends on unalloyed loyalty stemming from immutable national identity – identity for which there is no plausible or legitimate alternative. Countries' borders are not seen as coextensive with a comprehensive political community (Heisler, 2001:236).

Nowadays, Heisler (2001:237) concludes, "migration tends to attenuate territorial sovereignty, monolithic order, and identitive solidarity." In various ways, some of which are described below, the political dimensions of migrant transnationalism inherently involve questions of identity (Vertovec, 2001) and often raise contentious issues concerning civic order and the cohesiveness of 'host' societies (Vertovec, 1999).

With regard specifically to migrant transnational practices, David Fitzgerald (2000:10) observes that transnational migrants challenge nation-state ideals of identities, borders and orders in both sending and receiving countries. They do this not least by moving back and forth between states, sometimes circumventing state controls over borders and taxes. "Transnational migrants often live in a country in which they do not claim citizenship and claim citizenship in a country in which they do not live," he points out; "Alternatively, they may claim membership in multiple polities in which they may be residents, part-time residents, or absentees" (2000:10). This phenomenon is witnessed in examples of immigrants – even naturalized ones – going 'home' from Germany or the United States to vote in Turkey or the Dominican Republic.

Such trends run counter to orthodox assimilation theories that assumed immigrants would be less likely to continue involving themselves in the political concerns of their nation-state of origin. Instead, for many migrants with transnational networks and lifestyles, "the country of origin becomes a source of identity and the country of residence a source of right. . . . The result is a confusion between rights and identity, culture and politics, states and nations" (Kastoryano, 2002:160). Here the question of durability enters: are such border-crossing political identities merely an issue for first-generation migrants? Rainer Bauböck (2003:706) answers this by suggesting that "even if transnationalism remains a *transient* phenomenon for each migration cohort, the emergence of new legal and political conceptions of membership signifies an important *structural* change for the polities involved" (emphasis added).

Political dimensions of migrant transnationalism are deeply embedded in particular kinds of structural change currently underway and which can be seen particularly to put to the test longstanding ideals of identities-borders-orders. These especially involve migrants' practices around dual citizenship/nationality and homeland political affiliation.

Dual Citizenship/Nationality and 'Homeland' Politics

In much literature nationality and citizenship are treated as co-equivalent (although some scholars like Michael Jones-Correa [2001] argue that we should differentiate nationality as formal status of state membership and citizenship as rights and duties within the nation-state). In any case, it has been suggested that dual citizenship/nationality represents one of "the most fundamental questions about the relation between immigration and citizenship in the next century" (Pickus, 1998:xxvii).

Dual citizenship/nationality has a long history that is not always tied to the subject of immigration (*see* Koslowski, 2001). Dual citizenship or dual nationality can be claimed through birth, marriage, claiming ancestral lineage or through naturalization. Until recently there was a 'prevalent distaste' for dual nationality in states around the world; now, particularly post-Cold War, that distaste is dissipating, and we may be witnessing a long-term shift toward a more universal acceptance of dual nationality (Spiro, 2002:19–20). There is now an upward trend in claims for dual citizenship/nationality, produced especially through migration. The loosening of rules concerning dual citizenship represents a global trend, particularly among migrant sending countries (Hansen and Weil, 2002). "International and regional instruments," according to a United Nations report (UNPD, 1998), "also seem to be reconciling principles of nationality with the trends towards multiple identities. This is evident by the reorientation of instruments regarding dual or multiple nationality."

From an American perspective, Peter Schuck (1998:153) writes that "[w]ith current legal and illegal immigration approaching record levels, naturalization petitions quintupling in the last five years to almost two million annually, and legal changes in some of our largest source countries that encourage (and are often designed to encourage) naturalization in the United States, dual citizenship is bound to proliferate." It is estimated that more than a half million children born in the United States each year have at least one additional nationality (Aleinikoff and Klusmeyer, 2001). Among the one million people that naturalized in the United States in 1996, nine out of ten main countries of origin allow some form of dual nationality or citizenship (Fritz, 1998). Similarly, in 1996 seven of the ten largest immigrant groups in New York City had the right to be dual nationals (Foner, 2000).

In other Western states, official attitudes on dual citizenship or dual nationality vary considerably. The United Kingdom "is perfectly indifferent" while France is tolerant and increasingly liberalizing (Hansen and Weil, 2002:6–7). Even in countries like Germany that traditionally do not tolerate dual citizenship, Thomas Faist (2001) points out about one fourth to one third of all naturalizations from the 1970s to the 1990s resulted in multiple citizenship. Additionally, every seventh German marriage is with a foreigner, leading to two nationalities of the offspring under German law, and the millions of *Aussiedler* (ethnic German 'repatriates') who arrived since 1989 were not obliged to give up their Russian or Kazakh citizenship (Thränhardt, 2002).

On the migrant-sending-country side, dual citizenship has been difficult to push through many parliaments since domestic politicians see more disadvantage than advantage in allowing this (Østergaard-Nielsen, 2003b). They often feel that emigrant or diaspora participation in domestic politics is distinctly not welcome – particularly absentee voting which might give too much domestic oppositional influence to people actually living outside the country.

Notwithstanding political reluctance or outright resistance in many quarters, the incidence and impacts of dual citizenship/nationality are on the rise around the world. Migrant transnationalism plays a significant role in this growth. In addition to shaping actual practices of migrants, such a trend is having important outcomes in government policy. As T. Alexander Aleinikoff and Douglas Klusmeyer (2001:87) understand it, there is "an emerging international consensus that the goal [of state policies] is no longer to reduce plural nationality as an end in itself, but to manage it as an inevitable feature of an increasingly interconnected and mobile world."

Another aspect of political interconnection or overlap across borders is represented by the proliferation of 'homeland' political activity among today's migrants – sometimes, but not exclusively, conducted among dual nationals. It is well documented that over one hundred years ago many migrants maintained acute interest in the political plight of their place of origin (*e.g.*, Foner, 2000). Now such interests – and particularly the ability to act upon them – have been heightened due to advances in communication, cheapness of transport, and policy shifts such as the extension of dual citizenship/nationality.

Within and around transnational migrant communities, the politics of homeland can take a variety of forms (*see* Koopmans and Statham, 2001; Guarnizo *et al.*, 2003; Østergaard-Nielsen, 2003a). Such forms include: exile groups organizing themselves for return, groups lobbying on behalf of a homeland, external offices of political parties, migrant hometown associations, and opposition groups campaigning or planning actions to effect political change in the homeland. Some migrant organizations also manage to carry out dual programs of action aimed at both sending and receiving countries (Østergaard-Nielsen, 2001).

The kind and degree of participation in homeland politics differs with reference to a series of contextual factors, including the history of specific migration and settlement processes and political conditions in the country of residence. Overall, however, homeland political allegiance and engagement rests on the reconfiguration of identities-borders-orders, such that increasingly people from one or another particular place regard themselves as legitimate members of the collective identity and social order of that place even though they dwell outside its borders.

According to Fitzgerald (2000:106), such a reconfiguration posits "a model of citizenship that emphasizes rights over obligations, passive entitlements, and the assertion of an interest in the public space without a daily presence." There is a tension, he goes on to say, between "a reconceptualization of the polis as the transnational public space of the imagined community and the assertion that the polis should still be defined as a geographic space where citizens live together" (2000:106). Hence, we see governments of countries of emigration increasingly invoking national solidarity across state borders. This was exemplified by Vicente Fox's campaigning among Mexicans in California during 2000, in which he played upon the broader boundaries of an imagined nation and declared he would be the first president "to govern for 118 million Mexicans," including 100 million in Mexico and 18 million living outside the country (Rogers, 2000). Similarly, following the Los Angeles riots of 1992, South Korean politicians evoked images of Korean Americans as a 'colony' of the homeland (Shain, 1999:5), while in her 1990 inaugural address as Ireland's president, Mary Robinson proclaimed herself leader of the extended Irish family abroad. In addition to stimulating political interest, such rhetoric draws upon and reinforces migrants' sense of bifocality.

Pervasive rhetoric about extended nations abroad helps explain the fact that overseas communities are increasingly engaging themselves in the economic, social and political lives of their country of origin. Meanwhile, sending states are trying to channel this engagement to their own advantage (Østergaard-Nielsen, 2003b). There are a variety of reasons why specific countries develop certain policies toward expatriates (Levitt, 2003). Policies regarding overseas nationals are usually to encourage a sense of membership (but not return) among sending states toward their perceived national communities abroad. These include special ministries or government offices devoted to overseas nationals, special investment opportunities, special voting rights and, as we have seen, dual nationality/citizenship. Their effects, however, are broadly similar: "Such policies," Levitt (2003) believes, "are reinventing the role of states outside of territorial boundaries and in this way reconfiguring traditional understandings of sovereignty, nation, and citizenship."

Summary

The discussion in this section has endorsed the view, expressed by Held *et al.* (1999:9), that "the power of national governments is not necessarily diminished by globalization but on the contrary is being reconstituted and restructured in response to the growing complexity of processes of governance in a more interconnected world." Political features of migrant transnationalism – particularly surrounding dual citizenship/nationality and homeland allegiances – are contributing to a fundamental reconfiguration of the conceptual nexus identities-borders-orders.

Though conceptual, such reconfiguration has real impacts in policies, legal structures and national imaginations. This is apparent when we recall what each part of the analytical triad entails. Here, among other things, identities concern matters of membership, belonging, loyalty, and moral and political values; borders involve territoriality, admission, legal status and deportation; orders relate to sovereignty, implications of legal status, civil, social and political rights, obligations, and access to public resources. Migrants' transnational practices have direct implications for each of these areas of state interest.

ECONOMIC TRANSFORMATION: RE-INSTITUTIONALIZING DEVELOPMENT

Economic aspects of migrant transnationalism include numerous activities and diverse impacts. Some economic activities directly occupy migrants, such as transnational ethnic entrepreneurship (Portes *et al.*, 2002) or the facilitation of international trade (Light *et al.*, 2002). Others only indirectly engage migrants, especially spin-off industries catering to migrant transnational practices. There are industries or enterprises (such as supermarkets or breweries) that are based in migrant sending countries but reach out to customers in diaspora. In Ecuador, for instance, hundreds of new business services have been established catering to emigrants, including travel agencies, cyber cafes, and companies specializing in shipping abroad traditional Ecuadorian foods and medicinal herbs (Rogers, 2001c). Still other economic facets of migrant transnationalism involve government schemes to attract migrant's foreign currency, such as expatriate bonds, high interest foreign currency accounts, and tax exemptions for saving and investment.

Economically, however, by far the most transformative processes and phenomena of migrant transnationalism have concerned remittances, the money migrants send to their families and communities of origin. The following sections consider several aspects of remittances and their transformative effects and potentials, particularly for homeland development.

Remittances

"The most often-cited, tangible evidence and measuring stick for remittances have become the ties connecting migrants with their societies of origin," writes Guarnizo (2003:666). There are many studies probing the volume of remittances, their determinants and impacts in migrant sending contexts, and their channels of transference. Remittances are sent by all types of migrant workers: male and female, legal and undocumented, long term and temporary, manual and highly skilled. Money is transferred through banks, agencies of various kinds, directly on-line, through professional couriers or through social networks. Remittances have broad effects, including the stimulation of change within a variety of sociocultural institutions (such as local status hierarchies, gender relations, marriage patterns, and consumer habits; Vertovec, 2000). However, it is the economic impacts of remittances that receive most attention.

In numerous settings around the world, remittances are directly invested in small businesses such as manufacturing and crafts companies, market halls, bakeries, and transport agencies (Taylor, 1999; van Doorn, 2001). Among the reported negative impacts, migrant remittances are said to: displace local jobs and incomes; induce consumption spending (often on foreign imports); inflate local prices of land, housing, and food; create disparity and envy between recipients and nonrecipients; and create a culture of economic dependency.

It must be stressed that a large proportion of migrants send money to families for basic subsistence (Suro *et al.*, 2002). Also, schooling and other costs of education are often not factored into studies on the 'productive' use of remittances. "In any case," argues Peter Stalker (2000:81), "it can be argued that many forms of consumption, particularly on housing, better food, education, and health care, are a good form of investment that will lead to higher productivity." That itself could be called a significant kind of social, if not economic, transformation.

On the broadest scale, the recent increase in sheer volume of contemporary global remittances represents a highly significant type of economic transformation. Figures from the International Monetary Fund (IMF) show a massive increase in the amount of formal remittances worldwide, from less that $2 billion in 1970 to $54 billion in 1995 to over $105 billion in 1999 (*see* annual Balance of Payment Statistics). Over 60 percent of this amount goes to developing countries, and over the last decade total remittances have become a much larger source of income for developing countries than official development assistance (Gammeltoft, 2002). Such figures, however, must be taken as merely suggestive since the categories used to estimate them are contestable. Moreover, these figures are based on official transfers reported by central banks of receiving countries, who in turn rely on reports filed by remittance intermediaries. Therefore, the IMF estimates are likely to be considerably short of real remittance values – indeed, it has been suggested that officially recorded remittances represent "only the tip of the iceberg" (Puri and Ritzema, 1999:3). Beyond official figures, unofficial remittance transfers – by hand, informal couriers, *hawala* systems and other means – may amount to at least another $15 billion (*The Economist*, 2003a).

Whether through official or unofficial means, remittances mean a lot to the countries – to say nothing of the families and communities – that receive them. In 2000, remittances from abroad comprised more than 10 percent of the gross domestic product (GDP) of countries as diverse as Jamaica, Haiti, Ecuador, Eritrea, Jordan, and Yemen (UNPD, 2002). Remittances have exceeded the total value of exports in El Salvador and constitute more than half the value of exports in the Dominican Republic and Nicaragua (Orozco, 2001). Remittances are so important to the current and future economy of many nations, they are now used as a valuation instrument to upgrade the credit-worthiness of impoverished countries to secure large-scale international loans (Guarnizo, 2003).

However, experts agree that remittances by themselves are not a panacea for impoverishment. Indeed:

> remittances flowing to emigration areas often wind up producing what John Kenneth Galbraith called 'private affluence and public squalor,' or new homes reachable only over dirt roads. What is clearly needed is some way of harnessing some fraction of the remittances in order to develop the infrastructure that can help a region develop economically (Widgren and Martin, 2002:223).

Some economic advisers have suggested that migrant-sending countries could earmark, perhaps through an import tariff, a portion of remittances for a specific development fund. There have been failed attempts to create such funds in the Philippines, Pakistan, Thailand and Bangladesh (Puri and Ritzema, 1999). It is likely most migrants themselves are, or would be, skeptical of such schemes: this is due not only to anxieties over possible corruption, but also to past experiences and frustrations with the ineffective, preferential or nonexistent development programs of national governments and international agencies. Perhaps a more *laissez-faire* policy climate will suffice, others say, so that migrants and their families can find themselves the right ways to develop their communities and generate multiplier effects. This could be achieved perhaps with NGO advice, appropriate banking schemes, and government support (but not control). Another way of harnessing migrant remittances for broader economic development is collectively, through migrant organizations.

HTAs and MFIs

There is a long history of migrant associations sending money for collective benefit in the home town or village. Nancy Foner (2000:171–172) illustrates this by pointing to how, between 1914–1924, New York's Jewish *landsmanshaftn* or hometown associations sent millions of dollars to their war-ravaged communities of origin in Europe. Yet now "we are seeing a very specific type of home-town association, one directly concerned with socio-economic development in its communities of origin and increasingly engaging both governmental and civic entities in sending and receiving countries in these projects" (Sassen, 2002:226).

There has been a marked growth in the number and function of migrant hometown associations (HTAs) throughout the 1990s (*see, e.g.,* Orozco, 2000a, 2001; Lowell and de la Garza, 2000; Alarcón, 2001). For instance, in Chicago alone, the number of 'Mexican clubs' funneling money to specific localities in Mexico to build schools, roads and churches jumped from 35 in 1995 to 181 in 2002 (*The Economist,* 2003b). Perhaps this is a manifestation of both the transnational bifocality and political engagement emergent among migrants and described in earlier sections of this article. HTAs are said to represent the clearest evidence of recent processes surrounding the extensive institutionalization of transnational ties (Orozco, 2001).

HTA activities embrace charitable work such as donating clothes, goods for religious festivals, and construction materials for repairing the town church. They raise money for improving infrastructure such as sewage treatment plants and health care facilities. They support educational institutions, such as providing scholarships and library books. Yet another kind of HTA activity involves managing collective capital investment for income-generating projects in sending contexts that are often co-managed by locals and migrants (Orozco, 2000b; World Bank, 2001). HTAs also play a significant role in organizing disaster relief following catastrophes such as Hurricane Mitch in Central America in 1998 and the earthquakes in Turkey in 1999 and in Gujarat in 2001 (Rogers, 2001b).

HTAs are not of a single kind, nor are they the only mode of migrant transnationalism involved in collective remittance sending (*cf.* Mohan and Zack-Williams, 2002). Whatever the form of collective remitting, Alejandro Portes and Patricia Landolt (2000:543) observe, "Life conditions in munici-palities that receive 'grassroots transnational aid' confirm the economic relevance of this collective remittance strategy. Towns with a hometown association have paved roads, electricity, and freshly painted public buildings. . . . [T]he quality of life in transnational towns is quite simply better."

Such forms of migrant transnational organization and finance are so importantly engaged in local development that Smith (1998:227–228) believes they are generating "parallel power structures" that are "forcing the state to engage them in new ways, either in kind or degree, but engage the state they must." Some state and local governments work closely with, and match the funds raised by, HTAs in order to magnify their impact. Since 1993, one of the most noted programs of this type has been the 'two for one' initiative of the *Programa para las Comunidades Mexicanas en el Extranjero* (PCME, Program for Mexican Communities Abroad; *see* Smith, 1998; Goldring, 1998, 2001; Mahler, 2000). The program operates through a network of consulates and Mexican cultural centers in the United States. The idea of 'two for one' is that for every dollar raised by a hometown association abroad, the state (*e.g.*, of Zacatecas) and the federal government each put in a dollar for a community project. In 1995 in Zacatecas alone, the 'two for one' program added to the HTAs' $600,000 to provide $1.8 million towards 56 projects in 34 Mexican towns (Mahler, 1998).

'Two for one' was subsequently extended to a 'three for one' program, in which each migradollar is matched with one dollar from the federal government, one from the state government, and one from the municipal government. Between 1999–2001, migrants invested $2.7 million into such programs (World Bank, 2001). Despite some limitations, these initiatives in Mexico "have produced a deep impact in the local communities and have been recognized as new and effective forms of public-private collaboration" (World Bank, 2001:6). The ultimate objective, according to World Bank analysts, would be "to develop a self-sustainable private system for the development of projects and local programs financed totally or partially with remittances and savings from the Mexican community abroad. Available funds of international cooperation could be used for supporting some of the initiatives" (World Bank, 2001:7).

The collective remittance work of HTAs for development is not entirely rosy, however. Disagreements on how to use the funds raised by HTAs are endemic. For example, one HTA raised $2 million for Jalpa, a town of 13,500 in the state of Zacatecas, but got into a dispute over how to spend the money (*Migration News,* December 2002). Sarah Mahler (1998) and Luin Goldring (2001) both emphasize that while HTAs enjoy a veneer of altruism and democratic structure, they often significantly exclude women, reinforce existing power relations within a community, sometimes promote projects that are not the most needed but which generate the most symbolic power, and may be open to cooptation and exploitation by government. Further, Portes and Landolt (2000) point out problems of generating trust within HTAs due to suspicions of corruption, abuse of leaders' offices, and lack of democratic representation.

Relationships between HTAs and states of origin are not unproblematic, either. HTAs might be "left doing the lion's share of the government's work" in development while the government itself steps back from this responsibility (Levitt, 2001a:209). Sarah Mahler (2000) predicts that in Central America the region will see an ever-increasing amount of government activity concerning emigrants abroad, particularly regarding their remittances. "While such efforts are comprehensible,' she says, "they are drawing increasing criticism because they place responsibility for Central America's economic stability disproportionately on the shoulders of migrants" (2000:32). Additionally, the more governments attempt to control and channel remittances, the more migrants are pushed toward remitting via unofficial means (Meyers, 1998).

Relative to the amount of remittances sent through families, collective remittances channeled through HTAs and other migrant transnational frameworks are small. Despite this fact, and that of the sometimes problematic nature of such organizations and their relationship to the state, the forms of institutionalization they represent have much valuable potential for effectively directing remittances to highly needed and effective forms of local development. Other, newer forms of institutionalization in the shape of microfinance present important possibilities as well.

J. Edward Taylor (1999:74) proposes that "Migration is likely to have a larger effect on development where local institutions exist to gather savings by migrant households and make them available to local producers – that is, where migrants do not have to play the simultaneous roles of workers, savers, investors, and producers." National governments have sought to establish economic schemes, such as special investment funds or savings accounts, to channel remittances and encourage business development. These have met with very mixed results (Puri and Ritzema, 1999). Meanwhile, microfinance institutions (MFIs) may offer prospects for channeling migrant remittances in ways similar to those suggested by Taylor.

The idea of MFIs began in the 1970s but took off among development agencies and researchers during the 1990s. A core function of MFIs is to provide small, low-interest loans (microcredit, *e.g.*, from $10 to $3,000) and savings services to poor families – and often specifically to women – who ordinarily do not have access to formal financial institutions. Such loans are to help people engage in productive activities (involving, for instance, small farms, petty trading, craft enterprises or local business). MFIs offer credit, savings and insurance in often remote rural areas. They also may give financial and business advice and training. Many MFIs are nonprofit NGOs, credit unions or cooperatives, while there are also new commercial MFIs. Currently augmented by new information technologies, MFIs are growing in number, extent and function throughout the developing world.

One critical problem facing 'the microfinance revolution' is scarcity of capital (Robinson, 2001). Channeled remittances – especially pooled funds represented by HTAs – can go a long way toward supporting the establishment and work of MFIs. In contrast to rural credit programs which earlier absorbed large sums of money over several decades, many relevant agencies – such as the International Labor Organization, the World Bank and the Inter-American Development Bank – are increasingly interested in the potential interface between remittances and MFIs.

At one workshop on these issues convened by the International Labor Organization, it was agreed that microfinance institutions "appear particularly well suited to capture and transform remittances for several reasons: 1) they deal with small-scale transactions where personal relations were important, 2) they extensively involve groups and associations of intermediaries and 3) they integrate the formal and the informal sector practices" (ILO, 2000:15). The ILO workshop group also advocated a number of additional factors that should contribute to the successful linkage of MFIs and remittances, including the provision of a large number of local contact points, a wide range of financial services products at the local level, and the widening of partnerships between microfinance institutions and other organizations. The ILO group also believed that governments should at best mainly observe, but also act to create a positive regulatory framework and ideally provide matching funds to stimulate the use of MFIs for routing remittances for local community development.

One of the best ways to achieve remittance-MFI benefits may be through credit unions, which would use any transfer fees to reinvest in community development (Martin, 2001). Especially in comparison to banks and financial transfer agencies, credit unions are shown to offer some of the best practices in remitting opportunities to migrants (Rogers, 2001a; Grace, 2001; Orozco, 2002). MFIs are certainly not a solution to all economic problems in developing countries, and they are not without their own problems and failures (Jain and Moore, 2003). Nevertheless MFIs and the innovations in technology surrounding them have much potential for steering remittances – perhaps particularly collective ones – toward noteworthy forms of economic transformation in migrant sending contexts.

Summary

Drawing on a variety of studies for the Inter-American Development Bank, Manuel Orozco (2001:36) observes, "The links established through remittances suggest radical changes are remaking the look of countries' economies." Migrant sending countries themselves certainly recognize this. Consequently many have introduced policies to maximize their benefits; in this way, "[c]ooperation to increase remittances, reduce the cost of transferring money, and matching that share of remittances that are invested could open a new era in cooperative economic development" (Widgren and Martin, 2002:223).

The local and national economies of developing countries are changing for a variety of concurrent reasons, from the growing power of multilateral economic regimes and shifting international aid policies, through changing commodity markets and emerging patterns of global tourism, to expanding sources and impacts of foreign direct investment. This section has focused on ways in which patterns of migrant transnationalism – particularly surrounding remittances – are contributing to the reinstitutionalizing of local and national structures of development. Throughout many periods of migration, hometown associations have sent money back to villages for the repair of schools and churches. Now the sheer scale, kind and degree of institutionalization (increasingly involving HTAs and the sending state), along with the use of advanced telecommunications and new methods of financial transfer, have meant that remittances can transform the nature and pace of local development in migrant sending areas by, among other things, constructing infrastructures, providing equipment, and offering finance for enterprise.

Several significant questions continue to concern the place of remittances in national development, including how long remittances will continue to flow and whether high levels of international migration are needed to sustain remittance levels. Most remittances worldwide continue to be sent by individuals, and these may indeed decrease over time. Although this source of remittances will diminish, HTA or other forms of institutionalized collective remittance sending – perhaps increasingly utilizing microfinance institutions – may be better poised to persist and provide the broadest benefits directly to migrant sending communities.

CONCLUSION

The connection between migrant transnational practices and modes of transformation suggested in this article reflect the progression of changes considered by Portes (2001:191):

> Once migrant colonies become well established abroad, a flow of *transnational* economic and informational resources starts, ranging from occasional remittances to the emergence of a class of full-time transnational entrepreneurs. The cumulative effects of these dynamics come to the attention of national governments who reorient their *international* activities through embassies, consulates, and missions to recapture the loyalty of their expatriates and guide their investments and political mobilizations. The increased volume of demand created by migrant remittances and investments in their home countries support, in turn, the further expansion of the market for *multinationals* and encourage local firms to go abroad themselves, establishing branches in areas of immigrant concentration (emphasis in original).

Each set of changes entails small-scale and everyday practices of individuals and groups. Incrementally and cumulatively, these practices may generate far-reaching modes of transformation affecting migrants, their families and communities in places of origin, wider populations surrounding transnational networks, and entire societies permeated by migrant transnationalism.

Many forms of migrant transnationalism and their related modes of transformation are likely to widen, intensify and accelerate. The governments of migrant sending and receiving states will address a range of migrant transnational practices with greater attention and policy intervention. The rise in dual and multiple citizenships will continue to test the nature and reach of nation-states. Technological changes (especially the building and extension of infrastructures in developing countries) will make it ever easier and cheaper to communicate and exchange resources, including remittances, across borders and at long-distance. Hometown associations and other such diasporic organizations have become institutionalized to a degree that they will likely be sustained, and probably enhanced, at least over the next several years. Individuals within post-migration second and subsequent generations will probably not maintain the everyday bifocality and practices of their migrant forebears, but such parental orientations and practices are apt to have an enduring impression on their children's identities, interests and sociocultural activities.

As evident in the massive literature on globalization, an array of worldwide transformations are currently underway due to a convergence of contemporary social, political, economic and technological processes. Migrant transnational practices are stimulated and fostered by many of these globalization processes. In turn, transnational migrant practices themselves accumulate to augment and perhaps even amplify transformative global processes.

REFERENCES

Al-Ali, N. and K. Koser, eds.
2002 *New Approaches to Migration? Transnational Communities and the Transformation of Home.* London: Routledge.

Alarcón, R.
2001 "The Development of Home Town Associations in the United States and the Use of Social Remittances in Mexico." Washington, DC: Inter-American Dialogue, Final Report.

Albert, M., D. Jacobson and Y. Lapid, eds.
2001 *Identities, Borders, Orders: Rethinking International Relations Theory.* Minneapolis: University of Minnesota Press.

Albrow, M.
1997 *The Global Age: State and Science beyond Modernity.* Cambridge: Polity.

Aleinikoff, T. A. and D. Klusmeyer
2001 "Plural Nationality: Facing the Future in a Migratory World." In *Citizenship Today.* Ed. T. A. Aleinikoff and D. Klusmeyer. Washington, DC: Carnegie Endowment for International Peace. Pp. 63–88.

Ballard, R.
2003 "The South Asian Presence in Britain and Its Transnational Connections." In *Culture and Economy in the Indian Diaspora.* Ed. G. Singh, B. Parekh and S. Vertovec. London: Routledge. Pp. 197–222.

Bauböck, R.
2003 "Towards a Political Theory of Migrant Transnationalism," *International Migration Review,* 37(3):700–723.

—— 1994 *Transnational Citizenship: Membership and Rights in International Migration.* Aldershot: Edward Elgar.

Beck, U., W. Bonss and C. Lau
2003 "The Theory of Reflexive Modernization: Problematic, Hypotheses and Research Programme," *Theory, Culture and Society,* 20(2):1–33.

Bryceson, D. and U. Vuorela, eds.
2002 *The Transnational Family: New European Frontiers and Global Networks.* Oxford: Berg.

Carnoy, M. and M. Castells
2001 "Globalization, The Knowledge Society, and the Network State: Poulantzas at the Millennium," *Global Networks,* 1(1):1–18.

Castells, M.
1997 *The Power of Identity.* Oxford: Blackwell.

—— 1996 *The Rise of the Network Society.* Oxford: Blackwell.

Castles, S.
2002 "Migration and Community Formation under Conditions of Globalization," *International Migration Review,* 36(4):1143–1168.

2001 "Studying Social Transformation," *International Political Science Review,* 22(1):13–32.

The Economist
2003a "Special Report: Diasporas. A World of Exiles," January 4. Pp. 25–27.

2003b "Our Kinda Ciudad," January 11. P. 39.

Faist, T.
2001 "Dual Citizenship as Overlapping Membership." Malmö: School of International Migration and Ethnic Relations, Willy Brandt Series of Working Papers 3/01.

Fitzgerald, D.
2000 *Negotiating Extra-Territorial Citizenship: Mexican Migration and the Transnational Politics of Community.* La Jolla, CA: Center for Comparative Immigration Studies, Monograph Series No. 2.

Foner, N.
2000 *From Ellis Island to JFK: New York's Two Great Waves of Immigration.* New Haven: Yale University Press.

Fouron, G. and N. Glick Schiller
2001 "All in the Family: Gender, Transnational Migration, and the Nation State," *Identities,* 7(4):539–582.

Fritz, M.
1998 "Pledging Multiple Allegiances," *Los Angeles Times,* April 6.

Gammeltoft, P.
2002 "Remittances and other Financial Flows to Developing Countries," *International Migration,* 40(5):181–211.

Gardner, K.
1995 *Global Migrants, Local Lives: Travel and Transformation in Rural Bangladesh.* Oxford: Clarendon Press.

1993 "Desh-Bidesh: Sylheti Images of Home and Away," *Man,* 28(1):1–15.

Gardner, K. and R. Grillo
2002 "Transnational Households and Ritual: An Overview," *Global Networks,* 2(3):179–190.

Golbert, R.
2001 "Transnational Orientations from Home: Constructions of Israel and Transnational Space among Ukrainian Jewish Youth," *Journal of Ethnic and Migration Studies,* 27(4): 713–731.

Goldring, L.
2001 "The Gender and Geography of Citizenship in Mexico-U.S. Transnational Spaces," *Identities,* 7(4):501–537.

1998 "The Power of Status in Transnational Social Fields." In *Transnationalism from Below.* Ed. M. P. Smith and L. E. Guarnizo. New Brunswick, NJ: Transaction Publishers. Pp. 165–195.

Grace, D.
2001 "The Development Potential of Remittances and the Credit Union Difference." Paper presented at the Regional Conference Remittances as a Development Tool, Washington, DC: Multilateral Investment Fund, Inter-American Development Bank.

Guarnizo, L. E.
2003 "The Economics of Transnational Living," *International Migration Review*, 37(3):666–699.

1997 "The Emergence of a Transnational Social Formation and the Mirage of Return Migration among Dominican Transmigrants," *Identities*, 4(2):281–322.

Guarnizo, L. E., A. Portes and W. Haller
2003 "Assimilation and Transnationalism: Determinants of Transnational Political Action among Contemporary Migrants," *American Journal of Sociology*, 108(6):1211–1148.

Guillén, M. F.
2001 "Is Globalization Civilizing, Destructive or Feeble? A Critique of Five Key Debates in the Social Science Literature," *Annual Review of Sociology*, 27:235–260.

Hannerz, U.
1996 *Transnational Connections: Culture, People, Places.* London: Routledge.

Hansen, R. and P. Weil
2002 "Introduction: Dual Citizenship in a Changed World: Immigration, Gender and Social Rights." In *Dual Nationality, Social Rights and Federal Citizenship in the U.S. and Europe.* Ed. R. Hansen and P. Weil. Oxford: Berghahn. Pp. 1–15.

Heisler, M. O.
2001 "Now and Then, Here and There: Migration and the Transformation of Identities, Borders, and Orders." In *Identities, Borders, Orders.* Ed. M. Albert, D. Jacobson and Y. Lapid. Minneapolis: University of Minnesota Press. Pp. 225–247.

Held, D., A. McGrew, D. Goldblatt and J. Perraton
1999 *Global Transformations: Politics, Economics and Culture.* Cambridge: Polity.

Herrera, F.
2001 "Transnational Families: Institutions of Transnational Social Space." In *New Transnational Social Spaces.* Ed. L. Pries. London: Routledge. Pp. 77–93.

Hondagneu-Sotelo, P. and E. Avila
1997 " 'I'm Here, but I'm There': The Meanings of Latina Transnational Motherhood," *Gender and Society*, 11(5):548–571.

International Labour Organization (ILO)
2000 "Making the Best of Globalization: Migrant Worker Remittances and Micro-finance." Geneva, International Labor Organization, Social Finance Unit, Workshop Report.

Itzigsohn, J. and S. G. Saucedo
2002 "Immigrant Incorporation and Sociocultural Transnationalism," *International Migration Review*, 36(3):766–798.

Jain, P. and M. Moore
2003 "What Makes Microcredit Programmes Effective? Fashionable Fallacies and Workable Realities," Brighton: Institute of Development Studies Working Paper 177.

Jones-Correa, M.
2001 "Under Two Flags: Dual Nationality in Latin America and Its Consequences for Naturalization in the United States," *International Migration Review*, 35(4):997–1029.

Joppke, C., ed.
1999 *Immigration and the Nation-State: The United States, Germany and Great Britain.*
      Oxford: Oxford University Press.

————
1998 *Challenge to the Nation-State: Immigration in Western Europe and the United States.*
      Oxford: Oxford University Press.

Kastoryano, R.
2002 "Türken mit Deutschem Pass: Sociological and Political Aspects of Dual Nationality
      in Germany." In *Dual Nationality, Social Rights and Federal Citizenship in the U.S. and
      Europe.* Ed. R. Hansen and P. Weil. Oxford: Berghahn. Pp. 158–175.

Koopmans, R. and P. Statham
2001 "How National Citizenship Shapes Transnationalism: A Comparative Analysis of
      Migrant Claims-making in Germany, Great Britain and the Netherlands," Oxford:
      ESRC Transnational Communities Programme Working Paper WPTC-01-10.
      <www.transcomm.ox.ac.uk>.

Koslowski, R.
2001 "Demographic Boundary Maintenance in World Politics: Of International Norms on
      Dual Nationality." In *Identities, Borders, Orders.* Ed. M. Albert, D. Jacobson and Y.
      Lapid. Minneapolis, MN: University of Minnesota Press. Pp. 203–223.

Kyle, D.
2000 *Transnational Peasants: Migrations, Networks, and Ethnicity in Andean Ecuador.* Balti-
      more, MD: Johns Hopkins University Press.

Landolt, P.
2001 "Salvadoran Economic Transnationalism: Embedded Strategies for Household Main-
      tenance, Immigrant Incorporation, and Entrepreneurial Expansion," *Global Networks,*
      1(3):217241.

Lapid, Y.
2001 "Identities, Borders, Orders: Nudging International Relations Theory in a New Di-
      rection." In *Identities, Borders, Orders.* Ed. M. Albert, D. Jacobson and Y. Lapid.
      Minneapolis, MN: University of Minnesota Press. Pp. 1–20.

Levitt, P.
2003 "Transnational Migration and the Redefinition of the State: Variations and Explana-
      tions," *Ethnic and Racial Studies,* 26(4):587–611.

————
2001a "Transnational Migration: Taking Stock and Future Directions," *Global Networks,*
      1(3):195–216.

————
2001b *The Transnational Villagers.* Berkeley: University of California Press.

Levitt, P. and M. C. Waters
2002 "Introduction." In *The Changing Face of Home.* Ed. P. Levitt and M. C. Waters. New
      York: Russell Sage Foundation. Pp. 1–30.

Levitt, P. and N. Glick Schiller
2004 "Conceptualizing Simultaneity: A Transnational Social Field Perspective on Society,
      International Migration Review, 38(3):1002–1040.

Light, I., M. Zhou and R. Kim
2002 "Transnationalism and American Exports in an English-speaking World," *International
      Migration Review,* 36(3):702–725.

Lowell, B. L. and R. O. de la Garza
2000 'The Developmental Role of Remittances in U.S. Latino Communities and in Latin American Countries,' Washington, DC: Inter-American Dialogue, Final Project Report.

Mahler, S. J.
2000 "Migration and Transnational Issues: Recent Trends and Prospects for 2020," Hamburg: Instutut für Iberoamerika-Kunde, CA 2020 Working Paper No. 4.

1998 "Theoretical and Empirical Contributions toward a Research Agenda for Transnationalism." In *Transnationalism from Below*. Ed. M. P. Smith and L. E. Guarnizo. New Brunswick, NJ: Transaction Publishers. Pp. 64–100.

Maira, S. M.
2002 *Desis in the House: Indian American Youth Culture in New York City*. Philadelphia, PA: Temple University Press.

Martin, S. F.
2001 "Remittance Flows and Impact." Paper presented at the Regional Conference on Remittances as a Development Tool, Multilateral Investment Fund, Inter-American Development Bank, Washington, DC.

Menjivar, C.
2002 "Living in Two Worlds? Guatemalan-origin Children in the United States and Emerging Transnationalism," *Journal of Ethnic and Migration Studies*, 28(3):531–552.

Meyers, D. W.
1998 "Migrant Remittances to Latin America: Reviewing the Literature," Washington, DC: Inter-American Dialogue and the Tomás Rivera Policy Institute, Working Paper.

Migration News
2001 "Bush, Ids, Remittances," *Migration News*, 9(2). <http://migration.ucdavis.edu/mn>.

Mohan, G. and A. B. Zack-Williams
2002 "Globalisation from Below: Conceptualising the Role of the African Diasporas in Africa's Development," *Review of African Political Economy*, 92:211–236.

Mountz, A. and R. A. Wright
1996 "Daily Life in the Transnational Migrant Community of San Agustín, Oaxaca, and Poughkeepsie, New York, *Diaspora*, 5(3):403–428.

Orellana, M. F., B. Thorne, A. Chee and W. S. E. Lam
2001 "Transnational Childhoods: The Participation of Children in Processes of Family Migration," *Social Problems*, 48(4):572–591.

Orozco, M.
2002 "Attracting Remittances: Market, Money and Reduced Costs," Washington, DC: Multilateral Investment Fund of the Inter-American Development Bank, Report.

2001 "Globalization and Migration: The Impact of Family Remittances in Latin America." Paper presented at Inter-American Foundation/Un ECLAC/World Bank conference on Approaches to Increasing the Productive Value of Remittances, Washington, DC.

2000a "Latino Hometown Associations as Agents of Development in Latin America," Washington, DC: Inter-American Dialogue, Final Report.

2000b "Remittances and Markets: New Players and Practices," Washington, DC: Inter-American Dialogue and the Tomás Rivera Policy Institute, Working Paper.

Østergaard-Nielsen, E.

2003a *Transnational Politics: Turks and Kurds in Germany.* London: Routledge.

2003b "Sending Countries and International Migration: Key Issues and Themes." In *Sending Countries and International Migration.* Ed. E. Østergaard-Nielsen. Basingstoke: Palgrave.

2001 "Turkish and Kurdish Transnational Political Mobilization in Germany and the Netherlands," *Global Networks,* 1(3):261–282.

Pickus, N. M. J.

1998 "Introduction." In *Immigration and Citizenship in the Twenty-First Century.* Ed. N. M. J. Pickus. Lanham, MA: Rowman and Littlefield. Pp. xvii–xxxiii.

Portes, A.

2003 "Theoretical Convergencies and Empirical Evidence in the Study of Immigrant Transnationalism," *International Migration Review,* 37(3):874–892.

2001 "The Debates and Significance of Immigrant Transnationalism," *Global Networks,* 1(3):181–193.

Portes, A. and P. Landolt

2000 "Social Capital: Promise and Pitfalls of Its Role in Development," *Journal of Latin American Studies,* 32(2):529–547.

Portes, A., W. Haller and L. E. Guarnizo

2002 "Transnational Entrepreneurs: The Emergence and Determinants of an Alternative Form of Immigrant Economic Adaptation," *American Sociological Review,* 67:278–298.

Puri, S. and T. Ritzema

1999 "Migrant Worker Remittances, Micro-finance and the Informal Economy: Prospects and Issues." Geneva: International Labour Organization, Social Finance Unit, Working Paper 21.

Rapport, N. and A. Dawson, eds.

1998 *Migrants of Identity: Perceptions of Home in a World of Movement.* Oxford: Berg.

Robinson, M. S.

2001 *The Microfinance Revolution: Sustainable Finance for the Poor.* Washington, DC: The World Bank and the Open Society Institute.

Rogers, A.

2001a "Competition over Wire Transfer Business in N. America and Asia," *Traces,* 13. <www.transcomm.ox.ac.uk/traces/issue13.htm>.

2001b "Gujaratis Overseas Respond to Earthquake Disaster," *Traces,* 13. <www.transcomm.ox.ac.uk/traces/issue13.htm>.

2001c "Latin America: Migrants Flow Out, Remittances Flow In," *Traces,* 14. <www.transcomm.ox.ac.uk/traces/issue14.htm>.

2000 "Mexico's Historic Elections Spill over into the USA," *Traces,* 10. <www. transcomm.ox.ac.uk/traces/issue10.htm>.

Rouse, R.
1992 "Making Sense of Settlement: Class Transformation, Cultural Struggle, and Transnationalism among Mexican Migrants in the United States," *Annals of the New York Academy of Sciences,* 645:25–52.

Salih, R.
2003 *Gender in Transnationalism: Home, Longing and Belonging among Moroccan Migrant Women.* London: Routledge.

Sassen, S.
2002 "Global Cities and Diasporic Networks: Microsites in Global Civil Society." In *Global Civil Society 2002.* Ed. A. Anheier, M. Glasius and M. Kaldor. Oxford: Oxford University Press. Pp. 217–238.

1996 *Losing Control? Sovereignty in an Age of Globalization.* New York: Columbia University Press.

Schiffauer, W., G. Baumann, R. Kastoryano and S. Vertovec, eds.
2003 *Civil Enculturation: State, School and Ethnic Difference in Four European Countries.* Oxford: Berghahn.

Schuck, P. H.
1998 "Plural Citizenships." In *Immigration and Citizenship in the Twenty-First Century.* Ed. N. M. J. Pickus. Lanham, MA: Rowman and Littlefield. Pp. 149–191.

Shain, Y.
1999 *Marketing the American Creed Abroad: Diasporas in the U.S. and Their Homelands.* Cambridge: Cambridge University Press.

Smelser, N. J.
1998 "Social Transformations and Social Change," *International Social Science Journal,* 156: 173–178.

Smith, R.
2002 "Life Course, Generation, and Social Location as Factors Shaping Second-generation Transnational Life." In *The Changing Face of Home.* Ed. P. Levitt and M. C. Waters. New York: Russell Sage Foundation. Pp. 145–167.

2001 "Comparing Local-level Swedish and Mexican Transnational Life: An Essay in Historical Retrieval." In *New Transnational Social Spaces.* Ed. L. Pries. London: Routledge. Pp. 37–58.

1998 "Transnational Localities: Community, Technology and the Politics of Membership within the Context of Mexico and U.S. Migration." In *Transnationalism from Below.* Ed. M. P. Smith and L. E. Guarnizo. New Brunswick, NJ: Transaction Publishers. Pp. 196–238.

Soysal, Y. N.
1994 *Limits of Citizenship: Migrants and Postnational Membership in Europe.* Chicago: University of Chicago Press.

Spiro, P. J.
2002 "Embracing Dual Nationality." In *Dual Nationality, Social Rights and Federal Citizenship in the U.S. and Europe.* Ed. R. Hansen and P. Weil. Oxford: Berghahn. Pp. 19–33.

Stalker, P.
2000 *Workers without Frontiers: The Impact of Globalization on International Migration.* Geneva: International Labor Organization.

Strange, S.
1996 *The Retreat of the State: The Diffusion of Power in the World Economy.* New York: Cambridge University Press.

Suro, R., S. Bendixen, B. L. Lowell and D. C. Benavides
2002 "Billions in Motion: Latino Immigrants, Remittances and Banking," Washington, DC: Pew Hispanic Center and Multilateral Investment Fund, Report.

Taylor, J. E.
1999 "The New Economics of Labour Migration and the Role of Remittances in the Migration Process," *International Migration,* 37(1):63–88.

Thränhardt, D.
2002 "Prophecies, *Ius Soli* and Dual Citizenship: Interpreting the Changes in the German Citizenship System." Paper presented at the Workshop on Transnational Ties and Identities Past and Present, Netherlands Institute for Advanced Study, Wassenaar.

Tomlinson, J.
1999 *Globalization and Culture.* Cambridge: Polity.

UNPD/United Nations Population Division
2002 *International Migration 2002.* New York: Population Division, Department of Economic and Social Affairs, United Nations.

1998 *International Migration Policies.* New York: Population Division, Department of Economic and Social Affairs, United Nations.

van Doorn, J.
2001 "Migration, Remittances and Small Enterprise Development." Geneva: International Labour Organization.

Vertovec, S.
2001 "Transnationalism and Identity," *Journal of Ethnic and Migration Studies,* 27(4):573–582.

2000 "Rethinking Remittances," Oxford: ESRC Transnational Communities Programme Working Paper WPTC-2K-15. <www.transcomm.ox.ac.uk>.

1999 "Introduction." In *Migration and Social Cohesion.* Ed. S. Vertovec. Cheltenham: Edward Elgar. Pp. xi-xxxvii.

Vertovec, S. and R. Cohen, eds.
2002 *Conceiving Cosmopolitanism: Theory, Context and Practice.* Oxford: Oxford University Press.

Voigt-Graf, C.
2002 "The Construction of Transnational Spaces: Traveling between India, Fiji and Australia." PhD Thesis. Geography, University of Sydney.

Widgren, J. and P. Martin
2002 "Managing Migration: The Role of Economic Instruments," *International Migration,* 40(5):213–229.

Wiltshire, K.
2001 "Management of Social Transformations: Introduction," *International Political Science Review,* 22(1):5–11.

World Bank
2001 "Migrants Capital for Small-Scale Infrastructure and Small Enterprise Development in Mexico." Washington, DC: The World Bank.

Zhou, M.
1997 " 'Parachute Kids' in Southern California: The Educational Experience of Chinese Children in Transnational Families," *Educational Policy,* 12:682–704.

Chapter 7

CONCEPTUALIZING SIMULTANEITY[1]
A Transnational Social Field Perspective on Society

Peggy Levitt and Nina Glick Schiller

Social scientists have long been interested in how immigrants are incorporated into new countries. In Germany and France, scholars' expectations that foreigners will assimilate is a central piece of public policy. In the United States, immigration scholars initially argued that to move up the socioeconomic ladder, immigrants would have to abandon their unique customs, language, values, and homeland ties and identities. Even when remaining ethnic became more acceptable, most researchers assumed that the importance of homeland ties would eventually fade. To be Italian American or Irish American would ultimately reflect ethnic pride within a multicultural United States rather than enduring relations to an ancestral land.

Now scholars increasingly recognize that some migrants and their descendants remain strongly influenced by their continuing ties to their home country or by social networks that stretch across national borders. They see

---

[1] This is a co-authored article, jointly conceived and written by both contributors.

migrants' crossborder ties as a variable and argue that to understand contemporary migration, the strength, influence, and impact of these ties must be empirically assessed. They call for a transnational perspective on migration (Basch, Glick Schiller and Szanton Blanc, 1994). The resulting analyses, in combination with other scholarship on transnational dynamics, are building toward a new paradigm that rejects the long-held notion that society and the nation-state are one and the same.

This article is not intended as a comprehensive review of the transnational migration scholarship. In fact, a special volume of this journal, published in Fall 2003, does just that. Instead, we explore the social theory and the consequent methodology that underpins studies of transnational migration. We argue that central to the project of transnational migration studies, and to scholarship on other transnational phenomena, is a reformulation of the concept of society. The lives of increasing numbers of individuals can no longer be understood by looking only at what goes on within national boundaries. Our analytical lens must necessarily broaden and deepen because migrants are often embedded in multi-layered, multi-sited transnational social fields, encompassing those who move and those who stay behind. As a result, basic assumptions about social institutions such as the family, citizenship, and nation-states need to be revisited.

Once we rethink the boundaries of social life, it becomes clear that the incorporation of individuals into nation-states and the maintenance of transnational connections are not contradictory social processes. Simultaneity, or living lives that incorporate daily activities, routines, and institutions located both in a destination country and transnationally, is a possibility that needs to be theorized and explored. Migrant incorporation into a new land and transnational connections to a homeland or to dispersed networks of family, compatriots, or persons who share a religious or ethnic identity can occur at the same time and reinforce one another.

Our goals in this study are fourfold. First, we propose a social field approach to the study of migration and distinguish between ways of being and ways of belonging in that field. Second, we argue that assimilation and enduring transnational ties are neither incompatible nor binary opposites. Instead, we suggest thinking of the transnational migration experience as a kind of gauge which, while anchored, pivots between host land and transnational connections. Third, we highlight social processes and institutions that are routinely obscured by traditional migration scholarship but that become clear when we use a transnational lens. Finally, we locate our approach to migration research within a larger intellectual project, undertaken by scholars of transnational processes in a variety of fields, to reformulate the concept of society such that it is no longer automatically equated with or confined by the boundaries of a single nation-state.

FOUNDATIONAL APPROACHES TO THIS FIELD

There have already been several waves of transnational migration scholarship that have fine-tuned concepts and analyzed transnational relations in a much more nuanced manner than earlier formulations. Researchers have explored transnational identity formation and the economic, political, religious, and sociocultural practices that propel migrant incorporation and transnational connection at the same time (*see, e.g.,* Basch, Glick Schiller and Szanton Blanc, 1994; Smith and Guarnizo, 1998; Grasmuck and Pessar, 1991; Laguerre, 1998; Itzigsohn *et al.*, 1999; Smith, 2003; Levitt, 2001a, b; Glick Schiller and Fouron, 2001a, b; Ebaugh and Chafetz, 2002; Kyle, 2001; Ostergaard-Nielsen, 2003; Fitzgerald, 2003; Landolt, 2001; Goldring, 2002; Vertovec, 2003; Gold, 2002; Koopmans and Statham, 2001; Riccio, 2001; Van der Veer, 2001; Abelman, 2002; Morgan, 1999; Faist, 2000a, b; Schiffauer, 1999; Sklair, 1998; Itzigsohn, 2000; Portes, Guarnizo and Landolt, 1999; Kivisto, 2001; Mahler, 1998; Duany, 2000; Morawska, 2003b, Eckstein and Barberia, 2002). They have proposed typologies to capture variations in the dimensions of transnational migration. The extent to which transnational migration is a new phenomenon or whether it shares similarities with its earlier incarnations has been the subject of much debate (*see* Foner, 2000; Glick Schiller, 1999; Smith, 2002; Morawska, 2003b; Weber, 1999). Several studies examine the scope of transnational practices among particular immigrant populations (*see* Portes, Haller and Guarnizo, 2002; Guarnizo, Portes and Haller, 2003; Itzigsohn and Saucedo, 2002). Finally, an emerging body of research tries to explain variations in transnational practices across groups (Levitt, 2002b; Itzigsohn and Saucedo, 2002; Portes, Haller and Guarnizo, 2002; Guarnizo, Portes and Haller, 2003).

To develop our theory and methodology further and to address the implications of simultaneous incorporation, we begin with a brief synthesis of the scholarship on transnational migration to date upon which a new theoretical synthesis can be built. We see four distinct traditions developing among scholars of transnational migration: the research done by sociologists and anthropologists in the United States; studies done by the Transnational Community Programme based at Oxford University; a literature on transnational families; and an effort to reformulate notions of space and social structure. Underlying these developments is a fundamental problem of social theory – how to rethink society if we do not take national boundaries for granted.

Transnational migration scholarship in the United States has been shaped by its critique of the unilinear assimilationist paradigm of classical migration research (Glick Schiller, 1999; Basch, Glick Schiller and Szanton Blanc, 1994; Glick Schiller, Basch and Szanton Blanc, 1995). Some studies have focused on the kinds of networks that stretch between a sending community and its migrants (Grasmuck and Pessar, 1991; Levitt, 2001a; Rouse, 1992; Smith, 1998; Kyle 2001). Others have sought to determine the conditions under which migrants maintained homeland ties and identities and how commonplace transnational practices were among the migrant population as a whole (Morawska, 2003b; Levitt, 2003b; Basch, Glick Schiller and Szanton Blanc, 1994). These studies revealed that a small but nonetheless significant number of migrants engage in regular economic and political transnational practices (Portes, Haller and Guarnizo, 2002; Guarnizo, Portes and Haller, 2003) and that many more individuals engage in occasional transnational activities. Some studies explore the relationship between migration and development, categorizing transnational migration as a product of late capitalism which renders small, nonindustrialized countries incapable of economic autonomy and makes them dependent on migrant-generated remittances (Itzigsohn, 2000; Portes, 2003; M.P. Smith and Guarnizo, 1998). The ways in which sending and receiving states continue to play a critical role in migrants' lives has also received a good deal of attention (Smith, 1998; Goldring, 2002; Levitt and de la Dehesa, 2003). More recent research on the second generation is in many ways a continuation of the debate on assimilation, with proponents of the classic approach arguing that transnational migration is an ephemeral first-generation phenomenon. Meanwhile, some transnationalists speak of new forms of transnational connection or replace the term second generation with transnational generation to encompass youth in the homeland and the new land (Levitt and Waters, 2002; Glick Schiller and Fouron, 2002).

While many U.S. researchers have focused on homeland/newland connections, the Oxford Transnational Communities Programme used a much broader definition of transnational ties (*see, e.g.,* Koopmans and Statham, 2001; Riccio, 2001; Van der Veer, 2001; Abelman, 2002; Morgan, 1999; Faist, 2000a; Schiffauer, 1999; Sklair, 1998; Castles, 1998). In this project, transnational connections forged by businesses, the media, politics, or religion were all examined under the rubric of community. This work demonstrated that migrants are embedded in networks stretching across multiple states and that migrants' identities and cultural production reflect their multiple locations. Among the important findings of the Transnational Communities project was the need to distinguish between patterns of connection on the ground and the conditions that produce ideologies of connection and community (Gomez and Benton, 2002; Ostergaard-Neilsen, 2003).

Some of the U.S. and Oxford studies (Ballard, 2000) urge a reconceptualization of transnational kinship, although research in this area has developed a trajectory of its own (Chamberlin, 2002; Bryceson and Vuorela, 2002). Studies of transnational kinship document the ways in which family networks constituted across borders are marked by gendered differences in power and status. Kin networks can be used exploitatively, a process of transnational class differentiation in which the more prosperous extract labor from persons defined as kin. Kin networks maintained between people who send remittances and those who live on them can be fraught with tension.

A fourth group of scholars use a transnational approach to migration to challenge social theory. Morawska (2001a, 2003a) proposes a conceptualization of migration as structuration to posit the continuing dynamic between structure and agency that extends into a transnational domain. Faist (2000a, b), reasoning along similar lines, strives to conceptualize a domain of crossborder social relations he refers to as transnational social spaces. He privileges social relations and institutions, defining these spaces as characterized by a high density of interstitial ties on informal or formal, that is to say institutional, levels (Faist, 2000b:89). Guarnizo (1997) and Landolt (2001) refer to a transnational social formation.

Much of this work, however, views the social formations engendered by transnational migration as unique. Instead, we propose that they are one indication, among many, that the nation-state container view of society does not capture, adequately or automatically, the complex interconnectedness of contemporary reality. To do so requires adopting a transnational social field approach to the study of social life that distinguishes between the existence of transnational social networks and the consciousness of being embedded in them. Such a distinction is also critical to understanding the experience of living simultaneously within and beyond the boundaries of a nation-state and to developing methodologies for empirically studying such experiences.

BUILDING TO A TRANSNATIONAL SOCIAL FIELD THEORY OF SOCIETY

To further develop transnational migration studies, we revisit the concept of society as it has been generally deployed and put aside the methodological nationalism that has distorted many basic social science concepts (Martins, 1974; Smith, 1983). Methodological nationalism is the tendency to accept the nation-state and its boundaries as a given in social analysis. Wimmer and Glick Schiller (2003) identified three variants of methodological nationalism: 1) Ignoring or disregarding the fundamental importance of nationalism for modern societies. This tendency often goes hand and hand with 2) naturalization, or taking for granted that the boundaries of the nation-state delimit and define the unit of analysis. Finally, 3) territorial limitation confines the study of social processes to the political and geographic boundaries of a particular nation-state. According to Wimmer and Glick Schiller (2003:578), the three variants may intersect and mutually reinforce each other, forming a coherent epistemic structure, a self-reinforcing way of looking at and describing the social world.

Because much of social science theory equates society with the boundaries of a particular nation-state, researchers often take rootedness and incorporation in the nation-state as the norm and social identities and practices enacted across state boundaries as out of the ordinary. But if we remove the blinders of methodological nationalism, we see that while nation-states are still extremely important, social life is not confined by nation-state boundaries. Social and religious movements, criminal and professional networks, and governance regimes as well as flows of capital also operate across borders.

Recent developments in social theory have also challenged the nation-state container theory of society and provide insights into the nature of transnational flows that we build upon. Sassen, for example, reconfigured our understanding of the geography of cities by highlighting that some locations become global cities (Sassen, 1992). Discussing flexible capital accumulation, Harvey (1989) explored the time-space compressions that so revolutionize the objective qualities of space and time that we are forced to alter, sometimes in quite radical ways, how we represent the world to ourselves (p. 240). Other scholars have highlighted the interconnectedness of societies through flows of media, capital, and people (Held *et al.*, 1999). However, much of this work, according to Ulrich Beck (2000), continues to envision states as the primary unit and treats globalization as a process of interconnection between states. Such theories, Beck argues, continue "the container theory of society" on which most of the sociology of the first age of modernity is based. He calls for a new paradigm that changes not only the relations between and beyond national states and societies, but also the inner quality of the social and political itself which is indicated by reflexive cosmopolitization (p. 1).

Along with Beck, Faist (2000a), Urry (2000) and a growing number of social theorists, we seek ways to move beyond the container theory of society. Many of these scholars, however, tend to underplay the concept of the social as they reconfigure the concept of society. Beck's formulation of reflexive cosmopolitization and much of the related literature on cosmopolitanism, for example, largely abandons an exploration of social relations and social context. In Beck's (2000) cosmopolitanism, as in Luhmann's world society, communication technologies become key. Global media flows and consumerism lead to a new form of consciousness. Social relations and social positioning fall out of the analysis; the individual and the global intersect. Without a concept of the social, the relations of power and privilege exercised by social actors based within structures and organizations cannot be studied or analyzed. In addition, by trying to move beyond methodological nationalism, much of this theory-building neglects the continuing power of the nation-state. Transnational migration studies, with their concrete tracing of the movement and connection of people, provide a useful corrective to these oversights by highlighting the concept of social field.

We propose a view of society and social membership based on a concept of social field that distinguishes between ways of being and ways of belonging. The notion of social field exists in social science literature in several different forms. We draw here on those proposed by Bourdieu and by the Manchester school of anthropology. Bourdieu used the concept of social field to call attention to the ways in which social relationships are structured by power. The boundaries of a field are fluid and the field itself is created by the participants who are joined in struggle for social position. Society for Bourdieu is the intersection of various fields within a structure of politics (Jenkins, 1992:86). According to Bourdieu, either individuals or institutions may occupy the networks that make up the field and link social positions. While his approach does not preclude the notion of transnational social fields, he does not directly discuss the implications of social fields that are not coterminous with state boundaries.

The Manchester School also informs our framework because these scholars recognized that the migrants they studied belonged to tribal-rural localities and colonial-industrial cities at the same time. Migrant networks stretching between these two sites were viewed as constituting a single social field created by a network of networks. By understanding society in this way, these researchers focused on a level of social analysis beyond the study of the individual.

Despite its importance, the term social field within transnational migration research has not been well defined. Building on Basch, Glick Schiller and Szanton Blanc (1994), we define social field as a set of multiple interlocking networks of social relationships through which ideas, practices, and resources are unequally exchanged, organized, and transformed (*see also* Glick Schiller and Fouron, 1999; Glick Schiller, 1999, 2003). Social fields are multidimensional, encompassing structured interactions of differing forms, depth, and breadth that are differentiated in social theory by the terms organization, institution, and social movement. National boundaries are not necessarily contiguous with the boundaries of social fields. National social fields are those that stay within national boundaries while transnational social fields connect actors through direct and indirect relations across borders. Neither domain is privileged in our analysis. Ascertaining the relative importance of nationally restricted and transnational social fields should be a question of empirical analysis.

The concept of social fields is a powerful tool for conceptualizing the potential array of social relations linking those who move and those who stay behind. It takes us beyond the direct experience of migration into domains of interaction where individuals who do not move themselves maintain social relations across borders through various forms of communication. Individuals who have such direct connections with migrants may connect with others who do not. We should not assume that those with stronger social ties will be more transnationally active than those with weaker connections nor that the actions and identities of those with more indirect ties are less influenced by the dynamics within the field than those with direct transnational ties. In any given study, the researcher must operationalize the parameters of the field they are studying and the scope of the networks embedded within it, then empirically analyze the strength and impact of direct and indirect transnational relations.

For example, there may be one central individual who maintains high levels of homeland contact and is the node through which information, resources, and identities flow. While other individuals may not identify with or take action based on those ties, the fact that they are part of the same transnational social field keeps them informed and connected so that they can act if events motivate them to do so. Recognizing that this individual is embedded in a transnational social field may be a better predictor of future transnational behavior than if we simply locate him or her solely within a nationally delimited set of relationships.

The concept of social field also calls into question neat divisions of connection into local, national, transnational, and global. In one sense, all are local in that near and distant connections penetrate the daily lives of individuals lived within a locale. But within this locale, a person may participate in personal networks or receive ideas and information that connect them to others in a nation-state, across the borders of a nation-state, or globally, without ever having migrated. By conceptualizing transnational social fields as transcending the boundaries of nation-states, we also note that individuals within these fields are, through their everyday activities and relationships, influenced by multiple sets of laws and institutions. Their daily rhythms and activities respond not only to more than one state simultaneously but also to social institutions, such as religious groups, that exist within many states and across their borders.

A social field perspective also reveals that there is a difference between ways of being in social fields as opposed to ways of belonging (Glick Schiller, 2003; 2004).[2] Ways of being refers to the actual social relations and practices that individuals engage in rather than to the identities associated with their actions. Social fields contain institutions, organizations, and experiences, within their various levels, that generate categories of identity that are ascribed to or chosen by individuals or groups. Individuals can be embedded in a social field but not identify with any label or cultural politics associated with that field. They have the potential to act or identify at a particular time because they live within the social field, but not all choose to do so.

In contrast, ways of belonging refers to practices that signal or enact an identity which demonstrates a conscious connection to a particular group. These actions are not symbolic but concrete, visible actions that mark belonging such as wearing a Christian cross or Jewish star, flying a flag, or choosing a particular cuisine. Ways of belonging combine action and an awareness of the kind of identity that action signifies.

Individuals within transnational social fields combine ways of being and ways of belonging differently in specific contexts. One person might have many social contacts with people in their country of origin but not

[2]Some analysts, such as Thomas Faist (2000a), contrast social ties with "symbolic ties." By emphasizing ways of being, rather than social ties, we develop a concept that decouples social relationships from a notion of common interest or norms.

identify at all as belonging to their homeland. They are engaged in transnational ways of being but not belonging. Similarly, a person may eat certain foods or worship certain saints or deities because that is what their family has always done. By doing so, they are not signaling any conscious identification with a particular ethnicity or with their ancestral homes. Here again, they are not expressing a transnational way of belonging.

On the other hand, there are people with few or no actual social relations with people in the sending country or transnationally but who behave in such a way as to assert their identification with a particular group. Because these individuals have some sort of connection to a way of belonging, through memory, nostalgia or imagination, they can enter the social field when and if they choose to do so. In fact, we would hypothesize that someone who had access to a transnational way of belonging would be likely to act on it at some point in his or her life.

If individuals engage in social relations and practices that cross borders as a regular feature of everyday life, then they exhibit a transnational way of being. When people explicitly recognize this and highlight the transnational elements of who they are, then they are also expressing a transnational way of belonging. Clearly, these two experiences do not always go hand in hand.

Finally, locating migrants within transnational social fields makes clear that incorporation in a new state and enduring transnational attachments are not binary opposites (Morawska, 2003b; Levitt, 2003b). Instead, it is more useful to think of the migrant experience as a kind of gauge which, while anchored, pivots between a new land and a transnational incorporation. Movement and attachment is not linear or sequential but capable of rotating back and forth and changing direction over time. The median point on this gauge is not full incorporation but rather simultaneity of connection. Persons change and swing one way or the other depending on the context, thus moving our expectation away from either full assimilation or transnational connection but some combination of both. The challenge, then, is to explain the variation in the way that migrants manage that pivot and how host country incorporation and homeland or other transnational ties mutually influence each other. For example, Portes and his colleagues found that transnational entrepreneurs were more likely to be U.S. citizens, suggesting that by becoming full members of their new land, it became easier for them to run successful businesses involving their homeland. Similarly, some Latino communities use the same organizations to promote political integration in the United States that they use to mobilize around sending-country issues.

In this vein, Glick Schiller, Calgar and Karagiannis (2003) have pro-posed a useful distinction between mere connection and the kinds of con-nections that engage individuals institutionally in more than one nation-state. One can have friends, colleagues, or co-religionists with whom one communicates and exchanges information or objects across borders without ever coming into contact with the state or other institutions. But if one belongs to a church, receives a pension, or has investments in another land, one must necessarily negotiate his or her way through a set of public and private institutions that grounds those connections more firmly. His or her "pivot" is rooted in two or more legal and regulatory systems, encouraging a greater sense of embeddedness in the transnational social field and making the connections within it more likely to endure.

METHODOLOGY

Methodology and theory have an intimate relationship. To develop a trans-national framework for the study of migration, we need a methodology that allows us to move beyond the binaries, such as homeland/new land, citizen/noncitizen, migrant/nonmigrant, and acculturation/cultural persistence, that have typified migration research in the past. On the other hand, a framework that privileges transborder processes rather than incorporation-oriented ac-tivity may not capture the interrelationship between transnational connec-tion and social relationships within a single nation-state.

Using a transnational framework implies several methodological shifts. First, we need to focus on the intersection between the networks of those who have migrated and those who have stayed in place, whether in the new land, homeland, or some other diasporic location. This focus allows for comparisons between the experiences of migrants and those who are only indirectly influenced by ideas, objects, and information flowing across bor-ders. Although multi-sited research is ideal for studying these two different experiences, the impact of transnational relations can be observed by asking individuals about the transnational aspects of their lives, and those they are connected to, in a single setting.

Second, we need tools that capture migrants' simultaneous engagement in and orientation toward their home and host countries. And these dynam-ics cannot just be studied at one point in time. Transnational migration is a process rather than an event. Transnational practices ebb and flow in response to particular incidents or crises. A one-time snapshot misses the many ways in which migrants periodically engage with their home countries during election cycles, family or ritual events, or climatic catastrophes – their attention and energies shifting in response to a particular goal or challenge. Studying migrant practices longitudinally reveals that in moments of crisis or opportunity, even those who have never identified or participated transnationally, but who are embedded in transnational social fields, may become mobilized into action. Such a research strategy would help explain the transition from a way of belonging such as a diasporic identity – Armenian, Jewish, or Croatian – to direct engagement in transnational practices.

Each of the research methodologies used to study transnational migration has particular strengths. We believe that ethnography is particularly suited for studying the creation and durability of transnational social fields. Participant observation and ethnographic interviewing allow researchers to document how persons simultaneously maintain and shed cultural repertoires and identities, interact within a location and across its boundaries, and act in ways that are in concert with or contradict their values over time. The effects of strong and weak indirect ties within a transnational social field can be observed, and those connections, whether they take the form of institutional or individual actors, can be studied. Like surveys, ethnographic research can also begin with a random sample of persons who migrate and who have no intention of returning home.

POWER

When people belong to multiple settings, they come into contact with the regulatory powers and the hegemonic culture of more than one state. These states regulate economic interactions, political processes and performances, and also have discrete nation-state building projects. Individuals are, therefore, embedded in multiple legal and political institutions that determine access and action and organize and legitimate gender, race, and class status. Foucault (1980) wrote that the experience of power goes beyond mere contact with the law or the police. Rather, power pervades and permeates all social relations because what is legitimate, appropriate, and possible is strongly influenced by the state. People living in transnational social fields experience multiple loci and layers of power and are shaped by them, but they can also act back upon them.

Most migrants move from a place where the state has relatively little power within the global interstate system to a more powerful state. At the same time, many migrants gain more social power, in terms of leverage over people, property, and locality, with respect to their homeland than they did before migrating. It is this complex intersection between personal losses and gains that any analysis of power within transnational social fields must grapple with. Furthermore, migration often opens up the possibility for transnational migrants to contribute, both positively and negatively, to changes in the global economic and political system. For example, long distance nationalist movements have long influenced nation building and national transformation. Lithuania would not have become Lithuania without immigrants in the United States first imaging its emergence and then mobilizing to make it a reality (Glazer, 1954). Former Iraqi exiles are now playing a critical role in rebuilding the Iraqi state. Transnational migrants can also strengthen, alter, or thwart global religious movements like Islamic fundamentalism, Christian fundamentalism, or Hindu nationalism.

Not only can migrants potentially shift the position of states within the world economic order, they can also influence the internal functions of states as well. They may be forces for privatization because they want telephone systems that work and private schools and hospitals where their family members will be well attended. They may pressure states to institute conservative legislation that preserves traditional values. Acting within their transnational social fields, migrants may also fuel movements for rights, social justice, and anti-imperialist struggles.

Transnational migrants also shift power by redefining the functions of the host state. There are many instances, such as in the Cuban, Israeli, and Irish communities, in which migrants have successfully mobilized host country legislatures to support their homeland projects. The Mexican state and Mexican transnational migrants living in the United States have altered the ways in which some U.S. institutions categorize and process individuals. The Mexican state's issuing of the *matricula consular,* a consular ID card, to legal and unauthorized Mexican migrants in the United States has enabled migrants to pressure banks, motor vehicle bureaus, and car insurance companies to be more responsive to them.

Using a transnational social field perspective allows for a more systematic study of the social processes and institutions that have been routinely obscured by traditional migration scholarship and even by some studies of transnational migration. New perspectives emerge on a number of issues, including the effect of migration on gender hierarchies and racialized identities; family dynamics; the significance of nation-states, membership and citizenship; and the role of religion. In the following section, we discuss each in turn.

HOW CLASS, RACE, AND GENDER ARE MUTUALLY CONSTITUTED WITHIN TRANSNATIONAL SOCIAL FIELDS

Scholars have tended to study class, race, and gender as discrete realms of experience. Here we build on feminist theory by recognizing that since these social locations are mutually constituted, we must discuss them together. We approach all three as hierarchical positions that entail differential social power. Data on these varying statuses illustrate the analytical limits of methodological nationalism. Social scientists often use national income statistics to assess the socioeconomic status of migrants without considering the other statuses that they occupy. But when society differs from polity and is made up of sets of social relationships in intersecting and overlapping national and transnational social fields, individuals occupy different gender, racial, and class positions within different states at the same time. Recognizing that migrant behavior is the product of these simultaneous multiple statuses of race, class, and gender makes certain social processes more understandable.

For example, a transnational perspective can help explain contradictory data on the political attitudes and actions of immigrants. In some cases, immigrant women, who find themselves racialized in their new homes, appear to be quite conservative with respect to struggles for rights and recognition. Poor migrants of color in the United States, for example, often strive to differentiate themselves from African Americans rather than join efforts to advance minority group civil rights (Waters, 1999). They may re-enforce or even reinvent gender distinctions and hierarchies that are more rigid and traditional than those in their ancestral homes (Espiritu, 1997; Lessinger, 1995; Caglar, 1995). They accept low-status jobs in their new home, tolerate employment discrimination, and resist political projects or labor protests that would redress these wrongs. Ironically, this heightened gender stratification often occurs in households where immigrant women have entered the workforce and men have begun to share the responsibility for childrearing and housekeeping, thereby redefining other aspects of gender dynamics in more egalitarian terms.

Consideration of migrants' multiple positions within transnational social fields helps explain this seemingly conservative and contradictory behavior (Pessar and Mahler, 2003). When individuals elaborate markers of gender after they migrate, they may be preserving or creating status in other locations within the transnational social field. Conservative positions of women and men in relationship to struggles for rights or "family values" may be linked to the class position of migrants in the homeland. Migrants who are laborers, home health aides, or domestic workers in countries of immigration may also be educated and middle-class homeowners or business people in their homelands. Men who may have higher status than women at home are generally more interested in maintaining political homeland connections and identities (Grasmuck and Pessar, 1991). In contrast, women migrants may use income they earn abroad to improve their social standing at home. Transnational religious systems, such as Islam or Charismatic Christianity, also provide venues for asserting one's enhanced status and for acquiring social capital and resources (Peterson and Vásquez, 2001).

TRANSNATIONAL FAMILIES

Much work on globalization and transnational phenomena focuses on production. But reproduction also takes place across borders and is an important, if understudied, aspect of the migration experience. Just as transnational migration studies prompt us to rethink the terrain in which social processes take place, they also challenge our understanding of social reproduction.

Numerous studies illustrate the ways in which the boundaries of family life change over the life cycle. Members of the second and third generations in Europe and the United States continue to return to the Middle East and South Asia to find marriage partners (Hooghiemstra, 2001; Lesthaeghe, 2002; Levitt, 2002b). Increasing numbers of women have joined the ranks of men who head transnational families (Parrenas, 2001; Hondagneu-Sotelo and Avila, 2003). Transnational family life entails renegotiating communication between spouses, the distribution of work tasks, and who will migrate and who will stay behind via long distance (Pessar and Mahler, 2001). Nonmigrants also imagine the gendered lives of their migrant peers and change their ideas about successful marriages and suitable marital partners. Levitt (2001a) found that the young women in the Dominican village she studied only wanted to marry men who had migrated because they were considered the ideal breadwinner and life partner.

While adults make family decisions, children are the central axis of family migration and often a critical reason why families move back and forth and sustain transnational ties (Orellana et al., 2001; Zhou, 1998). Adult-centered studies obscure the ways in which child raising actively shapes families' journeys, the spaces they move in, and their experiences within those social fields. This is particularly true as children mature into young adults. Kandel and Massey (2002), for example, found a culture of migration so deeply embedded in the Mexican communities they studied that transnational migration became the norm. Young men, in particular, came to see migration as an expected rite of passage and as the way to achieve economically what they could not attain in Mexico.

The studies we describe attest to the fact that in migrant households that are constituted transnationally and across generations, living transnationally often becomes the norm (Nyberg Sorenson and Fog Olwig, 2002). How must we rethink conventional wisdom about the family in response? First, using a transnational lens reveals the changing nature of the family as a socioeconomic strategic unit and how family ties are worked and reworked over time and space. Deborah Bryceson and Ulla Vuorela (2002) use the term relativizing to refer to the ways in which individuals establish, maintain, or curtail ties to specific family members. Within transnational social fields, individuals actively pursue or neglect blood ties and fictitious kinship. Based on their particular needs, individuals strategically choose which connections to emphasize and which to let slide. Second, in many cases, socialization and social reproduction occur transnationally in response to at least two social and cultural contexts. Even children who never return to their parent's ancestral homes are brought up in households where people, values, goods and claims from somewhere else are present on a daily basis. Similarly, the children of nonmigrants are raised in social networks and settings entirely permeated by people, resources, and what Levitt (1999) has called social remittances from the host country. For these individuals, the generational experience is not territorially bounded. It is based on actual and imagined experiences that are shared across borders regardless of where someone was born or now lives.

Locating migrants and their families squarely within transnational social fields requires rethinking the notion of generation and the term second generation (Glick Schiller and Fouron, 2002). Conceptualizing generation as a lineal process, involving clear boundaries between one experience and the other, does not accurately capture the experience of living in a transnational field because it implies a separation in migrants' and nonmigrants' socialization and social networks that may not exist. It also fails to take into account that generational experiences are shaped by common experiences during youth that create a shared worldview or frame of reference which influences subsequent social and political activism (Mannheim, 1952; Eckstein, 2002).

While many researchers now acknowledge the salience of transnational ties for the immigrant generation, many predict these ties will weaken among their children. In the United States, these researchers find that the transnational activities of the second generation are confined primarily to certain groups who are, by and large, physically and emotionally rooted in the United States and lack the language, cultural skills, or desire to live in their ancestral homes. Since these individuals are only occasional transnational activists, and their activities are confined to very specific arenas of social life, they are likely to have minimal long-term consequences (Rumbaut, 2002; Kasinitz *et al.*, 2002).

But whether or not individuals forge or maintain some kind of transnational connection may depend on the extent to which they are reared in a transnational space. Clearly, transnational activities will not be central to the lives of most of the second generation, and those who engage in them will not do so with the same frequency and intensity as their parents. But surveys concluding that transnational practices will be inconsequential may be short sighted. They may overlook the effect of the many periodic, selective transnational activities that some individuals engage in at different stages of their lives (Levitt, 2002b; Glick Schiller and Fouron, 2002; Smith, 2002). They may also fail to differentiate between ways of being and possible ways of belonging – that the desire and ability to engage in transnational practices will ebb and flow at different phases of the lifecycle and in different contexts. At the point of marriage or child rearing, the same individuals who showed little regard for a parental homeland and culture may activate their connections within a transnational field in search of spouses or values to teach to their children (Espiritu and Tham, 2002). The children of Gujaratis who go back to India to find marriage partners, the second generation Pakistanis who begin to study Islam and Pakistani values when they have children, or the Chinese American business school students who specialize in Asian banking are doing just that.

THE NATION-STATE: THE POLITICAL LIMITS AND EXTENSIONS OF TRANSNATIONAL SOCIAL FIELDS

The use of a transnational social field perspective and the concept of simultaneity also draws attention to the changing nature of political activism and the nation-state and how these are shaped and shape the transnational social fields in which they are embedded. Both migrants and refugees continue to engage in a variety of cross-border political practices directed at their home and host countries. Some of the early work on transnational migration predicted that these activities would weaken or, in some cases, bring about the decline of the nation-state. Instead, what we see is a reformulation of the state as it assumes new functions, abdicates responsibilities for others, and redefines who its members are. Future research needs to explore why some states change in response to their increasingly transnational constituencies and others do not. We also need to ask which functions states abandon, under what conditions, and what new roles they assume. Finally, we need to identify the new kinds of organizations and collectivities that step in to fill the gap left by the changing state.

It is within sending states that we find the greatest changes in laws, state policy, and migrant practices on both the national and local levels. The vulnerable geopolitical position of many peripheral sending states, increasing poverty in the wake of structural adjustment policies, and the racial barriers migrants encounter explain recent trends toward extending the boundaries of citizenship (Basch, Glick Schiller and Szanton Blanc, 1994; Guarnizo, 2003; Itzigsohn, 2000). The governments of many states, even within Western Europe, see the utility of having access to populations settled elsewhere. Ireland, Greece, Italy and Portugal have recently developed both policies and rhetoric that embrace their communities abroad.

States have developed a range of policies that reflect who they are redefining as their membership. Some states pursue homelands policies that encourage state contact with temporary migrants to facilitate their return. Other states develop global nations' policies that encourage enduring links to permanent settlers abroad to ensure their continued national membership and loyalty rather than their return (Goldring, 2002; Smith, 1998). But not all sending states are the same. They vary with respect to how willing and able they are to encourage transnational activism and how willing they are to give emigrants and their descendants political rights, including the right to vote while living abroad. We suggest the following categorization to capture the variation in possible arenas and types of state responses toward emigrants. States vary with respect to law or the degree to which they extend political rights. They vary with respect to rhetoric or the kind of ideology of nationhood that is promulgated. And they vary with respect to public policy or the kinds of programs and policies that they pursue.

The Extension of Political Rights

The extension of rights is mandated by law. Some states distinguish between two categories of membership – citizenship and nationality. Citizenship delineates the character of a member's rights and duties within the national polity. Nationality legally delineates a category of belonging without granting full citizenship rights.

Sending states have promulgated a range of legal distinctions to delineate categories of citizenship and nationality: 1) the denial of dual citizenship or any form of dual access to rights – countries such as Haiti and Germany allow no dual sets of rights;[3] 2) dual nationality with the granting of some legal privileges to emigrants and their descendants but not full dual citizenship – Mexico and India have taken this position, legally recognizing nationals in some way; 3) dual citizenship in which emigrants and their descendants are accorded full rights, when they return to the homeland, even if they also hold the passport of another country – states as disparate as France, Ireland, Greece, the Dominican Republic, Brazil, Italy, and Portugal follow this policy; and dual citizenship with rights while abroad – people living abroad, from countries such as Colombia, have the right to elect representatives to the home-country legislature.[4]

The expansion of dual nationality or citizenship, in their different forms, means that even persons who are not active participants in transnational politics or even situated in transnational social fields, have access to those memberships if they want to claim them. As an identity strategy, an investment strategy, or even an exit strategy, multiple memberships endow the individual with several potential positions with respect to the state.

Ideology of Nationhood

States like China, Ireland, Portugal, and Haiti propose a national self-concept based on blood ties linking residents around the world to their respective homelands (Glick Schiller, forthcoming). They have redefined their territories to include those living outside them. They may do this, as in the Haitian case, without granting dual citizenship or nationality. For this reason, it is useful to distinguish legal connections from ideologies of long-distance nationalism. Building on Anderson's original concept, Glick Schiller and Fouron (2001a) define long-distance nationalism as a set of ideas about belonging that link together people living in various geographic locations and motivate or justify their taking action in relation to an ances-

---

[3]However, Germany allows dual citizenship for *Ausiedler*, Jews, and persons whose countries do not allow the repudiation of citizenship; and Haiti, without altering citizenship laws, considers its diaspora as a part of the Haitian nation.

[4]The number of countries permitting some form of dual belonging is increasing rapidly. In Latin America alone, ten countries allowed some form of dual nationality or citizenship in 2000 while only four countries had such provisions prior to 1991 (Jones-Correa, 2002). Other countries recognize dual membership selectively, with specific signatories.

tral territory and its government. As in other versions of nationalism, the concept of a territorial homeland governed by a state that represents the nation remains salient, but national borders are not thought to delimit membership in the nation. Citizens residing within the territorial homeland view emigrants and their descendants as part of the nation, whatever legal citizenship the émigrés may have.

These ideologies of nationhood shift over time, at different periods of nation building (Glick Schiller, forthcoming). Globally, before World War I, science endorsed the concept of nation as based on race. In the middle of the twentieth century, when the rhetoric of blood and race was discredited and the populations of nation-states became viewed as only those who lived within national territories, states tended not to make claims on their emigrant populations. Dictators such as Salazar of Portugal or Duvalier of Haiti denounced expatriates, who often organized in opposition to their regimes. Since the 1970s, during the current period of globalization, a language of blood has once again emerged and is deployed by a variety of states. Malaysia uses descent to differentiate populations considered native Malaysians with full citizenship rights from other populations such as persons of Chinese and Indian ancestry (Ong, 1999; Bunnell, 2003). Portugal has reclaimed its emigrant populations, allowing dual citizenship and organizing councils of Portuguese abroad. In promoting its case for entrance into the European Union, Portugal argued it would bring special access to countries like Brazil as well as special relation to Lusophonic populations in Africa (Feldman-Bianco, 2002).

Changing Functions of the State

States adopt some tasks and abandon others in response to transnational migration. In Levitt and de la Dehesa's (2003) review of transnational migration and redefinitions of the state, they found that Latin American governments instituted several different programs and policies toward emigrants. They reformed ministerial and consular services to be more responsive to emigrant needs. They put into place investment policies designed to attract and channel economic remittances. They granted dual citizenship or nationality, the right to vote from abroad, or the right to run for public office. They extended state protections or services to nationals living abroad that went beyond traditional consular services. Finally, they implemented symbolic policies designed to reinforce emigrants' sense of enduring membership.

Sending states institute these policies for a variety of reasons. For one thing, remittances far exceed the funds received for official development assistance or foreign portfolio investment in many less-developed countries (Naim, 2002). According to the Inter-American Development Bank (IDB), "in 2002, remittances to Latin America alone rose by 18 percent to $32 billion from 2001 levels, or 32 percent of the $103 billion worldwide estimated to be remitted to developing countries" (University of California, Davis, 2003). But sending nations' economic motivations to sustain strong ties to migrants go beyond remittances. Immigrants trade with their home countries and bring in large quantities of tourist dollars. Successful entrepreneurs from countries as diverse as India, Israel, China, Brazil, Taiwan, Mexico and Pakistan not only contribute money but entrepreneurial and technological energy and skills. Brain drain can become brain circulation or brain gain (Saxenian, 2002). Finally, states court emigrant loyalties because they see them as a potential political force in the host country that can advance their economic and foreign policy interests (Mahler, 2000; Levitt, 2001a). Some states even promote host-country political integration so that emigrants are better situated to act on their behalf.

States are not the only political actors that define their constituencies transnationally or that carry out activities across borders. Political parties may operate abroad, especially if emigrants have settled in sizeable numbers and with sufficient ties to influence elections in the homeland. Mexican, Dominican, and Haitian politicians campaign in the United States on a regular basis. Each of the three principal Dominican political parties has a U.S.-based organization trying to capture support among Dominicans along the eastern seaboard. In the Turkish case, parties with dominant religious and nationalist agendas, like the nationalist Milli Hareket Partisi or the religious Saadet Partisi, frequently send leaders to northern Europe to rally support (Ostergaard-Nielsen, 2003).

Regions of large countries, such as Brazil or India, may also begin to act as transnational agents, regardless of the national government's stance. This is especially true in situations where the majority of emigrants leave from a few regions or provinces. Substate policies are different from the transnational activities of national governments in that regional governments do not control immigration and formal citizenship and their transnational activities are driven by efforts to promote extraterritorial regional or local loyalties rather than nation-building (Baubock, 2003). In the Brazilian case, the municipal government of Governador Valadares and the state government of Minas Gerais created investment funds and business promotion schemes designed to build on migrants' localized loyalties. The money raised was used to support projects directed at municipal development. Likewise in India, the Gujarat State government has instituted a number of initiatives to encourage long-distance economic projects, including offering tax breaks and bureaucratic support to potential investors, that are separate from any efforts by the national government or political parties to stimulate Non-Resident Indian (NRI) involvement (Levitt, 2002b).

Even units as small as towns may define themselves transnationally and engage in development-oriented activities. In such cases, the actors are usually emigrants living abroad who organize hometown associations. For example, Mexican, Salvadoran, and Dominican hometown associations now fund and implement numerous community development projects that were previously the purview of the state (Goldring, 2002; Landolt, 2001). They assume this role in an age of neoliberalism in which states increasingly eschew roles they were rarely able to fulfill in countries beyond the capitalist core.

Based on their stances towards emigrants with regard to law, rhetoric, and public policy, we identify several broad categories of migrant-sending states.

Some states have become Transnational Nation-States in that they treat their emigrants as long-term, long-distance members. Consular officials and other government representatives are still seen as partially responsible for emigrants' protection and representation. These states also grant emigrants dual citizenship or nationality. Often these are states, or specific regions within them, that have become so dependent on remittances that transnational migrants' contributions and participation have become an integral part of national policy (Guarnizo, Portes and Haller, 2003). States such as El Salvador, Mexico, Portugal, the Dominican Republic, and Brazil fall into this category.

More common are Strategically Selective States that encourage some forms of long-distance economic and political nationalism but want to selectively and strategically manage what immigrants can and cannot do. Like transnational nation-states, these states also recognize the enormous political and economic influence migrants wield, on which they have come to depend. On the one hand, they want to ensure the continued home country involvement of emigrants, whom they recognize are unlikely to return. On the other hand, they want to maintain some level of control over emigrants' home ties, lest migrant interests conflict with those of the state. Such states offer partial and changing packages of tax privileges and services to emigrants, encourage long-distance membership, but never grant the legal rights of citizenship or nationality or the franchise. They walk a fine line between providing enough incentives to reinforce long distance membership while not over-serving migrants and making nonmigrants resentful. India, Barbados, Ireland, the Philippines, Haiti, and Turkey have all tried, at various times, to obtain support from populations abroad without granting full participation in their internal political activities.

These arrangements are by no means static. Diasporic agitation for dual citizenship led the Filipino government to pass legislation in 2003 that allows dual citizenship and restores Filipino citizenship to those people who previously lost their citizenship by becoming citizens of other countries. The Senate President remarked when the Citizenship Retention Bill was signed, "It is our affirmation to the age-old adage that 'once a Filipino, always a Filipino'" (Javellana-Santos, 2003). The same year, India granted persons four generations removed from migration and citizens of specific countries such as the United States and Great Britain dual citizenship (Khanna, 2004).

A third type of state is the Disinterested and Denouncing State. States adopting this stance treat migrants as if they no longer belong to their homeland. Any overtures migrants make vis a vis their ancestral home are viewed as suspect because migrants are seen as having abandoned the homeland or even as traitors to its cause. This stance was more common prior to the current period of globalization. Even today, however, when governments face vocal and powerful political opposition abroad, they may try to discredit emigrants' influence. Cuba's relationship to Cubans in the United States provides one such example that is particularly interesting since remittances factor so importantly in Cuba's economic life (Cervantes-Rodríguez, 2003; Eckstein and Barberia, 2002). Slovakia kept populations abroad at arm's-length following the Cold War, allowing them no representation within the new political system (Skrbi, 1999).

MEMBERSHIP AND CITIZENSHIP

Understanding migration from a transnational social field perspective also entails revisiting the meaning of nation-state membership (Yuval-Davis, 1997; Delgado and Stefanicic, 2003). While states grant membership through laws that accord legal citizenship and nationality, people also make demands of states regardless of their legal status. Therefore, persons without full citizenship may act as substantive or social citizens, claiming rights or assuming privileges that are, in principle, accorded to citizens (Flores and Benmayor, 2000). This is the case when immigrants without citizenship fight and die as members of a host country's military, protest in the streets about public policies, and access various social programs and services without being citizens. Individuals connected through social networks to a transnational social field make claims, take actions, and may even see themselves as members of a country in which they have not lived.

Substantive citizenship as exercised within transnational social fields differs from findings of proponents of post-national citizenship (Soysal, 1994). These scholars put aside the domain of nation-states and look to global rights regimes to protect and represent individuals living outside their homelands. Persons in transnational social fields who are refugees or religious or racial minorities may draw on plural legal systems in their quest for rights. But the international rights regime, as has often been noted, is still very much dependent on individual states for enforcement (Foblets, 2002; Woodman, 2002)

Persons living within transnational social fields may not make claims on states as legal or substantive citizens until a particular event or crisis occurs. They may engage in lobbying, demonstrating, organizing or campaigns of public information to influence either the government of the state in which they now reside, their homeland, or some other state to which they are connected. Simply focusing on legal rights and formal membership overlooks this broader set of people who, to varying degrees, act like members of a society while not formally belonging to it. By so doing, they influence and are influenced by the state. Glick Schiller and Fouron (2001a) propose the term "transborder citizens" to reflect those who may or may not be citizens of both their sending and receiving polities but who express some level of social citizenship in one or both.

Partial membership in two polities challenges core aspects of governance in at least two ways. First, dual belonging calls into question the very notion of governance because it is not readily obvious which state is ultimately responsible for which aspects of transnational migrants' lives. Where should those who live across borders get health care, pay taxes, or serve in the army? Which state assumes the primary responsibility for migrants' protection and representation? What happens when migrants are sentenced to the death penalty in their host country while the death sentence is prohibited in their country of origin?

Furthermore, transborder citizens' multiple experiences of governmentality and political socialization do not occur in isolation from one another. Persons in transnational social fields are exposed to different ideas of citizen rights and responsibilities and different histories of political practice. As a result, they enter the political domain with a broader repertoire of rights and responsibilities than citizens who live only within one state. The fact that migrants may also have direct experience with international rights regimes provides them with grist to reconceptualize their relationship to the state (Pessar, 2001; Levitt and Wagner, 2003). Migrants bring ideas about governance with them that transform host-country politics, they reformulate their ideas and practices in response to their experiences with host states, and they communicate these social remittances back to those in their homelands or members of their networks settled in other states. The kind of political culture that emerges and the kinds of claims made of states vary as a result. Haitian migrants, for example, infused the U.S. political system with calls for a Haitian government that was more responsible to its people (Glick Schiller and Fouron, 2001a). Shared experiences of democratic incorporation in the receiving state may feed back into transnational activities that lead to more transparent politics at home (Shain, 1999).

RELIGION: FIELDS OF BEING AND BELONGING WITHIN AND BEYOND THE STATE

While most scholars acknowledge the salience of migrants' transnational economic, political, and sociocultural practices, they have only recently begun to pay attention to the relationship between transnational migration and religion. In contrast to the other sections of this article, where we focus on the implications of research findings to date, our goal in this section is to summarize the emergent literature on religion and suggest directions for further work.

Religion as an ideology or as a set of practices is not coincident with the borders of nation-states. Its very lack of fit might partially explain why social scientists have largely ignored religion. Grand sociological theory in its various unilinear forms posited an evolution of society from religion to reason. Immigration theorists expected immigrants to develop religious institutions in the new land as part of the process of incorporation, but these institutions were expected to lose their force over several generations.

Religious cross-border connections are not all linked to migration; however, migrating populations may identify as religious diasporas rather than cling to a nation-state identity or use religious arenas to express membership in two polities. Conceptualizing society as intersecting transnational social fields that exist within and across the borders of states provides us with powerful tools for mapping and researching religious domains. Perhaps the

most productive distinction to be made is between religious ties that connect
people to a homeland state and religious ties that form transnational networks of connections that are not state based, such as charismatic Christianity. A fairly large body of work charts the course of Christian, Hindu,
and Muslim beliefs and institutions that cross national borders and link
various populations (Beyer, 2001; Robertson, 1991; Vertovec and Peach,
1997). Global religious institutions shape migrants' transnational experiences, while migrants chip away at and recreate global religions by making
them local. Migrant institutions are also sites where globally diffused models
of social organization and individuals' local responses converge and produce
new mixes of religious beliefs and practices. The study of transnational
migration and religion, therefore, provides an empirical window into ways of
being and belonging that cannot be encompassed by a nation-state (Levitt,
2003a). At the same time, these practices and ideas can be mobilized for
specific state projects by transnational migrant populations, as in the case of
support for Hindu nationalist politics on the part of Indian migrants who are
fully incorporated into the United States.

Research on transnational migrants' religious practices has addressed a
set of common themes and questions. Some of these studies are concerned
with the kinds of religious institutional connections produced by transnational migration (Ebaugh and Chafetz, 2002; Yang, 2002; Levitt, 2004).
Other studies ask how religion encourages or impedes transnational membership (Wellmeier, 1998; Menjívar, 1999; Peterson and Vásquez, 2001;
Kastoryano, 2000). A third set of questions focuses on the relationship
between religion and politics and how it changes when actors are engaged
transnationally. Such questions touch on ways of belonging, whether to two
or more states or to a transborder religious community, asking whether
access to the power of God or Gods is a way of gaining protection from the
power of states (Peterson and Vásquez, 2001; Menjívar, 2002). Migrants
denied citizenship and excluded from mainstream economic institutions
often look to their religious communities as sites for establishing alternative
identities (Guest, 2002). Transnational migrants often use religion to create
alternative geographies that may fall within national boundaries, transcend
but coexist with them, or create new spaces that, for some individuals, are
more meaningful and inspire stronger loyalties than politically-defined terrains (Levitt, 2003a). By doing so, they extend the boundaries of their
spiritual practices and superinscribe them onto the actual physical landscape
where they settle (McAlister, 2002). By building and conducting rituals at a
shrine to their national patron saint, Cuban exiles in Miami created what

Tweed (1999) calls transtemporal and translocative space. The rituals enacted within it enable migrants to recover a past when they lived in Cuba and to imagine a future when they will return.

EXPANDING THE CONVERSATION

Clearly, migration is only one of a range of social processes that transcends national boundaries. Numerous social movements, businesses, media, epistemic communities, and various forms of governance are also organized across boundaries. Persons living in transnational social fields can engage in multiple transnational processes at the same time. The transnational identities and institutions that emerge in response to these other processes are not well understood. Although they are the subject of an increasing body of scholarship, more often than not this research treats transnational economic, political, and social processes as if they were not connected to each other. We must explore how transnational practices and processes in different domains relate to and inform one another to understand how these developments are defining the boundaries of social life.

Migration scholars can begin this conversation by systematically examining the forms and consequences of different kinds of transnational activities and collectivities, analyzing how they relate to one another, and exploring how they define and redefine our world (Khagram and Levitt, 2004). How do migrant cross-border activities compare to those engaged in by indigenous rights proponents and religious group members? How do organizing strategies, diffusion of ideas, and cultural negotiations compare in transnational social movements to those undertaken in transnational professional groups or production networks? In what ways do these different kinds of transnational memberships complement or subvert one another? What are the rights and responsibilities that actors and institutions associate with transnational belonging?

New methodological and conceptual tools are needed to understand these processes. Because the social sciences originated in the nineteenth and twentieth centuries as part of the project of creating modern nation-states, terms like government, organization, and citizenship carry with them embedded nationalist assumptions that impair our capacity to see and understand transnational processes. Our conceptual categories implicitly take as given that the nation-state is the natural default category of social organization. The best that social science generally does is compare corporations, migrants, or institutions across national contexts rather than focus on firms and markets as parts of transnational fields of investment, production, distribution, and exchange. Persons can engage simultaneously in more than one nation-state and a nation-state does not delimit the boundaries of meaningful social relations. We need new analytical lenses that can bring to light the myriad social processes that cross boundaries. We need new conceptual categories that no longer blind us to these emergent social forms or prevent us from reconceptualizing the boundaries of social life.

REFERENCES

Abelman, N.
2002 "Mobilizing Korean Family Ties: Cultural Conversations across the Border." Working Paper, Transnational Communities Programme, WPTC – 0–11.

Ballard, R.
2000 "The South Asian Presence in Britain and Its Transnational Connections." Paper presented at the International Workshop on Transnational Research, sponsored by the Social Science Research Council and the Economic and Social Research Council (U.K.), Oxford University.

Basch, L., N. Glick Schiller and C. Szanton Blanc, eds.
1994 *Nations Unbound: Transnational Projects, Postcolonial Predicaments, and Deterritorialized Nation-States.* Langhorne, PA: Gordon and Breach.

Baubock, R.
2003 "Towards a Political Economy of Migrant Transnationalism," *International Migration Review,* 37(3):700–723.

Beck, U.
2000 "The Cosmopolitan Perspective: Sociology in the Second Age of Modernity," *British Journal of Sociology,* 5(1):79–107.

Beyer, P.
2001 "Introduction." In *Religion in the Process of Globalization.* Ed. P. Beyer. Wurzburg, Germany: Ergon Verlag. Pp. I–XLIV.

Bryceson, D. F. and U. Vuorela
2002 *The Transnational Family: New European Frontiers and Global Networks.* Oxford and New York: Berg.

Bunnell, T.
2003 "Repositioning Malaysia: High-tech Networks and the Multicultural Rescripting of National Identity," *Political Geography,* 21:105–124.

Caglar, A.
1995 "German Turks in Berlin: Social Exclusion and Strategies for Social Mobility," *New Community,* 21(3):309–323.

Castells, M.
1996 *The Rise of Network Society.* Cambridge, MA: Blackwell.

Castles, S.
1998 "New Migrations, Ethnicity, and Nationalism in Southeast and East Asia." Paper delivered to the Transnational Communities Programme Seminar Series at Oxford University. June 12.

Cervantes-Rodríguez, M.
2003 "Exile, Identities, and Cuba's Nation-building Project a Century Later." Unpublished paper.

Chamberlin, M.
2002 "Language, Identity and Caribbean Families: Transnational Perspectives." Paper presented at the Conference Caribbean Migration in Metropolitan Countries: Identity, Citizenship and Models of Integration, Maison de Sciences de l'Homme, Paris.

Delgado, R. and J. Stefanicic, eds.
2003 Critical Race Theory: The Cutting Edge. Second Edition. Philadelphia: Temple University Press.

Duany, J.
2000 "Nation on the Move: The Construction of Cultural Identities in Puerto Rico and the Diaspora," American Ethnologist, 27(1):5–30.

Ebaugh, H. R. and J. Chafetz
2002 Religion across Borders: Transnational Religious Networks. Walnut Creek, CA: Altamira Press.

Eckstein, S.
2002 "On Deconstructing and Reconstructing the Meaning of Immigrant Generations." In The Changing Face of Home: The Transnational Lives of the Second Generation. Ed. P. Levitt and M. Waters. New York: Russell Sage Publications. Pp. 367–399.

Eckstein, S. and L. Barberia
2002 "Grounding Immigrant Generations in History: Cuban Americans and Their Transnational Ties," International Migration Review, 36(3):799–838.

Espiritu, Y.
1997 Asian Women and Men: Labor, Laws, and Love. Thousand Oaks, CA: Sage.

Espiritu, Y. and T. Tran
2002 "Viet Nam, Nuoc Toi (Vietnam, My Country): Vietnamese Americans and Transnationalism." In The Changing Face of Home: The Transnational Lives of the Second Generation. Ed. P. Levitt and M. Waters. New York: Russell Sage Publication. Pp. 367–399.

Faist, T.
2000a The Volume and Dynamics of International Migration. New York: Oxford University Press.

2000b "Transnationalization in International Migration: Implications for the Study of Citizenship and Culture," Ethnic and Racial Studies, 23(2):189–222.

Feldman-Bianco, B.
2002 "Brazilians in Portugal, Portuguese in Brazil: Constructions of Sameness and Difference." In Colonial Continuities: The Portuguese Experience. Special Issue Identities: Global Studies in Culture and Power, 8(4).

Fitzgerald, D.
2003 "Beyond 'Transnationalism': Mexican Hometown Politics at an American Labor Union," Ethnic and Racial Studies, 27(2):228–247.

Flores, W. V. and R. Benmayor, eds.
2000 Latino Cultural Citizenship: Claiming Identity, Space, and Rights. Tempe, AZ: Bilingual Review Press.

Foblets, M. C.
2002 "Muslims, a New Transnational Minority in Europe? Cultural Pluralism, Fundamental Liberties and Inconsistencies in the Law." Paper delivered at the conference *Mobile People, Mobile Law: Expanding Legal Relations in a Contracting World.* Max Planck Institute for Social Anthropology, Halle, Germany. November 7–9.

Foner, N.
2000 *From Ellis Island to JFK: New York's Two Great Waves of Immigration.* New Haven: Yale University Press.

Foucault, M.
1980 *Power/Knowledge: Selected Interviews and Other Writings, 1972–1977.* New York: Pantheon.

Gabaccia, D. and F. Iacovetta, eds.
2002 *Women, Gender, and Transnational Lives: Italian Workers of the World.* Toronto: University of Toronto Press.

Glazer, N.
1954 "Ethnic Groups in America: From National Culture to Ideology." In *Freedom and Control in Modern Society.* Ed. M. Berger, T. Abel and C. Page. New York: Van Nostrand.

Glick Schiller, N.
Forthcoming "Transborder Citizenship: Legal Pluralism within a Transnational Social Field." In *Mobile People, Mobile Law: Expanding Legal Relations in a Contracting World.* Ed. F. Bender Beckman and K. Bender Beckman. London: Ashgate.

——— Forthcoming "Long Distance Nationalism." In *Encyclopedia of Diasporas: Immigrant and Refugee Cultures Around the World.* Vol. 10. Ed. M. Ember, C. R. Ember and I. Skoggard. New York: Kluwer Academic/Plenum Publishers.

——— Forthcoming "Blood and Belonging: Long-Distance Nationalism and the World Beyond." In *Complexities: Beyond Nature and Nurture.* Ed. S. McKinnon and S. Silverman. Chicago: University of Chicago Press.

——— 2004 "Transnational Theory and Beyond." In *A Companion to the Anthropology of Politics.* Ed. D. Nugent and J. Vincent. Malden, MA: Blackwell.

——— 2003 "The Centrality of Ethnography in the Study of Transnational Migration: Seeing the Wetland Instead of the Swamp." In *American Arrivals.* Ed. N. Foner. Santa Fe, NM: School of American Research.

——— 2003 "Transmigrants and Nation-States: Something Old and Something New in the U.S. Immigrant Experience." In *The Handbook of International Migration.* Ed. C. Hirshman, P. Kasinitz and J. DeWind. New York: The Russell Sage Foundation.

Glick Schiller, N., L. Basch and C. Blanc-Szanton
1995 "From Immigrant to Transmigrant: Theorizing Transnational Migration," *Anthropology Quarterly,* 68(1):48–63.

Glick Schiller, N., A. Calgar, and E. Karagiannis
2003 "Simultaneous Incorporation of Migrants." Paper delivered at the Max Planck Institute of Social Anthropology, Halle, Germany. July 17, 2003.

Glick Schiller, N. and G. Fouron
2003 "Killing Me Softly: Violence, Globalization, and the Apparent State." In *Globalization, the State and Violence.* Ed. J. Friedman. Oxford: Altamira.

——— 2002 "The Generation of Identity: Redefining the Second Generation within a Transnational Social Field." In *The Changing Face of Home: The Transnational Lives of the Second Generation.* Ed. P. Levitt and M. Waters. New York: Russell Sage Publications.

——— 2001a *Georges Woke Up Laughing: Long Distance Nationalism and the Search for Home.* Durham, NC: Duke University Press.

——— 2001b "I am Not a Problem without a Solution: Poverty, Transnational Migration, and Struggle." In *New Poverty Studies: The Ethnography of Politics, Policy and Impoverished People in the U.S.* Ed. J. Good and J. Maskovsky. New York: New York University Press.

——— 1999 "Terrains of Blood and Nation: Haitian Transnational Social Fields," *Ethnic and Racial Studies,* 22(2):340–366.

Gold, S.
2002 *The Israeli Diaspora.* Seattle: University of Washington Press.

Goldring, L.
2003 "Gender Status and the State in Transnational Spaces: The Gendering of Political Participation in Mexican Hometown Associations." In *Gender and U.S. Immigration.* Ed. P. Hondagneu-Sotelo. Berkeley: University of California Press.

——— 2002 "The Mexican State and Transmigrant Organizations: Negotiating the Boundaries of Membership and Participation," *Latin American Research Review,* 37(3):55–99.

Gomez, E. T. and G. Benton
2002 "Transnationalism and the Essentializing of Capitalism: Chinese Enterprise, the State, and Identity in Britain, Australia, and Southeast Asia." Paper delivered at Transnational Communities Final Conference, Keeble College, Oxford. July 2.

Grasmuck, S. and P. Pessar
1991 *Between Two Islands: Dominican International Migration.* Berkeley: University of California Press.

Guarnizo, L. E.
2003 "The Economics of Transnational Living," *International Migration Review,* 37(3):666–699.

——— 1997 "The Emergence of a Transnational Social Formation and the Mirage of Return Migration among Dominican Transmigrants," *Identities: Global Studies in Culture and Power,* 4(2):281–322.

Guarnizo, L. E., A. Portes and W. Haller
2003 "Assimilation and Transnationalism: Determinants of Transnational Political Action among Contemporary Migrants," *American Journal of Sociology,* 108(6):121–148.

Guest, K.
2002 "Transnational Religious Networks among New York's Fuzhou Immigrants." In *Re-*

ligion across Borders. Ed. H. R. Ebaugh and J. Chafetz. Walnut Creek: Altamira Press. Pp. 149–165.

Harvey, D.

1989 *The Condition of Postmodernity: An Enquiry into the Conditions of Cultural Change.* Oxford: Oxford University Press.

Held, D., A. McGrew, D. Goldblatt and J. Perraton

1999 *Global Transformations.* Cambridge: Polity.

Hondagneu-Sotelo, P. and E. Avila

2003 "I'm Here but I'm There: The Meaning of Latina Transnational Motherhood." In *Gender and U.S. Immigration.* Ed. P. Hondagneu-Sotelo. Berkeley: University of California Press.

Hooghiemstra, E.

2001 "Migrants, Partner Selection, and Integration: Crossing Borders?" *Journal of Comparative Family Studies,* 32(4):601–628.

Itzigsohn, J.

2000 Immigration and the Boundaries of Citizenship: The Institutions of Immigrants' Political Transnationalism, *International Migration Review,* 34(4):1126–1155.

Itzigsohn, J., C. Dore Cabral, E. Hernández Medina and O. Vázquez

1999 "Mapping Dominican Transnationalism: Narrow and Broad Transnational Practices," *Ethnic and Racial Studies,* 22(2):217–237.

Itzigsohn, J. and S. Giorguli Saucedo

2002 "Immigrant Incorporation and Sociocultural Transnationalism," *International Migration Review,* 36(3):766–799.

Javellana-Santos, J.

2003 "Citizenship Retention Act signed into Law," *Philippine News Online.* Accessed at: <http://www.philippinenews.com/news/view article.html?article id+70769de28b7244b86a587d6490538b>.

Jenkins, R.

1992 *Pierre Bourdieu.* London: Routledge.

Jones-Correa, M.

2002 "Under Two Flags: Dual Nationality in Latin America and Its Consequences for the United States," *International Migration Review,* 35(4):34–67.

Kandel, W. and D. Massey

2002 "The Culture of Mexican Migration: A Theoretical and Empirical Analysis," *Social Forces,* 80(3):981–1004.

Kasinitz, P., M. C. Waters, J. H. Mollenkopf and M. Anil

2002 "Transnationalism and the Children of Immigrants in Contemporary New York." In *The Changing Face of Home: The Transnational Lives of the Second Generation.* Ed. P. Levitt and M. Waters. New York: Russell Sage Publication. Pp. 96–122.

Kastoryano, R.

2000 "Settlement, Transnational Communities, and Citizenship," *ISSJ,* 165:307–312.

Khagram, S. and P. Levitt

2004 "Conceptualizing Transnational Studies." Hauser Center Working Paper No. 24. Harvard University.

Khanna, R.

2004 "Indian Parliament Approves Dual Citizenship." Accessed at: <http://www.immigration.com/newsletter1/dualpio.html>.

Kivisto, P.
2001 "Theorizing Transnational Immigration: A Critical Review of Current Efforts," *Ethnic and Racial Studies*, 24(4):549–578.

Koopmans, R. and P. Statham
2001 "How National Citizenship Shapes Transnationalism: A Comparative Analysis of Migrant Claims-making in Germany, Great Britain, and the Netherlands." Working Paper Transnational Communities Programme, WPTC-01–10.

Kyle, D.
2001 *Transnational Peasants*. Baltimore: Johns Hopkins University Press.

Laguerre, M.
1998 *Diasporic Citizenship*. New York: St. Martin's Press.

Lamont, M.
2002 "Ordinary Cosmopolitans: Strategies for Bridging Boundaries among Non-College Educated Workers." Working Paper Transnational Communities Programme, WPTC-2k-03.

Landolt, P.
2001 "Salvadoran Economic Transnationalism: Embedded Strategies for Household Maintenance, Immigrant Incorporation, and Entrepreneurial Expansion," *Global Networks*, 1:217–242.

Laslett, B. and J. Brenner
1992 "Feminism and the Family: Two Decades of Thought." In *Rethinking the Family: Some Feminist Questions*. Ed. B. Thorne and M. Yalom. Boston: Northeastern University Press. Pp. 3–30.

Lesthaeghe, R.
2002 Turks and Moroccans in Belgium: A Comparison. Seminar presented at the Center for Population and Development Studies, Harvard University.

Lessinger, J.
1995 *From the Ganges to the Hudson*. New York: Allyn and Bacon.

Levitt, P.
2004 "Redefining the Boundaries of Belonging: The Institutional Character of Transnational Religious Life," *Sociology of Religion*, 35(1):174–196.

2003a " 'You Know, Abraham Really Was the First Immigrant': Religion and Transnational Migration," *International Migration Review*, 37(3):847–873.

2003b "Keeping Feet in Both Worlds: Transnational Practices and Immigrant Incorporation." In *Integrating Immigrants in Liberal Nation-States: From Post-Nationals to Transnational*. Ed. C. Joppke and E. Morawska. London: Macmillan-Palgrave.

2002a "The Ties that Change: Relations to the Ancestral Home over the Life Cycle." In *The Changing Face of Home: The Transnational Lives of the Second Generation*. Ed. P. Levitt and M. Waters. New York: Russell Sage Publication. Pp. 123–144.

2002b "Why Should I Retire to Florida When I Can Go To Lahore?: Defining and Explaining Variations in Transnational Migration." Paper presented at the Emerging Architectures of Transnational Governance Conference, Harvard University. December 2002.

2001a *The Transnational Villagers*. Berkeley and Los Angeles: University of California Press.

2001b "Transnational Migration: Taking Stock and Future Directions," *Global Networks*, 1(3):195–216.

1999 "Social Remittances: A Local-Level, Migration-Driven Form of Cultural Diffusion," *International Migration Review*, 32(4):926–949.

Levitt, P. and R. de la Dehesa
2002 "Transnational Migration and a Redefinition of the State: Variations and Explanations," *Ethnic and Racial Studies*, 26(4):587–611.

Levitt, P. and S. Wagner
2003 "Refugee Rights and Wrongs: Global Cultural Diffusion among the Congolese in South Africa." Working Paper #23, Inter-University Committee on International Migration Rosemarie Rogers Working Paper Series. September.

Levitt, P. and M. Waters
2002 *The Changing Face of Home: The Transnational Lives of the Second Generation*. New York: Russell Sage Publications.

Mahler, S.
2000 "Constructing International Relations: The Role of Transnational Migrants and Other Non-State Actors," *Identities: Global Studies in Culture and Power*, 7:197–232.

1998 "Theoretical and Empirical Contributions toward a Research Agenda for Transnationalism." In *Transnationalism from Below: Comparative Urban and Community Research. Vol. 6.* Ed. M. P. Smith and L. Guarnizo. New Brunswick and London: Transaction Publishers.

Mannheim, K.
1952 "The Problem of Generations." In *Essays on the Sociology of Knowledge*. Ed. P. Kecksckemeti. New York: Oxford University Press.

Marshall, T. H.
1964 *Class, Citizenship, and Social Class: Essays by T. H. Marshall*. Garden City, NY: Doubleday and Co.

Martins, H.
1974 "Time and Theory in Sociology." In *Approaches to Sociology: An Introduction to the Major Trends in Sociology*. Ed. J. Rex. London and Boston: Routledge and Kegan Paul. Pp. 246–294.

McAlister, E.
2002 *Rara! Vadou, Power, and Performance in Haiti and its Diaspora*. Los Angeles and Berkeley: University of California Press.

Menjívar, C.
2002 "Living in Two Worlds? Guatemalan-Origin Children in the United States and Emerging Transnationalism," *Journal of Ethnic and Migration Studies*, 28(3):531–552.

1999 Religious Institutions and Transnationalism: A Case Study of Catholic and Evangelical

Salvadoran Immigrants," *International Journal of Politics, Culture, and Society,* 12(4): 589–611.

Morawska, E.

2003a "Disciplinary Agendas and Analytic Strategies of Research on Immigration and Transnationalism: Challenges of Interdisciplinary Knowledge," *International Migration Review,* 37(3):611–640.

2003b "Immigrant Transnationalism and Assimilation: A Variety of Combinations and the Analytic Strategy It Suggest." In *Toward Assimilation and Citizenship: Immigrants in Liberal Nation-States.* Ed. C. Joppke and E. Morawska. Hampshire, UK: Palgrave Macmillan. Pp. 133–176.

2001a "Structuring Migration: The Case of Polish Income-Seeking Travelers to the West," *Theory and Society,* 3:47–80.

1989 "Labor Migrations of Poles in the Atlantic World Economy, 1880–1914," *Comparative Study of Society and History,* 31(2):237–270.

1987 "Sociological Ambivalence: The Case of Eastern European Peasant-Immigrant Workers in America, 1880s-1930s," *Qualitative Sociology,* 10(3):225–250.

Morgan, G.

1999 "Transnational Communities and Business Systems." WPTC–99–14.

Naim, M.

2002 "The New Diaspora: New Links between Èmigrés and Their Home Countries Can Become a Powerful Force for Economic Development," *Foreign Policy,* 131:96–99.

Nyberg Sorenson, N. and K. Fog Olwig, eds.

2002 *Work and Migration: Life and Livelihoods in a Globalizing World (Transnationalism).* London: Routledge.

Ong, A.

1999 *Flexible Citizenship: The Cultural Logics of Transnationality.* Durham, NC: Duke University Press.

Orellana, M. F., B. Thorne, A. Chee and W. S. E. Lam

2001 "Transnational Childhoods: The Participation of Children in Processes of Family Migration," *Social Problems,* 48(4):572–592.

Østergaard-Nielsen, E.

2003 "The Politics of Migrants' Transnational Political Practices," *International Migration Review,* 37(3):760–786.

Parrenas, R. S.

2001 "Mothering From a Distance: Emotions, Gender, and Intergenerational Relations in Filipino Transnational Families," *Feminist Studies,* 27(2):361–391.

Pessar, P.

2003 "Anthropology and the Engendering of Migration Studies." In *American Arrivals: Anthropology Engages the New Immigrants.* Ed. N. Foner, Sante Fe, NM: School of American Research.

2001 "Women's Political Consciousness and Empowerment in Local, National, and Transnational Contexts: Guatemalan Refugees and Returnees." In *Gendering Transnational Spaces*. Ed. S. Mahler and P. Pessar. Special Issue. *Identities: Global Studies in Culture and Power*, 7(4):461–500.

Pessar, P. and S. Mahler

2003 "Transnational Migration: Bringing Gender In," *International Migration Review*, 37(3):812–843.

———

2001 "Gendered Geographies of Power: Analyzing Gender across Transnational Spaces." In *Gendering Transnational Spaces*. Ed. S. Mahler and P. Pessar. Special Issue. *Identities: Global Studies in Culture and Power*, 7(4):441–460.

Peterson, A. L. and M. Vásquez

2001 "Upwards: Never Down: The Catholic Charismatic Renewal in Transnational Perspective." In *Christianity, Social Change, and Globalization in the Americas*. Ed. A. Peterson, P. Williams and M. Vásquez. New Brunswick, NJ: Rutgers University Press.

Portes, A.

2003 "Conclusion: Theoretical Convergencies and Empirical Evidence in the Study of Immigrant Transnationalism," *International Migration Review*, 37(3):874–892.

Portes, A., L. Guarnizo and P. Landolt

1999 "Introduction: Pitfalls and Promise of an Emergent Research Field," *Ethnic and Racial Studies*, 22:463–478.

Portes, A., W. Haller and L. Guarnizo

2002 "Transnational Entrepreneurs: The Emergence and Determinants of an Alternative Form of Immigrant Economic Adaptation," *American Sociological Review*, (67):278–298.

Riccio, B.

2001 "Disaggregating the Transnational Community: Senegalese Migrants on the Coast of Emilia-Romagna." Working Paper, Transnational Communities Programme, WPTC-01-11.

Robertson, R.

1991 "The Globalization Paradigm: Thinking Globally." In *New Developments in Theory and Research: Religion and the Social Order Volume I*. Ed. D. G. Bromley. Greenwich, CT: JAI Press. Pp. 204–224.

Rouse, R.

1992 "Making Sense of Settlement: Class Transformation, Cultural Struggle, and Transnationalism among Mexican Migrants in the United States." In *Towards a Transnational Perspective on Migration: Race, Class Ethnicity and Nationalism Reconsidered*. Ed. N. G. Glick Schiller, L. Basch and C. Blanc Szanton. New York: New York Academy of Sciences.

Rumbaut, R.

2002 "Severed or Sustained Attachments? Language, Identity, and Imagined Communities in the Post-Immigrant Generation." In *The Changing Face of Home: The Transnational Lives of the Second Generation*. Ed. P. Levitt and M. Waters. New York: Russell Sage Publication. Pp. 43–95.

Sassen, S.

1992 *Global Cities*. Princeton, NJ: Princeton University Press.

Saxenian, A. L.

2002 "Local and Global Networks of Immigrant Professionals in Silicon Valley." Public Policy Institute of California.

Schiffauer, W.
1999 "Islamism in the Diaspora: The Fascination of Political Islam among Second Generation German Turks." Working Paper Transnational Communities Programme,
WPTC 99–06.

Shain, Y.
1999 *Exporting the American Creed Abroad.* New York: Oxford University Press.

Sklair, L.
1998 "Transnational Practices and the Analysis of the Global System." Paper delivered at the
Transnational Communities Programme Seminar Series. May.

Skrbis, Z.
1999 *Long Distance Nationalism: Diasporas, Homelands and Identities.* Aldershot, England:
Ashgate.

Smith, A. D.
1983 "Nationalism and Social Theory," *British Journal of Sociology,* 34(1):19–38.

Smith, M. P. and L. Guarnizo, eds.
1998 *Transnationalism from below: Comparative Urban and Community Research. Volume 6.*
New Brunswick and London: Transaction Publishers.

Smith, R.
1998 "Transnational Localities: Community, Technology, and the Politics of Membership
with the Context of Mexico-U.S. Migration." In *Transnationalism from Below: Comparative Urban and Community Research, Volume 6.* Ed. M. P. Smith and L. Guarnizo.
New Brunswick: Rutgers University Press.

Smith, R. C.
2003 "Diasporic Memberships in Historical Perspective: Comparative Insights from the
Mexican, Italian and Polish Cases," *International Migration Review,* 37(3):724–759.

2002 "Life Course, Generation and Social Location as Factors Shaping Second-Generation
Transnational Life." In *The Changing Face of Home: The Transnational Lives of the
Second Generation.* Ed. P. Levitt and M. Waters. New York: Russell Sage Publication.
Pp. 145–168.

Soysal, Y.
1994 *Limits of Citizenship: Migrants and Postnational Membership Europe.* Chicago and
London: University of Chicago Press.

Stichweh, P.
2000 "Systems Theory as an Alternative to Action Theory? The Rise of 'Communication' as
a Theoretical Option," *Acta Sociologica,* 43:(1):5–14.

Tweed, T.
1999 *Our Lady of Exile.* New York: Oxford University Press. University of California.

University of California, Davis
2003 Latin America, Remittances, *Migration News,* 10(2), Accessed at <http://
migration.ucdavis.edu/mn/more entireissue.php?idate=2003 04& number=2>.

Urry, J.
2000 "The Global Media and Cosmopolitanism." Paper presented at Transnational America
Conference, Bavarian American Academy, Munich, June 2000, published by the
Department of Sociology, Lancaster University at <http://www.comp.lancs.ac.uk/
sociology/soc056ju.html>.

Van der Veer, P.
2001 "Transnational Religion." Working Paper Transnational Communities Programme, WPTC-01-08.

Vertovec, S.
2003 "Migration and Other Modes of Transnationalism: Towards Conceptual Cross-Fertilization," *International Migration Review*, 37(3):641–665.

Vertovec, S. and C. Peach
1997 *Islam in Europe: The Politics of Religion and Community*. London: Macmillan Press, Ltd.

Waters, M. C.
1999 *Black Identities: West Indian Immigrant Dreams and American Realities*. New York and Cambridge, MA: Russell Sage Foundation.

Weber, D.
1999 "Historical Perspectives on Mexican Transnationalism: With Notes from Angumacutiro," *Social Justice*, 26(3):1043–1578.

Wellmeier, N. J.
1998 "Santa Eulalia's People in Exile: Maya Religion, Culture, and Identity in Los Angeles." In *Gatherings in Diaspora: Religious Communities and the New Immigration*. Ed. R. S. Warner and J. Wittner. Philadelphia: Temple University Press. Pp. 97–123.

Wimmer, A. and N. Glick Schiller
2003 "Methodological Nationalism, the Social Sciences and the Study of Migration: An Essay in Historical Epistemology," *International Migration Review*, 37(3):576–610.

Woodman, G. R.
2002 "Customary Laws of Ethnic Minorities in the U.K." Paper delivered at the conference *Mobile People, Mobile Law: Expanding Legal Relations in a Contracting World*. Max Planck Institute for Social Anthropology, Halle, Germany. November 7–9.

Yang, F.
2002 "Chinese Christian Transnationalism: Diverse Networks of a Houston Church." In *Religions across Borders: Transnational Religious Networks*. Ed. H. R. Ebaugh and J. Chafetz. Lanham, MD: Altamira Press. Pp. 175–204.

Yuval-Davis, N.
1997 *Gender and Nation*. London and Thousand Oaks: Sage Publications.

Zhou, M.
1998 "Parachute Kids in Southern California: The Educational Experience of Chinese Children in Transnational Families," *Educational Policy*, 12(6):682–704.

Chapter 8

Revisiting Ethnic Entrepreneurship[1]
Convergencies, Controversies, and Conceptual Advancements

Min Zhou

Ethnic entrepreneurship as a social phenomenon has long fascinated many social scientists and stimulated considerable research and debate. Ethnic entrepreneurs are often referred to as simultaneously owners and managers (or operators) of their own businesses, whose group membership is tied to a common cultural heritage or origin and is known to out-group members as having such traits; more importantly, they are intrinsically intertwined in particular social structures in which individual behavior, social relations, and economic transactions are constrained (Yinger, 1985; Aldrich and Waldinger, 1990).

[1]An earlier version of this article was presented at the session "The Continuing Debate on Immigrant Entrepreneurship and Ethnic Enclaves" of the Conference on Conceptual and Methodological Development in the Study of International Migration, Center for Migration and Development, Princeton University, May 23–25, 2003. I thank Nancy Foner, Riva Kastoryano, and Alejandro Portes for their insightful comments and Chiaki Inutake and Angela Sung for their research assistance.

In the layman's eye, however, ethnic entrepreneurs often carry images of petty traders, merchants, dealers, shopkeepers, or even peddlers and hucksters, who engage in such industries or businesses as restaurants, sweatshops, laundries, greengrocers, liquor stores, nail salons, newsstands, swap meets, taxicabs, and so on. Indeed, few would regard Computer Associates International (a large public firm specializing in computer technology based in New York) and Watson Pharmaceuticals (a large public firm based in Los Angeles) as ethnic businesses and their founders, Charles B. Wang, an immigrant from China, and Allen Chao, an immigrant from Taiwan, as ethnic entrepreneurs. These immigrant or ethnic group members appear to have successfully shed their ethnic distinctiveness and have incorporated their businesses into the core of the mainstream economy.

It is generally known that certain groups of immigrant and ethnic minorities are more entrepreneurial and more likely than others to adopt small business ownership as one of the most effective strategies in their quest for socioeconomic mobility (Glazer and Moynihan, 1963). In the past thirty years, many concepts and theories on ethnic entrepreneurship have been developed, challenged, and revised to provide a fuller account of the phenomenon. This article revisits the existing literature, focusing primarily on the research in the United States. I aim to address some of the conceptual and methodological issues and the controversies that have lingered around them and to highlight important advancements that have broken through conventional frameworks of this lasting subject matter.

CONCEPTUALIZING ETHNIC ENTREPRENEURSHIP

Middleman Minorities versus Enclave Entrepreneurs

The literature on ethnic entrepreneurship analytically distinguishes two main types of ethnic entrepreneurs: middleman minorities and enclave entrepreneurs. Middleman minorities are those ethnic entrepreneurs who trade in between a society's elite and the masses. Historically, they were sojourners, interested in making a quick profit from their portable and easily liquidated businesses and then reinvesting their money elsewhere, often implying a return home (Bonacich, 1973). Therefore, they most commonly established business niches in poor minority neighborhoods or immigrant ghettos in urban areas deserted by mainstream retail and service industries or by business owners of a society's dominant group. But in recent years, they have been found to open up businesses in affluent urban neighborhoods and middle-class suburbs and have shown up not only in the secondary sector but also in the primary sector of the host society's mainstream economy. Middle-man-minority entrepreneurs have few intrinsic ties to the social structures and social relations of the local community in which they conduct economic activities.

Enclave entrepreneurs, in contrast, include mainly those who are bounded by coethnicity, coethnic social structures, and location. In the past, they typically operated businesses in immigrant neighborhoods where their coethnic group members dominated and they themselves were also inter-twined in an intricate system of coethnic social networks within a self-sustaining ethnic enclave. In present times, as many ethnic enclaves evolve into multiethnic neighborhoods and new ones develop in affluent middle-class suburbs, those who run businesses in a particular location may simul-taneously play double roles – as middleman minorities and as enclave en-trepreneurs. For example, a Chinese immigrant who runs a fast food takeout restaurant in a Latino-dominant neighborhood is a middleman-minority entrepreneur, but he would become an enclave entrepreneur when he comes back to his other fast-food takeout in Chinatown. Similarly, a Korean im-migrant who opens up his business in Los Angeles' Koreatown may be an enclave entrepreneur to his Korean coethnics who live there. Yet, simulta-neously, to his Latino residents who make up the majority of that neigh-borhood, he is perceived as just one of many middleman-minority entre-preneurs.

The analytical distinction thus becomes sociologically meaningful as economic transactions of these two types of ethnic entrepreneurs are con-ditioned by different social structures and social relations. For example, the stone face of a Korean shop owner in a black neighborhood is often inter-preted as hostile and even racist. The effect of that facial expression can be exacerbated by a lack of English proficiency, but the same face is taken matter-of-factly by Koreans in Koreatown where a common language often eases potential anxiety.

The Ethnic Economy versus the Enclave Economy

Sociologists Bonacich, Modell, and Light were among the first to theoreti-cally develop the ethnic economy concept which broadly includes any im-migrant or ethnic group's self-employed, employers, and coethnic employees (Light, 1972, 1994; Bonacich and Modell, 1980; Bonacich, 1987). Light and his colleagues later rearticulated the concept to a higher level of gener-ality (Light et al., 1994; Light and Karageorgis, 1994; Light and Gold, 2000). The reconceptualized ethnic economy includes two key aspects: one is the ethnic group's maintenance of "a controlling ownership stake" and its coethnic labor force or unpaid family labor; and the other is the ethnic group's control over the employment network, which allows the channeling of coethnic members into non-coethnic firms and even into the public sector of the larger labor market (Light and Karageorgis, 1994:648). The ethnic economy concept, with its dual aspects of coethnic ownership and employment network, is thus a neutral designation for every enterprise that is either owned, or supervised, or staffed by racial/ethnic minority group members regardless of size, type, and locational clustering. It is also agnostic about the intensity of ethnicity, neither requiring nor assuming "an ethnic cultural ambience within the firm or among sellers and buyers" (Light and Karageorgis, 1994:649).

The ethnic economy concept thus encompasses businesses owned by middleman minorities, businesses owned by coethnics in ethnic enclaves, as well as all ethnic-owned or ethnic-controlled enterprises in the general economy. Under this conception, the groups that are known to have higher than average rates of self-employment, such as Jews, Japanese, Koreans, Chinese, Iranians, and Cubans, have their respective ethnic economies; the groups that are known to have low self-employment rates but have control over recruitment networks in certain industries in non-coethnic firms and even in the public sector, such as blacks, Mexicans, and Salvadorans, would also have their own ethnic economies. Such conception allows for two types of analyses: one is to account for variations in mobility outcomes among ethnic group members who create employment opportunities for themselves and their coethnic workers, and the other is to account for variations in the level of economic integration of group members who enter the general economy via coethnic employment networks. This conception also facilitates the comparison of mobility and economic integration of immigrant and ethnic minorities in different societal contexts (Light and Karageorgis, 1994). Moreover, it makes operationalization convenient, especially when using various sources of secondary data. For example, the ethnic economy may be operationalized by either coethnicity of owners and coworkers or coethnicity of supervisors and coworkers (Hum, 2000). It may also be measured by the degree of industrial or occupational clustering (Waldinger, 1996).

The enclave economy is a special case of the ethnic economy, one that is bounded by coethnicity and location. Not every group's ethnic economy can be called an enclave economy. Likewise, not every ethnic economy betokens a middleman minority (Light and Karageorgis, 1994). Portes and his colleagues were among the first to develop the enclave economy concept, drawing on the dual labor market theory (Wilson and Portes, 1980; Portes and Bach, 1985). In its original conceptualization, the enclave economy had a structural and a cultural component. As a distinct type of ethnic economy, it consisted of a wide range and diversity of economies activities that exceeded the limits of small businesses, trade and commerce, and traditional mom-and-pop stores, as well as ethnic institutions that mediated economic action, such as merchant associations, chambers of commerce, informal credit associations, and family/hometown associations. To a varying degree, it resembled some of the key characteristics of both primary and secondary sectors of the mainstream economy.

Unlike the ethnic economy concept that includes almost every business under an ethnic umbrella, the enclave economy has several unique characteristics. First, the group involved has a sizeable entrepreneurial class. Second, economic activities are not exclusively commercial, but include productive activities directed toward the general consumer market. Third, the business clustering entails a high level of diversity, including not just niches shunned by natives but also a wide variety of economic activities common in the general economy, such as professional services and production. Fourth, coethnicity epitomizes the relationships between owners and workers and, to a lesser extent, between patrons and clients. Last and perhaps most importantly, the enclave economy requires a physical concentration within an ethnically identifiable neighborhood with a minimum level of institutional completeness. Especially in their early stages of development, ethnic businesses have a need for proximity to a coethnic clientele which they initially serve, a need for proximity to ethnic resources, including access to credit, information and other sources of support, and a need for ethnic labor supplies (Portes and Manning, 1986).

The enclave economy also has an integrated cultural component. Economic activities are governed by bounded solidarity and enforceable trust – mechanisms of support and control necessary for economic life in the community and for reinforcement of norms and values and sanctioning of socially disapproved behavior (Portes and Zhou, 1992). Relationships between coethnic owners and workers, as well as customers, generally transcend a contractual monetary bond and are based on a commonly accepted norm of reciprocity. My own study of the garment workers in New York's Chinatown offers a concrete example. Immigrant Chinese women with little English and few job skills often find working in Chinatown a better option, despite low wages, because the enclave enables them to fulfill their multiple roles more effectively as wage earners, wives, and mothers.

In Chinatown, jobs are easier to find, working hours are more flexible, employers are more tolerant of the presence of children, and private child-care within close walking distance from work is more accessible and afford-able (Zhou, 1992). Such tangible and intangible benefits associated with the ethnic enclave is absent in the general secondary labor market, where co-ethnicity is atypical of owner-worker relationships and reciprocity is not an enforceable norm. Likewise, ethnic employers who run businesses in non-coethnic neighborhoods or who employ non-coethnic workers can effec-tively evade the social control of the ethnic community while causing un-intended consequences of heavier social costs such as interethnic conflicts.

In sum, the enclave economy is not any type of ethnic economies. The adjective "enclave" is not just there to invoke the concept of "ethnic economy," but refers to a specific phenomenon, one that is bounded by an identifiable ethnic community and embedded in a system of community-based coethnic social relations and observable institutions. The central idea of the enclave economy concept is that the enclave is more than just a shelter for the disadvantaged who are forced to take on either self-employment or marginal wage work in small business. Rather, the ethnic enclave possesses the potential to develop a distinct structure of economic opportunities as an effective alternative path to social mobility.

Each of the concepts that I have just discussed approaches ethnic entrepreneurship from different angles and captures some core aspects of the phenomenon. Any new sociological concept, especially the innovative ones, would naturally be subjected to scrutiny and critique in the field. How ethnic entrepreneurship is conceptualized has been and continues to be hotly debated. Some criticisms include that the middleman-minority concept overemphasizes the sojourning orientation of ethnic entrepreneurs and the consequential societal hostility and intergroup competition in which it re-sults, while overlooking ethnic social structures in which entrepreneurs are embedded. The ethnic economy concept is so expansive, ranging from eth-nic ownership, coethnicity of owners and workers, and ethnic density of a particular occupational niche regardless of ownership positions, that, as a sociological construct, it loses its analytical rigor. The enclave economy concept turns the traditional conceptions of residential segregation and labor market segmentation upside down, unveiling a set of nuanced ideas so unconventional and complex that it invokes much confusion in interpreta-tion and operationalization. In my view, these key concepts are useful analytically and are meaningful precisely because they capture the essence of some, not necessarily most, aspects of ethnic entrepreneurship.

EXPLAINING THE CAUSES AND CONSEQUENCES OF ENTREPRENEURSHIP: CONVERGENCIES AND CONTROVERSIES

Existing literature has sought to explain the causes and consequences of ethnic entrepreneurship. The central questions are twofold: Why are some immigrant groups more likely than others to engage in entrepreneurial activity; more specifically, what enables some groups to take on entrepreneurship and ensure their success in such an endeavor? Is ethnic entrepreneurship an effective means for social mobility, or what specific outcomes does entrepreneurship yield?

Determinants of Ethnic Entrepreneurship

Sociological research on ethnic entrepreneurship since the 1960s has given rise to a number of theoretical breakthroughs. Much of the literature seeks to explain why immigrants have a greater propensity for self-employment and why some groups are more likely than others to pursue self-employment as an alternative path to social mobility. Despite variations on the theme, major theories have converged on the independent and/or interactive effects of some key structural factors and group or individual characteristics that may either preexist before immigration or are adopted upon arrival in a host country. The "modes of incorporation" typology, developed by Portes and Rumbaut (1990) in their seminal work *Immigrant America,* is among one of the best analytical frameworks that cut across societal, group, and individual levels in dealing with the issue of intergroup variations in immigrant entrepreneurship. This typology refers to the ways in which different national-origin groups insert themselves into the U.S. society as labor migrants, entrepreneurs, or professionals, which are determined by the contexts of exit (*e.g.,* what immigrants bring with them – motivation, human capital, and financial/material resources; how they come – legal versus undocumented; and under what conditions they left their countries of origin) and the contexts of reception (*e.g.,* preexisting ethnic communities; government policies; societal reception). The central idea is that particular contexts of exit and reception can effect distinctive social environments and cultural conditions to the members of different national-original groups and offer opportunities or create constraints to the individual, independent of the individual-level human capital, structural, and cultural characteristics.

At the societal level, racial exclusion and discrimination erect structural barriers to prevent immigrants from competing with the native born on an equal basis in the mainstream economy. As a result, immigrants either take jobs that natives do not desire or carve out market niches for themselves, meeting the potential demands for specific goods and services unmet by the mainstream economy. Historically, anti-Semitism and legal exclusion of Jews from landownership and skilled-worker guilds in Europe forced the Jews into the position of a middleman trading minority as peddlers, shop-keepers, and money lenders (Bonacich, 1973). The Chinese Exclusion Act of 1882 pushed Chinese immigrants into their own enclave, developing marginal ethnic economies, such as restaurant and laundry businesses, for subsistence and self-protection (Wong, 1988).

More recent empirical research suggests that immigrants seek self-employment in greater proportion than do natives because of discrimination in the larger labor market and disadvantages associated with immigrant status, such as poor English proficiency and the depreciation of human capital (Mata and Pendakur, 1999). There are intergroup differences, however. For example, Korean business owners often consider business ownership as a strategy to cope with problems associated with blocked mobility, but do not want their children to take over their businesses. Hispanic entrepreneurs, in contrast, often view entrepreneurship not just as an instrument to overcome discrimination but also as a strategy for intergenerational mobility (Raijiman and Tienda, 2000).

In contemporary America where overt racism and discrimination is rendered illegal, various macrostructural forces have continued to influence the likelihood of engaging in entrepreneurial activity and its success. Aldrich and Waldinger highlighted two sets of such factors: market conditions and access to ownership. They argued that demands for ethnic consumer products stimulated both by growing ethnic populations and the changing tastes of nonethnics for things exotic and underserved nonethnic markets allowed certain group members to carve niches for self-employment. In this sense, the success of ethnic businesses hinged on the size of the ethnic population as well as on the access to customers beyond the ethnic community. They argued further that unique market conditions must interact with the access to ownership in the opportunity structures, which included levels of inter-ethnic competition for economic opportunities and state policies (Aldrich and Waldinger, 1990).

Others showed that ethnic market size interacted with immigrant disadvantages, such as the lack of English proficiency and linguistic isolation, in affecting self-employment (Evans, 1989). Still others showed that immigrants with limited English proficiency (LEP) became self-employed for different reasons, especially in a hostile context of reception. While LEP immigrants became self-employed because of limited labor market opportunities, those with fluent English proficiency did so for greater economic returns (Mora, 2002).

At the group level, the literature focuses on the group-specific cultural repertoire in the form of imported and reactive cultural values, behavioral patterns, distinct group traits, social structures, collective resources, and coping strategies. In his classic study of pre-War World II Chinese and Japanese ethnic economies, Light (1972) found that ethnic solidarism fostered interpersonal relations within the ethnic community, particularly within ethnic institutions such as clan or family mutual aid societies and rotating credit associations, which bore an "elective affinity" and functioned to collectively reinforce values and norms, mobilize resources, set prices, and regulate intraethnic competition for small business operation. Ethnic entrepreneurs preferred to partner with kin and coethnics as well as to hire coethnic labor because ethnic belonging constituted a framework of guiding decisionmaking and because the choice of partners or workers obeyed a logic based on trust, itself guaranteed by reputation.

In the Chinese enclave, for example, an "uncle" could testify for the reputation of the person organizing a rotating credit association (*hui*). Such a testimony was necessarily sufficient because the uncle was part of the informal social network that sanctioned cheating even if there were no penalties for possible transgression other than the exclusion of the swindler from interacting or doing business with other members of the community (Mung, 1996). My study of New York's Chinatown illustrated how informal reciprocal bonds are established between entrepreneurs and workers and how they functioned to nurture the entrepreneurial spirit and promote simultaneously the survival and growth of ethnic firms (Zhou, 1992).

Recent studies have examined in greater detail the relevant causal processes in the social structures of the ethnic community. Waldinger (1986) argued that the social structures of the ethnic community provide a mechanism of connecting organizations to individuals and stabilizing these relationships, which in turn enabled immigrant firms to remain competitive. Goldscheider (1986) found that the Jewish value of occupational independence as a mechanism of self-protection was carried over from Europe to the

United States and that it was the Jewish community's ties and networks, not the education or occupation of the parent generation, that reinforced the particular concentration of Jews in self-employment and ensured its continuity over generations. Cummings (1980) found that, among Poles and Slavs, fraternal mutual aid societies sponsored by the Catholic Churches contributed indirectly to ethnic businesses.

Light and his associates (1990) found that Korean *kyes*, or credit associations, helped fill some of the most urgent financial needs of entrepreneurs, promoting more entrepreneurship while strengthening coethnic network ties. Min (1992) found that Korean immigrant churches not only served as centers for social support and control but also acted as quasi business associations, or even as *kyes*, for entrepreneurs and prospective entrepreneurs. Findings about the role of *kyes* were mixed, however; among Koreans, personal savings were found to be a more important source of startup funds than kin and friendship ties (Kim and Hurh, 1985).

Group-level characteristics may be summed up in two concepts: "bounded solidarity" and "enforceable trust" (Portes and Zhou, 1992). Bounded solidarity is created by immigrants through virtue of their foreign status and by being treated as culturally distinct, which heightens the symbols of common origin, shared cultural heritage, and mutual obligations among coethnic owners, workers, and customers. I should stress that bounded solidarity among coethnic members need not be intimate. It is not spontaneous feelings of solidarity but the enforcement capacity of the ethnic community that constitutes the ultimate guarantee against breach of contract and violation of group norms (Portes and Zhou, 1992).

"Enforceable trust" is the key enforcement mechanism against malfeasance among prospective ethnic entrepreneurs and any violators of commonly accepted norms and standards. The sanctioning power of the community and its ability to confer status on individuals or exclude them depends on the organization of the ethnic community. These two group characteristics are embedded in ethnic social structures, forming an important source of social capital facilitating entrepreneurial growth. Other traits and cultural endowments that characterize a group's behavioral patterns include a sojourning orientation to the host society, an entrepreneurial tradition along with a sizeable entrepreneurial class in a group, the habit of saving, and the value of delayed gratification (Bonacich, 1973; Portes and Manning, 1986).

At the individual level, imported individual traits and behavior as well as an individual's demographic and socioeconomic characteristics, such as age upon arrival, marital status, education, jobs skills, and work experiences acquired abroad and those acquired in the United States, and English proficiency. These individual level characteristics have varied effects on self-employment depending on how they interact with societal, group and even individual-level factors. For example, Min (1986/87, 1988) examined why Koreans and Filipinos, having similar levels of education and similar timing of immigration, had vastly different rates of self-employment. He found that even though many Korean immigrants came from middle-class backgrounds, their lack of English proficiency blocked them from gaining entry into well-paying, white-collar professions in the mainstream labor market. Blocked mobility forced them to fall back on their own family and community solidarity and seek self-employment as the most effective means of getting ahead in their host society. Filipino immigrants, in contrast, were proficient in English, received a U.S.-style education, and often secured job offers prior to migration. Their high levels of acculturation and assimilation into mainstream institutions reduced the urgency in forming ethnic enclaves and fostering ethnic solidarity, leading to disincentives for self-employment.

While some of these determinants act independently, most interact with one another to account for the likelihood, success, and intergenerational continuity of entrepreneurship. It is interesting to note that the literature has generated more consensus than controversies on what determines entrepreneurship. There are disagreements, however. One point of disagreement is on the preference for coethnic labor. In his ethnographic study of Vietnamese ethnic businesses in Little Saigon, Gold (1994) found that Chinese and Sino-Vietnamese owners depended on access to local ethnic and overseas sources of credit, supplies, and markets, but increasingly turned to Mexicans and Central Americans as their preferred source of labor, even though jobs of trust and supervisory responsibilities are still in the hands of coethnics. Another point of disagreement is about opportunity structures. Instead of responding to existing host market conditions, ethnic entrepreneurs proactively create new opportunities. For example, the availability of low-skilled immigrant labor allows prospective entrepreneurs to develop new businesses in the lines of work that have already been outsourced abroad, such as the garment industry, and the types of work previously taken up by family labor rather than paid labor, such as gardening, housecleaning, and childcare. Moreover, the availability of highly skilled immigrant labor has also become a new source of entrepreneurship in the growing high-tech sector that redefines the mainstream economy.

Consequences of Ethnic Entrepreneurship

Theories explaining different outcomes of ethnic entrepreneurship are much more controversial than those accounting for intergroup differences in the rate of entrepreneurship. Five arguments are among the most significant and debatable. First, ethnic entrepreneurship creates job opportunities for the self-employed as well as for ethnic workers who would otherwise be excluded by mainstream labor markets. Light (1972) showed that low rates of Chinese and Japanese unemployment during the Great Depression of the 1930s were due to the ethnic community's efforts in helping coethnic workers become self-employed. The studies of Miami's Cuban enclave and my study in New York's Chinatown offered consistent evidence to support this argument (Perez, 1986; Portes, 1987; Zhou, 1992). Light and his associates (1994) took this argument even further, arguing that the numerical preponderance of the self-employed contributed to overall group employment beyond the ethnic enclave and that both workers and owners in the ethnic economy would earn more than if they were unemployed (Light *et al.*, 1994).

Second, ethnic entrepreneurship serves as a buffer in relieving sources of potential competition with native-born workers in the larger labor market. Light and Roach (1996) argued that a sizeable proportion of the foreign born entered the metropolitan labor market by creating their own employment opportunities rather than taking up jobs in the existing labor market or crowding out natives. Portes and Zhou (1999) analyzed the 1990 census data to examine the effect of immigrant entrepreneurship on immigrants and native minority. They found that the rise of immigrant economic enclaves did not detract from African American entrepreneurship and that the proliferation of small firms, rather than the size of the firm, created the necessary environment for the self-sustaining capacity of an entrepreneurial community, which in turn provided an alternative to social mobility.

Third, ethnic entrepreneurship not only fosters an entrepreneurial spirit and sets up role models among coethnics but also trains prospective entrepreneurs. In studying the garment industry in New York City, Waldinger observed that immigrant workers were offered training opportunities when they assumed supervisory positions (Waldinger, 1984, 1986). Later, in another analysis, Bailey and Waldinger (1991) found that bonds of solidarity in small ethnic firms and the presence of coethnic entrepreneurs encouraged informal business apprenticeships, which had social effects beyond pure economic gain of the individual. They concluded that informal training systems were formed through close contacts between owners and workers in ethnic enclaves as well as in spatially dispersed ethnic economies, enabling potential entrepreneurs to eventually start out on their own.

Fourth, and perhaps most controversially, there is a significant earnings advantage of self-employment over other forms of employment net of other observable effects of human capital and demographic characteristics. The economists Borjas (1990) and Bates (1997) flatly dismissed any significant earnings benefits associated with self-employment. Other economists, such as Fairlie and Meyer (1996), found that a high self-employment rate of an ethnic or racial group was strongly associated with a high average income for that group. Analyses conducted by many sociologists also suggested that groups with high rates of self-employment also showed higher than average rates of educational and occupational intergenerational mobility and that their descendants enjoyed individual and family incomes higher than the national averages (Goldscheider, 1986; Portes and Bach, 1985; Portes and Jensen, 1987; Portes and Zhou, 1992 and 1996; Waldinger, 1996).

Portes and Zhou (1996) addressed the contradictory findings by examining how the choice of functional forms – loglinear (relative returns) versus linear (absolute dollar values) – of the earnings equations produced contradictory outcomes concerning the superior or inferior earnings of the self-employed relative to wage/salaried workers. When the loglinear form was used, there was a negative, but statistically insignificant, earnings effect of self-employment, which supported Borjas' claim. But when the linear form was used, the effect became significantly positive. They also found that the preponderance of the self-employed was among positive outliers and thus argued that the use of the loglinear form, which was favored by most economists, sacrificed substantive knowledge about ethnic entrepreneurship because it excluded all the outliers and evened out the earnings of the most successful entrepreneurs.

The earnings return on human capital in ethnic enclaves has also been hotly debated. Portes and Bach (1985) found that, compared to immigrants employed in the secondary sector of the mainstream economy, those in the enclave had occupations that corresponded more closely with their educational attainment and earnings that corresponded more closely with their occupational status. Their original study implied but did not directly test the hypothesis that earnings return to human capital was greater in the enclave than outside. Others disagreed, finding that workers participating in enclave economies suffered from a significant earnings penalty (Sanders and Nee, 1987; Hum, 2001). Logan and his associates (2003) examined the effects of self-employment in ethnic and nonethnic sectors of the metropolitan economies in New York and Los Angeles. They found mixed results on being at work, hourly wages, and annual wages, depending on model specification and varying across groups. They concluded that the self-employed worked longer hours and generally at lower hourly rates than those employed by others and that the effects of self-employment in ethnic niches were more disadvantaged than that in the mainstream economy. I think that, while these mixed results are certainly due to data limitations constraining a more accurate operationalization of the enclave, there is a considerable confusion on the part of the researchers who fail to distinguish between the enclave economy and the ethnic economy concepts.

Lastly, ethnic entrepreneurship affects the economic prospects of in-group members as well as out-group members. Again, results are mixed. In an analysis of how group self-employment rate influenced the earnings of coethnic workers, Spener and Bean (1999) found a positive effect of Mexican self-employment on the earnings of their coethnic workers in labor markets where the size of the coethnic labor force was relatively large. However, the effect was negative in labor markets where the size of ethnic labor force was small. They concluded that such discrepancy was due to the nature of niches in which the self-employed were concentrated. In labor markets with high coethnic density, niches in which the self-employed were engaged were likely to be more diverse and profitable. In contrast, in labor markets with low coethnic density, niches were likely to concentrate in manual occupations. Fairlie and Meyer (1998) found only a small negative but insignificant effect of immigrant self-employment on black self-employment. In another analysis, however, they found that immigrant self-employment had a significantly negative effect on the prospect of native nonblacks' self-employment but increased the earnings of nonblack self-employed (2000). They speculated that the displacement effect of immigrant self-employment might concentrate on the marginal, low-income self-employed.

While debates on ethnic entrepreneurship are largely productive and mixed findings about outcomes are a natural process of knowledge production, I should point out that too much attention on the technical details may sometimes detract us from the big picture and is likely to corner us into an intellectual dead end, leaving gaps in a fuller understanding the substantive meaning and practical implications of ethnic entrepreneurship. What matters most is that self-employment is an option over unemployment, that it creates job opportunities for an individual as well as for others in or out of the ethnic group, that it provides economic resources for the family and children, that it empowers group members with economic independence, and that it opens up a viable path to social mobility for individual group members and their groups as a whole (Washington, 1971; Boyd, 1990; Butler, 1991; Light *et al.*, 1994; Portes and Zhou, 1992).

NEW DYNAMISMS IN ETHNIC ENTREPRENEURSHIP AND CONCEPTUAL ADVANCEMENTS

Theories and empirical research that I have reviewed so far presuppose a national context within which the structure of opportunities for ethnic entrepreneurship emerges and economic mobility for immigrant groups occurs. Sweeping economic globalization and rising rates of international migration since the 1970s have brought about unprecedented changes in immigrant communities and ethnic economic activities in the United States. These trends have led researchers to think beyond the constraints of existing conceptual and analytical frameworks in understanding the causes and consequences of ethnic entrepreneurship. Here, I highlight two interrelated advancements – transnational entrepreneurship and the synergy of entrepreneurship in community building.

Transnationalism and Entrepreneurship

Historically, movements back and forth between sending and receiving countries have been a fact of life for many immigrant groups. What is new about contemporary transnationalism is that the scale, diversity, density, and regularity of such movements and the socioeconomic consequences that they have brought about are unmatched by the phenomena of the past, thanks to jet flights, long-distance telephone and fax services, the Internet, and other high-tech means of communication and transportation, but most importantly to the restructuring of the world economy along with the globalization of capital and labor. Today, a garment design conceived in New York may be transmitted electronically to a factory in some remote country in Asia, and the first batches of the products can be shipped to San Francisco in a week's time (Castells, 1980). It has become apparent that growing numbers of migrants of certain national origins are participating in the political, social, and economic lives of their countries of origin even as they put down roots in the United States (Levitt, 2001). Such processes are likely to give rise to new structures and forces that determine ethnic entrepreneurship.

In the United States, the emerging literature on the relationship between transnationalism and entrepreneurship has come primarily from ethnographic case studies, with the exception of a few small-scale surveys (Grasmuck and Pessar, 1991; Portes and Guarnizo, 1991; Mahler, 1995; Chin *et al.*, 1996; Durand *et al.*, 1996; Gold, 1997, 2001; Guarnizo, 1997; Li, 1997; Guarnizo and Smith, 1998; Itzigsohn *et al.*, 1999; Kyle, 1999; Landolt *et al.*, 1999; Landolt, 2001; Levitt, 2001; Light *et al.*, 2002; Portes *et al.*, 2002; Tseng 1995, 1997; Yoon, 1995). These case studies have covered a wide variety of transnational entrepreneurship. The first type is related to financial services that include informal remittance handling agencies, or *financierasi*, and investment banks. The second type is import/export of raw material, semi-processed products, manufactured durable and nondurable goods, and exotic or folk handicrafts that include informal couriers (*viajeros* who deliver mail and supplies to immigrant kin on a monthly basis or "suitcase" entrepreneurs who travel back and forth with packed suitcases of goods to be traded in street markets on both ends) and formal air, sea, and land shipping companies and trading firms.

The third type entails various cultural enterprises, ranging from trading music, movies, video or digital compact discs, importing and reproducing ethnic language media in print, television, and radio, to organizing musical, dancing, sports teams and tourist groups of various purposes to visit immigrant sending and receiving countries. The fourth type includes manufacturing firms, operating either as separate units of a firm or as one single firm across national boundaries, such as a garment factory in Dongguan, China that belongs to the same owner in New York's Chinatown. The fifth type are return migrant microenterprises, such as restaurants, video stores, laundromats, auto sales and repairs, and office supplies, which are established in places of origin with migrant wages and personal savings in the United States (Landolt *et al.*, 1999). Existing case studies show that many immigrants in the United States are building bases abroad rather than aiming at the permanent return and that they have bought real estate, opened bank accounts, and established business contacts abroad from which they create new economic opportunities for themselves and organize their transnational lives in both the sending and receiving countries by strengthening their transnational networks that sustain regular back-and-forth movements, including cyclical migration (Portes and Guarnizo, 1991).

An understanding of the levels of scale and formality of these various types of transnational economic activities requires a new perspective that goes beyond the one centering on the host country (Levitt and Glick Schiller, 2003). Transnationalism is generally defined as "the processes by which immigrants forge and sustain multi-stranded social relations that link together their societies of origin and settlement" (Basch *et al.*, 1994:6). Portes (1994) argues that it is the intensity of exchanges, not just the occurrences themselves (trips, occasional contacts or activities), that becomes a justifiable topic of investigation. Portes and his associates (1999) advance a typology of three sectors of transnationalism (economic, political, sociocultural) at two levels of institutionalization (high versus low) and define transnationalism as measurable occupations and activities that require regular and sustained social contacts over time across national borders for their implementation.

Recent research has shown that many of the same causal processes affecting ethnic entrepreneurship have also influenced transnationalism, such as structural disadvantages associated with immigrant status: racial prejudice, discrimination, and exclusion. Human capital (*e.g.*, education, job skills, citizenship status) and other key demographic characteristics (*e.g.*, age, sex, and marital status) are important determinants too, affecting not so much the likelihood of engaging in transnational activities as the formality and scale of such activities. Highly educated immigrants have been found quitting their well-paying salaried jobs to pursue entrepreneurship because they can better utilize their skills, bicultural literacy, and transnational networks to reap material gains, as in the case of Israelis, Chinese, Taiwanese, and Colombians, and many of their transnational businesses tend to be formal and based in host countries, using transnational entrepreneurship as an effective means of maximizing their human capital returns and expanding their middle-class status (Gold, 2001; Guarnizo *et al.*, 1999; Light *et al.*, 2002; Zhou and Tseng, 2001).

Low-skilled immigrants from Mexico, El Salvador, Guatemala, and the Dominican Republic have also shown a similar tendency toward transnational entrepreneurship, but their transnational practices seem to be oriented more toward sending countries and tend to be limited to sending remittances home regularly to support families and kin, buying land or building houses for their own transnational lives, and establishing small, sustainable businesses in their homelands as effective ways to convert their meager wages earned in the United States to material gains and social status recognition in their countries of origin (Diaz-Briquets and Weintraub, 1991; Portes and Guarnizo, 1991; Itzigsohn, 1995; Goldring, 1996; Popkin, 1999). However, the same groups that are found to engage in small-scale, informal types of transnational economic activities also show signs of large-scale, government and corporation-sponsored transnational entrepreneurship, such as the Mexicans and Dominicans (Guarnizo, 1997; Itzigsohn *et al.*, 1999).

One of the foci of the emerging research on transnational entrepreneurship emphatically highlights the significance of state policies. Roberts and his associates (1999) found that the North American Free Trade Agreement (NAFTA) of the early 1990s and the General Agreement on Tariffs and Trade (FATT) in 1998 instituted the free movement of capital and goods between the two countries, but not of labor, which they argued has profound implications for the development of formal and large-scale transnational entrepreneurship and the migration of the professional and entrepreneurial class. Zhuang's in-depth historical analysis of the Chinese trade diaspora and immigration in Southeast Asia since the sixteenth century showed how restrictive emigration policies of Chinese government shaped the formality and types of migrant transnational business activities and the formation of different business groups, including pirates who controlled territories at sea to safeguard their illegal channels of trade with China (Zhuang, 2001). Zhuang also showed that China's open-door policy and government mandated economic reform in the late 1970s renewed, consolidated, and expanded the transnational and multinational ties between China and centuries-old Chinese trade diaspora in Southeast Asia, which resulted in tremendous capital investment in China.

The levels of economic development in the countries of origin are also important determinants, as they shape particular structures of opportunities unique to national-origin groups and determine who is engaged in what type of transnational activities. For example, in countries where industrialization and development were at their early stages, informal trade and *viajeros* seemed to dominate as in the case of Mexicans, Salvadorans, and Dominicans who traveled back and forth to engage in informal activities that bypass existing laws and the regulatory agencies of the state in both sending and receiving countries and take advantage of differential demands and prices on both sides (Portes and Guarnizo, 1991).

At more advanced stages of economic development in sending countries, formal and large-scale transnational activities, such as import/export, transnational banking and investment in both knowledge-intensive and labor-intensive industries are likely to dominate, as in the case of Taiwanese and Koreans (Min, 1986/87; Yoon, 1995; Li, 1997; Zhou and Tseng, 2001). These transnational economic activities, in turn, have positive impact on state policies, as many nation states have come to depend on migrant remittances and capital investments as a reliable source of foreign exchange, collateral for the solicitation of international loans, and capital mobilization for economic development (Portes, 2003).

Another point of emphasis in recent research is the significances of ethnic networks and their enduring moral ties to ethnicity and the countries of origin. As networks facilitate processes of migration and settlement in lowering risks and costs of the initial journey, they also play a crucial role in facilitating transnational entrepreneurship and promoting their growth (Guarnizo et al., 2003). Once again, traditional trade and economic networks are based on trust and enduring moral ties dictated by a common ethnicity or a cultural heritage – origin, religion, and language. At the individual level, however, these networks may not necessarily be as closely knit as those based on family and kin, and many manifest themselves in the form of weak ties rather than strong ties, which allows for more vertical rather than horizontal linkages of ethnic entrepreneurship (Yoon, 1995). Also, transnational networks tend to be diverse: some are oriented more toward sending countries while others more toward receiving countries; some have relatively more open boundaries while others are more exclusive in membership (Gold, 2001).

There are direct economic and noneconomic benefits to individual transnational entrepreneurs in terms of employment security, economic independence, favorable earnings, and social recognition in sending countries. However, these individual gains do not automatically accrue to group mobility. For example, despite extensive and well-documented transnational ties, some groups, such as Dominicans, Salvadorans, and Mexicans, have continued to face economic hardships and suffer from group disadvantages in the United States (Gold, 2001). Also, while transnational entrepreneurship creates more opportunities for individual group members to become self-employed, its impact on the group or the ethnic community as a whole varies. For example, the Dominican community in Washington Heights in New York is marked by the most serious social pathologies despite the presence of thriving ethnic businesses (Hernandez and Torres-Saillant, 1996).

Findings and conclusions about transnational entrepreneurship appear to be indefinite at the moment since they have come primarily from ethnographic case studies of a limited number of national-origin groups. Researchers warn that transnational entrepreneurial activities are regularly undertaken only by a small minority of group members and that they range from broad to narrow in scale, producing varied outcomes (Itzigsohn et al., 1999; Portes et al., 2002). Moreover, transnational entrepreneurship may

impose a whole new set of obstacles and difficulties; not all forms of transnational practices bring about positive effects for group social mobility in
host societies (Gold, 2001).

Nevertheless, a transnational perspective has advanced our thinking on
ethnic entrepreneurship in some important ways. First, potential immigrant
entrepreneurs, low-skilled and highly-skilled alike, do not merely react to
structural disadvantages they face in their host countries but actively look for
opportunities and market niches beyond the national boundaries of the
receiving countries, utilizing their bicultural skills and preexisting binational
ethnic networks. While globalization creates new opportunities, those with
bicultural literacy and binational experiences are more likely than others to
act as agents to initiate and structure global transactions.

Second, transnational entrepreneurship does not necessarily impact the
group or the ethnic community in a similar way as it does individuals or
individual families, even when it boosts the rate of self-employment for the
group. However, when transnational entrepreneurship is linked to an existing enclave economy, the effect on the group becomes significant. On the
one hand, transnationalism opens up international capital, labor, and consumer markets beyond the constraints imposed by the host society and
economy and thus expands the economic base by diversifying industries,
creating potential for the enclave economy to integrate both horizontally and
vertically and making it more competitive and viable. On the other hand, the
expanded enclave economy provides greater material support for existing
social structures of the ethnic community, which in turn strengthens the
basis for social capital formation.

Third, ethnic networks are important social capital resources for transnational entrepreneurship, but their effects are unequal. Networks that pivot
around family or kin relations are manifested in trust-based strong ties.
These strong ties may be less beneficial and of less value than those occu-
pationally-based weak ties.

Fourth, even though transnational entrepreneurs may conduct their
routine activities across national borders, it is possible that they weigh their
future orientation and permanent settlement more on the host country than
on the sending country or vice versa, hence a sojourning orientation to their
economic activity on one side and a more settler's orientation on the other.

Examining two industrial sectors – high tech firms and accounting
firms – in Los Angeles' Chinese immigrant suburb, known as "ethnoburb,"
Zhou and Tseng (2001) found that Chinese transnational activities with the
economic base in Los Angeles stimulated the growth of other traditional

low-wage, low-tech businesses in the suburban enclave. They concluded that transnational practices necessitated deeper localization rather than deterritorialization and contributed to strengthening the economic base of the existing ethnic enclave. When transnational entrepreneurs orient toward the ancestral homeland, they may overlook the importance of building and strengthening social structures that help enhance their future well-being in the host country.

Entrepreneurship and Community Building: A Focused Look at the Enclave Economy

The burgeoning research on ethnic entrepreneurship has been more concerned with the causes and effects of entrepreneurship on economic integration among immigrant and ethnic minorities than with its influence on the social contexts mediating ethnic economic life and has largely overlooked its noneconomic effects. Some noneconomic effects, such as serving as an alternative means to social status recognition, nurturing entrepreneurial spirit, providing role modeling that inspires others to follow suit, and strengthening social networks locally and internationally, are noted in existing literature but lack further investigation. Just through what mechanisms and under what conditions these noneconomic effects are produced is unclear, leaving a substantial conceptual gap. Examining how a particular ethnic community may be affected by entrepreneurship can help fill this gap.

Before illustrating the relationship between ethnic entrepreneurship and community building, I shall once again reiterate the conceptual distinction between the ethnic economy and the enclave economy, even though the latter is a type included in, and often mistaken as the same as, the former. As I have discussed in the first section of this article, the ethnic economy is an umbrella concept that takes into consideration not simply job creation by ethnic entrepreneurs, but also access to existing jobs in the general economy by ethnic networks. Such an inclusive concept runs the risk of decontextualization and a loss of analytical rigor when examining group-level processes, particularly variations in ethnic social structures and social capital formation among disadvantaged immigrant and ethnic minorities.

For example, Korean entrepreneurs running businesses as middleman minorities in non-Korean neighborhoods do not tend to invest in the social structures of the neighborhoods they are serving because they are not bounded by social relationships with local residents and because their businesses serve a singular function – trade or commerce – with little attachment to any significant social structures there (Min, 1996). Quite the contrary, Korean entrepreneurs running businesses in Koreatown have a "stake" in the community and are intertwined in multiple social relationships with coethnic residents and multiple ethnic social structures there. Therefore, I argue that it is the social embeddedness of ethnic economic activities, rather than the ethnic economy *per se,* that affects a unique social context for group mobility. The enclave economy concept is useful for us to examine the noneconomic effects of entrepreneurship and to explain why social contexts affecting group mobility vary by national origins or race/ethnicity and why ethnic communities vary in their capacities to protect group members from disadvantages and move them up in society.

My recent study of Los Angeles's Koreatown is a case in point (Zhou *et al.*, 2000; Zhou, 2002).[2] It demonstrates that ethnic entrepreneurship can have social effects that go well beyond the economic success of individual entrepreneurs and that an enclave economy, rather than merely a concentration of ethnic businesses, provides a critical material base for the ethnic community to function effectively. In inner-city minority neighborhoods, many viable social institutions are gone with the out-migration of the middle class to suburbs, leaving the "truly disadvantaged" trapped in social and economic isolation (Wilson, 1987). Urban public schools, churches, nonprofit organizations, and other publicly funded agencies are not, by themselves, up to the task of protecting children from falling down into permanent poverty. Despite multiple risks, however, not all poor urban neighborhoods are predestined to ghettoization.

Los Angeles's Koreatown is a typical urban neighborhood that has a concentration of racial minorities and the poor; yet it is an unusual immigrant enclave since it is multiethnic, with sizeable subpopulations of Mexicans, Salvadorans, Guatemalans, Koreans, and a few others. Only about one fifth of the residents are Korean and two thirds Latino, but no single national-origin group constitutes a numerical majority. Koreatown is known for its high concentration of Korean-owned businesses, churches, and other cultural and social institutions. The Korean-owned businesses encompass both traditional mom-and-pop stores serving local residents and upscale

---

[2]Koreatown is part of my comparative ethnographic study of three immigrant neighborhoods in Los Angeles, based on intensive one-on-one interviews and extensive field observations conducted in 1998–2000. The other two neighborhoods are Chinatown and Pico Union (a Mexican/Central American neighborhood) (*see* Zhou *et al.*, 2000, for more detail).

retail and professional establishments catering to the tastes and needs of suburban middle-class Korean families and, to a lesser extent, tourists.

The two modern shopping malls – Koreatown Plaza and Koreatown Galleria, a handful of expensive Koreatown restaurants, and two indoor golf driving ranges, along with many large and small churches and numerous professional and social services, all owned or run by Koreans – form the core of the Korean enclave. This enclave has become a magnet attracting Korean immigrants and their families who have settled elsewhere in suburban Los Angeles to shop, entertain, socialize, and conduct various aspects of their ethnic lives on a regular basis. The return of the middle class, in turn, promotes further coethnic business investment and the proliferation of a wide range of cultural, religious, and social institutions.

The organization of economic activities and other ethnic institutions in Koreatown suggests that Koreans and Latinos of this inner-city neighborhood are actually living in two very different social worlds. Korean residents, who are poor and mostly recent immigrants, are in a social environment in which they have convenient access to jobs and ethnic goods and services and are also in frequent contact with their suburban middle-class coethnics and benefit from such contact via multilevel participation in the economic and social life of the ethnic enclave. To Latino residents, however, Koreantown is simply a place where they live, and Koreatown entrepreneurs are merely middleman minorities. The Korean ethnic environment accrues ample tangible or intangible benefits within the easy reach of Korean residents, but it is not equally accessible to Latino residents.

It is apparent that social environments are not defined by the neighborhood's characteristics, nor by residents' socioeconomic status, nor by institutions that are located there, but by a complicated set of interrelated social relationships between various institutions and residents bounded by ethnicity, which has significant consequences facilitating or constraining possibilities for social mobility. Koreatown's unique social context for Koreans is a direct outcome of the enclave economy. Let me elaborate further on how Korean entrepreneurship shapes an ethnic environment conducive to education that benefits Korean immigrant children to the exclusion of Latino children sharing the same neighborhood.

In Koreatown's enclave economy, there is a visibly high concentration of Korean-owned and Korean-run businesses targeting children and youth, most noticeably the *hagwons* (after-school tutoring), college preparation schools, Korean language centers, preschool daycare centers, businesses offering music, dance and karate classes and vocational training, and recreational facilities. These private businesses constitute an effective system of supplementary education (Bhattacharyya, 2003), functioning as any other for-profit businesses to meet a particular demand, but serving important social functions as well. First, the concentration of educational enterprises in Koreatown gives suburban middle-class Korean immigrants a reason to go to Koreatown other than for shopping because they believe that the ethnic system of education is best for their children. When the middle-class suburbanites come to Koreatown, they come for multiple purposes – sending their children to *hagwons,* going to church, playing golf, eating real Korean food, shopping, and even for a facial or massage or haircut. The presence of the middle class, in turn, stimulates not only more entrepreneurial investment in businesses of varying scales, but also the development of religious and cultural institutions.

Second, the ethnic system of supplemental education reinforces the overriding importance of education and facilitates educationally-relevant information flows among the children of Korean immigrants. We noticed in our interviews that Korean adolescents in Koreatown have a more sophisticated understanding of the educational system and are more informed of college options than their Latino peers. They seem to know what the specific paths to higher education are, such as which middle school is a feeder school to a better high school, which high school offers sufficient AP courses, how to prepare for AP and SAT tests, and when to take these standardized tests. Many mentioned that they had to take SAT tests early so that they had time to retake them if necessary. They also mentioned the names of prestigious colleges, such as Harvard, Princeton, Cal Tech, and Stanford, and had concrete remarks about how colleges were ranked; high school seniors reported they had visited the web sites of many colleges.

With regard to structured after-school academic or recreational activities, our Korean teenage respondents would say that taking more AP tests, having higher SAT scores, or playing musical instruments made them "look good on college applications," that participating in after-school activities could connect them to those who "know about college admission and financial aid stuff," or those who "can write you recommendation letters for college." They also would say that voluntary work in the community could help them "make up for bad grades in school." A Korean low-achiever told us why he got involved in a service club, "Well, I like to help people, but mostly it's for college, because my grades aren't too good. They [colleges] like to see some of that extra stuff."

Third, multiple purposes for community participation lead to involvement in multiple institutions, hence broadening the basis for social interaction between local Korean residents and their suburban coethnics. Such relationships, though more secondary and instrumental than primary and intimate, create channels for information exchange and thus ease the negative consequences of social isolation associated with inner-city living. For example, Korean parents, often non-English speaking, are able to obtain detailed information about high school and college requirements, school and college rankings, scholarship and financial aid, and other education-related matters through their casual contacts with a more informed group of coethnics in churches, restaurants, beauty salons, and other ethnic institutions and also through the Korean language media. They can find tutors and after-school programs from a range of options offered by for-profit businesses which are advertised in Korean-language newspapers. The ethnic media routinely announces and honors Korean children and youths who win national or regional awards and competitive fellowships, get accepted into prestigious colleges, and score exceptionally well on SAT and other scholastic standardized tests.

The case of Koreatown offers insights into the understanding of the role of the enclave economy in community building and social capital formation. First, social structures in an ethnic community require the support of an enclave economy, not just any type of ethnic economies. For Latinos, Koreatown's ethnic businesses are not connected to the social structures of their ethnic community, be it Mexican, Salvadoran, or Guatemalan. Korean business owners are merely middleman minority entrepreneurs. Even Latino business owners tend to be middleman minority entrepreneurs of their own ethnic groups because of the lack of development of diversity and scale of Latino-owned businesses that can stimulate the development of other social structures in the Latino community.

Second, the development of the enclave economy increases the level of institutional completeness in an ethnic community, which in turn stimulates more diverse community investment. However, Koreatown's enclave economy does not help build an ethnic community for Latino residents who live and work there. Some for-profit Korean-owned educational or social service enterprises are not even accessible to Latinos because of cultural and language barriers.

Last but not least, a high level of institutional completeness intertwined with the enclave economy creates a physical site where coethnics of diverse class backgrounds meet one another face-to-face and rebuild social networks that have been disrupted through the process of immigration. New ties may not be as intimate as those based on family and kin, but they are nonetheless bridge ties centering on the enclave while having many outlets branching from it. Mixed-class interactions among coethnics tend to generate more beneficial social relations and more valuable social capital from these social relations, which in turn effectively reduces the level of social isolation in the inner-city and leads to effective and practical means to social mobility.

In sum, my study contributes to the literature on ethnic entrepreneurship by shifting the focal point from ultimate mobility outcomes – earnings or employment opportunities – to intermediate social processes – community building and social capital creation. I argue that social organization in immigrant neighborhoods varies by ethnicity and that the presence of an enclave economy, not just the concentration of a variety of local ethnic businesses, influences not only the economic life but also the social environment of coethnic group members. The vitality of the ethnic community and its ability to generate resources conducive to the acquisition of skills and information necessary for social mobility depend largely on the development of the enclave economy.

Varied levels of enclave economic development among different immigrant groups affect institutional completeness, which in turn creates differences in the availability and access to neighborhood-based resources, especially those pertaining to the education of immigrant children. Social capital formed in different social contexts appears to have different values, and what appears to be social capital for one ethnic group may not equally benefit another sharing the same neighborhood. In this respect, the enclave economy concept is superior for investigating the social contexts and processes of group mobility. It allows for a more focused and detailed examination of varied social contexts and their effects on mobility outcomes, hence unpacking the black box of ethnicity.

A fuller account of the variations in social contexts can offer a better explanation of why the ethnicity variable has a positive effect on outcome for some groups and a negative effect for others in the same model. It also allows for the development of a theoretical conception to understand more precisely how social resources are produced and reproduced in the ethnic community.

CONCLUSION

Unlike the past, when ethnic entrepreneurship conjured up images of small, informal, and family-owned businesses, contemporary entrepreneurial activities among immigrant groups in the United States have become increasingly heterogeneous in scale, range, intensity, and levels of formality or institutionalization. As in the past, today's immigrants have continued to exploit entrepreneurship as an effective alternative to circumvent labor market barriers and to move up socioeconomically in the host society, but, they have done so more proactively, taking advantage of new opportunities that are open to them in the processes of economic globalization and international migration. The literature seems to converge on the various causes of ethnic entrepreneurship, paying ample attention to interactive effects of various levels of determining factors.

There is much debate about what consequences ethnic entrepreneurship produces and how it affects individuals as opposed to groups. In my opinion, the intellectual disagreements and mixed findings are due primarily to conceptual confusion and inconsistent operationalization of the key concepts under investigation. Because of data limitations, researchers sometimes collapse qualitatively different concepts into a single conceptual category and measure it as if it is intrinsically coherent. I should stress that the concepts of middleman minority and enclave economy are analytically distinct categories, while the ethnic economy is an inclusive umbrella.

The two conceptual advancements that I have discussed highlight some of the most dynamic processes underlying ethnic entrepreneurship. An emerging transnational perspective has pushed the subject matter to a higher level of complexity, stimulating new ways of thinking about how contexts of exit and reception intertwine to affect the probability of self-employment, what constitutes the structure of and access to opportunities, what enables individuals of diverse socioeconomic backgrounds from the same national origin or ethnic group to engage in transnational business, how transnational entrepreneurship affects or is affected by the immigrant's past and present experience in the middleman minority situation, ethnic enclaves, or ethnic niches in the host country, and why immigrants and native minorities differ in their rates of self-employment.

Similarly, emphasizing the noneconomic effects of ethnic entrepreneurship develops an important idea which is noted in the literature but has not been taken seriously, namely that immigrant enterprise can have social effects that go well beyond the economic success of individual entrepreneurs. This approach has also enabled us to see how the enclave economy is a valuable concept as opposed to the concept of the ethnic economy. Linking ethnic economic activities to community and network building helps explain not only why entrepreneurial activities necessarily lead to varied outcomes and why economic success of individual entrepreneurs do not automatically imply group success, but also how group-level economic activities can affect unique social contexts conducive to the adaptation of the second generation and how valuable bridge ties that cut across class and spatial boundaries can emerge to prevent social isolation among disadvantaged coethnic group members. The increasing visibility of entrepreneurial activities among immigrant groups and the surging interest in research suggest that we, as sociologists, should be able to hold on to our jobs for quite some years to come. The challenge is how we advance beyond, or bypass, the constraints posed by the existing theoretical and conceptual frameworks of this intellectual enterprise.

REFERENCES

Aldrich, H. E. and R. Waldinger
1990 "Ethnicity and Entrepreneurship," *Annual Review of Sociology*, 16:111–135.

Bailey, T. and R. Waldinger
1991 "Primary, Secondary, and Enclave Labor Markets: A Training System Approach," *American Sociological Review*, 56(4):432–445.

Basch, L., N. Glick-Schiller and C. Blanc-Szanton
1994 *Nations Unbound: Transnational Projects, Post Colonial Predicaments and Deterritorialized Nation States.* Langhorne, PA: Gordon and Breach.

Bates, T.
1997 *Race, Self-Employment, and Upward Mobility: An Illusive American Dream.* Washington, DC: Woodrow Wilson Center Press.

Bhattacharyya, M.
2003 "Korean Supplementary Education in Los Angeles: An Urban Community's Resource for Families." In *Supplementary Education.* Ed. E. W. Gordon, A. S. Meroe and B. L. Bridglall. Denver, CO: Rowman and Littlefield.

Bonacich, E.
1987 "'Making It' in America: A Social Evaluation of the Ethics of Immigrant Entrepreneurship," *Sociological Perspectives*, 30:446–466.

———
1973 "A Theory of Middleman Minorities," *American Sociological Review*, 38:583–594.

Bonacich, E. and J. Modell
1980 *The Economic Basis of Ethnic Solidarity: Small Business in the Japanese-American Community.* Berkeley, CA: University of California Press.

Borjas, G. J.
1990 *Friends or Strangers: The Impact of Immigrants on the U.S. Economy.* New York: Basic Books.

Boyd, R. L.
1990 "Black and Asian Self-Employment in Large Metropolitan Areas: A Comparative Analysis," *Social Problems*, 37(20):258–274.

Butler, J.
1991 *Entrepreneurship and Self-Help among Black Americans: A Reconsideration of Race and Economics.* Albany, NY: State University of New York Press.

Castells, M.
1980 "Multinational Capital, National States, and Local Communities." I.U.R.D. Working Paper. University of California, Berkeley.

Chin, K., I. Yoon and D. Smith
1996 "Immigrant Small Business and International Economic Linkage: A Case of the Korean Wig Business in Los Angeles, 1968–1977, *International Migration Review*, 30(2): 485–510.

Cummings, S.
1980 *Self-Help in Urban America: Patterns of Minority Economic Development.* Port Washington, NY: Kennikat Press.

Diaz-Briquets, S. and S. Weintraub, eds.
1991 *Migration, Remittances, and Small Business Development: Mexico and Caribbean Basin Countries.* Boulder, CO: Westview Press.

Durand, J., E. A Parrado and D. S. Massey
1996 "Migradollars and Development: A Reconsideration of the Mexican Case," *International Migration Review*, 30(2):423–444.

Evans, E. D. R.
1989 "Immigrant Entrepreneurship: Effects of Ethnic Market Size and Isolated Labor Pool," *American Sociological Review*, 54:950–962.

Fairlie, R. W. and B. D. Meyer
2000 "The Effect of Immigration on Native Self-Employment." National Bureau of Economic Research Working Paper Series #7561. <http://www.nber.org/papers/7561 (viewed on April 10, 2003).

_____ 1998 "Does Immigration Hurt African-American Self-Employment?" In *Help or Hindrance? The Economic Implications of Immigration for African Americans.* Ed. D. S. Hamermesh and F. D. Bean. New York: Russell Sage Foundation. Pp. 185–221.

_____ 1996 "Ethnic and Racial Self-Employment Differences and Possible Explanations," *Journal of Human Resources,* 31(4):757–793.

Glazer, N. and D. P. Moynihan
1963 *Beyond the Melting Pot.* Cambridge, MA: MIT Press.

Gold, S. J.
2001 "Gender, Class, and Networks: Social Structure and Migration Patterns among Transnational Israelis," *Global Networks,* 1(1):19–40.

_____ 1997 "Transnationalism and Vocabularies of Motives in International Migration: The Case of Israelis in the United States," *Sociological Perspectives,* 40:409–427.

_____ 1994 "Chinese-Vietnamese Entrepreneurs in California." In *The New Asian Immigration in Los Angeles and Global Restructuring.* Ed. P. Ong, E. Bonacich and L. Cheng. Philadelphia, PA: Temple University Press. Pp. 196–226.

Gold, S. J. and I. Light
2000 "Ethnic Economies and Social Policy," *Research in Social Movements, Conflicts and Change,* 22:165–191.

Goldring, L.

1996 "Blurring Borders: Constructing Transnational Communities in the Process of Mexico-U.S. Immigration," *Research in Community Sociology*, 6:69–104.

Goldscheider, C.

1986 *Jewish Continuity and Change: Emerging Patterns in America*. Bloomington, IN: Indiana University Press.

Grasmuck, S. and P. Pessar

1991 *Between Two Islands: Dominican International Migration*. Berkeley: University of California Press.

Greenfield, S.M., A. Strickon and R. T. Aubey

1979 *Entrepreneurs in Cultural Context*. Albuquerque, NM: University of New Mexico Press.

Guarnizo, L. E.

1997 "The Mexican Ethnic Economy in Los Angeles: Capitalist Accumulation, Class Restructuring, and the Transnationalization of Migration." La Jolla, CA: Center for U.S. Mexico Studies, University of California, San Diego.

Guarnizo, L. E., A. Portes and W. Haller

2003 "Assimilation and Transnationalism: Determinants of Transnational Political Action among Contemporary Migrants," *American Journal of Sociology*, 108(6):1121–1148.

Guarnizo, L. E., A. Sanchez and E. Roach

1999 "Mistrust, Fragmented Solidarity, and Transnational Migration: Colombians in New York and Los Angeles," *Ethnic and Racial Studies*, 22:367–396.

Guarnizo, L. E. and M. P. Smith

1998 "The Locations of Transnationalism." In *Transnationalism from Below*. Ed. M. P. Smith and L. E. Guarnizo. New Brunswick, NJ: Transaction. Pp. 3–14.

Hernandez, R. and S. Torres-Saillant

1996 "Dominicans in New York: Men, Women, and Prospects." In *Latinos in New York: Communities in Transition*. Ed. G. Haslip-Viera and S. L. Baver. South Bend, IN: University of Notre Dame Press. Pp. 30–56.

Hum, T.

2001 "The Promises and Dilemmas of Immigrant Ethnic Economies." In *Asian and Latino Immigrants in a Restructuring Economy: The Metamorphosis of Southern California*. Ed. M. Lopez-Garza and D. R. Diaz. Stanford, CA: Stanford University Press. Pp. 77–101.

2000 "A Protected Niche: Immigrant Ethnic Economies and Labor Market Segmentation." In *Prismatic Metropolis: Inequality in Los Angeles*. Ed. L. D. Bobo, M. L. Oliver, J. H. Johnson and A. Valenzuela, Jr. New York: Russell Sage Foundation Press. Pp. 279–314.

Itzigsohn, J.

1995 "Migrant Remittances, Labor Markets, and Household Strategies: A Comparative Analysis of Low-Income Household Strategies in the Caribbean Basin," *Social Forces*, 74(2):633–657.

Itzigsohn, J., C. Dore, E. Hernandez and O. Vazquez

1999 "Mapping Dominican Transnationalism," *Ethnic and Racial Studies*, 22:316–339.

Kim, K. C. and W. M. Hurh

1985 "Ethnic Resources Utilization of Korean Immigrant Entrepreneurs in the Chicago Minority Area," *International Migration Review*, 19(1):82–111.

Kyle, D.
1999 "The Otavalo Trade Diaspora: Social Capital and Transnational Entrepreneurship," *Ethnic and Racial Studies*, 22(2):422–446.

Landolt, P.
2001 "Salvadoran Economic Transnationalism: Embedded Strategies for Household Maintenance, Immigrant Incorporation, and Entrepreneurial Expansion," *Global Networks*, 1:217–242.

Landolt, P., L. Antler and S. Baires
1999 "From 'Hermano Lejano' to 'Hermano Mayor': The Dialectics of Salvadoran Transnationalism," *Ethnic and Racial Studies*, 22:290–315.

Levitt,P.
2001 *The Transnational Villagers*. Berkeley, CA: University of California Press.

Levitt, P. and N. Glick Schiller
2003 "Transnational Perspectives on Migration: Conceptualizing Simultaneity." Paper presented at the Conference on Conceptual and Methodological Development in the Study of International Migration, Center for Migration and Development, Princeton University, May 23–25.

Li, W.
1997 "Spatial Transformation of an Urban Ethnic Community from Chinatown to Chinese Ethnoburb in Los Angeles." Ph.D. Dissertation. Department of Geography. University of Southern California.

Light, I.
1994 "Beyond the Ethnic Enclave Economy," *Social Problems*, 41(1):601–616.

1972 *Ethnic Enterprise in America: Business and Welfare among Chinese, Japanese, and Blacks*. Berkeley, CA: University of California Press.

Light, I. and S. J. Gold
2000 *Ethnic Economies*. San Diego, CA: Academic Press.

Light, I. and S. Karageorgis
1994 "The Ethnic Economy." In *The Handbook of Economic Sociology*. Ed. N. J. Smelser and R. Swedberg. Princeton, NJ: Princeton University Press. Pp. 647–669.

Light, I., I. J. Kwuon and D. Zhong
1990 "Korean Rotating Credit Associations in Los Angeles," *Amerasia Journal*, 16(2):35–54.

Light, I. and E. Roach
1996 "Self-Employment: Mobility Ladder or Economic Lifeboat." In *Ethnic Los Angeles*. Ed. R. Waldinger and M. Bozorgmehr. Berkeley, CA: University of California Press. Pp. 193–213.

Light, I., G. Sabagh, M. Bozorgmehr and C. Der-Martirosian
1994 "Beyond the Ethnic Enclave Economy," *Social Problems*, 41:65–80.

Light, I., M. Zhou and R. Kim
2002 "Transnationalism and American Exports in an English-Speaking World," *International Migration Review*, 36(3):702–725.

Logan, J. R., R. Alba and B. J. Stults
2003 "Enclave and Entrepreneurs: Assessing the Payoff for Immigrants and Minorities," *International Migration Review*, 37(2):344–373.

Mahler, S. J.
1995 *American Dreaming, Immigrant Life on the Margins.* Princeton, NJ: Princeton University Press.

Mar, D.
1991 "Another Look at the Enclave Economy Thesis: Chinese Immigrants in the Ethnic Labor Market," *Amerasia Journal*, 17(3):5–21.

Mata, R. and R. Pendakur
1999 "Immigration, Labor Force Integration, and the Pursuit of Self-Employment," *International Migration Review*, 33(2):378–402.

Min, P. G.
1996 *Caught in the Middle: Koreatown Communities in New York and Los Angeles.* Berkeley, CA: University of California Press.

_____
1992 "The Structure and Social Functions of Korean Immigrant Churches in the United States," *International Migration Review*, 26(4):1370–1394.

_____
1988 *Ethnic Business Enterprise: Korean Small Business in Atlanta.* Staten Island, NY: Center for Migration Studies.

_____
1986
1987 "Filipino and Korean Immigrants in Small Business: A Comparative Analysis," *Amerasia Journal*, 13(1):53–71.

Model, S.
1985 "A Comparative Perspective on the Ethnic Enclave: Blacks, Italians, and Jews in New York City," *International Migration Review*, 19(1):64–81.

Mora, M. T.
2002 "A Re-Evaluation of the Effects of Ethnic Market Size and Isolated Labor Pools on Immigrant Entrepreneurship." Department of Economics and Finance. University of Texas-Pan American.

Mung, E. M.
1996 "Ethnic Economy and Diaspora." Paper presented at the ISSCO conference on the Ethnic Chinese, History and Perspectives: Ethnic Chinese at the Turn of the Centuries. November 18–22, Xiamen University, China.

Nee, V., J. Sanders and S. Sernau
1994 "Job Transitions in an Immigrant Metropolis: Ethnic Boundaries and the Mixed Economy," *American Sociological Review*, 59:849–872.

Perez, L.
1986 "Immigrant Economic Adjustment and Family Organization: The Cuban Success Story Reexamined," *International Migration Review*, 20(1):4–20.

Popkin, E.
1999 "Guatemalan Mayan Migration to Los Angeles: Constructing Transnational Linkages in the Context of the Settlement Process," *Ethnic and Racial Studies*, 22(2):267–289.

Portes, A.
2003 "Conclusion: Theoretical Convergencies and Empirical Evidence in the Study of Immigrant Transnationalism," *International Migration Review*, 37(3):872–890.

1994   "Paradoxes of the Informal Economy: The Social Basis of Unregulated Entrepreneurship." In *Handbook of Economic Sociology*. Ed. N. J. Smelser and R. Swedberg. Princeton, NJ: Princeton University Press. Pp. 426–449.

1987   "The Social Origin of the Cuban Enclave Economic of Miami," *Sociological Perspectives*, 30(4):340–372.

Portes, A. and R. L. Bach
1985   *The Latin Journey: Cuban and Mexican Immigrants in the United States*. Berkeley, CA: University of California Press.

Portes, A. and L. E. Guarnizo
1991   "Tropical Capitalists: U.S.-Bound Immigration and Small Enterprise Development in the Dominican Republic." In *Migration, Remittances, and Small Business Development: Mexico and Caribbean Basin Countries*. Ed. S. Diaz-Briquets and S. Weintraub. Boulder, CO: Westview Press. Pp. 101–131.

Portes, A., L. E. Guarnizo and W. J. Haller
2002   "Transnational Entrepreneurs: An Alternative Form of Immigrant Economic Adaptation," *American Sociological Review*, 67:278–298.

Portes, A., L. E. Guarnizo and P. Landolt
1999   "Introduction: Pitfalls and Promise of an Emergent Research Field," *Ethnic and Racial Studies*, 22(2):217–237.

Portes, A. and L. Jensen
1987   "What's an Ethnic Enclave? The Case for Conceptual Clarity," *American Sociological Review*, 52:768–771.

Portes, A. and R. D. Manning
1986   "The Immigrant Enclave: Theory and Empirical Examples." In *Comparative Ethnic Relations*. Ed. S. Olzak and J. Nagel. Orlando, FL: Academic Press. Pp. 47–68.

Portes, A. and R. G. Rumbaut
1990   *Immigrant America: A Portrait*, First Edition. Berkeley, CA: University of California Press.

Portes, A. and M. Zhou
1999   "Entrepreneurship and Economic Progress in the Nineties: A Comparative Analysis of Immigrants and African Americans." In *Immigration and Opportunity: Race, Ethnicity, and Employment in the United States*. Ed. F. D. Bean and S. Bell-Rose. New York: Russell Sage Foundation. Pp. 143–171.

1996   "Self-employment and the Earnings of Immigrants," *American Sociological Review*, 61(2):219–230.

1992   "Gaining the Upper Hand: Economic Mobility among Immigrant and Domestic Minorities," *Ethnic and Racial Studies*, 15(4):491–522.

Raijiman, R. and M. Tienda
2000   "Immigrants' Pathway to Business Ownership: A Comparative Ethnic Perspective," *International Migration Review*, 34(3):682–706.

Roberts, B. R., R. Frank and F. Lozano-Ascencio
1999   "Transnational Migrant Communities and Mexican Migration to the U.S.," *Ethnic and Racial Studies*, 22(2):239–266.

Sanders, J. and V. Nee
1987 "Limits of Ethnic Solidarity in the Enclave Economy," *American Sociological Review*, 52:745–773.

Saxton, A.
1971 *The Indispensable Enemy: Labor and the Anti-Chinese Movement in California*. Berkeley, CA: University of California Press.

Schiller, N. G., L. Basch and C. Blanc-Szanton
1992 "Transnationalism: A New Analytical Framework for Understanding Migration." In *Toward a Transnational Perspective on Migration*. Ed. N. G. Schiller, L. Basch, and C. Blanc-Szanton. Pp. 1–24.

Spener, D. and F. D. Bean
1999 "Self-Employment Concentration and Earnings among Mexican Immigrants in the United States," *Social Forces*, 77(3):1021–1047.

Tseng, Y.
1997 "Immigrant Industry: Immigration Consulting Firms in the Process of Taiwanese Business Immigration," *Asian and Pacific Migration Journal*, 6:275–294.

1995 "Beyond Little Taipei: the Development of Taiwanese Immigrant Businesses in Los Angeles," *International Migration Review*, 29(1):33–58.

Waldinger, R.
1996 *Still the Promised City? African-Americans and New Immigrants in Postindustrial New York*. Cambridge, MA: Harvard University Press.

1986 *Through the Eye of the Needle: Immigrants and Enterprise in New York's Garment Trades*. New York: New York University Press.

1984 "Immigrant Enterprise in the New York Garment Industry," *Social Problems*, 32(1): 60–71.

Washington, B. T.
1971 *The Negro in Business*. New York: AMS Press.

Wilson, K. and A. Portes
1980 "Immigrant Enclaves: An Analysis of the Labor Market Experience of Cubans in Miami," *American Journal of Sociology*, 86:295–319.

Wilson, W. J.
1987 *The Truly Disadvantaged: The Inner City, the Underclass, and Public Policy*. Chicago: University of Chicago Press.

Wong, B. P.
1988 *Patronage, Brokerage, Entrepreneurship and the Chinese Community of New York*. New York: AMS Press.

Yinger, J. M.
1985 "Ethnicity," *Annual Review of Sociology*, 11:151–180.

Yoon, I.
1995 "The Growth of Korean Immigrant Entrepreneurship in Chicago," *Ethnic and Racial Studies,* 18(2):315–335.

Zhou, M.
2002 "How Neighborhoods Matter for Immigrant Adolescents," *CPRC Brief (California Policy Research Center)* 14(8):1–4. December.

_____
1992 *Chinatown: The Socioeconomic Potential of an Urban Enclave.* Philadelphia, PA: Temple University Press.

Zhou, M. with J. Adefuin, A. Chung and E. Roach
2000 "How Community Matters for Immigrant Children: Structural Constraints and Resources in Chinatown, Koreatown, and Pico-Union, Los Angeles." Project final report submitted to the California Policy Research Center.

Zhou, Y. and Y. Tseng
2001 "Regrounding the 'Ungrounded Empires': Localization as the Geographical Catalyst for Transnationalism," *Global Networks,* 1(2):131–153.

Zhuang, G.
2001 *On Relations between Overseas Chinese and China.* Guangzhou: Guangdong Higher Education Press.

Part IV

Unauthorized Immigration and the Second Generation

Chapter 9

MEASURING UNDOCUMENTED MIGRATION

Douglas Massey and Chiara Capoferro

As fertility and mortality have fallen throughout the developed world, international migration has emerged as a major force for demographic change. In the United States, for example, more than a third of total population growth during the 1990s (34%) came from immigration, and by the end of the decade the share had climbed to 40 percent (Kent and Mather, 2002). Given even lower rates of fertility and mortality in Europe and Japan, the contribution of immigration to the growth and structure of their populations was greater. Now, more than ever, it is important to understand the causes and consequences of international migration and to measure accurately and reliably the numbers and characteristics of immigrants.

As the volume of immigration has grown, however, governments in developed countries have sought to impose more restrictive policies with respect to entry and settlement (*see* Castles, 2004). The imposition of tighter restrictions in the face of a persisting supply of and demand for immigrant labor has led to the emergence of undocumented migration as a universal phenomenon throughout the developed world (Joppke, 1998; Hollifield, 2004). In the United States, spending on border enforcement increased by a factor of twelve between 1980 and 2000, and the number of U.S. Border

Patrol officers rose four times, even though the U.S. and Mexican economies were rapidly integrating under the North American Free Trade Agreement (Massey, Durand and Malone, 2002). Despite the militarization of the border, however, the number of Mexicans in the United States increased by 450 percent over the same period, and the share of the immigrant population that was unauthorized continued to expand. By the year 2000, around a quarter of all foreigners present in the United States were undocumented, up from just 10 percent a decade earlier (Massey and Bartley, 2004).

As undocumented migration comes to comprise a larger share of total immigration to developed countries, an increasing fraction of demographic growth will lie outside the usual avenues of statistical measurement, creating major problems for demographers seeking to forecast the size and composition of national populations (Heckmann, 2004) and serious headaches for social scientists seeking to study the determinants and processes of immigration and immigrant incorporation (Rumbaut, 2004). In this article, we review data sources used by demographers and statisticians to study immigration and discuss their inadequacies with respect to measuring unauthorized migration. We then review an alternative methodology, known as the ethnosurvey, that we originally developed to study patterns and processes of undocumented migration from Mexico. After validating the ethnosurvey for Mexico, we discuss its use in other sending countries and conclude with a discussion of its broader applicability.

PROBLEMS WITH EXISTING DATA SOURCES

Demographers possess a variety of instruments to compile data on immigrants, both documented and undocumented. The most common sources of data include population censuses, intercensal surveys, registration systems, and specialized surveys. As discussed below, however, all of these potential data sources have serious drawbacks for the study of legal immigrants, and as sources of information about those without legal documents, they are even more seriously compromised.

Population Censuses

The most widely available and commonly used source of data on immigrants is no doubt the population census, which most countries administer on a regular decennial cycle. Census forms typically include a question on place of birth, enabling researchers to identify people born outside a nation's boundaries. Such persons are assumed to be "immigrants," and their social, economic, and demographic characteristics may be tabulated to construct a profile of the immigrant population, which can be broken down by country or region of origin. If the census also includes a question on year of arrival in the host country, researchers can define synthetic cohorts and tabulate immigrant characteristics by period of entry and duration of residence to make inferences about patterns and processes of assimilation.

A *de jure* census enumerates people at their places of legal residence, and since undocumented migrants by definition have no legal residence, they are most likely excluded by this enumeration method. A *de facto* census enumerates people wherever they happen to be on the census day and in theory covers undocumented migrants, even if imperfectly. In the United States, enumeration occurs at the place of "usual" residence and efforts are made to enumerate all residents regardless of legal status. Despite its attempt to include undocumented migrants, the U.S. census has serious problems as a source of data on their numbers and characteristics.

A major drawback is that the census form includes no question on legal status. Although many undocumented migrants may be enumerated, researchers do not know which respondents are in the country legally and which are not. If patterns and processes of assimilation are conditioned by legal status, as is logical, then researchers are not in a position to measure this effect. Moreover, if the share of undocumented migrants varies across time and by nationality, then comparative analyses will be compromised. For example, if Mexicans in the United States earn less than Cubans, we cannot tell whether the difference is attributable to greater discrimination against Mexicans in the labor market or a higher proportion of undocumented migrants among them compared to Cubans. This problem cannot be solved simply by including a question on legal status, as such a query would be very threatening to most undocumented migrants and thus depress response rates and undermine cooperation to produce incomplete and inaccurate data.

A second problem with census data is that no matter how hard authorities work to include undocumented migrants, some inevitably are missed, and since neither the census nor the post-enumeration survey is in a position to ask a question on legal status, there is no way to estimate the degree of underenumeration. Given their marginal position in the host society and their resultant exposure to the risk of apprehension and deportation, undocumented migrants obviously have a strong incentive to avoid enumeration. As modern censuses come to depend on the compliant behavior of respondents to return mail-out census forms, the overall level of underenumeration can be expected to rise. Whatever one assumes about their behavior, the extent of the undercount will be greater for undocumented migrants than for other hard-to-enumerate groups, and it is virtually certain that within any given census a significant number will not be captured.

A third problem with census data is that they are inherently cross-sectional, so that census-year snapshots and synthetic cohorts constructed to chart immigrants' progress over time are inevitably biased by selective emigration and mortality. Those included in a census represent a residual of all foreigners who entered in earlier years – specifically those who survived and remained in the country to be enumerated on census day; and the earlier the date of entry, the greater the potential for bias. If immigrant decisions about whether to stay or return are influenced by economic success, health, and other socioeconomic characteristics, as is reasonable to assume, then inferences about patterns and processes of assimilation are fatally biased. The commonly observed pattern of wages rising with time spent in the host country may reflect the accumulation of country-specific human capital, or it may reflect the selective out-migration over time of migrants who are less successful economically. Health and mortality likewise vary by socioeconomic status, further exacerbating the potential for bias.

Another drawback of censuses is that they generally occur only once a decade (although a some occur on a five-year timetable). The decennial administration of most population censuses means that data on immigrants are perpetually out of date. During periods of rapid immigration, this problem becomes especially serious, as in the final years before the administration of a new census the information will be eight to ten years out of date. Moreover, the time and effort required to tabulate census data means that detailed information on the foreign born will not be available for one to two years after the census, leaving a relatively small window during which census-based estimates are both available and timely.

Although it is not an inherent problem of censuses, most ask few or no questions about the characteristics of immigrants before they arrive in the host country. It is thus impossible to address critical questions about the selectivity of migration, the gains or losses that people experience when they become immigrants, or the various kinds and amounts of capital that immigrants bring with them. From census data alone, we may be able to learn something about the characteristics of immigrants, but we can never learn how those of immigrants compare to those of others left behind.

Intercensal Surveys

Data on immigrants may also be compiled from surveys that most national statistical bureaus field regularly between censuses. These surveys routinely ask respondents to report information about their demographic and employment characteristics, but it has been relatively uncommon for them to include questions on place of birth and year of entry. It was not until 1995, for example, that the U.S. Current Population Survey asked these questions in its annual demographic supplement, and their inclusion on the questionnaire only came about as a result of intense lobbying by demographers inside and outside of government.

Intercensal surveys that contain questions on place of birth and year of entry do solve the timeliness problem inherent in census enumeration by providing a regular assessment of changes in the size and composition of the foreign-born population. Even when they include the requisite questions, however, intercensal surveys still suffer from the other limitations of census data: a cross-sectional design, no information on legal status; underenumeration of undocumented migrants; and no information on immigrant background. In addition to these deficiencies, moreover, intercensal surveys suffer the burden of small sample size. In most countries, immigrants are still a relatively small share of the total population and therefore require either an extremely large survey or deliberate oversampling to develop reliable estimates of immigrant characteristics, particularly if they are to be reported separately by national origin.

Registration Systems

A small number of countries maintain population registries that require individuals to notify government officials whenever they change addresses. While such registers have been employed to study patterns and processes of internal migration, they generally have not been used to study international migration, and they are particularly unsuited to the study of undocumented migration. It is unrealistic to expect people who are present in a country without authorization to report themselves voluntarily to governmental representatives upon arrival. Moreover, undocumented migrants often live in irregular housing and frequently sublet rooms or even floor space in homes and apartments registered in the names of others. Often these arrangements are illegal, which virtually guarantees that the unauthorized residents will be unreported.

Although relatively few countries maintain a population register, all have in place systems to record the arrival of foreigners. The United States, for example, tabulates information on the arrival of permanent legal immigrants (those admitted for permanent residence) and nonimmigrants (those admitted for temporary stays). Foreigners seeking to enter the United States on nonimmigrant visas fill out I-94 forms before departure and turn them in to inspectors upon arrival. When compiled and tabulated, these forms yield a count of nonimmigrant entries that can be classified by class of admission (tourist, business, student, exchange, etc.), country of origin, age, and gender, but few other characteristics, as little information beyond these rudimentary variables is included on the form.

Some of those arriving on nonimmigrant visas will go on to violate the terms of that visa by taking jobs or staying beyond the specified time limit, thus becoming unauthorized immigrants (Heckmann, 2004). It is impossible, however, to know in advance which of the arriving nonimmigrants will eventually end up in illegal status. In theory, nations that maintain a system to register nonimmigrant departures could conduct searches to match entries and exits and classify nonmatches as undocumented migrants. However, imperfections in record keeping create considerable potential for error, the process of record matching is costly and time consuming even in an age of computers, and the number of characteristics available from entry and exit forms is typically very limited. In the United States, these imperfections are moot as the government abandoned all exit controls in 1957, and since that date U.S. authorities have not maintained any statistics on departures from the United States by anyone, documented or otherwise.

Most nations undertake efforts to compile information about people who arrive from abroad with the intention of settling permanently. In the United States, for example, data on legal immigrants come from applications for permanent residence, which include age, sex, country of birth, country of last residence, occupation, place of intended residence, and class of admission. Although these data provide a count of arriving immigrants and a sketch of their characteristics, they also have many problematic features.

First, many pieces of information of importance to social science research are not gathered on the visa application. Surprisingly, even so fundamental a variable as education is not included on the form. Second, the data only cover immigrants at the moment they become resident aliens, not when they actually entered the country. Each year thousands of foreigners who originally entered in some nonimmigrant category (student, temporary worker, parolee, asylum recipient, or undocumented migrant) "adjust status" to become current resident aliens, and it is at this moment that they are counted as having "immigrated" to the United States, not at the point when they actually entered, which could have been years before.

Finally, the registration of foreigners as they enter a country provides no information on what happens to them after they arrive. Given that immigrant adaptation, incorporation, and assimilation are among the most important topics studied by social scientists and policymakers, the ultimate utility of entry statistics is rather limited. Moreover, in the absence of a record of departures, the registration of entries provides no information on the size, nature, or selectivity of return migration; and as already mentioned, even when there are comparable registries of entries and exits, matching to determine who has emigrated is time consuming, cumbersome, and error-prone, and it can only produce information on selectivity with respect to the limited array of variables available from arrival and departure forms.

Specialized Surveys

Some of the most important advances in social science in recent years have come from the analysis of longitudinal datasets such as the National Longitudinal Survey and the Panel Study of Income Dynamics in the United States and the Socioeconomic Panel in Germany. To date, however, U.S. longitudinal surveys have been of limited utility for studying immigrants. Although they generally oversample minorities and the poor to achieve adequate representation and sufficient statistical power to study these groups, they have not incorporated immigrants into their sample designs. Given the modest size of most longitudinal surveys, without oversampling immigrants their number will be too small to sustain meaningful analysis. In Germany, however, the Socioeconomic Panel, which has been in the field since 1984, deliberately oversampled guestworkers from Turkey, Yugoslavia, and elsewhere in the European Union, yielding sufficient numbers of cases for detailed studies of immigrant adaptation and assimilation and even emigration (Constant and Massey, 2002).

Despite the potential of the German Socioeconomic Panel, however, it is of no value in considering patterns and processes of undocumented migration because all of the foreigners it surveyed were legal guestworkers. Given the intrusive nature and ongoing burden inherent in longitudinal surveys, it is unlikely that many undocumented migrants would be willing to become respondents, and those who captured in the baseline certainly would be at heightened risk of dropping out, either deliberately or as a by-product of their high rate of geographic mobility.

In the United States, a new effort is underway to create a specialized longitudinal survey of legal immigrants to the United States (*see* Jasso *et al.*, 1999). The New Immigrant Survey will interview roughly 11,000 immigrants to the United States as they become permanent resident aliens during 2003 and follow them for five years while conducting follow-up interviews at regular intervals. These data, of course, pertain only to documented migrants. However, an analysis of data from the pilot project done for the New Immigrant Survey found that a large share of "new" immigrants to the United States were actually in the country beforehand. Massey and Malone (2003) showed that two thirds of new resident aliens had prior experience in the United States and that nearly a third had lived there in unauthorized status. Thus, the full sample of 11,000 migrants can be expected to yield around 3,600 former undocumented migrants for study.

These former undocumented migrants, of course, are not representative of all persons who reside in the United States without documents – only those who managed to possess or acquire the social and economic characteristics required to attain legal status in the year 2003. An earlier specialized survey covering a subset of the U.S. undocumented population is the Legalized Alien Population Survey, which is a representative sample of migrants who legalized under the amnesty provisions of the 1986 Immigration Reform and Control Act (*see* Smith, Kramer and Singer, 1996). The survey was conducted in two waves in 1989 and 1992. The first wave covered 6,193 respondents and the second reinterviewed 4,012 of the original panel. Although these data provide relatively detailed information about the characteristics of former undocumented migrants before and after their arrival in the United States, they nonetheless have serious limitations. First, only two waves of data were collected, and the information they contained is now quite dated. Second, the baseline survey did not ask country of origin, so tabulations by nationality can only be done for the subsample contacted in the second wave. Among those respondents, 70 percent are from Mexico, leaving too few from other countries for reliable analysis. Moreover, the data cover a very unusual subset of undocumented migrants – those able to document at least five years of continuous U.S. residence through 1986 (the criterion for legalization).

One final source of information of data on undocumented migration is special surveys conducted within migrant sending countries. Beginning in 1992, for example, the Mexican Statistical Institute added questions on international migration to its biannual National Survey of Population Dynamics, asking whether any current or former household member had lived or worked in the United States during the five years prior to the interview. The information gathered on recent emigrants is rather limited, however, being confined to age, sex, marital status, and departure date for those still abroad at the time of the survey. Although additional socioeconomic data are available on former migrants who have returned to the household, the survey asks no specific questions about their migratory experience and does not capture migrants who have settled in the United States or who travel within entire households. The data thus offer regular but rather incomplete data on Mexican immigrants, but contain no information on the crucial variable of legal status, precluding an accurate assessment of the number or characteristics of undocumented migrants.

THE ETHNOSURVEY IN THEORY

The foregoing review suggests a need for sources of information that can: 1) identify undocumented migrants and compare their characteristics and behavior to those of documented migrants; 2) measure trends in the characteristics of documented and undocumented migrants over time; 3) support longitudinal analyses of the migration process; 4) discern the background and characteristics of migrants before they enter the host country and follow their progress after they arrive; 5) provide sufficient numbers of migrants for detailed analysis and cross-tabulation by national origin; 6) study transitions between different legal statuses and model selective movements back and forth across the border; and 7) provide an ongoing source of longitudinal data capable of monitoring the effects of policy changes on a timely basis.

None of the datasets reviewed above satisfies all or even most of these criteria, even for the United States where data on immigration are generally most plentiful. To circumvent the deficiencies encountered in standard datasets, social scientists have turned to alternative sources of data on Mexico-U.S. migration. One alternative method is the ethnosurvey, a multi-method data-gathering technique that simultaneously applies ethnographic and survey methods within a single study. Developed initially by Massey, Alarcón, Durand and González (1987) to study emigration from Mexico, ethnosurveys have since been applied in a variety of locations throughout that country to create a large, reliable, and valid database on immigration to the United States.

Unlike other sources of information on Mexican immigration, ethnosurveys yield data that allow investigators to: 1) compare the characteristics and behavior of documented and undocumented migrants; 2) measure trends in the characteristics of both groups over time; 3) undertake longitudinal studies of the migration process; 4) discern the background and characteristics of migrants before and after they enter the United States; 5) undertake detailed cross-tabulations of Mexicans based on large samples; 6) study transitions between different legal statuses and model selective movements back and forth across the border; and 7) provide an ongoing source of longitudinal data capable of monitoring the effects of shifting U.S. and Mexican policies.

Philosophy of the Ethnosurvey

The basic idea underlying an ethnosurvey is that qualitative and quantitative procedures complement one another, and when properly combined, one's weaknesses become the other's strengths, yielding a body of data with greater reliability and more internal validity than would be possible to achieve using either method alone. Whereas survey methods produce reliable quantitative data for statistical analysis, generalization, and replication, in guaranteeing quantitative rigor they lose historical depth, richness of context, and the intuitive appeal of real life. Ethnographic studies, in contrast, capture the richness of the phenomenon under study. Oral histories supplemented with archival work provide historical depth, and first-hand experiences in the field give insight into the real life of a community. The lack of quantitative data, however, makes it difficult to demonstrate the validity of conclusions to other scientists, and subjective elements of interpretation are more difficult to detect and control. Qualitative field studies are also difficult to replicate.

The ethnosurvey was developed to capitalize on the strengths of both methods while minimizing their respective weaknesses. It shifts back and forth between quantitative and qualitative modes during all phases of design, data collection, and analysis. Consequently, ethnographic and survey methods inform one another throughout the study. Once a site is selected for study, the ethnosurvey begins with a phase of conventional ethnographic fieldwork, including participant observation, unstructured in-depth interviewing, and archival work. Early materials from this fieldwork are then made available for use in designing the survey instrument.

After the instrument has been designed, it is applied to a probability sample of respondents selected according to a carefully designed sampling plan. During the implementation of the survey, qualitative fieldwork continues or resumes after the survey's completion. The flow of analysis is organized so that preliminary quantitative data from the survey are made available to ethnographic investigators before they leave the field so that patterns emerging from quantitative analysis shape qualitative fieldwork, just as insights from early ethnographies guide later statistical studies.

The Interview Schedule

In an ethnosurvey, quantitative data are gathered using a semi-structured interview schedule that lies midway between the highly structured instrument of the survey researcher and the guided conversation of the ethnographer. When interviewing respondents about sensitive subjects or clandestine behaviors such as undocumented migration, rigidly structured instruments and closed-form questions are inappropriate, impractical, and excessively obtrusive, yet some standardization is essential in order to collect comparable information across subjects. The ethnosurvey questionnaire is a compromise instrument that balances the goal of unobtrusive measurement with the need for standardization and quantification. It yields an interview that is informal, nonthreatening, and natural, but one that allows the interviewer some discretion about how and when to ask sensitive questions. Ultimately, it produces a standard set of reliable information that carries greater validity than that obtained using normal survey methods.

The interview schedule is laid out in a series of tables with variables arranged in columns across the top and the rows referring variously to persons, events, years, or other meaningful categories. The interviewer holds a natural conversation with the subject and fills in the cells of the table by soliciting required information in ways that the situation seems to demand, using his or her judgment as to the timing and wording of specific questions or probes. Each table is organized around a particular topic, giving coherence and order to the "conversation," and certain specialized probes may be included to elaborate particular themes of interest.

The usual place to begin is with a simple roster or table that describes the household's demographic and social composition, where each household member is listed in rows down the side, and columns give each person's sex, relationship to household head, year of birth, place of birth, marital status, schooling, current labor force status and occupation, and present income. Special probes are included to make sure that household members temporarily absent from the home are not overlooked.

Since the interview schedule is semi-structured and does not employ fixed-question wording, it is crucial that each fieldworker has the same understanding of what information is being sought and why. Thus, interviewer training assumes great importance in an ethnosurvey. Rather than being trained by rote to ask specific questions exactly as written, interviewers are educated to be conversant with the goals, background, and nature of the study. Rather than following a scripted interaction, they tailor the interview to the respondent in ways the situation seems to demand.

Life Histories

A fundamental feature of any ethnosurvey is the collection of life histories. Within the quantitative survey, the semi-structured questionnaire is readily adapted to compile event histories on various aspects of social and economic life, such as employment, migration, marriage, childbearing, and property ownership. Different facets of a respondent's life are covered by different tables in the event history questionnaire. Rows refer to specific years or periods in the respondent's life, and columns correspond to variables relating to the facet of life under investigation. These tables provide structure to the gathering of life histories by guiding the flow of conversation between interviewer and respondent.

For each table, the interviewer begins at an appropriate starting point in the respondent's life and moves chronologically forward in time, asking about the timing of events and changes in status. When one aspect of life has been exhausted by reaching the present, the next facet of life is considered in parallel fashion. To compile a labor history, for example, each row of the table would list a specific job, spell of unemployment, or period of non-labor force activity. Moving from age 15 to the present, the columns would give the year when the job or spell of nonwork began, the respondent's age at the time, the duration of the job or spell, the place where the job or spell transpired, the respondent's occupational category, his or her industrial category, and when relevant the wages or salary earned. When all information on the first job or spell has been collected, the interviewer asks about the next job or spell and compiles the same information about it, proceeding systematically up to the present. When the labor history is done, the investigator might direct the conversation to other issues, compiling the respondent's marital history, for example, by asking about his or her first marriage or cohabitation and moving forward to more recent relationships. When the marital history is done, the interviewer may turn to a fertility history, then to a residence history, and so on.

Event histories gathered from randomly selected respondents yield a representative sample of a community's recent social history. When properly compiled and coded, the various event histories (employment, marriage, fertility, etc.) can be combined with the aid of a computer to construct a comprehensive life history for each respondent, summarizing key events for each person-year of life from birth (or some other relevant starting point) to the survey date. The construction of such retrospective life histories takes the ethnosurvey design considerably beyond the cross-sectional approach usually applied to census or survey data, and permits the estimation of dynamic, developmental models using sophisticated methods of longitudinal data analysis.

Multilevel Data Collection

Although individuals may be the ultimate units of analysis, their decisions are typically made within larger social and economic contexts. These contexts structure and constrain individual decisions so that analyses conducted only at the microlevel are perforce incomplete. The ethnosurvey design is therefore explicitly multilevel, compiling data simultaneously for individuals, households, communities, and even the nations in which they reside.

In the case of migration, although individuals ultimately make the decision to go or stay, it is typically reached within some larger family or household unit. Likewise, households exist within larger communities that influence family decision-making. Examples of community-level variables likely to influence the migration decision include local employment opportunities, wage levels, land tenure arrangements, inheritance systems, transportation and communication linkages, access to community facilities, economic and political power structures, climatic factors, governmental policies, and kinship networks.

The ethnosurvey is designed to collect such data for multi-level statistical analysis. Information is solicited from all household members, which enables the estimation of household contextual variables like dependency, family income, lifecycle stage, and kinship connections to other migrants. At the same time, other modules gather information on variables that pertain directly to households themselves, such as property ownership, dwelling construction, home furnishings, length of residence, and tenure in the home.

If communities themselves are sampling units, and quantitative information is gathered on multiple communities as part of a cluster sampling design, then fieldworkers also complete community inventories that later enable researchers to construct aggregate-level data files. Individual, household, and community-level data may be organized into separate datasets, or combined into a single multi-level file. Either way, variables defined at various levels are available for analysis. This file structure enables the systematic statistical evaluation of community on household outcomes and household context on individual decision-making.

Representative Multisite Sampling

A distinguishing feature of the ethnosurvey is the careful selection of sites and the use of representative sampling methods within them. The sites may be chosen according to specific criteria designed to enable comparative analysis between settings, or they may be chosen randomly from a universe of possible sites in order to represent a population of interest. The latter procedure yields a representative cluster sample that generates unbiased statistical estimates. Whether chosen randomly or according to *a priori* specifications, however, both internal and external validity are greatly enhanced by multiple field sites. A variety of sites also enhances the strength of inference in qualitative as well as quantitative analyses.

Parallel Sampling

Mexico-U.S. migration is very much a transnational social process (Levitt and Glick Schiller, 2004). Whenever a social process transcends distinct geographic or cultural areas, parallel sampling is recommended (Vertovec, 2004). Parallel sampling involves the gathering of contemporaneous samples in the different geographic locations that serve as loci for the social or economic process under study. In the case of migration, representative samples of respondents are surveyed in both sending and receiving areas.

This strategy is necessary because migration, like most social and economic processes, is selective. The population of people with U.S. migratory experience contains two very different classes of beings: those who have returned home and those who have remained abroad. Since the decision to stay or return is highly selective of different characteristics and experiences, neither class is representative of all those with migrant experience. The use of origin or destination samples alone produces biased statistical analyses and misleading statements about migratory processes (Lindstrom and Massey, 1994).

Multiplicity Sampling

Parallel sampling raises certain troubling technical issues, however. Whereas it is straightforward to design a representative sample of returned migrants who live in a particular sending community, it is more difficult to generate a representative sample of settled emigrants from that community who reside elsewhere. The main difficulty lies in constructing a sampling frame that includes all out-migrants from a community, since they are typically scattered across a variety of towns and cities, both domestic and foreign. New techniques of multiplicity sampling, however, solve the main problems of parallel sampling (Kalton and Anderson, 1986).

In a multiplicity sample of out-migrants, respondents in sending communities provide information not only about themselves and others in the household, but also about some well-defined class of relatives – usually siblings – who live outside the community. When the survey of households in the sending community is complete, a sampling frame for settled out-migrant siblings will have been compiled, and a random sample of emigrants may be chosen from it. Researchers then return to households containing relatives of the sampled siblings to obtain information necessary to locate them in destination areas. Then they go to these destination areas to administer the interview schedule, yielding a representative sample of the out-migrant community.

THE ETHNOSURVEY IN PRACTICE

The ethnosurvey was first developed for implementation in four Mexican communities and U.S. branch settlements during 1982–1983. Designed to serve as a demonstration project, these ethnosurveys yielded detailed information about patterns and processes of documented and undocumented migration to the United States, as well as transitions between these legal statuses. The data were analyzed and the results summarized in Massey, Alarcón, Durand and González (1987) and a series of related articles (reviewed and included in the bibliography of Massey *et al.*, 1998). The methodology for an ethnosurvey was first laid out by Massey (1987).

Having demonstrated the potential of ethnosurveys to gather data on subjects resistant to study using the normal sources, Douglas Massey and his Mexican colleague, Jorge Durand, joined together in 1987 to propose a new project that would annually survey selected communities throughout Mexico to build up, over time, a large and reliable base of data about the characteristics and behavior of documented and undocumented migrants to the United States. This proposal was funded by the National Institute of Child Health and Human Development and ultimately became the Mexican Migration Project (MMP).

The Mexican Migration Project

Soon after its initial funding, the MMP was granted a MERIT Award by NICHD which allowed for automatic renewal (subject to administrative approval) for a second five-year period. It was renewed competitively again in 1997 and 2002 and presently is completing its sixteenth year of continuous support. Including the four communities originally surveyed in 1982–1983, the MMP to date has surveyed 81 Mexican communities and U.S. branch settlements to build a binational database that contains information on 17,625 current or former migrants to the United States, 59.8 percent of whom (10,549 persons) were undocumented on their most recent U.S. trip. Among household heads, 5,512 had been to the United States, yielding 258,910 person-years of information. Data and documentation are publicly available via the project website, which can be accessed by typing "Mexican Migration Project" into any search engine.

Basic information about the communities surveyed by the MMP and its samples are shown in Table 1, grouped according to the geographic classification scheme derived by Durand (1998). As can be seen, the MMP covers a variety of Mexican states, focusing on those that comprise the traditional heartland for U.S. migration – the western states of Aguascalientes, Colima, Guanajuato, Jalisco, Michoacán, Nayarit, San Luís Potosí, and Zacatecas. As far back as data exist, these states have accounted for at least half of all migrants to the United States (Durand, Massey and Zenteno, 2001). More recently, the project has broadened its coverage to incorporate newer sending states in Mexico's south-central region (Guerrero, Oaxaca, and Puebla), as well as the north (Baja California, Chihuahua, Durango, and Sinaloa).

Following standard procedures, within each state investigators selected a range of different-sized communities for study, from small rural villages of 1,000 or less to major metropolitan centers with populations in the millions, and all sizes in-between. In selecting communities for study, the goal was not to find international migrants, but to incorporate a wide range of different kinds of communities with contrasting patterns of social and economic organization, and then to enumerate whatever migrants turned up at each site. The success of the ethnosurvey in securing respondent cooperation is indicated by the low refusal rates encountered by MMP interviewers, which ranged from zero in several communities to 18.6 percent in one community in the state of Guerrero (that happened to be near a zone of guerilla activity). The average refusal rate was just 4.7 percent.

TABLE 1
INFORMATION ON COMMUNITY SAMPLES INCLUDED IN THE MEXICAN MIGRATION PROJECT

No.	State	1990 Population	2000 Population	Survey Year	Mexican Sample	U.S. Sample	Refusal Rate
1	Guanajuato	52,000	65,000	1987	200	21	0.034
2	Guanajuato	868,000	1,135,000	1987	200	0	0.119
3	Jalisco	4,000	5,000	1988	200	22	0.140
4	Guanajuato	17,000	18,000	1988	200	22	0.057
5	Guanajuato	2,000	2,000	1988	150	10	0.085
6	Jalisco	5,000	6,000	1988	200	20	0.115
7	Jalisco	3,000	4,000	1988	200	15	0.010
8	Michoacán	6,000	8,000	1989	200	20	0.050
9	Michoacán	32,000	36,000	1989	200	20	0.037
10	Michoacán	2,000	1,000	1990	150	20	0.152
11	Nayarit	20,000	25,000	1990	200	20	0.029
12	Nayarit	12,000	13,000	1990	200	20	0.010
13	Guanajuato	21,000	25,000	1990	200	20	0.047
14	Michoacán	7,000	8,000	1990	200	20	0.057
15	Guanajuato	265,000	319,000	1991	200	20	0.057
16	Guanajuato	1,000	1,000	1991	100	10	0.029
17	Jalisco	31,000	35,000	1991	200	20	0.044
18	Zacatecas	8,000	7,000	1991	365	20	0.127
19	Michoacán	428,000	550,000	1991	200	20	0.083
20	Jalisco	3,000	3,000	1982	106	0	0.038
21	Jalisco	2,000	2,000	1982	94	0	0.037
22	Michoacán	7,000	7,000	1982	200	0	0.015
23	Jalisco	12,000	18,000	1982	200	0	0.038
24	Jalisco	1,650,000	1,646,000	1982	200	16	0.048
25	Jalisco	1,000	1,000	1992	100	7	0.029
26	Guanajuato	34,000	34,000	1992	200	15	0.095
27	Guanajuato	24,000	22,000	1992	200	15	0.127
28	Jalisco	73,000	85,000	1992	200	20	0.074
29	Michoacán	188,000	226,000	1992	200	13	0.083
30	Zacatecas	1,000	1,000	1991	187	0	0.025
31	Guerrero	83,000	105,000	1993	100	12	0.089
32	S. L. Potosí	489,000	629,000	1993	200	25	0.048
33	Colima	7,000	8,000	1994	200	20	0.087
34	Zacatecas	2,000	2,000	1994	149	0	0.063
35	Zacatecas	100,000	114,000	1994	239	10	0.142
36	S. L. Potosí	13,000	13,000	1994	201	5	0.024
37	S. L. Potosí	1,000	1,000	1994	102	5	0.000
38	S. L. Potosí	42,000	47,000	1994	200	15	0.052
39	S. L. Potosí	1,000	1,000	1994	100	0	0.000
40	Zacatecas	34,000	38,000	1995	201	30	0.107
41	Guerrero	7,000	6,000	1995	153	11	0.186
42	Guerrero	1,000	1,000	1995	100	0	0.107
43	Guerrero	515,000	621,000	1995	200	0	0.074
44	S. L. Potosí	1,000	1,000	1995	99	17	0.000
45	S. L. Potosí	1,000	1,000	1996	142	11	0.000
46	Zacatecas	1,000	1,000	1995	111	0	0.142
47	S. L. Potosí	3,000	4,000	1996	197	11	0.032
48	S. L. Potosí	3,000	4,000	1996	94	0	0.021
49	Oaxaca	1,000	1,000	1996	100	0	0.000
50	Oaxaca	1,000	1,000	1996	100	10	0.000

TABLE 1 (CONTINUED)
INFORMATION ON COMMUNITY SAMPLES INCLUDED IN THE MEXICAN MIGRATION PROJECT

No.	State	1990 Population	2000 Population	Survey Year	Mexican Sample	U.S. Sample	Refusal Rate
51	Oaxaca	9,000	9,000	1997	199	0	0.083
52	Oaxaca	213,000	252,000	1996	200	9	0.087
53	Sinaloa	2,000	1,000	1998	100	6	0.020
54	Puebla	1,007,000	1,272,000	1997	201	1	0.016
55	Guanajuato	1,000	1,000	1997	80	8	0.000
56	Guanajuato	1,000	1,000	1998	87	9	0.033
57	Jalisco	4,000	6,000	1998	201	20	0.057
58	Jalisco	1,000	1,000	1998	100	10	0.029
59	Puebla	2,000	2,000	1997	100	0	0.010
60	Puebla	2,000	3,000	1997	100	0	0.010
61	Puebla	9,999	9,999	1998	199	0	0.050
62	Sinaloa	3,000	4,000	1998	150	11	0.020
63	Baja Cal. N.	699,000	1,149,000	1998	150	8	0.068
64	Baja Cal. N.	699,000	1,149,000	1998	150	7	0.011
65	Baja Cal. N.	699,000	1,149,000	1998	150	8	0.085
66	Baja Cal. N.	699,000	1,149,000	1998	152	7	0.080
67	Colima	3,000	4,000	1998	72	10	0.029
68	Colima	1,000	1,000	1998	100	10	0.000
69	Aguascal.	18,000	4,000	1998	150	1	0.013
70	Sinaloa	5,000	6,000	1998	202	0	0.010
71	Aguascal.	2,000	2,000	1997	100	6	0.010
72	Guanajuato	41,000	41,000	2000	155	16	Pending
73	Durango	16,000	23,000	1999	203	24	Pending
74	Durango	9,000	9,000	1999	151	11	Pending
75	Durango	1,000	1,000	1999	101	6	Pending
76	Durango	348,000	427,000	1999	200	20	Pending
77	Nuevo León	198,000	226,000	2000	200	0	Pending
78	Chihuahua	4,000	5,000	2000	200	0	Pending
79	Chihuahua	3,000	4,000	2000	150	0	Pending
80	Chihuahua	516,000	516,000	2000	201	0	Pending
81	Chihuahua	1,000	1,000	2000	100	0	Pending

Source: MMP, 2003.

Because communities were not themselves randomly selected, the MMP does not yield a probability sample of Mexico, even for the states in which the samples are located. Technically, the 81 community samples are representative only of the combined population of those communities. Thus a relevant question is how accurate a portrait the MMP sample paints of U.S. migrants and their characteristics. Massey and Zenteno (2000) used Mexico's 1992 National Survey of Population Dynamics to validate the accuracy of the MMP. As described above, this survey included a question to identify those members or former members of selected households aged 12 and over who had been to the United States working or looking for work during the five years prior to the survey, thus yielding a nationally representative population of persons with U.S. migratory experience with which similarly defined migrants captured by the MMP could be compared. Their analysis showed that apart from geographic background, the MMP captured very accurately the characteristics and behavior of U.S. migrants.

Here we update that earlier study by comparing the current MMP database of 81 communities with the most recently available round of Mexico's National Survey of Population Dynamics (known by its Spanish acronym ENADID), which was fielded in 1997. Table 2 compares the regional distribution of U.S. labor migrants aged 12 and over identified from both sources. Given the purposive selection of communities for the MMP, it is hardly surprising that its migrants are not geographically representative of all U.S. migrants in Mexico. Given that the MMP started in Mexico's historical region of migration and only later branched out to embrace other locations, the western states are clearly over-represented in the MMP data. Whereas 86 percent of all migrants in the latest version of the MMP were from the historical region, only 48 percent of those captured by ENADID were from this zone.

Although the border and central regions are under-represented with respect to their actual contribution of migrants to the national population, their experience is nonetheless included in the MMP. Whereas 28 percent of all Mexican migrants to the United States originated in the border region and 22 percent were from the central region, the respective figures among migrants identified by the MMP were 8 percent and 7 percent. Only the relatively unimportant southern region, which contributes very few (2%) migrants to the national pool, is still unrepresented in the MMP.

More relevant than geography are the social characteristics of Mexican migrants. Table 3 assesses how accurately the MMP sample represents the traits and behaviors of the population of migrants to the United States. As can be seen, the only MMP distribution to depart markedly from that found in ENADID is for community size. Compared with the national population of U.S. migrants, the MMP under-represents those in rural communities with fewer than 2,500 inhabitants (only 10% compared with 36% in ENADID) as well as metropolitan centers of one million or more (14% compared with 30%). Migrants from the two middle categories (2,500–20,000 and 20,000–100,000) are correspondingly over-represented.

Aside from this distinctive feature of the MMP, which follows from its nonrandom sample selection method, the distributions of other variables are quite close. According to the MMP, U.S. migrants are 86 percent male, whereas according to ENADID the figure is 84 percent. Likewise, the median age of migrants was 40 in the MMP and 38 in the ENADID, and mean ages were even closer, with respective figures of 43 and 42. With respect to

TABLE 2
MIGRANTS IDENTIFIED BY THE MEXICAN MIGRATION PROJECT (MMP) AND MEXICO'S 1997
NATIONAL SURVEY OF POPULATION DYNAMICS (ENADID)

Region and State	ENADID	MMP
Historical Region	47.5%	85.5%
Aguascalientes	1.6	2.3
Colima	1.0	2.4
Durango	3.8	4.3
Guanajuato	9.3	16.1
Jalisco	14.0	16.7
Michoacán	8.6	14.3
Nayarit	1.9	3.1
San Luís Potosí	3.6	11.0
Zacatecas	3.9	15.3
Border Region	28.2%	7.9%
Baja California Norte	5.8	3.2
Baja California Sur	0.2	0.0
Coahuila	2.8	0.0
Chihuahua	6.0	2.7
Nuevo León	3.8	0.4
Sinaloa	2.5	1.6
Sonora	3.0	0.0
Tamaulipas	4.1	0.0
Central Region	22.0%	6.5%
Distrito Federal	3.9	0.0
Guerrero	3.5	2.6
Hidalgo	1.7	0.0
Mexico	4.6	0.0
Morelos	2.0	0.0
Oaxaca	2.1	2.3
Puebla	2.5	1.6
Queretaro	1.3	0.0
Tlaxcala	0.4	0.0
Southern Region	2.3%	0.0%
Campeche	0.1	0.0
Chiapas	0.3	0.0
Quintana Roo	0.2	0.0
Tabasco	0.1	0.0
Veracruz	1.2	0.0
Yucatan	0.4	0.0

Source: ENADID, 1997; MMP, 2003.

marital status, ENADID shows that 79 percent of all U.S. migrants are married, compared with 78 percent among those identified by the MMP. The educational distributions were also quite similar. According to the MMP sample of migrants, 50 percent had fewer than six years of schooling; 27 percent had six to eight; 13 percent had nine to eleven years; and 10 percent had twelve or more, compared with respective figures of 46 percent, 29 percent, 16 percent, and 8 percent in the ENADID sample. These two distributions yielded mean educations of 5.1 for migrants identified by the MMP and 5.6 among those identified by ENADID.

TABLE 3

SOCIAL CHARACTERISTICS OF U.S. MIGRANTS IDENTIFIED BY THE MEXICAN MIGRATION PROJECT
(MMP) AND MEXICO'S 1997 NATIONAL SURVEY OF POPULATION DYNAMICS (ENADID)

Characteristic	ENADID	MMP
Size of Community		
Under 2,500	36.06%	9.7%
2,500–19,999	20.56	35.4
20,000–99,999	13.50	40.9
Over 100,000	29.87	14.0
Gender		
Male	84.4%	86.0%
Female	15.6	14.0
Age		
Median Age	38.0	40.0
Mean Age	42.2	43.1
Standard Deviation	16.2	16.8
Relation to Household Head		
Household Head	73.4%	71.6%
Spouse	8.8	7.5
Son/Daughter	13.1	19.0
Other	4.7	1.9
Marital Status		
Currently Married	78.8%	77.8%
Never Married	12.3	16.7
Formerly Married	8.9	5.5
Years of Schooling		
Under 6	46.4%	50.1%
6–8 Years	28.6	26.7
9–11 Years	16.4	13.4
12+ Years	8.0	9.8
Median	6.0	5.0
Mean	5.6	5.1
Duration of Last Trip		
Median	7.0	8.0
Mean	17.6	18.7
Number of Unweighted Cases	8,297	6,766

Source: ENADID, 1997; MMP, 2003.

The only distribution to differ between the two sources was that for household position. In general, the MMP contains a larger number of sons and daughters compared to the ENADID. Whereas 19 percent of migrants in the MMP were children of the household head, the figure was only 13 percent in ENADID; but Massey and Zenteno (2000) determined that this difference occurred because the MMP, owing to its careful procedures for determining household membership, was more successful in enumerating absent sons and daughters (mostly the former) who had been away for some time but who were expected to rejoin the household upon their return.

In a study of international migration, perhaps the most important variables are those associated with migratory behavior itself. The only indicator of migratory behavior available from ENADID is the duration of last trip to the United States. For the MMP, the average trip had a mean of nineteen months with a median of eight months, indicating a long-tailed distribution skewed to the left. Trip durations reported by migrants identified by the ENADID likewise displayed a mean of seven and a median of eighteen, suggesting essentially the same distribution. Figure I presents the cumulative distribution of U.S. trips by duration for both the MMP and ENADID to demonstrate how closely the two sets of data correspond.

Figure I.   **Months Spent by Return Migrants on Last Trip to the U.S., Cumulative Percentage**

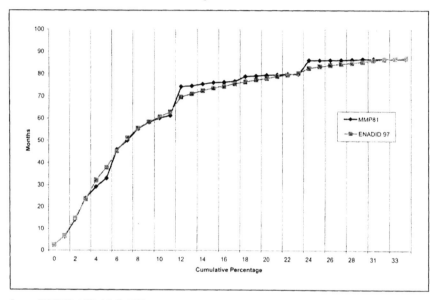

Source: ENADID, 1997; MMP, 2003.

The foregoing systematic comparison suggests that, despite the non-representative nature of the MMP's selection of sample communities, it nonetheless captures the social and economic characteristics of U.S. migrants quite accurately, including the timing of their departures and returns. The great advantage of the MMP, however, is that it allows investigators to identify those migrating with and without documents, thus permitting detailed analyses of the characteristics and behavior of unauthorized migrants. Massey and Espinosa (1997), for example, analyzed migrant decisionmaking by separately modeling the determinants of initial undocumented migration, repeat undocumented migration, and, among migrants present in the

United States, the decision to return. The MMP's multi-level life history data allowed them to determine, for each year in the life of each male household head, his personal characteristics, the characteristics of his household, the structure and organization of the community in which he lived, conditions in potential U.S. regional labor markets, and basic conditions in the political economies of both Mexico and the United States. This comprehensive analysis revealed that: 1) U.S. policies were ineffective in discouraging migration to the United States; 2) the strongest predictors of departure were social connections to friends or relatives with U.S. experience; 3) migrants tended to come from communities with relatively high wages and levels of industrial development; 4) the decision to make a first U.S. trip was more strongly predicted by Mexican interest rates than wage differentials with the United States; and 5) potential access to U.S. social services did not motivate migration to the United States.

In addition, the MMP asks a detailed series of migration-specific questions (about social ties to other migrants and use of border smugglers, for example) that are simply unavailable from standard demographic surveys such as the ENADID. Using these data, Singer and Massey (1998) were able to estimate a quantitative model of undocumented border crossing. They showed that having a social tie to a U.S. migrant increased the likelihood of using a paid crossing guide, which lowered the probability of apprehension by the Border Patrol; that as migrants accumulated multiple U.S. trips they increasingly substituted their own knowledge and experience for the services of paid smugglers; and that arrest did not deter migrants from making additional attempts at clandestine entry.

Ethnosurveys in Other Countries

Although Mexicans constitute nearly 60 percent of all legal immigrants from Latin America and around 80 percent of all immigrants who arrive without documents (see Bean et al., 1998; Woodrow-Lafield, 1998), many thousands of immigrants arrive each year from other Latin American nations. In order to expand the base for empirical generalization and theory testing, in 1998 Massey and Durand launched the Latin American Migration Project. To date, the LAMP has carried out ethnosurveys in 35 communities located in Puerto Rico, the Dominican Republic, Nicaragua, Costa Rica, Haiti, Guatemala, Peru, and Paraguay. Table 4 summarizes the sampling information for these communities. A preliminary analysis comparing rates and patterns of U.S. migration from these four countries to rates and patterns observed in Mexico has been carried out by Massey and Sana (2004).

TABLE 4
ETHNOSURVEY DATA POTENTIALLY AVAILABLE TO STUDY INTERNATIONAL MIGRATION FROM
SELECTED COUNTRIES

Country	Investigator(s)	Communities Surveyed	Households Surveyed
Latin America			
Mexico	Durand and Massey	81	13,970
Puerto Rico	Durand-Massey-Duany	5	646
Dominican Republic	Durand-Massey-Silié	7	978
Costa Rica	Durand-Massey-Vargas	4	1,017
Nicaragua	Durand-Massey-Vargas	5	811
Paraguay	Durand-Massey-Cerrutti-Parrado	2	300
Haiti	Durand-Massey-Lundy	3	300
Peru	Durand-Massey-Valencia	4	676
Guatemala	Durand-Massey-Lindstrom	7	578
Europe			
Lithuania	Sipaviciene and Frejka	4	255
Poland	Okolski and Frejka	4	900
Ukraine	Pyrozhkov and Frejka	3	440
Poland	Kalter and Iglicka	4	1,400
Asia			
Fujian, China	Liang	14	3,120
Total Households Potentially Available		146	25,391

With financing from the United Nations Population Fund, Tomas Frejka at the Population Activities Unit of the Economic Commission for Europe sponsored a round of ethnosurveys in Poland, Lithuania, and Ukraine (*see* Frejka, Okolski and Sword, 1998, 1999). The communities ranged in size from 3,400 to 17,000 inhabitants, and as shown in Table 4, yielded ethnosurveys of 900 households. The Polish data have been subject to detailed analyses to paint a rather clear picture of patterns and processes of international migration emanating from Central and Eastern Europe (*see* Jazwinska and Okolski, 1996; Iglicka and Sword, 1999; Iglicka, 2001).

Zai Liang, of the State University of New York at Albany, is in the process of applying ethnosurvey methods to study emigration from China, focusing on three regions in Fujian Province which are known to send large numbers of migrants to the United States. As in earlier projects, he selected sites at different points on the continuum of urbanism. In one city of 670,000 he selected four of seventeen districts; he also selected two of 22 towns in a semi-urbanized county of 610,000 inhabitants and two of four villages in a rural district of 153,000, for a total of eight communities. The project will also interview 40 migrants from each of the eight locations currently living the New York and Philadelphia metropolitan areas, and a second round of ethnosurveys of 1,200 additional households in six communities is currently being gathered. Ultimately Liang's China Migration

Project should contain data on 3,120 households located in fourteen Fujianese communities and their foreign destinations.

Most recently, Frank Kalter of the University of Mannheim and Krystyna Iglicka of the University of Warsaw have proposed a new round of ethnosurveys in Poland, selecting four communities that vary not only according to urbanism, but also with respect to distance to the German border. Within Proszan (a small city close to Germany) and Warsaw (which is further away), specific neighborhoods will be demarcated and sampled, and two rural communities located 20–50 kilometers from each site will also be surveyed. Within each community, 300 households will be interviewed, and 50 additional migrant households from each location will be surveyed at points of destination in Germany, yielding a total sample size of around 1,400.

CONCLUSION

Immigration has become a key component of population growth in developed countries, and a rising share of immigrants to these nations are undocumented, creating serious problems of measurement. We reviewed standard sources of demographic data – censuses, intercensal surveys, registration systems, and specialized surveys – to show how all fell short in providing accurate and timely data on immigrants, particularly those without documents. Our review uncovered a need for data sources that could: 1) identify undocumented migrants and compare their characteristics and behavior to those of documented migrants; 2) measure trends in the characteristics of documented and undocumented migrants over time; 3) support longitudinal analyses of the migration process; 4) discern the backgrounds and characteristics of migrants before they enter the host country and follow their progress after they arrive; 5) provide sufficient numbers of migrants for detailed analysis and cross-tabulation by national origin; 6) study transitions between different legal statuses and model selective movements back and forth across the border; and 7) provide an ongoing source of longitudinal data capable of monitoring the effects of policy changes on a timely basis.

We suggest that the ethnosurvey provides a useful tool that fulfills these desiderata. The ethnosurvey blends anthropological and survey research methods to conduct in-depth surveys of specific communities chosen to represent an array of sizes and patterns of social and economic origins. An ethnosurvey applies a semi-structured instrument to interview a random sample of respondents from purposively selected communities. A key component of the ethnosurvey is the gathering of a detailed life history that allows for the construction of retrospective event history analysis that can sustain longitudinal analysis. Individual data are supplemented with event history data compiled at the household, community, national, and international levels to enable multi-level analyses, and to mitigate selection biases parallel sampling is conducted, whereby out-migrants who have settled abroad are located, interviewed, and incorporated into the final database.

Ethnosurveys have been most extensively applied in Mexico, yielding a rich and detailed research literature on patterns and processes of Mexican migration to the United States, both documented and undocumented. More recently, ethnosurveys have been carried out in places other than Mexico: in other Latin American countries, in Central and Eastern Europe, and in China, and a round of surveys are currently planned for Poland in 2003–2004. When they are finally available, they will potentially provide data on patterns and processes of international migration from 146 communities and more than 25,000 households located in fourteen different countries.

With such comparable multi-level event history data compiled across so many settings, analysts will be in a better position than in the past to 1) determine which theoretical explanations predominate in which circumstances; 2) find out why various migratory processes are expressed in different ways in different settings; and 3) identify the structural as opposed to the individual determinants of international migration. We recommend that other social scientists from around the world use ethnosurvey methods to develop comparable databases for their countries, which can then be pooled with those described here to create a global source of data to measure accurately and reliably patterns and processes of both documented and undocumented migration.

REFERENCES

Bean, F. D., R. Corona, R. Tuirán and K. A. Woodrow-Lafield
1998 "The Quantification of Migration between Mexico and the United States." In *Migration between Mexico and the United States, Binational Study, Volume I: Thematic Chapters*. Washington, DC: U.S. Commission on Immigration Reform.

Constant, A. and D. S. Massey
2002 "Return Migration by German Guestworkers: Neoclassical versus New Economic Theories," *International Migration*, 40:5–38.

Durand, J.
1998 "Nuevas Regiones Migratorias?" In *Población, Desarrolo, y Globalización*. Ed. R. Zenteno. México, D.F.: Sociedad Mexicana de Demografia y El Colegio de la Frontera Norte.

Durand, J., D. S. Massey and R. Zenteno
2001 "Mexican Immigration to the United States: Continuities and Changes," *Latin American Research Review*, 36:107–127.

Frejka, T., M. Okolski and K. Sword
1999 *In-Depth Studies on Migration in Central and Eastern Europe: The Case of Poland.* Economic Studies No. 12, Economic Commission for Europe. New York and Geneva: United Nations.

———— 1998 *In-Depth Studies on Migration in Central and Eastern Europe: The Case of Poland.* Economic Studies No. 11, Economic Commission for Europe. New York and Geneva: United Nations.

Heckmann, F.
2004 "Illegal Migration: What Can We Know and What Can We Explain? The Case of Germany," *International Migration Review*, 38(3):1103–1125.

Iglicka, K.
2001 *Poland's Post-War Dynamic of Migration.* Aldershot, UK: Ashgate.

Iglicka, K. and K. Sword
1999 *The Challenge of East-West Migration for Poland.* London: MacMillan.

Jasso, G., D. S. Massey, M. Rosenzweig and J. P. Smith
1999 "The New Immigrant Survey Pilot Study: Overview and New Findings about U.S. Legal Immigrants at Admission," *Demography*, 37:127–138.

Jazwinska, E. and M. Okolski
1996 *Causes and Consequences of Migration in Central and Eastern Europe.* Warsaw: Institute for Social Studies, University of Warsaw.

Joppke, C.
1998 "Why Liberal States Accept Unwanted Immigration," *World Politics*, 50:266–293.

Kalton, G. and D. W. Anderson
1986 "Sampling Rare Populations," *Journal of the Royal Statistical Society A*, 149–182.

Kent, M. M. and M. Mather
2002 "What Drives U.S. Population Growth?" *Population Bulletin*, 57(4):1–40.

Levitt, P. and Glick Schiller, N.
2004 "Conceptualizing Simultaneity: A Transnational Social Field Perspective," *International Migration Review*, 38(3):1002–1039.

Lindstrom, D. P. and D. S. Massey
1994 "Selective Emigration, Cohort Quality, and Models of Immigrant Assimilation," *Social Science Research*, 23:315–349.

Massey, D. S.
1987 "The Ethnosurvey in Theory and Practice," *International Migration Review*, 21(4): 1498–1522.

Massey, D. S., R. Alarcón, J. Durand and H. González
1987 *Return to Aztlan: The Social Process of International Migration from Western Mexico.* Berkeley, CA: University of California Press.

Massey, D. S., J. Arango, G. Hugo, A. Kouaouci, A. Pellegrino and J. E. Taylor
1998 *Worlds in Motion: International Migration at the End of the Millennium.* Oxford: Oxford University Press.

Massey, D. S. and K. Bartley

Forthcoming "The Changing Legal Status Distribution of Immigrants: A Caution," *International Migration Review*, 39(2), Summer.

Massey, D. S., J. Durand and N. Malone

2002 *Beyond Smoke and Mirrors: Mexican Immigration in an Age of Economic Integration.* New York: Russell Sage.

Massey, D. S. and K. Espinosa

1997 "What's Driving Mexico-U.S. Migration? A Theoretical, Empirical and Policy Analysis," *American Journal of Sociology*, 102:939–999.

Massey, D. S. and N. J. Malone

2003 "Pathways to Legalization," *Population Research and Policy Review*, 21:473–504.

Massey, D. S. and M. Sana

2004 "Patterns of U.S. Migration from Mexico, the Caribbean, and Central America," *Migraciones Internacionales*, forthcoming.

Massey, D. S. and R. Zenteno

2000 "A Validation of the Ethnosurvey: The Case of Mexico-U.S. Migration," *International Migration Review*, 34(3):765–792.

Singer, A. and D. S. Massey

1998 "The Social Process of Undocumented Border Crossing," *International Migration Review*, 32(3):561–592.

Sipaviciene, A.

1997 *International Migration in Lithuania: Causes, Consequences, Strategy.* Vilnius: Lithuanian Institute of Philosophy and Sociology.

Smith, S. J., R. G. Kramer and A. Singer

1996 *Characteristics and Labor Market Behavior of the Legalized Population Five Years Following Legalization.* Washington, DC: U.S. Department of Labor.

U.S. Immigration and Naturalization Service

2003 *2001 Statistical Yearbook of the Immigration and Naturalization Service.* Washington, DC: U.S. Government Printing Office.

Woodrow-Lafield, K.

1998 "Estimating Authorized Immigration." In *Migration between Mexico and the United States, Binational Study, Volume 2: Research Reports and Background Materials.* Washington, DC: U.S. Commission on Immigration Reform.

Chapter 10

ILLEGAL MIGRATION: WHAT CAN WE KNOW AND WHAT CAN WE EXPLAIN?[1]
The Case of Germany

Friedrich Heckmann

Imagine two scenes at the German-Czech border. Scene 1: it is night, a group of illegal migrants from Moldavia is sneaking through the bushes, led by a villager from a Czech border village, trying to cross the border to get into Germany. Their goal is to work there in the shadow economy. But they are spotted by a night vision camera of the border police, arrested and questioned, and some are sent back while others are brought into court. Scene 2: The next morning a group of Romanians, comfortably sitting in leather seats on their bus, present their passports to the border officers and are allowed into the country. Their intention, however, is not tourism in

[1]Conference "Conceptual and Methodological Developments in the Study of International Migration."

Germany, but – like the Moldavians – to work there in the shadow economy.

While scene 1 is what one commonly associates with illegal immigration,[2] scene 2 is a case that occurs more and more frequently. The difference between the two groups: Moldavians need visas to travel to Germany, Romanians no longer need visas. Other groups cross the border with falsified documents. We shall see below, in a more detailed way, that there are many forms of illegal immigration. Illegal or undocumented migration is a multifaceted phenomenon.

As the related term "undocumented migration" suggests, there are not and there cannot be any exact figures on the size and kinds of migrants of this type. The first methodological problem this article addresses is whether there are some ways to at least estimate the size of this form of migration. Are there any indicators that allow for an estimate of the size and/or for trends in the development of the phenomenon? We argue that illegal migration is not completely undocumented, that there are indicators, but that the indicators available depend largely on nationally specific conditions. The focus of the discussion here will be conditions and indicators in Germany.

Experts agree that most undocumented migration in the modern world is done through different forms of human smuggling and that human smuggling is a business. Little is known, however, in a systematic way, about the organization of the smuggling process. The idea of an internationally operating, highly organized and centralized, pyramid-like mafia organization that not only trades in migrants, but also in prostitutes, weapons and drugs, is very popular, but it has not been convincingly verified by police investigations or by research (Içduygu and Toktas, 2002:26; Kyle and Koslowski, 2001:13). Conceptual terms used for the analysis of the smuggling process imply a variety of theoretical ideas: "migration merchants" (Kyle and Dale, 2001), "large and well-organized transnational criminal organizations" (Kyle and Koslowski, 2001:11), "crime that is organized" (Finckenauer, 2001: 173), "mom-and-pop operators" (Finckenauer, 2001:183) or "smuggling industry" (Meyers III, 1997:108), to name a few.

If methodology in the sense referred to above is related to questions of measurement, a second methodological focus concerns ways to theorize on the phenomena to be analyzed. Thus, a second methodological-theoretical

---

[2]In accordance with most literature in Germany, we use the term "illegal migration" synonymously with "undocumented" or "irregular" migration.

problem this article addresses is the development of concepts for analyzing the smuggling process.

There is a growing research interest in illegal migration and human smuggling from different disciplines and different perspectives, such as legal and criminological perspectives, labor market and social policy views, national security and control of immigration aspects, or focusing on issues of human rights. The research interest discussed herein is primarily the social organization of the smuggling process.

This shall be done by looking at general concepts from sociology and economics and asking whether they can be applied to explain phenomena of human smuggling and, if so, in which ways. The phenomena to be studied concern the entire smuggling operation, including mobilization in the country of origin, the travel-transport phase, and "integration" or insertion into the immigration country. The social organization and technology of human smuggling are in a constant process of adapting to new environmental conditions. To explain the dynamics of this change is another focus of the study.

The context from which I have written this paper is an ongoing project at the *European Forum for Migration Studies* (EFMS) at the University of Bamberg, called "Human Smuggling and Trafficking in Migrants. Types, Origins and Dynamics in a Comparative and Interdisciplinary Perspective," financed by the National German Research Foundation within the framework of a "European Collaborative Research Project."[3] We begin by discussing the measurement aspects of the topic.

ESTIMATING TRENDS IN ILLEGAL IMMIGRATION INTO GERMANY

Illegal immigration takes on many different forms that greatly depend on existing legal regulations, policing, border regimes, reactions of smugglers and migrants towards these conditions, and physical characteristics of the border areas. There are, however, three basic forms or types of illegal migration that may have many subtypes and variations, depending upon the conditions mentioned (Figure I). Apart from the illegal and clandestine crossing of a border there is – according to police experts – the increasingly

---

[3]The project partners are: IMIS (University of Amsterdam), Centro Studi di Politica Internazionale (Rome), ICMPD (Wien), SFM (Neuchatel) and Instituto Universitario de Estudos sobre Migraciones (Madrid). The EFMS project team consists of Friedrich Heckmann, Thomas Müller-Schneider and Matthias Neske.

Figure I.   **Basic Forms of Illegal Migration**

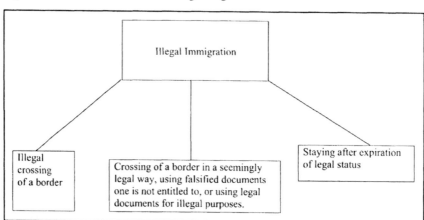

important crossing of a border in a seemingly legal way, either by using falsified documents, by using legal documents one is not entitled to, or by using legal documents for illegal purposes. The third form is – in a strict sense – not so much a form of immigration, but of not re-migrating and staying in a country after one's legal status has expired, for instance a tourist or temporary student visa ("overstayers").

The quantitative side of the phenomenon of illegal immigration has been approached in some countries on the basis of amnesty measures for illegal immigrants. Such amnesty or legalization campaigns have been organized in Belgium, France, Greece, Italy, the Netherlands, Portugal, Spain and the United States (Lederer, 2003:194). Depending upon the scope and the "generosity" or openness of such programs, more or less accurate estimates of the stock of the population can be gained for a particular moment in time. These stock data, however, become quickly outdated, since amnesty programs form an incentive for new migrants to come in the same way, hoping or believing they will gain legal status in the future. Germany has not had and will most probably not have such programs, which means that this method of measurement is not and will not be available.

How much the recording of illegal immigration is dependent upon very specific historic national and regional conditions may be demonstrated by another example from research at the U.S.-Mexican border in the 1980s. Bustamante (1989:100) was interested in flow data. He writes that a photographic technique "systematically examines the habitual gatherings of people once they have crossed the U.S.-Mexican border 'without inspection' by U.S. immigration authorities. . . . Photographic slides of the two principal gathering places for undocumented immigrants crossing through Tijuana are systematically taken each day." The research was undertaken to evaluate possible effects of the 1986 legislation, which provided for sanctions against firms employing illegal migrants. It seems questionable whether this technique ever could be regarded as valid and reliable. With operations like "Gatekeeper" and "Hold the Line" and the total change in the control regime at the U.S.-Mexican border, this method certainly could not be repeated.

Researchers in the United States have used – among other methods – census data to estimate the stock of illegal migrants in the country (Heer, 1990, in Lederer, 2003:203). The rationale behind this is convincing evidence that a substantial portion of the illegal migrants would be registered in the census. It is unthinkable that such a method could be utilized in Germany, since anyone without legal status detected in the census data collection would have to be reported to the authorities.

The *European Forum for Migration Studies* at the University of Bamberg has been writing reports on immigration into Germany for the federal government (Beauftragte, 2001). When reporting on illegal immigration, we work with the basic idea that illegal immigrants are traceable, to some degree, in certain data and statistics. These data, like apprehension statistics, can never, of course, measure exactly the size of illegal immigration into the country. But they can be analyzed for trends. Comparing the United States and Great Britain on one side and Germany (and Austria or Switzerland) on the other, it can be stated that official statistics come closer to the true numbers of illegal migrants in the latter case. This is due to the much greater density of internal controls by law enforcement agencies in the latter countries. We first look at some statistics that indicate flow, then at others that indicate stock of illegal immigrant population.

Flow Data

Data indicating flow of illegal immigration may be divided into statistics that indicate unsuccessful attempts of illegal border crossing and data that indicate "successful" illegal border crossings. The data on unsuccessful attempts all stem from the German Border Police. The most important statistic is apprehensions for illegal border crossing. Figure II shows apprehensions at German borders from 1990 to 2001.

The number of apprehensions was four times higher in 2001 than in

Figure II.   **Apprehensions of Foreigners Attempting to Cross National Land and Sea Borders Illegally, 1990–2001**

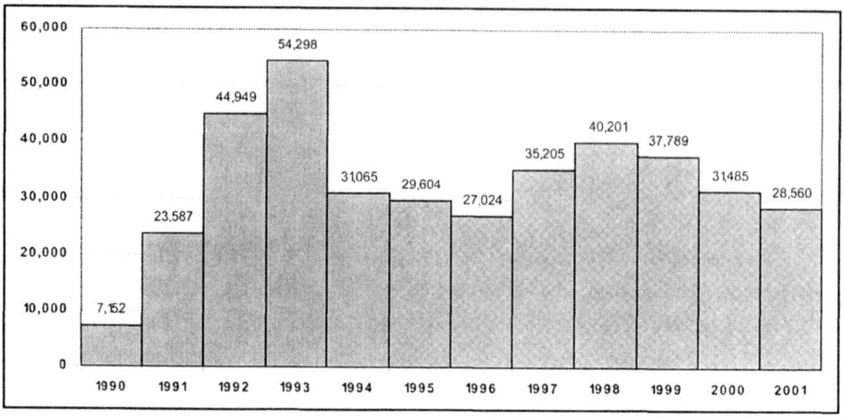

Source. Federal Border Guard (Bundesgrenzschutz)

1990. A very sharp increase occurred between 1990 and 1993, from 7,152 to 54,300 cases. Since 1993, the numbers have gone down, and remain at a relatively consistent lower level. Figure III shows apprehensions of smugglers and smuggled persons from 1990 to 2001. The numbers for smuggled people are five times higher in 2001 than in 1990, and there has been a rather continuous increase. Whether this is due to an increase in smuggling or an intensification of border controls, or both, we cannot infer from these statistics.

If these statistics indicate unsuccessful attempts at illegal border crossings, asylum statistics indicate "successful" illegal crossing of the border. The statistic referred to in this context is people asking for asylum within the country (Figure IV). Due to the safe-third-country regulation of 1993, any person asking for asylum at a land border would be turned back, since Germany is surrounded only by "safe" countries in which a person might find asylum and would not have to go to Germany to be safe from political persecution. Once a person is in the country, asks for asylum, and does not tell authorities about the true route and mode of traveling or of being smuggled into the country, an asylum procedure is started. Authorities know the person applying for asylum has illegally entered the country across a land or sea border, but they accept it within the asylum-seeking process. A "regular" way to get access to the asylum procedure without crossing the border illegally is to arrive by arriving by air or sea.

Between 1990 and the end of 2002, almost 2 million persons applied

Figure III.   **Apprehensions of Human Smugglers and Smuggled Migrants at German National Borders, 1990–2001**

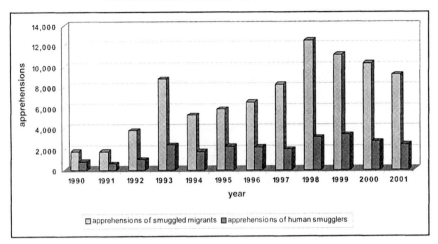

Source: Federal Border Guard (Bundesgrenzschutz)

Figure IV.   **Asylum Applications ("Erstanträge"), 1990–2002**

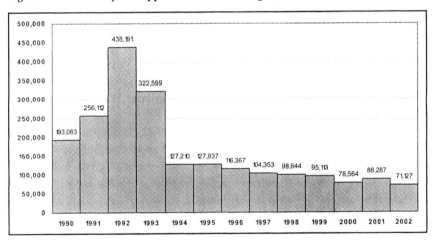

Source: Federal Office for the Recognition of Foreign Refugees (BAFl)

for political asylum in Germany. Since 1993, application figures have been decreasing continuously, mainly due to the reform of asylum law, the stabilization of Eastern European countries, and the resolution of the conflict in former Yugoslavia (*Beauftragte,* 2001:39). The remarkable feature of asylum migration in Germany is that one gets a (temporary) legal status for the asylum procedure despite an illegal crossing of the border, which "normally" constitutes a criminal act.

Stock Data

Unlike in the United States, long-term or even permanent illegal stay in the country is very difficult in Germany. The country is much smaller and controls are more effective and regarded as legitimate (ID cards, "*verdachtsunabhängige Kontrollen,*"[4] for example). Thus, in most cases, illegal immigration and stay in Germany is temporary, or a kind of pendulum movement. Welfare organizations and churches in Germany recently have begun to recognize the existence of a population of illegal immigrants in need of help. They have started certain programs for these migrants, and authorities, who would be obliged by law to record such cases and take action against illegal migrants, seem to tolerate such activities. Social workers who work with this population can help to estimate the size of the illegal population in the country. This, of course, is a "soft" indicator, but some social workers in urban areas are among the very few who have knowledge of this hidden population.

Another indicator is found in crime statistics, looks more exact, and gives numbers and time-series data: suspected criminal offenses of foreigners without legal resident status. German police continuously collect data on suspected criminal offenses of all kinds and record the resident status of foreign citizens suspected of crimes. The number of suspects without legal resident status marks the bottom line of the illegal migrant population in the country (Figure V).

In 2001, for instance, there were about 122,500 apprehensions of people without legal documents. Subtracting the number of apprehension cases at the border that are also recorded in this statistic, one arrives at a number of about 94,000 people without a legal stay for the year 2001 who are suspected of having committed crimes.[5] Looking at the statistic of suspected criminal offenses of people without legal title to stay in the country during the 1994 to 2001 period (Figure V), one could determine the numbers remain at a rather constant level.

---

[4]Checking on a person who has not behaved in a suspicious way. Such controls are possible for instance in airports, railway or bus stations.

[5]Since this statistic records cases and not only persons, the number of people for which this statistic stands must be somewhat smaller; a few people will have been apprehended twice or even more often.

Figure V.   Persons Suspected of a Criminal Offense Without a Legal
                  Residence Status in Germany, 1994–2001

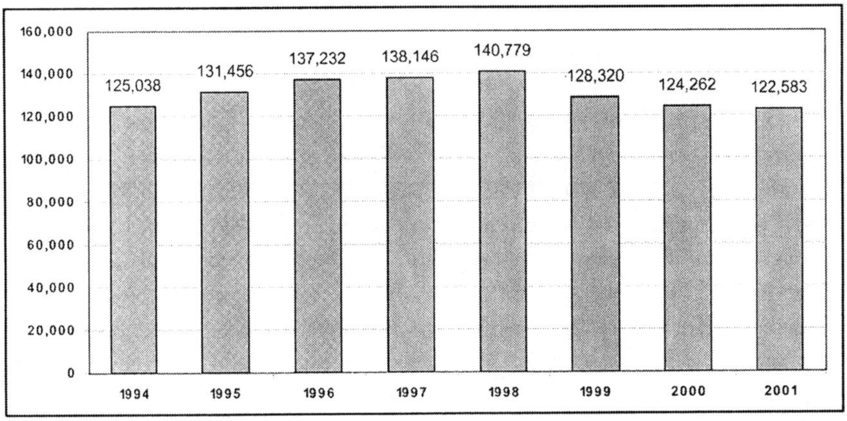

Source: Federal Office of Criminal Investigation (Police Crime Statistics)

Other statistics that reflect, to a certain degree, the number of illegal migrants in the country are cases of document fraud by foreigners, false marriages, illegal employment, and illegal work. All of these data rose sharply in the first half of the 1990s and remained at a rather constant lower level in the second half of the decade (Lederer, 2003:232–247). What do we know from the different data about illegal immigration to Germany? In terms of stock data, we have a minimum number of people that must live in the country. We may infer that at present the population of illegal migrants is at least about 94,000. As to flow data, a trend can be identified: a steep increase in the first three to four years after 1990 and a somewhat lower and rather constant level for the second half of the 1990s.[6]

ILLEGAL MIGRATION AND HUMAN SMUGGLING

Illegal migration can be organized in different ways. We may discern forms of illegal migration that are totally self-organized by the migrating person(s).

[6]The statistic on smugglers and smuggled people caught does correspond to this trend in the first half of the 1990s, but not to the second half. Whether this is due to a rather continuous increase in smuggling or reflects tighter controls by the border police or both, we do not know. What can be stated with certainty is that border controls have strongly and continuously been intensified at the Schengen borders.

In other cases, migrants may "buy" certain smuggling services necessary at certain points or intervals "en route." A third type could be a network or an organization that controls the entire smuggling operation – from recruitment to insertion – and operates both in the country of origin and in the immigration country.

Self-organization of the illegal migration process to Europe is more of an exception in modern times. Illegal migration mostly involves organized human smuggling of some kind and to some degree. Human smuggling is planned and performed in quite different ways. In terms of methodology and theory, we are interested in concepts and theories that could help explain the existence and functioning of different forms of organization of the smuggling process. Before discussing concepts for the analysis of human smuggling, I first turn to possible sources of information that could help describe the phenomenon, with particular reference to Germany.

Data Sources

The following data sources may be used: interviews with smuggled people; experts' interviews (police, social workers, health services personnel); final reports of police investigations; reports by public prosecutors; and court records.

Interviews with smuggled persons – for obvious reasons – are possible only after the person has achieved a safe and legal status. In countries with legalization programs and amnesties, such interviews are possible. Germany is not a country with legalization programs, but those whose asylum applications have been positively decided might be ready for interviews.

Police, social workers and supporting health services personnel are the main experts on illegal immigration. Churches and welfare organizations in Germany have started, in the last two or three years, to realize the need for programs helping illegal migrants. Authorities are interested in avoiding the development of problematic situations and tolerate the work of the welfare organizations. Thus, expertise in illegal migration and the social situations of these migrants is developing among small groups of professionals, particularly in big cities. The most valuable information for our research project has come from the police and the Federal Border Police. Expert interviews with police investigators have proven very informative. The other source used for our research is final reports of police investigations on cases of human smuggling and trafficking that are sent to the public prosecutor. Court verdicts are another source of information.

Cases of Human Smuggling

Before approaching the discussion of possible concepts for the analysis of human smuggling, we describe three cases of smuggling that have been reconstructed from twelve intensive experts' interviews with police investigators within the EFMS project.[7] A fourth case has been taken from the literature. These cases demonstrate the broad variety of the phenomenon of human smuggling.

Case 1: Mr. A is standing at the railway station in Prague waiting for customers. He approaches people who, in his opinion, might be potential clients for his smuggling services. Judging that they are interested in getting to Germany, he offers to organize the transport to the German border for $300. He tells them they would be brought to a pub near the border where they would surely meet on-foot smugglers who would lead them through the forest across the border. If a "customer" accepts the offer, the following day Mr. A. picks him up by car. He collects the money and takes the person, as previously agreed upon, to the pub near the border.

Case 2: Mr. B. lives as a foreigner in Germany and organizes the smuggling of fellow countrymen from the Middle East. A relative in his home village is his contact person for the organization at the beginning of a smuggling operation. Many people in the village have plans to migrate, and the activities of Mr. B's relative are well known. A person who wishes to be smuggled pays Mr. B. for the first stage of the journey via a form of shadow banking, which is called *Hawala.*[8] The person to be smuggled receives a mobile phone

---

[7]The interviews have been conducted by Matthias Neske; he has also reconstructed the cases. The interviews were done with officers from the *Bundesgrenzschutzinspecktion Furth im Wald, Bundesamt für die Anerkennung ausländischer Flüchtlinge, Kriminalpolizei Nürnberg, Bundesgrenzschutzpräsidium Süd Müchen, Bundesgreznschutzamt Schwandorf, Bundesgrenzschutzpräsidium Ost Berlin, Bundesnachrichendienst Pullach, Bundesgrenzschutzamt Frankfurt Oder, Bundesgrenzshutzdirektion Koblenz, Landeskriminalamt Niedersachsen Hannover, Landeskriminalamt Bayern Müchen* and *Bundeskriminalamt Wiesbaden.*

[8]*Hawala* is based on the principle of two "containers": one in the country of origin and one in the country of destination. As an example: Mr. A., who works in Hamburg, wants to transfer money to Mr. B. in Kabul. He approaches a *Hawala* banker in Hamburg and gives him the amount of money. The banker charges a commission and calls his banker colleague in Kabul, with Mr. B. standing next to him in the Kabul bank, and confirms that the amount has just been paid in Hamburg. The banker in Kabul pays the money to Mr. B. The proceedings are based on complete mutual trust among all participants and have the advantage of being considerably faster, more effective, and cheaper than Western bank transfers.

with the number of Mr. B. so he may contact him in case of complications. The crossing of the first border is eased by Mr. B.'s contact bribing the border guard. After that, the migrant is left on his own. Mr. B. has further contact people in Ankara, Istanbul and Athens. The smuggled person approaches these people after receiving orders from Mr. B. via phone and pays a required sum of money for the next stage of the trip. He then continues to travel to Patras, where he manages to hide under the tarpaulin of a truck and reaches Italy. Mr. B. then sends his uncle with a hired camper van to Italy to pick up the smuggled person near the harbor and take him to Germany. Upon arrival, the smuggled person has to pay the final sum. In Germany, the smuggled person is received by his relatives.

Case 3: Two Afghans met at a Czech university and now live in Hamburg and Moscow. As they were sent to Europe during Soviet times and were supported by the regime, they could not return to Afghanistan after the fall of the communist regime. They have developed numerous contacts with fellow countrymen in many other countries. Without having been involved in criminal activities before, they now use their contacts to organize human smuggling operations. All along the route from Afghanistan to Hamburg, they have cooperating contacts who help them. Only the two smugglers know all of these persons.

The smugglers use the method of recruitment to get customers. The recruitment activities are carried out in Kabul by local accomplices, and the journey begins as soon as Hamburg relatives of the person to be smuggled have paid the first installment for the trip via *Hawala*. Those being smuggled are driven out of the country in a minibus and taken care of along the route to Moscow by the different accomplices of the two Afghans, who provide them with food and lodging and who bribe the border guards. After arrival in Moscow, a Moscow-based Afghan organizes a trip with other Afghans to Prague. The smuggled group carries a mobile phone during the whole journey, enabling them to contact the two core smugglers in case of problems. No names are used. In Prague, the smugglers use the assistance of locals to organize rides to the border and the last stage of smuggling—on foot to Germany. Upon arrival in Germany, the final sum is paid.

There are no written traces of the transfer so that incriminate funds can be transferred, too. In order to balance the two cash "containers," couriers with money fly from Hamburg to Kabul. Imports or exports are another form of balancing the assets (Neske, Müller-Schneider and Heckmann, 2002:4).

Case 4: This case from Meyers (1997:108)[9] deals with smuggling from Fujian province in China:

> Fujianese migration began a slow but steady increase as it entered the . . . phase in 1986. Spurred by the Taiwanese development of the transportation networks, the smuggling industry developed the basic structure that exists today. Networks created by *guanxi* partnerships made access to illicit transportation easier, and *guanxi* wove globally distributed specialist entrepreneurs into highly flexible networks to form the smuggling industry. Mostly by letter, frequently through a returning relative, and sometimes by phone, pleas and demands for migration assistance from Fujianise in the source villages poured into the U.S. Fujianese community. The members of that community were established, had the funds and obligations, and, most importantly, had *guanxi* with the smugglers. . . .[T]he market for smuggling services was in the United States, not Fujian Province. Manhattan's Chinatown . . . was the point of contact for those seeking illicit transportation services and those brokering them. . . . The terms, almost always oral, included a total payment, usually U.S.$18,000; a down payment, usually U.S.$1,000; undertakings of performance by the broker; and a final balance due on delivery. . . . Because broker and client had a *guanxi* relationship . . . neither could breach their obligations without incurring a loss of face . . . and a resultant social and economic ostracism, or risking rectification of a breach by a progression of informal means, culminating in terror – induced performance at the hands of a criminal gang retained by the aggrieved party.

Concepts for Analyzing the Organization of Smuggling Operations

The cases described represent different forms of organization of the human smuggling processes. In terms of general sociological and economic theory (working with the assumption that human smuggling is a business), what kind of structures and processes can we identify here? In a methodological sense, the literature on human smuggling is rather weak and often uses vague and *ad hoc* concepts when approaching this question: smuggling industry, networks of smugglers, migrant merchants, mom-and-pop-smugglers, organized crime, or crime that is organized, to name a few. Often the term used does not seem to be more than a metaphor. First attempts to describe the organizational structures of human smuggling and trafficking in a publication by the International Organization for Migration (Juhász, 2000:196–197; Okólski, 2000:261) look rather "voluntaristic"; in addition, the empirical basis for the argument is not made clear.

The public perception of organized human smuggling conveys the notion that pyramid-like, hierarchical organizations of a mafia type domi-

[9] While cases 1–3 were drawn from the experts' interviews with police experts in an ongoing EFMS research project, case 4 is from Meyers, III (1997, 108–109).

nate the smuggling process. ". . . [H]uman trafficking and even smuggling are often visualized as a global business involving well organized criminal, mafia-type formations involving countries of origin, of transit and of destination world wide" (Içduygu and Toktas, 2002:29). Many law enforcement agencies and jurists seem to share that view and speak of organized crime (*see, e.g.,* Albrecht, 2002; Nowotny, 2002; Yates, 1997). The cases we have described, however, clearly demonstrate a variety of forms of human smuggling. This does not necessarily mean that the pyramid type of organization does not exist: organizational purposes, a membership structure, a hierarchy and a division of labor, rules and sanctions, and definitions of what one has to do for the organization and what one can expect in return. We have, however, not seen convincing evidence so far that the pyramid-like criminal mafia organization exists.

Trying to identify the cases in terms of general theoretical concepts, Case 1 is about a single actor and seems to be the very opposite of case 4. While in case 4 we have a large organized structure with complete "service" from recruiting to insertion in the country of immigration, only a partial service is being offered by a provider in a market-type situation. The provider is in competition with other providers of similar or identical services.

Are there any special characteristics of this form of market versus "more normal" markets? Market is an exchange process that is based on the interest of the actors. Market exchange processes, particularly in well functioning markets, are not based on interest alone, but require certain rules that help to minimize risks involved in the exchange. These rules could be given by the state in the form of market regulations or by a system of market morals and mutual trust (Esser, 2000:172). The particular risks in a smugglers' market as described in case 1 seem to be constituted by a lack of such rules and by the fact that the exchange usually is a single exchange that gives the buyer little sanctioning power. He could only inform other potential migrants about the case, but it would be difficult for them to use this information. Thus the smugglers' market with an exchange of a limited and short-term service is a market with high risks involved for the "customers" and a high probability of the migrants being cheated.

The actions of certain "*pateros,*" *i.e.,* single smugglers at the Mexican border with Texas, may serve as an illustration of this risk:

> This type of smuggler can frequently be found loitering around international bridges in addition to the bus stations of Mexican border cities. Migrants who are unaware of the realities of the journey they have undertaken are often victimized by these smugglers, who take their money in advance, lead them across the river, and

abandon them to their fate once they are on the Texas side. This fate usually includes quick apprehension by the Border Patrol and often includes assault and worse by bandits who lurk in the darkness near the river on the U.S. side. A frequent complaint is that the assailants in these cases include the smugglers themselves (Spener, 2001:135–136).

Police experts and literature (Içduygu and Toktas, 2002) tell us that cases 2 and 3, and variants of these, quantitatively have become the most important contemporary forms of organized human smuggling operations. In sociological terms, what kind of structures do these cases have? How do they rise, how can we explain its functioning and its adaptation to changing environmental conditions? A first and general answer is that the two cases represent network relations among smugglers. Concepts of network analysis can help to describe and understand these relations.

A network consists of units and their relationships. With reference to cases 2 and 3, we could say that there is a unit of an initiating and organizing individual or of a (small) group of individuals who are the "entrepreneurial" part of the network. The other units are locally and internationally spread out "helpers" or "contacts." Since human smuggling in present times almost exclusively is a business, the relationship between "entrepreneur" and "helpers" is characterized by mutual economic interest. In case the relationships are kin and/or ethnic relations, communication in the net is eased, and the relationships could be more stable. This is what may explain the ethnic homogeneity of the smugglers' networks. The difference between case 2 and case 3 is that case 2 has this type of closer relationship, which is further strengthened by kin and ethnic ties. Case 2 has a higher degree of multiplexity. Also, there are elements of self-organization of the migration process in case 2. Kin and ethnic ties are connected by obligations of solidarity, which can be mobilized for the network activity. In case 3, it is "only" a relationship among members of the same ethnic or national group, bound together by their economic interests.

Despite kin and ethnic relationships, the human smugglers' network is one of high asymmetry. The entrepreneurial core person(s) clearly dominate and profit most from the network or even exploit the helpers. The smugglers' network, in addition, is highly centralized. In terms of network concepts, it represents a star configuration. All relationships are from the core to the other units, but there are no relations among the other units. This constitutes a singular power for the core.

On the basis of an analysis by Phillip Bonacich on the different effects of power versus prestige relationships, Hartmut Esser (2000:196–197) distinguishes networks of *"negativer Verbundenheit"* or "negative union" from networks of *"positiver Verbundenheit"* or "positive union." They constitute very different "worlds" in which very different strategies of action are prevalent. Networks of *positiver Verbundenheit* are characterized by relationships of prestige, mutual sympathy, trust, and help; hence they are mutually supportive and complementary. The value of an actor's relation to another actor increases with the value of this actor's relationships and resources. Networks of negative union are characterized by unequal power relations and competition for the control of scarce goods among the actors. Despite the ethnic bond in the network of case 3, the smugglers' network is a case of *negativer Verbundenheit*. The function that ethnicity plays is one of easing communication, but not of establishing mutual relationships of sympathy and help. Case 2 could be said to have elements of both *"negativer"* and *"positiver Verbundenheit."*

The difference between positive and negative union is helpful in explaining the difference between networks in which human smuggling is a business – which is today's normal – and idealistic networks of human smugglers. The network that smuggled German-Jewish intellectuals and artists out of Germany during the Nazi rule or the student groups of *"Fluchthelfer"* from the Free University of Berlin who smuggled East Germans through the Wall after 1961 clearly are characterized by different relations of positive union than contemporary commercial smuggling networks.

Let us now turn to the analysis of case 4, the case of Chinese human smugglers. Is this a case of a large, hierarchical, pyramid-like mafia organization that we hear so much about, or does it have network characteristics? Looking at cases 2 and 3 versus case 4, we could first say that case 4 has a much larger and globally more extensive structure. Its elements have, at least partly, the characteristics of an organization – for example, the transportation organization – but the structure of operations as a whole does not seem to show one organization, but rather the interconnected organizations. It is a network that consists of organizations, hence an interorganizational network.

Most of the numerous publications referring to human smuggling as an activity of organized crime assume the existence of a large organization performing the operation. Neither the hypothesis of organized crime nor that of the existence of large total organizations "doing the job" have been convincingly verified. We rather follow Ko-lin Chin, who has interviewed more than 300 smuggled people and concludes: ". . . immigrant smuggling . . . is a global business initiated by Chinese Americans of Fuzhou extraction and supported not only by Taiwanese but also by Chinese and non-Chinese in numerous transit countries. In short, the human trade is in many ways like any other legitimate international trade, except that it is illegal. Like any trade, it needs organization and planning, but it does not appear to be linked with traditional "organized crime" groups (Chin, 2001: 225). Europol states in its report for the years 1996–1997 that "there is no clear proof that illegal immigration is . . . organized by internationally acting criminal groups" (Salt and Hogarth, 2000:54).

Returning to case 4 and continuing to work with the assumption that human smuggling is a business, we have a network of business organizations. Gerum (2001) has carried out a broad theoretical analysis of the network concept with special emphasis on networks of business organizations – *Unternehmensnetzwerke* – that can be applied to explain the workings of the case 4 relationships. His analysis refers to relationships between legal businesses. We assume that a network of businesses engaged in illegal activities follows the same or similar basic pattern.

To understand the functioning of networks between business organizations, it is helpful to differentiate these from markets and hierarchies. Markets and hierarchies represent ideal types of coordination of economic activities. Analyzing a broad sociological and economic literature, Gerum (2001:11–13) argues convincingly that networks represent an independent form of coordination of economic activities. He lays down the basic functional principles of such interorganizational networks: networks of organizations are formed by self-reliant, independent actors and usually are based on long-term relationships. There is – at least partially – a common interest between the organizations, yet cooperation coincides with competition in the relationship. The relationship is stable as long as profit gained from cooperation in the network is greater than profit gained from truly competitive behavior by each individual organization. This creates mutual dependency. Complementary resources are the basis for the creation of a network among organizations. The value of the network as a whole is dependent upon the actions of all partners, which determines the specific network risk.

The distribution of profit in an organizational network is another interesting point. In a market – under conditions of perfect information – the distribution of profit is regulated *ex ante* with the conclusion of a contract. In a hierarchy or formal organization, the profit is distributed according to an employment contract and, in case of several owners, according to the charter of the company. The employment contract regulates clearly the amount and size of income, while the charter (*Gesellschaftsvertrag*) could only regulate the distribution of (potential) profits. During the formation of a network, however, neither the size of profit nor the mode of distributing profits are known. Negotiations *ex post* are therefore necessary for the regulation of these issues. Hence, high risks are involved in network structures of organizations. This applies to any interorganizational network. The risks are even higher for organizations engaged in illegal activities. As a consequence of illegal activities, smugglers and traffickers operate in a clandestine way and use particular techniques to hide their activities, such as forging documents or continuously changing mobile phones to ensure secrecy of communication.

Decisions have to be made under conditions of limited information and uncertain outcomes. In this situation, organizations in the network have to resort to trust. "Trust is the central coordinating mechanism in a network" (Gerum, 2001). In the example of case 4, this relationship is called *guanxi* – a relationship of trust between people not related by kinship. Whereas, in networks of *positiver Verbundenheit*, sympathy and trust are founding principles of the network; in case 4 trust is a necessity resulting from the logistics of the business. Portes (1995:14) called this mechanism "enforceable trust." It refers to a situation in which "economic transfers can proceed with confidence that others will fulfill their obligations lest they be subjected to the full weight of collective sanctions" (Portes, 1995:13).

The Interaction between Law Enforcement and Smugglers: The Development of an Arms Race

While in the previous section we have been interested primarily in the possibilities of analyzing different types of social organizations of human smuggling, in this section we add some elements for a possible explanation of the dynamics. Human smuggling arises out of the existence of borders and because border crossing is possible only under certain defined legal conditions, while the motivation for global migration exceeds the given legal possibilities. At the same time, the abilities of states to control immigration are limited, and migration policies often fail to achieve their intended objectives (Castles, 2004).

Experts agree that the process of human smuggling is under constant pressure to adapt. The dynamism in the social organization of smuggling evolves from the relationship between law enforcement and smugglers' networks. The basic pattern is an interaction process: the action of one actor provokes a reaction from the other, which in turn leads to another action. Each action is influenced by the actor's anticipation of possible reactions from the other actor. The whole process takes on the form of an arms race.

The state's and law enforcement's actions and measures generally include: an increase in financial means and personnel for border control; an increase in material and technological resources; changes in legislation and administrative rules; and cooperation with other states and training of their personnel.

These elements do not come all at once, but rather in phases and lead to a spiral in the intensity of competition with the smugglers.

The smugglers' response and arsenal of reactions include: changes of routes; increase in technological sophistication; professionalization and specialization; increase of juridical sophistication; development of marketing strategies such as more systematic recruitment and improvement of "services"; guaranteed smuggling and special fees for certain groups; and attempts to corrupt state officials.

From general theory of economic competition we can infer that the intensity of competition is evident in the speed with which one side can make up for the advantages of the other side (Kantzenbach, 1967). The level and intensity of competition between law enforcement and smugglers results, on the one hand, from its nature as an interactive process. On the other hand, when looking at each side separately and at the endogenous part of the process, cumulative causation and a pattern of path dependency seem to operate. Path dependency is a concept that denotes the influence of past states on present conditions (Portes, 1995:17). Since one has decided to engage in a particular process in the past and has invested in it, one cannot easily withdraw from it. The costs would be quite high.

An arms race will end with the exhaustion of one of the competitors. In human smuggling, however, we seem to be far from that moment. What Peter Andreas (2001) has found for the U.S.–Mexican border – a conflict and simultaneously a kind of symbiotic relationship between law enforcement and smuggling – is most probably true for the European scene as well. As the demand for smuggling services and the risks of illegal migration have grown the price for smuggling has risen. This has enhanced the wealth and power of smuggling groups, but not of all groups. Better controls have removed some smugglers from the business, but improved the market position of others. "Moreover, many of those arrested are the lowest-level and most expendable members of smuggling organizations – the border guides and drivers who are the 'foot soldiers' of the business" (Andreas, 2001:117).

From the migrants' perspective, the risks for illegal migration have grown for those with few resources.

Law enforcement and migration policy decisionmakers are well aware of the dilemma. Apart from cumulative causation and path dependency, the state has additional and significant reasons for not withdrawing from the arms race: control over territory, population and borders are core aspects of a state's sovereignty. For a union of states – like the Schengen States within the EU, who have removed border controls among them – the same holds true for the policies regarding their common outside borders.

CONCLUSION

The article consists of two parts: an analysis of possibilities to empirically trace illegal or undocumented migration, with special reference to Germany, and a discussion of the ability of certain concepts and hypotheses to describe and explain the social organization of human smuggling. In this volume, Massey (2004) has described an impressive range of methods to document the number of illegal aliens which seem to have some universal applicability. At the same time, it is evident that the possibilities to empirically trace this type of migration depends on nationally and historically specific conditions. Referring to Germany, we have argued that official statistics on apprehensions, asylum applications, and criminal offenses indicate trends of illegal migration and allow for the estimation of a minimum number of illegal migrants in the country. These possibilities are related to the existence of a rather strict border and an internal control regime in Germany.

Much of the discussion on human smuggling is dominated by the hypothesis of mafia type, pyramid-like organizations performing the operations. We have given evidence for a variety of forms that represent different types of human smuggling. We have discerned single actors, networks of smugglers, and interorganizational networks. Each type of social organization operates under particular conditions, with particular implications for the smugglers as well as for their customers. In ongoing research investigating files of police investigations and court verdicts, we will further differentiate our models of the human smuggling organizations. Evidence for the activities of large-scale criminal organizations has not been found as yet. A connection between the smuggling of humans and of drugs and/or weapons has not been empirically established.

REFERENCES

Albrecht, H. J.
2002 "Eine Kriminologische Einführung zu Menschenschmuggel und Schleuserkriminalität." In *Illegale Migration und Schleusungskriminalität. Schriftenreihe der Kriminologischen Zentralstelle Wiesbaden, Band 37.* Ed. E. Minthe. Pp. 29–53.

Andreas, P.
2001 "The Transformation of Migrant Smuggling across the U.S.-Mexican Border." In *Global Human Smuggling. Comparative Perspectives.* Baltimore and London: Johns Hopkins University Press. Pp. 107–128.

Beauftragte der Bundesregierung für Ausländerfragen
2002 Migration Review. English Version of Beauftragte 2001 on CD ROM. The CD can be ordered from EFMS <www.uni-bamerg.de/efms>.

2001 *Migrationsbericht der Ausländerbeauftragten im Auftrag der Bundesregierung.* Berlin: Bonn.

Bustamante, J. A.
1989 "Measuring the Flow of Undocumented Immigrants." In *Mexican Migration to the United States.* Ed. W. Cornelius and J. Bustamante. San Diego, CA: University of California Press. Pp. 95–106.

Castles, S.
2004 "The Factors that Make and Unmake Migration Policies," *International Migration Review,* 38(3):852–884.

Chin, K. L.
2001 "The Social Organization of Chinese Human Smuggling." In *Global Human Smuggling. Comparative Perspectives.* Ed. D. Kyle and R. Koslowski. Baltimore and London: Johns Hopkins University Press.

Esser, H.
2000 *Soziologie. Spezielle Grundlagen. Band 4: Opportunitäten und Restriktionen.* Frankfurt and New York: Campus.

Europol
1999 "General Situation Report 1996–1997: Illegal Immigration." The Hague. File No. 2562–52.

Finckenauer, J. O.
2001 "Russian Transnational Organized Crime." In *Global Human Smuggling. Comparative Perspectives.* Ed. D. Kyle and R. Koslowski. Baltimore and London: Johns Hopkins University Press.

Gerum, E.
2001 "*Unternehmensnetzwerke: Ein Grundlagenstreit. Vortag im Workshop der Kommission Wissenschaftstheorie des Verbandes der Hochschullehrer für BWL.*" Augsburg.

Heer, D. M.
1990 *Undocumented Mexican Americans in the United States.* Cambridge: Cambridge University Press.

Içduygu, A. and S. Toktas
2002 "How Do Smuggling and Trafficking Operate via Irregular Border Crossings in the

Middle East? Evidence from Field Work in Turkey," *International Migration*, 40(6): 25–54.

Juhász, J.
2000 "Migrant Trafficking and Human Smuggling in Hungary." In *IOM 2000: Migrant Trafficking and Human Smuggling in Europe. A Review of the Evidence with Case Studies from Hungary, Poland and Ukraine*. Geneva: IOM Publication.

Kantzenbach, E.
1967 *Die Funktionsfähigkeit des Wettbewerbs*. Göttingen.

Kyle, D. and J. Dale
2001 "Smuggling the State Back In. Agents of Human Smuggling Reconsidered." In *Global Human Smuggling. Comparative Perspectives*. Ed. D. Kyle and R. Koslowski. Baltimore and London: Johns Hopkins University Press. Pp. 30–57.

Kyle, D. and R. Koslowski, eds.
2001 "Introduction." In *Global Human Smuggling. Comparative Perspectives*. Ed. D. Kyle and R. Koslowski. Baltimore and London: Johns Hopkins University Press. Pp. 1–25.

Lederer, H. W.
2003 *Indikatoren der Migration. Manuskript der Dissertation*. Universität Bamberg.

v. Liempt, I.
2003 "Human Smuggling." In "Migrants: Towards a Typology." Unpublished Paper IMES, University of Amsterdam.

Massey, D. S.
2004 "Measuring Undocumented Migration," *International Migration Review*, 38(3):1075–1102.

Myers, W. H., III
1997 "Of Quinging, Qinshu, Guanxi and Shetow: The Dynamic Elements of Chinese Irregular Population Movement." In *Human Smuggling. Chinese Migrant Trafficking and the Challenge to America's Immigration Tradition*. Ed. P. J. Smith. Washington, DC: The Center for Strategic and International Studies. Pp. 93–133.

Neske, M., T. Müller-Schneider and F. Heckmann
2002 "The Social Organisation of Human Smuggling." EFMS Project Paper.

Nowotny, K.
2002 In *Illegale Migration und Schleusungskriminalität. Schriftenreihe der kri-minologischen Zentralstelle Wiesbaden, Band 37*. Ed. E. Minthe. Pp. 98–104.

Okólski, M.
2000 "Migrant Trafficking and Human Smuggling in Poland." In *IOM 2000: Migrant Trafficking and Human Smuggling in Europe. A Review of the Evidence with Case Studies from Hungary, Poland and Ukraine*. Geneva: IOM Publiction. Pp. 233–328.

Portes, A.
1995 "Economic Sociology and the Sociology of Immigration: A Conceptual Overview." In *The Economic Sociology of Immigration*. Ed. A. Portes. New York. Pp. 1–41.

Salt, J. and J. Hogarth
2000 "Migrant Trafficking and Human Smuggling in Europe: A Review of the Evidence." In *IOM 2000: Migrant Trafficking and Human Struggling in Europe. A Review of the Evidence with Case Studies from Hungary, Poland and Ukraine*. Geneva: IOM Publication. Pp. 11–164.

Singer, A. and D. S. Massey
1998 "The Social Process of Undocumented Border Crossing among Mexican Migrants," *International Migration Review*, 32(3):561–592.

Spener, D.
2001 In *Global Human Smuggling. Comparative Perspectives*. Ed. D. Kyle and R. Koslowski. Baltimore and London: Johns Hopkins University Press. Pp. 129–165.

Yates, K.
1997 "Canada's Growing Role as a Human Smuggling Destination and Corridor to the United States." In *Human Smuggling. Chinese Migrant Trafficking and the Challenge to America's Immigration Tradition*. Ed. P. J. Smith. Washington, DC: The Center for Strategic and International Studies. Pp. 156–168.

Chapter 11

DOES THE 'NEW' IMMIGRATION REQUIRE A 'NEW' THEORY OF INTERGENERATIONAL INTEGRATION?[1]

Harmut Esser

In terms of the immigration flows to (Western) Europe after World War II, the phenomenon of "new" immigration is, in fact, anything but new. From the outset, and all the way up to the present day, these migration flows have involved the (permanent) immigration of large population groups from the less developed countries of southeastern Europe or from former colonies, some of which display major social, cultural, and religious differences from the receiving countries. At least in part, and even after protracted residence in their host countries extending into subsequent generations, these immigrants stayed in close contact with their countries of origin. Soon they were confronted – again at least partially – by distinct social distances in their receiving countries, began stressing their ethnic and national identities rather more strongly in the course of time, and occasionally imported certain political conflicts from their countries of origin into the receiving countries. In the meantime, there are also indications of the establishment of institutionally stabilized and complete ethnic communities (especially in some urban quarters), of the "segmented" assimilation of subsequent generations in deviant subcultures, and of a neo-feudal ethnic substratification of host countries. In addition, for certain groups, integration no longer seems to be simply a matter of time and the sequence of generations.

[1]This article is based on a paper presented at the conference on Conceptual and Methodological Developments in the Study of International Migration, Princeton, May 23 and 24, 2003.

This appears to be true, for instance, of Turkish immigrants in Germany (*e.g.*, Alba, Handl and Müller, 1994; Esser, 1986a, 1990, 1991; Granato and Kalter 2001; Kalter and Granato, 2002; Nauck, 1995; Noll, Schmidt and Weick, 1998; for comparable processes in other European countries, *see* the contributions in Heckmann and Schnapper, 2003). Consequently, when the sociology of migration in Europe started to deal with this topic (*cf.* Hoffmann-Nowotny, 1973; Esser, 1980; Heckmann, 1981), there was a debate from the outset that in fundamental terms immigration flows to (Western) Europe cannot be compared with the processes observable in "classical" immigration countries, *e.g.*, the United States, Canada, or Australia. For this reason alone, it was argued that classical assimilation theory, for instance in the sense of Gordon (1964), could not be applied to these "new" migration processes in (Western) Europe. Such an approach would, in fact, represent an inappropriate ideological determination and an obstacle to the establishment of peaceful multiculturalism within Western European countries (*cf.* Wilpert, 1980 or the recent contributions by Favell, 2002 or Pott, 2002). This discussion was (and still is) similar to the ongoing controversy within the American (and international) sociology of migration on whether classical assimilation theory is obsolete for the sociological analysis of the new immigration and the integration of the new second generation (*cf.* Massey *et al.*, 1998; Portes, 1995, 1996, 1999; Rumbaut, 1999; Schmitter Heisler, 2000; Zhou, 1999; with regard to transnationalism *see* Faist, 2000; Foner, 1997; Glick Schiller, 1999; Pries, 2001).

The general aim of this article is to find a way to overcome these debates. Its main concern is to outline a comprehensive model of intergenerational integration. The basic idea follows the logic of the model of sociological explanation[2] and can be described as follows. Migrations and subsequent social processes of integration are (mostly indirect) consequences of situationally reasonable reactions of the involved actors to the respectively given societal conditions. These situationally shaped individual responses lead to – mostly unintended – structural consequences (at different societal levels), which themselves create a new situation logic for the actors. Under

---

[2]The model of sociological explanation is an advancement of the concept of situational logic proposed by Max Weber and Karl R. Popper. The concept was further developed and applied in sociology by, *e.g.*, Robert K. Merton, James S. Coleman, Raymond Boudon, Siegwart Lindenberg and Reinhard Wippler, as well as more recently by John Goldthorpe. On the connection between this concept and the idea of "generative mechanisms," *see* Hedström and Swedberg, 1998. On the subsumption under details of general sociology, *see* Esser, 1993, 1999.

certain conditions, typical trajectories of social processes and, sometimes, typical equilibria result, which can then be observed as typical structural patterns of (dis)integration. Assimilation of individual immigrants, ethnic homogenization or pluralization of the host society, segmented assimilation, or the emergence of stable transnational networks would represent such typical patterns. Like the classical model of assimilation, they represent an (explainable) special case in this concept. In contrast to more inductive attempts, like typologies of certain structural conditions and (observed) outcomes, for instance for special ethnic groups, it first specifies a general causal mechanism generating some basic processes, and then it applies this general mechanism deductively to the specific conditions with regard to characteristics of sending and receiving countries, ethnic groups, and individual migrants and their relations. The main advantages of such models are that they represent not only descriptive generalizations, but also full explanations in the sense of the Hempel-Oppenheim scheme. With their aid, it is possible to explicate the generative causal processes behind the empirical generalizations and to derive new implications about possible processes that have hitherto passed unobserved.

THEORIES OF INTERGENERATIONAL INTEGRATION AND THE PROBLEM OF INCOMPLETENESS

Recently, Richard Alba and Victor Nee have vehemently opposed the hypothesis that the new immigration requires new concepts for the description and explanation of the processes involved (Alba, 1999; Alba and Nee, 1999; *see also* Gans, 1999:169; Perlmann and Waldinger, 1999; Brubaker, 2001). Basically, in their defense of the assimilation concept, Alba and Nee assume that there is still an institutional and cultural core in the host society, which above and beyond all differences and distances acts as a kind of irresistible centripetal force on immigrants (of all generations), ultimately forcing one generation after another – by virtue of their own objective interests – to follow the path of assimilation to this core (*cf.* Alba, 1985 on these processes for the old immigration to the United States). But this is precisely the claim that is contested by those who insist that the classical assimilation concept no longer applies. They deny that this unequivocal core still exists, especially in the face of the historically quite recent establishment of supranational institutions and of worldwide interdependencies between different cultures. Other centers, for example societies of origin or those of a transnational community, are of similar if not superior strength and attractiveness. Accordingly, the old mono- and ethnocentristic assimilation theory is quite simply unable to deal with this (new) multilevel polycentrism.

In short, this controversy rages between two clearly distinct theories with very different assumptions and conclusions. The problem that emerges is one with which sociology in general is all too familiar. For the analysis and explanation of social phenomena, certain general concepts or even "sociological laws" based on observed regularities are assumed, for example, the world's inevitable cultural and social homogenization or the final assimilation of immigrants over cohorts. However, empirically there are always exceptions and deviations, and sometimes completely new times seem to set in, apparently involving the necessity of a complete change of the respective laws and a radical paradigmatic shift to a completely new theory. In terms of the methodology of sociological explanation, this problem is referred to as the problem of incompleteness (*see* Wippler and Lindenberg, 1987:137). The way out of the problem of incompleteness is not, however, an endless controversy between paradigms, or the modification and adaptation of concepts, or the construction of descriptive typologies. The only recourse is an alteration of the sociological method itself. Inductive generalized observations of certain covariations or trends and typologies of conditions and outcomes are not the *explanans* for empirical processes, but represent themselves an *explanandum* that still has to be explained by some deductively derived theoretical arguments and the corresponding empirical (initial) conditions. The question is now why the given correlation or trend exists – for example a race relation cycle, the pattern of segmented assimilation, or certain generational effects – together with the deviations therefrom. This necessarily implies the modeling of some general generative mechanism and thus of the interaction of multilevel relations, especially those between actions, on the one hand, and structures on the other. In the meantime, some developments in general theoretical sociology provide a well-elaborated methodology for that purpose: one of them is the model of sociological explanation. It is the core of the following reconstruction of different patterns and outcomes of intergenerational integration within the framework of one general generative mechanism for these phenomena. However, first of all, the *explanandum* has to be clarified.

DIMENSIONS AND PATTERNS OF INTERGENERATIONAL (DIS)INTEGRATION

Every theory about the (intergenerational) integration of migrants refers to three different but interdependent aspects. The first is the social integration of immigrants into a social system as individual actors, for instance inclusion in the labor market of the host society, as a member of an ethnic community, or as part of a transnational network. The second aspect is the emergence of certain social structures, especially with regard to patterns of social inequality and social differentiation. Social inequality refers to differences in certain traits within aggregates of (nonrelated) individual actors, for instance with regard to income, occupations, or cultural lifestyles; social differentiation refers to differences with regard to the various social systems within a broader societal context, for instance in the form of the various functional subsystems of the societal division of labor, of communities, networks, and organizations, or regional subsocieties. Both these elements of social structure have horizontal and vertical dimensions depending on whether or not the respective aggregates or social systems are not only different, but equal in their evaluation. The third aspect is, following a distinction by David Lockwood (1964), related to the societal integration of a whole society (or a broader, perhaps transnational system) with regard to certain structural cleavages and (latent or open) conflicts.

Assimilation can then have two meanings. First, it refers to the (process of) social integration or the inclusion of individual immigrants into the various subsystems of the host society and/or their (increasing) similarity to individual actors in comparable segments of the native population, *e.g.*, by the adoption of certain cultural traits, the placement in the native (primary) labor market, intermarriage, or even emotional identification with the host society or parts of its subculture(s). We call this individual assimilation.

Second, assimilation refers to a specific pattern of the social structure of a society (or a larger system of societal units). We distinguish two central aspects of the social structure of a societal system: social inequality and social differentiation. With regard to social inequality, assimilation designates the (process of an) increasing similarity in the distribution of certain characteristics between ethnic groups as aggregates, for instance the complete disappearance of between-group variances in education, occupations, and income between ethnic groups. That includes, of course, the existence of social inequalities in general, but the remaining inequalities consist completely of individual within-group variances, and all ethnic-group variance has disappeared. Note that this process of assimilation can take place via changes on both sides, and by processes of so-called pluralistic assimilation. It only means that the distributions of certain characteristics are becoming similar between ethnic groups, regardless of the direction, place, or initiator of this process. With regard to social differentiation, assimilation refers to the (process of) decrease of the ethnic institutionalization and ethnic coding of societal (sub)systems (and not just aggregates of populations), like, for instance, the dissolution of institutionally complete ethnic communities and/or the decline of ethnic boundaries and collective feelings of social distances and identifications. We subsume both structural processes under the label of societal assimilation. As the object of a sociological theory of intergenerational integration, these processes of societal assimilation as structural outcomes are the only ones relevant. However, every explanation of these outcomes has to deal with processes of individual assimilation and also the respective actions and experiences of individual actors, because the structural outcomes are the – not always intentional – results of the individuals' actions.

Societal assimilation as a de-emergence of systematic ethnic structurations, however, is not the only possible societal outcome of immigration processes, as the debate about the new immigration demonstrates. After the two dimensions of social structures mentioned above (social inequality and social differentiation), two other possible structural outcomes can be distinguished as alternatives to societal assimilation: ethnic inequality and ethnic differentiation. Ethnic inequality means the persistence of between-group variances in the individual traits of ethnic aggregates. In this context, we speak of ethnic pluralization if ethnic inequality refers to the horizontal dimension and to traits with equal evaluations, *e.g.*, with respect to lifestyles and professions with similar prestige. In contrast, ethnic stratification is characterized by vertical differences in the evaluation of traits, *e.g.*, differences in education and income or professions with different degrees of prestige, where distribution varies systematically between ethnic groups. What is most important, however, is that both aspects of ethnic inequality can be considered as purely individual differences between the ethnic groups and that they are not very much more than an ethnically biased individualistic pluralization in terms of lifestyles or the control of (economic) resources. By contrast, ethnic differentiation refers to the ethnic organization (and the cultural coding of certain ethnic boundaries) of social systems, *e.g.*, of an ethnic economy, an ethnic colony (with more or less perfect institutional completeness in the sense of Breton, 1964), a (transnational) ethnic network that transcends and connects various places regardless of national and territorial boundaries, or a regional ethnic subsociety. Ethnic segmentation designates a horizontal ethnic differentiation, *e.g.*, in the form of (regional) "parallel societies" or ethnic subcultures existing side by side without any further evaluation of power, prestige, and privileges. In contrast, ethnic (neo)feudalism also encompasses a vertical order and closure of these ethnic (sub)systems. The most extreme example here is an (ethnic) caste system.

Societal assimilation, ethnic inequality, and ethnic differentiation can (and must) be thought of as (theoretically) independent of the third aspect of the integration of immigrants: the problem of the societal integration of a complete societal system or the emergence of cleavages and conflicts. Cleavages and conflicts can (and do) occur, of course, both in ethnically homogeneous and in ethnically heterogeneous societies, as the example of class conflict indicates. But societal (dis)integration in the form of ethnic conflicts must, of course, also be one of the objects of any theory of inter-generational integration.

The main objective and the minimal aim of any general theory of intergenerational integration is, then, to specify the mechanisms and (initial) conditions governing the emergence of one or the other of these structural outcomes, probably as a sequence of typical stages. The complications are obvious. There are innumerable possible combinations of conditions and sequences and a large number of possible interdependencies and feedback-loops between the diverse structural outcomes and the individual behavior that creates and is shaped by them. The main problem of any theoretical model of intergenerational integration is, then, to detect a basic and maxi-mally simple situational logic for typical patterns of (dis)integration of im-migrants over generations. In the following sections, we try to specify a general generating mechanism for the processes of intergenerational integra-tion, drawing upon some (selected) elements of the model of sociological explanation. The rest of the article is devoted to using these elements to model typical conditions and processes as simply as possible, leading to the different possible outcomes described and typified above. For reasons of space, we largely refrain, in the later stages of the article, from modeling the emergence of ethnic conflicts, concentrating instead on the contribution made by aspects of individual and societal assimilation or the emergence and stabilization of ethnic inequality and ethnic differentiation and on interac-tion processes taking place between them.

INTERGENERATIONAL INTEGRATION AND THE MODEL OF SOCIOLOGICAL EXPLANATION

The *explanandum* at issue in the model of sociological explanation is made up of certain collective phenomena or correlations and trends.[2] In this concept, every collective phenomenon is, in principle, conceived of as a (more or less complicated) aggregated consequence of individual actions, which are the result of (more or less rational) decisions by human beings geared to and shaped by socially structured situations. In its most basic form, the model consists of three elementary steps or logics: the logic of situation for the actors, the logic of selection, and the logic of aggregation. The logic of situation connects objective societal structures with subjective parameters guiding the actions of individual actors. The logic of selection specifies a rule about the (causal) connection between these parameters and the selection of a certain behavior. The resulting individual effects are part of the third step, the logic of aggregation toward a certain collective outcome, which in most cases deviates from the actors' intentions. Thus, the model systematically connects the macro level of social structures with some of the micro processes of actors and actions, and back again with the macro level of social structures. This elementary model can be extended in two directions. It may include one or more other levels of social systems, *e.g.*, markets, organizations, communities, social groups, or networks. In addition, it can be combined with processual sequences that connect chains into sequences of an extended situational logic, including feedback processes of cumulative causation or (process) equilibria, for instance in connection with chain migrations and the emergence of ethnic communities and transnational systems. Apart from these more general methodological points, the model of sociological explanation makes some substantial propositions that guide the specification of the three logics. We shall adopt and apply them to our specific problem: the explanation of different trajectories and structural outcomes of intergenerational integration.

Social Production Functions and Cultural Goals

The first step concerns the logic of situation the actors are facing. Any general theory of intergenerational integration must include a strong argument indicating why certain structural characteristics of a social environment display – at least sometimes – a systematic and objective influence on this logic and on the respective definition of the situation – and when and why this "irresistible" structural logic loses its strength or is replaced by another one of similar objectivity. The answer to this question is the concept of social production functions. The concept is based upon ideas in the household production theory proposed by Lancaster (1966) and Becker (1965) and its sociological elaboration, notably by Lindenberg (1989, 1992). It rests on the general assumption that, directly or indirectly, every (social) action has to do with the fulfillment of certain general (everyday) needs. Two such general needs are assumed to exist: physical well-being and social approval. To satisfy these two needs, actors must achieve or produce certain commodities. Commodities are goods that are able to produce physical well-being and/or social approval directly. This makes them preeminent among the actors' interests, and thus they represent the dominant goal of all their activities in a certain social field, like a family or an ethnic group, in a functional subsystem, like the sphere of politics, or in an entire society. In addition, they have to be produced by investing in other resources or goods and by spending (real) time. Since these input factors are instrumental to the production of the commodities, they are means that become (intermediate) goals themselves. As a consequence, social behavior can be understood as a chain of production in which lower-level means are invested as input factors to produce higher-level goal(s). The important point here is that the dominant goal and the conditions of its production by certain means are not idiosyncratic and not universal for all societies or historical periods. Rather, they are systematically structured by the (formal and/or informal) constitution of the respective society or another social system that the actors are part of. Therefore, the dominant goal can (and does) change and vary between societies and other social contexts. The socially constituted dominant goal is, by the way, nothing other than what Robert K. Merton called a "cultural goal": a "frame of aspirational reference," a "thing worth striving for" or the "design for group living" (Merton, 1967:132). It shapes the primary interests and orientations of all actors living within the boundaries of the respective (societal or group) constitution. This is true even for those who do not accept it as appropriate or legitimate. Merton assumed economic success as the cultural goal in modern Western societies. Cultural goals and institutionalized means constitute the main elements of the objective logic of the situation for the actors, and the constitution of the respective social production functions forms the frame that shapes the actors' subjective orientations and interests and hence govern the definition of the situation and the framing of alternatives and actions.

For the analysis of processes of intergenerational integration, the concept of social production functions is relevant in that it offers a straightforward and simple argument about why people – even of very different social and cultural backgrounds – have very good reasons to gear their actions to the prevailing constitution and cultural goal(s) in the host society and why it is worthwhile for them to invest in (institutionalized) means of gaining control over them (*cf.* Kalter and Granato, 2002:201; *see also* Nee and

Sanders, 2001). To this extent, immigrants have (or should have) an objective interest in assimilative actions and investments in receiving country capital, like formal education or the acquisition of the host society's language, and one would expect the same investment strategies to apply as for the indigenous population. The problems migrants (and their offspring) face (in relation to most sections of the indigenous population) are obvious: what they mainly have at their disposal is ethnic group capital, like the sending country's language or ethnic social capital. However, ethnic group capital is clearly less efficient than receiving-country capital. By comparison, it is, in most cases, specific capital, because its usability depends on special circumstances, such as the existence of an ethnic community or a transnational network. By contrast, receiving country capital is (again by comparison and in most cases) generalized capital that is highly efficient within the whole scope of the respective constitution and sometimes beyond it, or even worldwide, for example in the case of financial or human capital. There are several reasons for the lower efficiency of (most) ethnic group capital. The most important ones seem to be lack of relevant (input) means – like abilities and knowledge – that could be used in the new environment, and (overt or covert) discrimination (*cf.* Kalter, 2003: 81; on the effects of language (dis)abilities on the prospects of structural assimilation, *see, e.g.,* Dustman and van Soest, 2002; Pendakur and Pendakur, 2002). Precisely because of these structural (and/or institutional and cultural) disadvantages, gaps and delays in the achievement of the prevailing cultural goals and the production of physical well-being and social approval have to be expected from the pursuit of assimilative strategies alone. Therefore, under certain circumstances, the tendency to use the less efficient ethnic capital and to improve its productivity may become a reasonable option, *e.g.,* by investment in an ethnic business, cultivation of ethnic networks, or even the organization of an ethnic movement aimed at changing the constitution of the (host) society and the prevailing social production functions in favor of the controlled ethnic capital.

Resources, Options and Strategies

Immigrants and their offspring have several options. In the simplest case they can decide between (individual) assimilation or segmentation, and also between acceptance of the prevailing constitution and seeking to change it through political action. All these options result in certain structural outcomes. Therefore, the second step in the model of sociological explanation requires the specification of a logic of selection for these options, which allows for the consideration of the particularities of the respective logic of the situation and of different social production functions. The Expected Utility (EU) Theory is especially well suited for this purpose. According to this theory, actors will prefer that option for which the product of each goal's value and the expectation that the respective option will attain the goal (the sum of all intended goals) is relatively higher (for details and criticism, *see*, *e.g.*, Abelson and Levi, 1985; Schoemaker, 1982). A clear simplification of the modeling process results from the consideration that many decisions display a specific simple structure in terms of the actors' bounded rationality: it is a choice between an attendant option with a secure gain and a – more or less – risky and costly investment. The options are labeled "niv" and "inv," "niv" meaning the (attendant) waiving of an active investment and "inv" the engagement in a risky investing activity. EU weights for this decision can be derived as follows (*cf.* Riker and Ordeshook, 1973:22):

$$(1a)\ EU(niv) = U(squ)$$

$$(1b)\ EU(inv) = pU(inv) + (1 - p)U(squ) - C.$$

U(squ) denotes the (securely) expected gain from keeping the status quo without any investment, and U(inv) the expected gain for a successful investment. The subjective probability of success is p, while C denotes the certain investment costs. If the investment is not successful (with the probability of (1-p)), one can still expect the status-quo payoff. We then have the following condition for a transition from the niv option to the inv option:

$$(2)\ U(inv) - U(squ) > C/p.$$

The term on the left-hand side stands for the investment motive, the one on the right stands for the investment risk. The success expectation p is of particular importance in overcoming the investment risk. If p decreases, the transition threshold increases disproportionately, and if it approaches zero, then even extremely high incentives for investment have no effect.

In principle, this model can be applied to all decisions of relevance to intergenerational integration. The decisions involved in the processes of intergenerational integration are of three kinds. First, we have the decision to invest in resources and capital, both of which are directly related to the social production functions of the receiving country. Alternatives here are investment in the acquisition of receiving-country capital (option rcc) or noninvestment. The respective incentive is denoted by U(rcc), the success expectation by p(rcc), and investment costs by C(rcc). The (successful) investment then means social integration into the host society and hence a form of (individual) assimilation. The most relevant and prototypical example is investment in formal education with its major significance for opportunities in the receiving country's labor market. Second, there is the decision to improve utility production through investment in ethnic group capital, brought along into the receiving country (option egc). Here, the most important and significant examples are starting an ethnic business or founding an ethnic organization. The respective gain is denoted by U(egc), the success expectation by p(egc), and investment costs by C(egc). What investments in receiving-country capital and in ethnic group capital have in common is the fact that the comprehensive framework is established by the (unquestionable) orientation to the (major) cultural goal of the receiving country, which in Western industrial societies is usually economic advancement. To this extent, all investments are made in strict acceptance of the prevailing, nonethnic social production function. A third kind of investment can then relate to the change of prevailing production functions (option csp) in favor of a reevaluation of the ethnic group capital already in stock. Therefore, it is a kind of political investment within the scope of the mobilization of an ethnic conflict. The respective gain is denoted by U(csp), the success expectation by p(csp), and the costs for participation in the ethnic movement by C(csp).

We assume that the actors will compare all three investment options with each other and with the inactivity option "niv." The respective EU weights can then be summarized as follows:

$$(3a)\ EU(niv) = U(squ)$$

$$(3b)\ EU(rcc) = p(rcc)U(rcc) + (1 - p(rcc))U(squ) - C(rcc)$$

$$(3c)\ EU(egc) = p(egc)U(egc) + (1 - p(egc))U(squ) - C(egc)$$

$$(3d)\ EU(csp) = p(csp)U(csp) + (1 - p(spf))U(squ) - C(csp).$$

Naturally, the model in its general form cannot predict which of the options will actually be selected. For that purpose the model's parameters have to be connected with the structural conditions of the logic of situation via special bridge hypotheses. Such bridge hypotheses can (and must) be formulated for each structural variable relevant for the different constructs of the decision model. The attractiveness of investment in receiving country capital U(rcc), for example, depends on economic opportunities within the host society or on the cultural evaluation of, say, education. Success expectations p(rcc) correlate with the availability of information, which increases with the duration of stay, and costs C(rcc) are influenced by cultural and social distances that have to be overcome. Accordingly, the evaluation of investment in ethnic group capital U(ecg) increases with the market opportunities and productivities of ethnic businesses, and hence indirectly with the number of immigrants in an ethnic group. The success probability p(egc) increases with entrepreneurial experience and with the availability of ethnic social capital. In addition, costs C(egc) decrease with an increasing opportunity for exploiting ethnic solidarities. With regard to the political option csp, it can be assumed that 1) the value of a constitutional change U(csp) rises with increasing ethnic discrimination and after futile investment in receiving country capital, 2) the success probability p(csp) increases with (ethnic and particularly non-ethnic) competencies and (ethnic) social relations that can be mobilized, and 3) the costs C(csp) of political investment will decrease in the presence of an organizational (ethnic) infrastructure.

Justifying the respective bridge hypotheses on the relation between situational conditions and the constructs of the EU model represents a constant challenge in its own right. Correlations are frequently neither direct nor linear, for example those between group size and ethnic market opportunities, or success expectations increasing with education, and they also change with societal and historical conditions. This is the main reason why correlations between different variables encountered in the research on migration display little stability and also why some classical correlations have already changed before the new immigration came about, *e.g.*, the correlation between language ability, economic advancement, and identification with the host society. However, one can generally predict that the niv option will always become likely (compared to each of the three investment strategies) if the success expectation p is low – regardless of certain incentives or costs. This should apply to immigrants of the first generation and those with exclusively specific capital and should apply, in fact, with regard to all three investment strategies.

Aggregation and Emergence

The actors' (investment) decisions and their individual effects always lead to some structural consequences. In the simplest case, they aggregate to simple distributions of traits within a population of otherwise unconnected actors, as in the case of ethnic inequality. However, we often have to deal with complicated emergences connected with the unintended consequences of actions. An example would be the formation of ethnic communities and transnational systems as an indirect and unintended consequence of investment in an ethnic (niche) economy with the aim of achieving the given primary cultural goal (*e.g.*, economic security) by using ethnic group capital. The emergent situation created by the given logic of the situation and the logic of selection thus structures a new logic of the situation for all participants, with attendant consequences for the parameters of the decision model and the subsequent actions. This can lead to typical trajectories of social (initial) conditions, situation logics structured by those conditions, (investment) actions controlled by them, and new social consequences developing in their wake. There are several instruments available for the modeling of such structured processes, like models of diffusion and contagion (also dependent on network structures), models of the origin of segregations, the emergence of vertical stratifications and of the inheritance of social inequality, or (game-theoretical) models of collective action. These instruments can also be applied directly at certain points of the explanatory reconstruction of patterns of intergenerational integration. There is no hard-and-fast rule for the specification of a certain logic of aggregation. But there are several instruments that are especially useful for the modeling of typical constellations of processes of intergenerational integration. We shall be using some of them in the following reconstruction.

THE BASIC MODEL OF INTERGENERATIONAL INTEGRATION

Taking its bearings from the model of sociological explanation, the basic model of intergenerational integration explains different structural outcomes of immigration – societal assimilation, ethnic inequality/ethnic differentiation, ethnic conflicts – as aggregated consequences of the immigrants' rational "situation-logical" actions geared to the prevailing circumstances. The starting point is the concept of social production functions, which states that these actions (ultimately) serve to secure physical well-being and social approval by investment in socially defined cultural goals with institutionalized means whose efficiencies are also socially determined. Then (for simplicity) we assume two options: 1) assimilative actions geared to the standards of the receiving country's social production functions (rca) according to equation 3b and 2) all ethnic alternatives (ega), *i.e.*, passive adherence to the status quo or efforts to secure or improve the ethnic social production function (according to equations 3a, 3c, and 3d). Ethnic activities will be preferred if their EU weight is higher than the EU weight of one of the assimilative alternatives: EU(ega) > EU(rca).

The Basic Functions

The differences between EU(rca) and EU(ega) and action resulting from them thus represent the micro-theoretical core of the processes. They are not, however, their causes. They are rather the structural conditions of the respective logic of situation that have to be connected systematically with the parameters of both EU weights via bridge hypotheses. In principle, the model of intergenerational assimilation takes account of all the conceivable structural conditions on all levels, like the institutional and social conditions of the country of origin and the receiving country, available ethnic networks, social capital and ethnic communities and institutions in the receiving country, and the immigrant's individual traits, resources, different forms of capital and attitudes, as determined by the country of origin and the individual migration biography, including certain cultural and social distances. A very specific assumption, moreover, is that – *ceteris paribus* – the number of immigrants with the same ethnic membership systematically influences the value of both EU weights. The theoretical argument for this assumption is derived from the opportunity theory of Blau (1977, 1994), which states that intergroup relations are objectively structured by opportunities determined by (relative) group size. There are two reasons for this assumption. On the one hand, opportunities for within-group interactions increase with number. On the other hand, higher numbers provoke conflicts between the groups and hence create (mutual) closure tendencies. It can thus (*ceteris paribus*) be expected that as group size increases the EU weight for ethnic orientation also increases, while the EU weight for assimilative orientation to the host society decreases.

Against this background, two (ideal-) typical relations between differences in EU weights and their change as a function of group size and other structural conditions are specified. They are summarized in Figure I. Functions 1a and 1b describe differences and changes in EU weights for assimilative activities and functions 2a and 2b those for ethnic activities. The presentation is a variant of the tipping-point model according to Schelling (1978), which Laitin (1995) applied to explain especially the persistence of ethnic marginality, for instance in the case of middleman minorities (for a similar model, *see* Esser, 1986b).

Function 1a reflects a strong tendency to assimilation, which barely decreases even in the case of increasing group size N and inner ethnic opportunities. It describes the structural situation of immigrants with low cultural and social distances toward the receiving country and with high

Figure I.   **The Basic Model of Intergenerational Integration[a]**

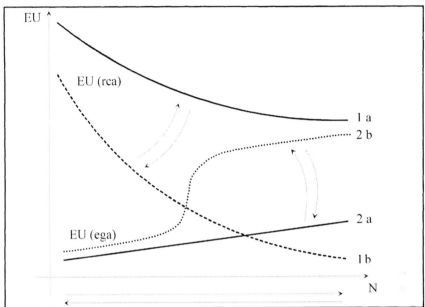

Note: 'EU denotes values of the expected-utility weight of the alternatives. N represents variations in group size. EU(rca) refers to actions oriented toward the recipient country with different functional connections to N (functions 1a and 1b), EU(ega) to ethnic group oriented actions, also with different functional connections to N (functions 2a and b).

amounts of generalized capital that can be efficiently used within the scope of the host society's social production functions. Of special note is the way in which the success expectation p for effective inclusion in the host society increases with generalized capital (with regard to the relevant equation 3b). Even an increasing number of ethnic competitors barely influences opportunities, while low cultural and social distances keep costs C for assimilative efforts low. In the case of ongoing immigration and increasing group size, these costs also remain low if there are neither traditions of social distance nor current reasons for dissociative closures in the host society. Function 1b describes the exact opposite: higher cultural and social distance and little available generalized capital that can be used in the receiving society. Small numbers of immigrants of whatever cultural origin are given a rather friendly reception and initially have good chances of integration into the receiving society. But as group size increases, these chances are clearly slighter from the start, and competition for structurally limited positions also claimed by other immigrants will soon ensue.

Accordingly, functions 2a and 2b indicate differences and changes in the EU weight for the ethnic option when group size N increases. It is generally assumed that the correlation between group size and the EU weight for the ethnic option becomes stronger if an ethnic organization takes shape. Against this background, function 2a describes the situation in which chances for an ethnic organization are low. Immigrants constitute an otherwise disconnected aggregate of individual and individualized actors or families. Though (again in line with Blau's opportunity theory) chances for inner-ethnic relations increase (and hence the value of ethnic orientations), this increase is weak because it is geared solely to the statistical probability of encountering opportunities. Here we see the difference over and against function 2b, which describes the situation of immigrants who are embedded in ethnic networks and who possess extensive ethnic social capital. Once a certain critical mass is reached, an ethnic organization will emerge much more easily. Spatial segregations and the collective solidarities and identifications always present in ethnic networks support this process. With a successful ethnic organization, all parameters for the EU weight of the ethnic option then change in their turn. The value U of the ethnic option and the probability p for the success of any further ethnic investment increase, while costs C decrease. This is especially true for the investment in an inner-ethnic economy or in ethnic institutions, but it also applies to the mobilization of ethnic movements: the structural demand for ethnic supplies increases in proportion to the size of the group, while the supplies themselves become cheaper to produce.

The clear increase in function 2b after the take-off phase also represents certain cumulative processes of ethnic institutionalization (not modeled here). Once launched, a successful ethnic organization reinforces – *ceteris paribus* – the further organization, and once established, the ethnic networking and creation of an inner-ethnic moral system further accelerate this process. In addition, cumulative interactive effects connected with spatial segregation achieve greater significance. Though at first they may be due solely to selective migration by otherwise unconnected actors, they now increasingly contribute to (further) ethnic organization and social distance (*cf.* Massey, 1985; Massey and Denton, 1998; for the general dynamics of segregation processes even in the absence of any discrimination, *see* Schelling, 1971).

However, the increase in the EU weight for the ethnic option flattens out again with further increase in group size. The organization of ethnic networks and of the strong ties they require becomes more and more difficult in large groups. In addition, the upper limit of the attainable value of ethnic investment is soon reached. We assume that the reason for this is that ethnic organized capital is (mostly) specific capital, its usability in the scope of the receiving country's social production functions is only limited, and even if the ethnic organization expands further, its value remains more or less clearly below that of the receiving country capital attainable by assimilative means.

Differences, Changes, and Dynamics

Differences between the EU weights of the two options can be thus related to three structural conditions and functional correlations: first, changes in EU weights for both options due to group size N; second, changes in the assimilative option's EU weight according to the level of cultural and social distances or the controlled generalized capital (function 1a and b), and third, changes in the EU weight for the ethnic option according to the level of embeddedness in ethnic networks (functions 2a and b). The three structural conditions themselves are not static, but change – partly endogenously – with the process itself.

The group size changes (under otherwise constant structural conditions) as a result of further immigration on the part of those who had originally stayed behind in their countries of origin and by the absorption of assimilated immigrants in the receiving society (leaving aside remigrations). Follow-up immigration increases group size, absorption reduces it. Changes in group size due to follow-up immigration and absorption can themselves be based on (endogenous) cumulative processes, particularly chain migration or chain absorption. The larger the number of other persons who have already emigrated from the areas of origin or have already been absorbed, the lower the risk will appear for one's own decision to take this (risky) step, and the more unattractive it becomes to stay in one's country of origin or one's own ethnic group. Very different developments and equilibria are possible. Three typical cases call for special mention: the – more or less cumulative – increase in group size through major, ongoing follow-up immigration; the decrease of a formerly high number through the dwindling of follow-up immigration (or increasing remigration) and continuous absorption of following generations; or an equilibrium of continuous replenishment through new immigration and concomitant absorption (or remigration) of formerly migrant persons.

It should be added that not only the size but also the composition of ethnic groups and hence their respective functions change with these processes. Accordingly, another argument for the increase of function 2b after reaching a certain critical magnitude can be derived. Follow-up immigrants are mostly persons with low levels of individualization, and – *e.g.*, in the course of family reunion – they provide for the completion of everyday ethnic life routines even without further ethnic organization and, accordingly, for an enhancement of the value of the ethnic option. These processes of change in group sizes are symbolized in Figure 1 by the two opposite arrows on the x axis.

Changes in cultural and social distances or in the generalized capital determining the EU weight of the assimilative option (functions 1a and 1b) can be explained – in the simplest case – by differences in exposure to the receiving society, caused, for example, by the duration of stay and/or interethnic contacts. The central theoretical argument is a simple learning-theoretical extension of Blau's opportunity theory. The acquisition of assimilative traits (such as command of the language spoken in the host society, knowledge of norms and values, availability of information, and interethnic friendships) is initially a matter of (learning) opportunities. Accordingly, it can be assumed – again *ceteris paribus* – that the EU weight of (individual) assimilation increases with the level of the (temporal and social) exposure to the receiving society, as caused, for example, by duration of stay and/or developments over generations. Hence, it becomes evident that it is not time or generation *per se* that causes this change. Opportunities and rewarding reinforcements must really come about, and it is therefore not unimportant in which sector of the receiving society the exposure takes place. For example, an increase in the EU weight for investment in receiving country capital will not be expected if exposure takes place within a deviant or marginalized subculture of the host society. Other changes in given structural conditions, *e.g.*, the availability of positions in the course of business cycles or changes in social distances due to public campaigns of welcome or of xenophobia, have similar effects. These processes are depicted by the twin arrow in functions 1a and 1b.

Ethnic networks are the central structural condition for differences in the EU weight of the ethnic option (functions 2a and b). Thus, a shift of the situation from function 2b to function 2a implies the erosion of ethnic networks. This erosion results from processes of migrants' individualization and notably from increasing independence of ethnic networks and ethnic social capital, for example due to an initial economic advancement or to interethnic contacts. Here, cumulative processes of de-institutionalization and the breakdown of ethnic communities are also possible, *e.g.*, via processes of chain absorption (of the offspring) of ethnic entrepreneurs who had initially provided the basis for ethnic organization and who are now using the capital thus accumulated for their individual assimilative advancement. Conversely, as individual independence decreases, ethnic associations of formerly individualized members of an ethnic group become likely. These changes are depicted as twin arrows between functions 2a and 2b in Figure I.

The relations described in functions 1a, 1b, 2a, and 2b indicate four (extremely) simplified special cases of structural conditions and processes of (intergenerational) integration or assimilation, respectively, for which all kinds of deviations and combinations can result in individual cases. The prototypical case for the model is the structural dimension of (intergenerational) integration, more especially the use of investment to achieve inclusion in a primary labor market of the receiving society versus (noninvestive) integration into an ethnic economy oriented to the ethnic status quo. Of particular importance here is the demonstration of the possibility in principle to relate different variables of the sociology of migration to one general basic process, to specify them as initial conditions of a basically uniform process, and then to derive the structural outcome of (intergenerational) integration that one can theoretically expect, according to the empirical conditions prevailing in the given case.

VARIANTS OF INTERGENERATIONAL INTEGRATION

According to the model of intergenerational integration, there is no universal process for the development of interethnic relations in the course of international immigration. All structural outcomes are possible: (societal) assimilation, horizontal and vertical ethnic inequality and segmentation, and the emergence of ethnic conflicts with the aim of changing the receiving country's constitution. In the following, we shall draw on the relations suggested by the model of intergenerational integration to describe various typical conditions and trajectories leading to these different kinds of structural outcomes. We begin with the classic process of assimilation over generations. Then we address the emergence of ethnic structuring in the receiving society in the form of ethnic inequality and segmentation and their interplay. For reasons of space, however, we shall refrain here from deriving the conditions and processes operative in the emergence and mobilization of ethnic conflicts.

Assimilation

The model of intergenerational integration shows that the classic case of assimilation actually only occurs under quite special conditions. This becomes obvious in a reconstruction of the race-relation cycle of Robert S. Park (1950:49). As is generally known, Park postulates a typical sequence in the development of interethnic relations as a consequence of immigration. After an initially friendly phase of contact, conflicts over scarce resources soon occur, which are then defused by the emergence of spatial segregations and ethnic divisions of labor in a process of so-called accommodation. The fourth phase is the emergence of (societal) assimilation – regarded as "irresistible" and "irreversible" – taking the form of the gradual disappearance of the relevance of the ethnic dimension in the course of generations.

The model of intergenerational integration can easily reconstruct this process. It is obviously assumed that the process of migration has only just started and that at first the respective ethnic group is very small. Additionally, it seems to proceed on the assumption that there are rather marked cultural and social distances and low generalized capital, on the one hand (function 1b), and ethnic social embeddedness (function 2b) and continuous increase in group size N, *e.g.*, by processes of chain migration, on the other. Initially, and as long as the group size is small, competition and distances are low, and immigrants will also tend toward assimilative contact, a feature that is simply due to a lack of ethnic opportunities. Then, with continuous follow-up migration and increasing group size, we find increasing competition, distinctive closures, and a clear decrease in assimilative propensities. These processes constitute a phase of intensifying conflict bound up with an increase in group size. At the same time, tendencies toward ethnic segmentation increase, which can also be organized through the available ethnic networks. The establishment of ethnic divisions of labor and ethnic communities once again mitigates competition with members of the host society and the visibility of immigrants mitigates again. In this way, the accommodation of henceforth separate and self-sufficient groups postulated by Park can arise. The fourth stage – (societal) assimilation over generations – would, of course, not be arrived at under otherwise constant circumstances. We have now to assume that the basic situation of the respective actors changes, whatever processes may be responsible for that. The model specifies two mechanisms for this: on the one hand, exposure to the host society (function 1b), and on the other, the dissolution of social embeddedness (function 2b). In the course of the generations we can at least assume increasing exposure to the receiving society, over and against the first generation. With the change to function 1a that this implies, (societal) assimilation does indeed become all but inevitable – even if group size stays large or increases further.

Assimilation would also occur in spite of the continuing existence of ethnic segmentations, due, for example, to the ongoing replenishment of ethnic communities by follow-up migrations. However, everything depends on whether exposure to core areas of the receiving society actually occurs. Similar processes would have to be assumed for changes in ethnic social embeddedness.

The reconstruction of the race-relation cycle shows that, though the hypotheses about its generality and irreversibility are certainly not accurate in the sense in which they are postulated, they are not totally unfounded. The implicit assumption about the way things develop over time is frequently corroborated empirically. There is a steady and "irreversible" increase in group size (e.g., due to processes of chain migration), latent cultural and social distances between immigrants and natives are (initially) substantial and increase with group size, the endowment with generalized capital is low, information on particular aspects of the receiving society is absent, spatial segregation, social embeddedness in ethnic networks, and corresponding ethnic solidarities quickly set in, thus allowing for and accelerating the organization of an ethnic community once the critical mass with respect to group size has been reached. All these conditions are still common to most instances of (international) immigration. Therefore, the controversy has rather been about the (implicit) assumption that in the course of the generations the necessary exposure to the receiving society does indeed arise (inevitably), which explains the transition from function 1b to 1a, or that individualization and the dissolution of ethnic networks do indeed occur, thus explaining the transition from function 2b to 2a. However, these are not theoretical questions that can be answered in a general way, but questions pertaining to the given empirical circumstances and thus to the specific initial conditions of the general model of intergenerational integration.

Ethnic Inequality

Any persistent systematic differences in socially relevant features caused by ethnic membership would contradict the assimilation hypothesis. We have distinguished two forms of ethnic structuring: 1) ethnic inequality as ongoing distribution differences in aggregates of populations according to ethnic membership and 2) ethnic differentiation as the formation of ethnic (sub)-systems within or alongside receiving (and sending) countries. Ethnic inequality is a special case of social inequality in populations; ethnic differentiation is a special case of social differentiation in societal systems in general.

In the light of more general sociological concepts seeking to explain social inequalities and social differentiations, we assume that the explanation of assimilative and/or ethnic investments (as expressed in equations 3a, 3b, and 3c) constitutes the (micro-) theoretical core of these processes, *e.g.*, investments in formal education and/or in the effort of setting up an ethnic business. Figure II illustrates the general conditions governing the transition

Figure II.   **Conditions for the Change from Inactivity to Investment[a]**

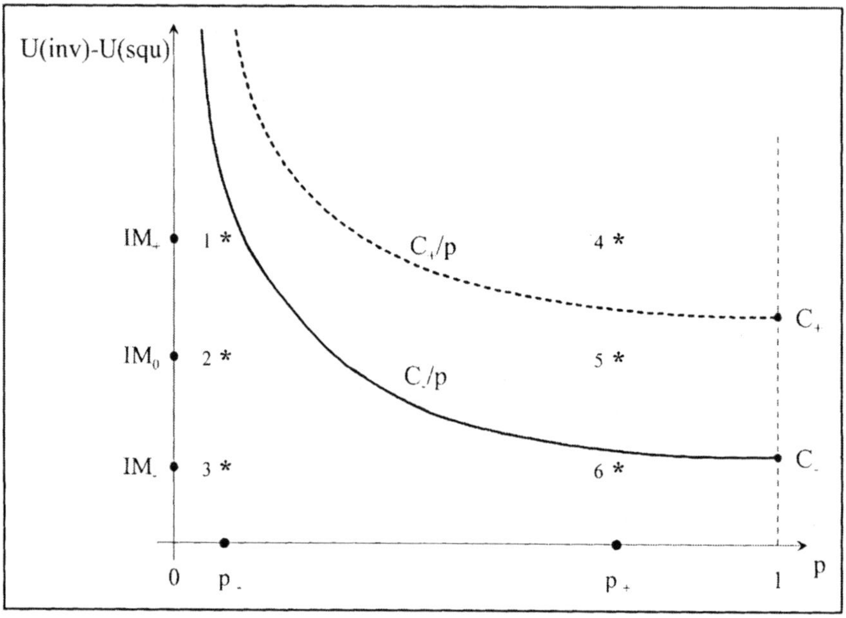

Note. [a]IM refers to three different levels of the investment motive U(inv)-U(squ) following eq. (2) in paragraph 3, p to subjective expectations of success in investments, and C to investment costs. C/p represents the perceived investment risk and hence the threshold condition for an investment. Points 1 to 6 refer to typical constellations of different values for IM, p, and C.

to one of these two investments. The most important parameters are both related to the functions of the basic model of intergenerational integration and used to explain the different structural outcomes.

Following equation 2 and summarized for both forms of investment, Figure II describes the increase of investment risk C/p as a function of different values for success expectation p over and against the given investment costs C. The prototypical case drawn upon to explain the emergence of stable ethnic inequalities is that of educational investments EU(rcc) according to equation 3b, compared to EU(squ) according to 3a. In merito-cratic societies and in the course of capitalist globalization, these investments are perhaps the most important investments made in generalizable capital and, accordingly, one of the most significant means for achieving relevant cultural goals in general. We begin with educational decisions of typical immigrants of the second generation whose parents had relatively low levels of education and little information on the host society when they first entered the country. We assume that, in principle, even for first-generation immigrants' children the value of IM+ would be maximally achievable. However, the special immigration situation makes the investment appear unlikely, as the parents' low levels of information strongly reduce success expectations. Even in the case of such a strong investment motive (and even if investment costs equal zero), the investment in question would therefore not be made (constellations 1 through 3). The threshold could be only overcome by a clear increase in success expectations. This is one of the assumptions implicit in the hypothesis of intergenerational assimilation. Exposure to the receiving society increases, and both information and other conditions for educational success improve in the course of the generations. Success expectation rises to approximately p+, thus causing an investment to be made (constellation 4). But this would only happen in the case of maxi-mal investment motive (IM+). It needs to be said, however, that these are frequently unlikely conditions – even for the following generations. The parents' low educational levels, the whole migration background, the "wrong" cultural capital, and the low degree of embeddedness in nonethnic networks all reduce the overall usability potential of the investment to some-thing like IMo. The threshold C/p would only be crossed if there were a lowering of costs to C-, e.g., by reducing social distances (constellation 5).

Though educational investments represent one core factor in the sta-bilization of ethnic inequalities, they are not the only mechanism. Dynamics of endogenous stabilization or of reinforcement of formerly weak differences may also develop (on such models, see Kalter, 2003:72). Here we need only refer to Raymond Boudon's classic model for the explanation of the (en-dogenous) stabilization of existing educational inequalities (1974:146). With an approximately constant supply of higher positions available on the labor market, the queue for better positions becomes longer, while the higher supply of (formally) qualified applicants devaluates the educational certifi-cates – and hence increases the relevance of symbolic qualification signals and of a certain kind of cultural capital. This is why participation in higher education usually displays only a minor effect on intergenerational mobility.

In the case of immigrants, (visible) ethnic membership exacerbates the situation by counting as a (negative) symbol for the actual value of an educational certificate.

All this strongly suggests that even after several generations in so-called "open" societies, ethnic disadvantages must be expected for the majority of immigrants of alien ethnic origins. However, this is not inevitably the case. If certain ethnic groups (*e.g.*, Jewish immigrants of the old and Asian immigrants of the new immigration to the United States) assign a special value of their own to education (increase of IM in the model) and are able to ensure high success rates through family structures (increase in p), ethnic disadvantages (in this respect, at least) should soon vanish – or else make way for quite another kind of ethnic inequality, the kind caused by disproportionate advancement and success. And if following generations are exposed to more marginalized and deviant segments of the receiving society, thus reducing the evaluation of education and the success expectations, then clear mobility restraints are to be anticipated despite a certain degree of cultural assimilation, *e.g.*, language acquisition as a result of exposure to the host society.

Ethnic Differentiation

Investment in an ethnic business is the prototypical case for the emergence of ethnic differentiation, initially perhaps in the form of an ethnic niche economy. This may then result in the establishment and the complete institutionalization of a (self-sufficient) ethnic community. The investment involved need not be aimed at the establishment of such ethnic segmentation. From the individual actors' point of view, it is frequently nothing other than an alternative strategy to assimilation as a way of attaining the receiving society's cultural goals (or securing the individual's own livelihood). It is chosen simply because it promises to be more successful than assimilative investment. Hence, the point at issue here is whether or not to engage in any kind of investment activity at all (according to equation 3a), and, if so, whether to make an assimilative investment in receiving country capital (according to equation 3b) or an ethnic investment (according to equation 3c). The attractiveness of an ethnic investment for (specific) members of an ethnic group is directly evident from the model. The gain achievable by an assimilative investment is clearly higher (IM+) than the gain promised by an investment in an ethnic business (IMo). But (under certain circumstances) other investment conditions clearly favor the ethnic option. For example, exploiting ethnic solidarities (and difficulties), can clearly cut down on production costs. In addition, no costs are incurred for overcoming social distances (C-). However, with success expectations (p-) still very low, this is not a sufficient basis for the investment decision. Here, the market chances become a decisive factor. The chances of success will not increase before the potential demand for products of an ethnic business reaches a critical mass. Spatial segregations and ethnic networks promote the attainment of such a critical mass. Ethnic social capital, especially in the form of trust and informational relations, increases the individual entrepreneur's chances of success (cf. Aldrich and Waldinger, 1990:128), as does experience with the business in question and – in general terms – endowment with generalizable capital like education, financial resources, and general business experience. With such improved chances of success (e.g., p+), the investment risk C/p can easily be exceeded, despite the comparatively lower revenues generated by the ethnic business (constellation 5).

Against this background, the emergence of transnational ethnic differentiations in the course of the immigration processes also becomes intelligible. The most important structural reason is the recent clear reduction in transport, communication, and transaction costs for ethnic investments, even over long distances. This generates further potential for reducing costs and risks, including the outsourcing of production to indigenous regions, the expansion of sales markets for (ethnic) products, and the cultivation and utilization of geographically wide-ranging ethnic networks. On the other hand, such transnational enterprises demand higher organizational effort in comparison to local ethnic communities. The findings of Portes, Haller, and Guarnizo (2002:290) to the effect that transnational entrepreneurs differ appreciably from their local counterparts on account of their higher education and higher professional experience can also be readily interpreted in terms of the model. And it is easy to understand why transnational ethnic entrepreneurs take a continued interest in the (political) concerns of their countries of origin. The circumstances there directly affect the conditions governing the productivity and the potential success of their business enterprise.

The Interaction between Ethnic Differentiation and Ethnic Inequality

Once established, an ethnic infrastructure reduces costs for further ethnic investment and increases both their prospects of success and the value of attainable gains. Thus, in general terms, the development of institutionally

complete ethnic communities initiated and possibly cumulatively reinforced
in this way will enhance the value of the ethnic option, and, more especially,
the value of noninvesting acceptance of the given situational circumstances
of ethnic segmentation from core spheres of the receiving society. From this
there results an important connection between the emergence of ethnic
differentiations and the (possibly permanent) consolidation of vertical ethnic
inequality, as well as with the dynamics described in the basic model of
intergenerational integration. Let us therefore return to the model of investment in receiving-country capital, taking educational investments as an example. We assume a rather cautious estimation of the attainable gain from
(IMo). The first generation faces the usual low success chances, therefore no
investment will be made (constellation 2). For the next generation, success
chances have risen to p+, perhaps due to stronger exposure to the receiving
country, and social distances are no longer high (C-). The value of the
noninvestment option U(squ), however, increases with the development of
the ethnic community (induced by follow-up migrations). Accordingly, the
investment motive U(inv)-U(squ) decreases, for example to IM- (constellation 6). The result of this is that, despite clearly improved chances of success
and only low cultural and social distances, the following generation will not
invest in the relevant receiving-country capital – with all the indirect and
unintended structural consequences that this immobility involves. Norbert
F. Wiley (1970) has referred to this phenomenon as the "ethnic mobility
trap." It is the stabilization of ethnic inequalities without any discrimination,
because its rests exclusively on voluntary decisions which the actors have very
good reasons for making. This model seems to have been forgotten in the
recent debates on the different paths and outcomes of intergenerational
integration.

   This connection between the establishment of ethnic differentiations
and the consolidation of (vertical) ethnic inequalities can also explain the
frequently observed emergence and consolidation of vertically evaluated ethnic differentiations (*see also* Fong and Ooka, 2002), all the way up to
(quasi-)caste systems of an ethnic form of (neo)feudalism and segmented
ethnic ghettos in societies recipient to international immigration (*cf.* for
instance, Berreman, 1960 and Massey and Denton, 1998 on the case of
blacks in the United States). This applies especially if group size continuously increases by chain migrations, if no absorption takes place, *e.g.*, due to
the cumulative processes of re-evaluation in connection with the ethnic
option, or if absorption is balanced or outnumbered by replenishment from
follow-up migrations.

To be sure, the emergence of vertical ethnic differentiations and in-equalities need not be an inevitable consequence of ethnic investments. The generalizable capital also attainable via ethnic investments, like money in-come and human capital, improves the conditions for more profitable in-vestments in receiving country capital, especially for following generations. Their withdrawal from ethnic enterprises and their absorption into the receiving society can themselves result in processes leading to a dwindling of ethnic differentiation, *e.g.*, in the form of cumulative chain absorption, because now the attractiveness of the ethnic option will decline for people who have remained within the ethnic community. The likelihood of such (possibly cumulative) processes involving the intergenerational dissolution of ethnic segmentations and subsequently of (clear) ethnic inequalities will increase with the attractiveness of assimilative cultural goals and the effec-tiveness of the assimilative means and forms of capital required for the purpose in the host society. And one can safely assume that these charac-teristics of assimilative goals and means are structurally inherent in them.

CONCLUSIONS: DECLINE OR RETURN OF ASSIMILATION(-THEORY)?

This article took its initial bearings from a number of more or less recent debates on different concepts of intergenerational integration, notably those between (classical) assimilation theory and several different criticisms of it, such as the various multiculturalist, differentialist, or pluralist approaches, the concept of segmented assimilation, and current approaches on transna-tionalism. The aim was to outline a general model of intergenerational integration from which different structural outcomes of international im-migration could theoretically be derived. Accordingly, the question raised in the title of this article can be answered as follows: A new theory of inter-generational integration is indeed required, but the model proposed here is not completely new. It integrates several well-known correlations that have frequently been tacitly assumed, or have been part of descriptive typologies, into the methodology employed by the model of sociological explanation. Methodologically, the most important feature is the systematic reference of the respective variables and conditions of intergenerational integration to a coherent (micro-)theoretical model of (investment) decisions by the actors involved, as well as the modeling (not described here in detail) of emergent structural effects deriving from the actions thus explained, including longer sequences, structural equilibria, and the immigration process itself. Intergenerational assimilation is one of the possible structural outcomes in this model, but it is not the only one. And (classical) assimilation theory – like the alternative concepts – is only a special case, with particular but well specifiable preconditions in its substance.

Is there anything we can say at this stage about the controversy over the decline or return of assimilation, the range of (classical) assimilation theory, and the more normative question of appropriate migration and integration policies? We believe that there is. And we intend to couch this belief in the form of a daring and certainly controversial hypothesis. It has to do with one of the central theoretical foundations of the model of intergenerational integration: the concept of social production functions and the subsequent differentiation between specific and generalized capital. The hypothesis states that in all immigration processes there is a structural change in the institutional and cultural conditions for productive actions, making certain resources and investments more efficient than others for the attainment of the respective cultural goals. Despite all the transnational and supranational processes taking place, the relevant national institutions and cultures still play a central role here, *e.g.*, within the educational systems. And if the nation- state is not directly involved, there are still the given regional and local circumstances asserting their relevance. To this extent, there are always certain institutional and cultural cores to which actors should orientate themselves, for it is in their own interests to do so. And this is precisely what we can observe empirically. In most cases, the ethnic resources used and produced in this process make up a comparatively (more or less) specific form of capital with only limited usability and productivity. Therefore, more generalized forms of capital, like a universally usable language, social relations not bound to ethnic limits, or human capital in the form of technical and administrative knowledge, maintain their status as the constitutional core of investments, even under the conditions of the new immigration.

REFERENCES

Abelson, R. P. and A. Levi
1985 "Decision Making and Decision Theory." In *Handbook of Social Psychology, Volume I: Theory and Method, 3rd edition.* Ed. G. Lindzey and E. Aronson. New York: Random House. Pp. 231–309.

Alba, R. D.
1999 "Immigration and the American Realities of Assimilation and Multiculturalism," *Sociological Forum,* 14:3–25.

——————
1985 *Italian Americans. Into the Twilight of Ethnicity.* Englewood Cliffs, NJ: Prentice Hall.

Alba, R. D., J. Handl and W. Müller
1994   "Ethnische Ungleichheit im Deutschen Bildungssystem," *Kölner Zeitschrift für Soziologie und Sozialpsychologie,* 46:209–237.

Alba, R. D. and V. Nee
1999   "Rethinking Assimilation Theory for a New Era of Immigration." In *The Handbook of International Migration: The American Experience.* Ed. C. Hirschman, P. Kasinitz and J. DeWind. New York: Russell Sage Foundation. Pp. 135–160.

Aldrich, H. E. and R. Waldinger
1990   "Ethnicity and Entrepreneurship," *Annual Review of Sociology,* 16:111–135.

Becker, G. S.
1965   "A Theory of the Allocation of Time," *The Economic Journal,* 75:493–517.

Berreman, G. D.
1960   "Caste in India and the United States," *American Journal of Sociology,* 64:120–127.

Blau, P. M.
1994   *Structural Contexts of Opportunities.* Chicago: University of Chicago Press.

1977   *Inequality and Heterogeneity. A Primitive Theory of Social Structure.* New York: Free Press.

Boudon, R.
1974   *Education, Opportunity, and Social Inequality. Changing Prospects in Western Society.* New York: Wiley.

1964   "Institutional Completeness of Ethnic Communities and the Personal Relations of Immigrants," *American Journal of Sociology,* 70:193–205

Brubaker, R.
2001   "The Return of Assimilation? Changing Perspectives on Immigration and Its Sequels in France, Germany, and the United States," *Ethnic and Racial Studies,* 24:531–548.

Dustman, C. and A. van Soest
2002   "Language and the Earnings of Immigrants," *Industrial and Labor Relations Review,* 55:473–492.

Esser, H.
1999–2002 *Soziologie. Spezielle Grundlagen, Volume 1–6.* Frankfurt/M. and New York: Campus.

1993   *Soziologie. Allgemeine Grundlagen.* Frankfurt/M. and New York: Campus.

1991   "The Integration of Second Generation Immigrants in Germany: An Explanation of 'Cultural' Differences." In *Education for Democratic Citizenship: A Challenge for Multi-Ethnic Societies.* Ed. R. S. Sigel and M. Hoskins. Hillsdale, NJ: Lawrence Erlbaum Associates Publishers. Pp. 45–69.

1990   "Nur Eine Frage der Zeit? Zur Frage der Eingliederung von Migranten im Generationen-Zyklus und zu Einer Möglichkeit, Unterschiede Hierin Theoretisch zu Erklären." In *Generation und Identität. Theoretische und Empirische Beiträge zur Migrationssoziologie.* Ed. H. Esser and J. Friedrichs. Opladen:Westdeutscher Verlag. Pp. 73–100.

1986a "Social Context and Inter-Ethnic Relations: The Case of Migrant Workers in West German Urban Areas," *European Sociological Review*, 2:30–51.

1986b "Ethnic Segmentation as the Unintended Result of Intentional Actions." In *Paradoxical Effects of Social Behavior. Essay in the Honor of Anatol Rapoport*. Ed. A. Diekmann and P. Mitter. Heidelberg and Wien: Physica-Verlag. Pp. 281–296.

1980 "Aspekte der Wanderungssoziologie. Assimilation und Integration von Wanderern, ethnischen Gruppen und Minderheiten." *Eine handlungstheoretische Analyse*. Darmstadt and Neuwied: Luchterhand Verlag.

Faist, T.
2000 *The Volume and Dynamics of International Migration and Transnational Spaces*. Oxford: Clarendon Press.

Favell, A.
2002 "Multicultural Nation-building: 'Integration' as Public Philosophy and Research Paradigm in Western Europe," *Swiss Political Science Review*, 7:116–124.

Foner, N.
1997 "What's New About Transnationalism? New York Immigrants Today and at the Turn of the Century," *Diaspora*, 6:355–375.

Fong, E. and E. Ooka
2002 "The Social Consequences of Participating in the Economic Economy," *International Migration Review*, 36(1):125–146.

Gans, H. J.
1999 "Toward a Reconciliation of 'Assimilation' and 'Pluralism': The Interplay of Acculturation and Ethnic Retention." In *The Handbook of International Migration: The American Experience*. Ed. C. Hirschman, P. Kasinitz, and J. DeWind. New York: Russell Sage Foundation. Pp. 161–171.

Glick Schiller, N.
1999 "Transmigrants and Nation-States: Something Old and Something New in the U.S. Immigrant Experience." In *The Handbook of International Migration: The American Experience*. Ed. C. Hirschman, P. Kasinitz, and J. DeWind. New York: Russell Sage Foundation. Pp. 94–119.

Gordon, M. M.
1964 *Assimilation in American Life. The Role of Race, Religion, and National Origins*. New York: Oxford University Press.

Granato, N. and F. Kalter
2001 "Die Persistenz Ethnischer Ungleichheit auf dem Deutschen Arbeitsmarkt. Diskriminierung oder Unterinvestition in Humankapital," *Kölner Zeitschrift für Soziologie und Sozialpsychologie*, 53:497–520.

Heckmann, F.
1981 *Die Bundesrepublik: Ein Einwanderungsland? Zur Soziologie der Gastarbeiterbevölkerung als Einwandererminorität*. Stuttgart: Klett-Cotta.

Heckmann, F. and D. Schnapper, eds.
2003 *The Integration of Immigrants in European Societies. National Differences and Trends of Convergence*. Stuttgart: Lucius & Lucius.

Hedström, P. and R. Swedberg
1998   "Social Mechanisms: An Introductory Essay." In *Social Mechanisms: An Analytical Approach to Social Theory.* Ed. P. Hedström and R. Swedberg. Cambridge: Cambridge University Press. Pp. 1–31.

Hoffmann-Nowotny, H.-J.
1973   *Soziologie des Fremdarbeiterproblems.Eine Theoretische und Empirische Analyse am Beispiel der Schweiz.* Stuttgart: Enke Verlag.

Kalter, F.
2003   *Chancen, Fouls und Abseitsfallen. Migranten im Deutschen Ligenfußball.* Opladen:Westdeutscher Verlag.

Kalter, F. and N. Granato
2002   "Demographic Change, Educational Expansion, and Structural Assimilation of Immigrants. The Case of Germany," *European Sociological Review,* 18:199–216.

Laitin, D. D.
1995   "Marginality. A Microperspective," *Rationality and Society,* 7:31–57.

Lancaster, K. J.
1996   "A New Approach to Consumer Theory," *The Journal of Political Economy,* 74:132–157.

Lindenberg, S.
1992   "Cohorts, Social Production Functions and the Problem of Self Command." In *Dynamics of Cohort and Generations Research.* Ed. H. A. Becker. Amsterdam: Thesis Publishers. Pp. 283–308.

1989   "Social Production Functions, Deficits, and Social Revolutions. Prerevolutionary France and Russia," *Rationality and Society,* 1:51–77

Lockwood, D.
1964   "Social Integration and System Integration." In *Explorations in Social Change.* Ed. G. K. Zollschan and W. Hirsch. London: Routledge & Kegan Paul. Pp. 244–257.

Logan, J. R., R. D. Alba and W. Zhang
2002   "Immigrant Enclaves and Ethnic Communities in New York and Los Angeles," *American Sociological Review,* 67:299–322.

Massey, D. S.
1985   "Ethnic Residential Segregation: A Theoretical Synthesis and Empirical Review," *Sociology and Social Research,* 69:315–350.

Massey, D. S. and N. A. Denton
1998   *American Apartheid: Segregation and the Making of the Underclass.* 8th edition. Cambridge: Harvard University Press.

Massey, D. S. *et al.*
1998   *New Migrations, New Theories.* In *Worlds in Motion: Understanding International Migration at the End of the Millennium.* Ed. D. S. Massey *et al.* Oxford: Clarendon Press. Pp. 1–16.

Marx, K. and F. Engels
1992   *The Communist Manifesto.* Oxford and New York: Oxford University Press.

Merton, R. K.
1967   "Social Structure and Anomie." In *Social Theory and Social Structure.* 11th edition. Ed. R. K. Merton. New York and London: Free Press. Pp. 131–160.

Nauck, B.
1995 "Educational Climate and Intergenerational Transmission in Turkish Families: A Comparison of Migrants in Germany and Non-Migrants." In *Psychological Response to Social Change. Human Development in Changing Environments*. Ed. P. Noack, M. Hofer and J. Youniss. Berlin: de Gruyter. Pp. 67–85.

Nee, V. and J. Sanders
2001 "Understanding the Diversity of Immigrant Incorporation: A Forms-of-Capital Model," *Ethnic and Racial Studies*, 24:386–411.

Noll, H.-H., P. Schmidt and S. Weick
1998 "Ethnic Groups and Migrants in Germany. Towards a Multicultural German Society?" In *Monitoring Multicultural Societies: A Siena Group Report*. Ed. J. Bühlmann, P. Röthlisberger and B. Schmid. Neuchatel: BFS. Pp. 139–171.

Park, R. E.
1950 "The Nature of Race Relations." In *Race and Culture*. Ed. R. E. Park. Glencoe, IL: Free Press. Pp. 81–116.

Pendakur, K. and R. Pendakur
2002 "Language as Both Human Capital and Ethnicity," *International Migration Review*, 36(1):147–177.

Perlmann, J. and R. Waldinger
1999 "Immigrants, Past and Present: A Reconsideration." In *The Handbook of International Migration: The American Experience*. Ed. C. Hirschman, P. Kasinitz and J. DeWind. New York: Russell Sage Foundation. Pp. 223–238.

Portes, A.
1999 "Immigration Theory for a New Century: Some Problems and Opportunities." In *The Handbook of International Migration: The American Experience*. Ed. C. Hirschman, P. Kasinitz and J. DeWind. New York: Russell Sage Foundation. Pp. 21–33.

————, ed.
1996 *The New Second Generation*. New York: Russell Sage Foundation.

———
1995 "Economic Sociology and the Sociology of Immigration: A Conceptual Overview." In *The Economic Sociology of Immigration. Essays on Networks: Ethnicity, and Entrepreneurship*. Ed. A. Portes. New York: Russell Sage Foundation. Pp. 1–41.

Portes, A., W. J. Haller and L. E. Guarnizo
2002 "Transnational Entrepreneurs: An Alternative Form of Immigrant Economic Adaptation," *American Sociological Review*, 67:278–298.

Pott, A.
2002 *Ethnizität und Raum im Aufstiegsprozeß. Eine Untersuchung zum Bildungsaufstieg in der Zweiten Türkischen Migrantengeneration*. Opladen:Leske + Budrich.

Pries, L., ed.
2001 *New Transnational Social Spaces. International Migration and Transnational Companies*. London: Routledge.

Riker, W. H. and P. C. Ordeshook
1973 *An Introduction to Positive Political Theory*. Englewood Cliffs, NJ: Prentice Hall.

Rumbaut, R. G.
1999 "Assimilation and its Discontents: Ironies and Paradoxes." In *The Handbook of Inter-*

national Migration: The American Experience. Ed. C. Hirschman, P. Kasinitz and J. DeWind. New York: Russell Sage Foundation. Pp. 172–195.

Schelling, T. C.
1978 *Micromotives and Macrobehavior.* New York and London: Norton.
1971 "Dynamic Models of Segregation," *Journal of Mathematical Sociology,* 1:143–186.

Schmitter Heisler, B.
2000 "The Sociology of Immigration. From Assimilation to Segmented Integration, from the American Experience to the Global Arena." In *Migration Theory: Talking across Disciplines.* Ed. C. B. Brettell and J. F. Hollifield. New York and London: Routledge. Pp. 77–96.

Schoemaker, P. J.
1982 "The Expected Utility Model: Its Variants, Purposes, Evidence and Limitations." *The Journal of Economic Literature,* 20:529–563.

Wiley, N. F.
1970 "The Ethnic Mobility Trap and Stratification Theory." In *The Study of Society: An Integrated Anthology.* 2nd edition. Ed. P. I. Rose. New York and Toronto: Random House. Pp. 397–408.

Wilpert, C.
1980 *Die Zukunft der Zweiten Generation.* Königstein: Athenäum.

Wippler, R. and S. Lindenberg
1987 "Collective Phenomena and Rational Choice." In *The Midro-Macro Link.* Ed. J. C. Alexander, B. Giesen, R. Münch and N. J. Smelser. Berkeley, Los Angeles and London: University of California Press. Pp. 135–152.

Zhou, M.
1999 "Segmented Assimilation: Issues, Controversies, and Recent Research on the New Second Generation." In *The Handbook of International Migration: The American Experience.* Ed. C. Hirschman, P. Kasinitz and J. DeWind. New York: Russell Sage Foundation. Pp. 196–212.

Chapter 12

AGES, LIFE STAGES, AND GENERATIONAL COHORTS[1]
Decomposing the Immigrant First and Second Generations in the United States

Rubén Rumbaut

The study of the long-term consequences of international migration for receiving countries has focused increasingly on the process of adaptation of the immigrants' children (Boyd and Grieco, 1998; Caplan *et al.*, 1991; Gans, 1992; Hernández and Charney, 1998; Levitt and Waters, 2002;

[1]Revision of paper presented at the international conference on "Conceptual and Methodological Developments in the Study of International Migration," Princeton University, May 23–24, 2003, sponsored by the Center for Migration and Development, Princeton University, in collaboration with the *International Migration Review* and the International Migration Program of the Social Science Research Council. I gratefully acknowledge the support provided to the Children of Immigrants Longitudinal Study (CILS) by research grants from the Russell Sage Foundation and the Andrew W. Mellon, Spencer, and National Science Foundations, to Alejandro Portes and Rubén G. Rumbaut, Principal Investigators; and the research assistance of Charlie V. Morgan of the University of California, Irvine.

Perlmann and Waldinger, 1997; Portes, 1996; Portes and Zhou, 1993; Portes and Rumbaut, 2001; Rumbaut and Cornelius, 1995; Rumbaut and Ima, 1988; Suárez-Orozco and Suárez-Orozco, 2002; Sung, 1987; Zhou, 1997; Zhou and Bankston, 1998). The "new second generation" is rapidly growing and diversifying through continued immigration, natural increase and intermarriage, complicating its contours and making it increasingly important, for theoretical as well as programmatic and public policy reasons, to clarify who and what is encompassed by that term and to measure its size and composition. Similarly problematic is the definition, depiction and measurement of the immigrant "first generation," a large segment of which is composed of persons who migrated as children and who are often regarded as members of the "second" generation.

Many theoretical questions can be and have been raised about the incorporation of children of immigrants vis-à-vis that of their parents: about their "coming of age" in the United States, their modes of acculturation and ethnic identity (and ethnic group) formation, patterns of language use and mother-tongue shift, and their social, residential, reproductive, marital, educational, occupational, economic, civic and political trajectories into adulthood. As with issues of language and national loyalties, questions have been raised as well about whether and to what extent the "transnational" attachments of their parents are sustained in the generation of their children, particularly those born in receiving countries such as the United States, who lack the memories and the symbolic "birth connection" of their emigrant parents. All of these are open empirical questions, but each of them presupposes a clear operational definition of what is meant by second generation vis-à-vis the first generation, and even of something as basic as the ethnicity of first- versus second-generation persons. However, while there is a consensus about the import of intergenerational analysis for the study of the long-term impact of immigration, there is no such consensus on the meaning and measurement of generations (Oropesa and Landale, 1997).

Although these may appear to be simple and straightforward matters, they become complex and elusive on closer inspection. To begin with, the term generation brings with it a variety of meanings. In a kinship context, it refers to a stage in a natural succession comprising those who are of the same genealogical remove from an ancestor (*e.g.*, the generations of the parents, children, and grandchildren). It is also used as a synonym for cohort, a term preferred by demographers to refer to a set of people born at about the same time (Ryder, 1965; Riley, 1987). In his seminal essay "The

Problem of Generations," Karl Mannheim ([1928] 1996) distinguished between individuals of the same age group (which he termed a "generational location") and a "generation as an actuality" – contemporaries (typically compatriots as well) who are exposed to and defined by the effects of a powerful historical stimulus (especially during the years of the transition to adulthood when "personal experimentation with life begins") and develop a shared consciousness about it[2] – while noting that members of a generation may react differently to the common historical stimulus, forming different "generational units" within the same actual generation.

Immigrant families and communities themselves are often acutely conscious of the generational status of their members and of generational differences between them – perhaps none more so than the Japanese in the United States, who have specific terms for the first four generations since the initial migrations of the late nineteenth and early twentieth centuries (*issei, nisei, sansei, yonsei*), and another term (*nikkei*) to describe all four generations of people of Japanese ancestry. How recent Japanese immigrants fit into this closed generational scheme is another matter altogether, since the scheme posits an original migration (a first generation), in terms of which all subsequent U.S.-born generations are genealogically defined and counted. But the imagery is suggestive: international migration is a powerful and transformative force, producing profound social changes not only in the sending and receiving societies, but, above all, among the immigrants themselves and their descendants. Those effects may begin to fade over time and generation, the greater the remove from the original migrations and the conditions that produced them. But how to grasp and measure that "remove" – including the evolution over time and place of the ethnic self-identities of the referent populations, in widely different and rapidly changing circumstances and often in a context of continuing immigration – is problematic.

An example may be instructive. The complexity of some of these issues was raised in our Children of Immigrants Longitudinal Study (CILS) as soon as we set about to analyze the first wave of survey data collected in 1992 (Portes and Rumbaut, 2001; Rumbaut and Portes, 2001). The CILS baseline sample consisted of 5,262 teenage respondents on both coasts of the United States, most born in 1977 or 1978, representing 77 different nationalities. Half were foreign-born youths who had immigrated to the United States before age 12 (the "1.5 generation"), and half were U.S.-born

---

[2]The idea echoes Erik Erickson's later (1964) concept of identity formation within a common "psycho-historical actuality."

children of at least one immigrant parent (technically the second generation). Among the foreign-born youth, the sample was also evenly split by age at arrival: about half had lived in the United States for ten years or more (that is, they were preschool-age at arrival), while the other half had lived in the United States nine years or less (that is, they had reached elementary school age in their native country but arrived in the United States before reaching adolescence and secondary schooling). Time in the United States for these immigrant children thus was not solely a measure of length of exposure to American life, but also an indicator of qualitatively different life stages and sociodevelopmental contexts at the time of immigration.

The determination of ethnicity for CILS respondents was mostly straightforward and unambiguous among foreign-born youths and those whose parents were co-nationals (born in the same foreign country), except for ethnic minorities (such as the Hmong from Laos, the ethnic Chinese from Vietnam) or in cases involving unique historical circumstances. But in one fourth of the cases in the CILS sample, the parents were born in different countries, and in over half of those cases –accounting for 13 percent of the overall sample – one of the parents was U.S. born. In the case of the latter, ethnicity was assigned on the basis of the national origin of the foreign-born parent, whether it was the father or the mother (*see* Oropesa and Landale, 1997; Waters, 1990).

In the case of the former – in mixed marriages where the parents were born in different foreign countries – the nationality of the mother took precedence in the assignment of ethnicity, reflecting both the mother's more influential role in the children's socialization and the fact that fathers were absent in 30 percent of the homes in the sample (Rumbaut, 1994). Of course, what is a methodological problem to the researcher is a central psychosocial issue to an adolescent in arriving at a meaningful ethnic self-definition during a stage of the life cycle concerned with "identity crisis" and its resolution (Erikson, 1968). Over time, as those adolescents come of age, marry and have children of their own, issues of ethnic identity and the determination of ethnicity in comparative research studies can be confidently predicted to become more complicated still and their measurement and analysis methodologically more challenging.

Taking off from the preceding observations, this article is intended as a conceptual, methodological, and empirical contribution to the cognate research literature. It seeks to specify the size and composition – and definition – of what are loosely referred to as the first and second generations in the United States, identifying such populations empirically, and to advance our research and understanding based on specific operational definitions of distinctive generational cohorts and on new survey data from representative national and regional samples. In particular, it will address the question of the utility and validity of "lumping" versus "splitting" such generational cohorts in the study of immigrant adaptation, including that of foreign-born immigrant children and the native-born children of immigrants.

DEFINING AND REDEFINING THE FIRST AND SECOND GENERATIONS

Differences in nativity (of self and parents) and in age and life stage at arrival, which are criteria used to distinguish between generational cohorts, are known to affect significantly the modes of acculturation of adults and children in immigrant families, especially with regard to language and accent, educational attainment and patterns of social mobility, outlooks and frames of reference, ethnic identity and even their propensity to sustain transnational attachments over time (*cf.* Cropley, 1983; Rumbaut, 1991, 1998a, 2002; Rumbaut and Ima, 1988). To carry out such analyses – and setting aside for the time being the problem of the determination of "ethnicity" – the measurement of first and second generations requires at a minimum data sources that contain information on the country of birth of the respondent; and, if foreign born, the age and date of arrival; and, if native born, the country of birth of the mother and father.

Spurred by the mass migration of the 1840s to the United States, the 1850 census was the first to collect data on the nativity of the population; beginning with the 1870 census, a question on parental nativity was added as well and collected in each decennial U.S. census until 1970 (*see* Gibson and Lennon, 1999). However, the study of the second generation and of the intergenerational mobility of immigrant-origin groups in the United States was severely undercut after 1970 when the U.S. Census Bureau dropped the question on parental nativity from the long-form questionnaire of its decennial census, the largest and most reliable nationally-representative data source for the analysis of the myriad of immigrant groups. As a result, ironically, just at the very moment when a new era of mass migration made the collection of such data indispensable in the United States, the last three censuses (1980, 1990, 2000) have permitted only a detailed examination of the foreign-born population by country of birth and date of arrival, but not of their U.S.-born children. The only exception in this regard has been the innovative use of the Public Use Microdata Samples (PUMS) of the decennial census to construct child files for all children under 18 residing in households with at least one foreign-born parent, and then concatenating information on the parents and household to each record (Jensen and Chitose, 1994; Oropesa and Landale, 1997); however, those efforts are limited only to those children still residing with their (foreign-born) parents and cannot consider any second-generation persons 18 and older.

Fortunately, in 1994 the questions on paternal and maternal nativity were incorporated in the annual (March) supplement of the Current Population Surveys (CPS) conducted by the Census Bureau for the Bureau of Labor Statistics. The CPS has since become the main national-level data set in the United States permitting more refined intergenerational analyses (from the first to the second and third-and-beyond generations) – but the sample size for a given year, while substantial, is not large enough to provide reliable information on smaller immigrant populations or for comparative analyses by national origin and by generational cohorts defined by age-at-arrival and parental nativity. This limitation can be addressed to some extent by merging annual demographic data files for several consecutive years to generate sufficient sample sizes for analytical purposes – a methodological strategy that will be pursued below.

Aside from the problem of relevant data sources and data needs, the measurement of the size and composition of the first and second generations, which together comprise the country's "immigrant-stock" or foreign-parentage population, depends on what is meant by these terms, which have not been uniformly defined in the literature or operationalized in research studies. When referring to the first generation, immigration scholars in the United States commonly have in mind persons born and socialized in another country who immigrate as adults, although the term technically includes the foreign born regardless of their age at arrival. Similarly, the second generation technically refers to the U.S.-born and U.S.-socialized children of foreign-born parents, although under this rubric immigration scholars also often, if imprecisely, lump together foreign-born persons who immigrated as children as well as U.S.-born persons with one U.S.-born parent and one foreign-born parent, treating them together as a *de facto* second generation.

Indeed, the expression "second-generation immigrants" is a commonplace in the literature – although it is technically an oxymoron, inasmuch as persons born in the United States cannot also be immigrants to the United States. Still, none of these conventional usages accurately captures the experience of youths who fall in the interstices between these groupings nor, among those born abroad, takes into account their different ages and life stages at the time of migration.

That there are fundamental differences in the pace and mode of adaptation between persons who immigrate as adults and those who do so as children is a well-established observation – indeed, it is the stuff of a rich popular literature and culture – and wider still are the differences in adaptive outcomes vis-à-vis the native-born children of foreign-born parents (*cf.* Berrol, 1995; Child, 1943; Ebaugh and Chafetz, 2000; Nahirny and Fishman [1965] 1996; Piore, 1979:65–68). By 1914, Robert Park could write convincingly, "In America it has become proverbial that a Pole, Lithuanian, or Norwegian cannot be distinguished, in the second generation, from an American born of native parents" (Park and Burgess, [1921] 1924:757–758).

His colleagues W. I. Thomas and Florian Znaniecki, writing over 80 years ago in *The Polish Peasant in Europe and America,* referred in passing to the "half-second" generation to describe foreign-born youths coming of age in the United States in contrast to second-generation native-born youths ([1918–20] 1958:1776). Warner and Srole, in *The Social Systems of American Ethnic Groups* (1945), distinguished the foreign-born – whom they called the "parental" or "P" generation – from the U.S.-born generations – the first of which (the offspring of the immigrants) was dubbed the "filial first" or "F1" generation, the second (the grandchildren of the immigrants) was dubbed "F2," and so on. They divided the immigrant generation, in turn, into those who entered the United States after the age of 18 (labeled the "P1" generation) and those who entered at age 18 or younger (the P2 generation). Both the P2 and the half-second concepts are akin to the terms "one-and-a-half" or "1.5 generation," which I coined in studies of Cuban and then Southeast Asian youths (*cf.* Rumbaut, 1976, 1991; Rumbaut and Ima, 1988).

Those segments of the immigrant first generation that Warner and Srole labeled P1 (adults) and P2 (children) can each be decomposed and further refined into distinct types, depending on their ages and life stages at migration. Unique historical circumstances notwithstanding (such as the case of war-torn refugees), among those who immigrate as adults (P1) their general orientation and processes of adjustment and incorporation can be expected to vary significantly depending on whether they immigrated during early, middle, or older adulthood. For example, unlike the youngest of these (ages 18–24) who are more likely to be making their transitions to adulthood, young adults aged 25–34 generally migrate after having completed their educations, at the beginning of their work careers, and in their peak childbearing and family-formation years – but both bring a future-oriented outlook to their new arrangements.

By contrast, mid-adulthood immigrants (aged 35–54) come with years of prior work experience, by and large have already had their children, and indeed are often motivated to migrate by the search for opportunities for their children; they are unlikely to shed their native languages, customs and identities in the process of their accommodation to the new society. Older adults (55 and older), who are relatively rare in immigrant (and even refugee) flows, are already near or at the end of their work careers, and tend to be followers of children; they lack the plasticity of young migrants and are least likely to learn the new language or acculturate other than superficially to their new environment.

Similarly, those immigrants who arrive as children – what Warner and Srole called the P2 generation – can be further refined into three distinct groups, depending on whether their migration occurred during early childhood (ages 0–5), middle childhood (6–12), or adolescence (in their teens). Foreign-born adolescents, elementary-school-age children, and pre-school children are at starkly different life stages at the point of migration, begin their adaptation processes in very different social contexts, and can be classified accordingly. More specifically: 1) those who arrive in early childhood (ages 0–5) – whom I have elsewhere labeled the 1.75 generation because their experience and adaptive outcomes are closer to that of the U.S.-born second generation – are pre-school children who retain virtually no memory of their country of birth, were too young to go to school to learn to read or write in the parental language in the home country (and typically learn English without an accent), and are almost entirely socialized here; 2) those who arrive in middle childhood (ages 6–12) – the classic 1.5 generation – are pre-adolescent, primary-school-age children who have learned (or begun to learn) to read and write in the mother tongue at schools abroad, but whose education is largely completed here; and 3) those who arrive in their adolescent years (ages 13–17), who may or may not come with their families of origin, either attend secondary schools after arrival or in the older ages may go directly into the workforce – a 1.25 generation whose experiences and adaptive outcomes are hypothesized to be closer to the first generation of immigrant adults than to the native-born second generation (Rumbaut, 1997a).

In a rigorous empirical test of this classification, which they referred to as "decimal" generations, Oropesa and Landale (1997) found significant differences between each of these generational cohorts and strong cohort effects on language outcomes (being bilingual, or English or Spanish mono-lingual) in multivariate analyses of native-born and foreign-born second-generation children of Latin American origin, suggesting that these are distinctive populations and that it is inappropriate to combine them, at least when the focus of the analysis is on language or on adaptive outcomes affected by language competencies.

While more precise distinctions based on age and life stage at arrival are not only possible but theoretically important for the analysis of modes of acculturation among immigrant parents and their children – including those variants we have labeled "dissonant," "consonant," and "selective" acculturation (Portes and Rumbaut, 1996, 2001) – the aim here is more limited. For purposes of estimating and depicting the size and composition of the immigrant-stock population of the United States, I distinguish first by nativity between the first and second generations (or P and F1, in Warner and Srole's scheme) and contrast them to the third-and-beyond generation of native parentage (F2 in Warner and Srole's terminology). A demographic and geographic profile of the immigrant-origin population is then presented, broken down by detailed national origins. Second, I decompose the foreign-born first generation (by applying the above age-based typology to both adults and children at different life stages at arrival in the United States) and the native-born second generation (by distinguishing between persons born in the United States of two foreign-born parents versus persons born in the United States of one foreign-born parent and one U.S.-born parent) and estimate the size of these generational cohorts by national origin. The data are drawn from an analysis of merged CPS annual demographic files for the five years of 1998 to 2002, yielding an overall sample of about 740,000 cases.[3]

Third, to explore the utility of the proposed typology, I examine differences in a variety of outcomes among these generational cohorts, relying on three data sources. Using the merged CPS data, I first compare the educational and occupational attainments of these cohorts for the largest immigrant population (that from Mexico) and for types of immigrant groups who arrive with sharply different levels of human capital. Next, I

---

[3]Of course, the accuracy of the estimates decreases as the sample size decreases, and thus care should be taken when interpreting the results presented below, especially for the smaller national-origin groups. For a discussion of sampling and nonsampling error in the March CPS, *see* Schmidley, 2001; Schmidley and Robinson, 1998. *See also* <http://www.bls.census.gov/cps/ads/2002/S&A 02.pdf>.

focus on patterns of linguistic assimilation among the generational cohorts composing the foreign-born population, using the 5 percent PUMS from the 2000 U.S. Census (since data on language are not available from the CPS). A last section compares differences in acculturation and identity among the cohorts composing "the new second generation," based on new longitudinal findings from the CILS survey.

THE SIZE, COMPOSITION, AND CONCENTRATION OF THE FIRST AND SECOND GENERATIONS

Based on the 1998–2002 CPS merged data files, Table 1 provides a simple tabulation of the first, second, and third-plus generations, classified solely by nativity,[4] broken down by self-reported "race" and Hispanic origin. The table shows both the weighted estimates for these populations and the un-weighted number of cases (sample size). For the total U.S. population at the turn of the century, the CPS estimated a first generation of some 32 million, a second generation of about 29 million, and a third-and-beyond generation of 211 million.[5] Thus, over 60 million people, or 22 percent of the total U.S. population, were of foreign birth or parentage around the year 2000 – including 70 percent of the Mexican-origin population, 95 percent of the Cubans, Central and South Americans, and 90 percent of the Asians, reflecting the relative recency of their migrations. By contrast, only about one in ten of "non-Hispanic whites" and "non-Hispanic blacks" were of immigrant origin. Short of examining the specific national origins of the foreign born (to which we will turn next), this is the most detailed available generational picture of the American ethnoracial mosaic, consisting largely of one-size-fits-all panethnic categories ("white," "black," "Asian") that conceal

[4]The first-generation estimate includes nearly 2 million persons who were born in a foreign country but had at least one parent who was a U.S. citizen. The U.S. Census Bureau classifies such persons as part of the "native-born population" and excludes them from the "foreign-born" population, even though many are in fact recent U.S. arrivals. Most of them come from Mexico, Canada, Germany, Great Britain, Japan, the Philippines, and Korea (countries from which immigration to the United States via marriages with U.S. citizens is common).

[5]The estimates apply to the civilian noninstitutionalized resident population of the 50 states and the District of Columbia. Given the focus on immigrant generations, American Indians and Alaska Natives are not included in Table 1. Included under first generation are island-born Puerto Ricans and other U.S. islanders who are U.S. citizens at birth, and under second generation are mainland-born Puerto Ricans of island-born parents. These figures do not include the 3.8 million who resided in Puerto Rico, nor the population of the other U.S. territories.

TABLE 1
The Population of the United States, 1998–2002, by Immigrant Generation and Self-Reported Race and Hispanic Origin:[a] Weighted CPS Estimates and Unweighted CPS Cases

Race and Hispanic Origin	Immigrant Generation[b]									Foreign Parentage (% 1st and 2nd Generation)
	First		Second		Third+		Total			
	Weighted Estimate	CPS Sample Size	Weighted Estimate	CPS Sample Size	Weighted Estimate	CPS Sample Size	Weighted Estimate	CPS Sample Size		
Hispanic	14,559,468	51,380	10,337,124	36,264	8,416,598	30,551	33,313,190	118,195		75
Mexican	8,457,887	28,798	7,016,435	23,695	6,503,121	21,820	21,977,443	74,313		70
Puerto Rican[c]	1,229,780	4,715	1,144,343	4,383	671,745	2,571	3,045,868	11,669		78
Cuban	905,626	3,181	338,565	1,250	74,763	274	1,318,954	4,705		94
Central-South American	3,295,509	12,112	1,296,310	4,887	218,938	823	4,810,757	17,822		95
Other Spanish	670,666	2,574	541,471	2,049	948,031	5,063	2,160,168	9,686		56
Non-Hispanic	17,513,047	42,178	18,540,381	47,985	202,892,992	525,248	238,946,420	615,411		15
White, non-Hispanic	8,341,444	20,661	14,339,679	37,805	170,899,381	452,792	193,580,504	511,258		12
Black, non-Hispanic	2,156,234	4,983	1,290,433	2,944	30,924,468	68,031	34,371,135	75,958		10
Asian, non-Hispanic	7,015,369	16,534	2,910,269	7,236	1,069,143	4,425	10,994,781	28,195		90
Total Population	32,072,515	93,558	28,877,505	84,249	211,309,590	555,799	272,259,610	733,606		22

Source: Merged Current Population Survey (CPS) annual demographic files (March), 1998 through 2002.

[a]Based on self-reported responses to CPS questions on "race" and "Hispanic origin." American Indians and Alaska Natives are not included in this table.

[b]Immigrant generations defined as follows: First = foreign-born; Second = U.S.-born of foreign-born parents; Third-and-beyond: U.S.-born of U.S.-born parents.

[c]Persons born in Puerto Rico are U.S. citizens; "first" and "second" generations here refer to island versus mainland nativity of self or parents.

far more than they reveal about the extraordinary ethnic diversity subsumed under those labels.

Moreover, as a methodological caveat, it is worth noting that the data on race and Hispanic origin are subjective self-reports chosen from a list of ethnoracial categories specified by the survey (and by the federal government) and may be susceptible to changes in self-definition over time and circumstance. Consider, for example, the findings of an exploratory analysis of merged 1996–97 CPS data (Rumbaut, 1998b), which focused on Cubans, Mexicans, and Puerto Ricans – the only distinctive Hispanic groups for which the CPS permits a self-report of ethnic identity (the rest are lumped under Central/South Americans or Other Spanish). Against that subjective measure of ethnicity, I contrasted an alternative, objective measure based on the country of birth of respondents and of their mother and father. By using both approaches to "define" who is Cuban, the data yielded a weighted 1997 "subjective" estimate of about 1.2 million Cubans in the United States (based on the self-report of respondents who said they were Cuban), in contrast to an "objective" estimate of 1.6 million Cubans (based on the data on nativity – *i.e.*, if either the respondent or one or both of the parents were born in Cuba, they were classified as of Cuban origin).

I dubbed this "The Case of the 400,000 Missing Cubans," pointing out that subjective self-reports may miss large numbers of people who, as a result of intermarriage and assimilation, especially by the third generation, may stop identifying ethnically as such and fade into what Richard Alba (1985, 1990) has called the "twilight of ethnicity" – or disappear into panethnic and racial categories, much as Haitians, Jamaicans and other West Indians have been observed to begin to "fade to black" by the second generation (Kasinitz et al., 2001; Waters, 1999). The "missing Cubans" tended to be U.S. born, living outside of the dense Miami enclave, more likely to be children of mixed marriages, and did not self-report as "Cuban" to the CPS question on Hispanic origin.

For the Cuban sample, that was a large discrepancy (close to a 25% difference between the subjective and the objective measures of ethnicity). But for Mexicans and Puerto Ricans, the comparisons between subjective and objective definitions yielded only small single-digit discrepancies in size estimates, suggesting (perhaps) that those groups were more likely to maintain "thick" ethnic identities over time and generation. Naïve intergenerational studies relying on self-report measures of ethnicity alone may thus underestimate the generational slippage and the erosion or "thinning" of ethnicity that may occur among differentially advantaged or disadvantaged groups by the third generation.

Table 2 focuses on the first and second generations only, but replaces the race and Hispanic origin classification for the specific countries of birth of the respondents (or, for the U.S.-born second generation, of their parents). The result yields a vastly different panorama, revealing the extraordinary diversity of national origins that comprises the so-called "foreign-stock" or immigrant-origin population of the United States. Note that in Table 2 Puerto Ricans and other U.S. islanders, who have birthright citizenship, are listed at the bottom of the table and not included with the immigrant-origin totals, to separate these different citizenship categories (although island born vs. mainland born first and second generations are reported for them as well). Again the table provides both weighted estimates for each group, as well as the CPS sample sizes. Each of the groups listed have total sample sizes at least in the thousands (the data for the first- and second-generation Mexicans are based on a merged sample size of over 51,000 cases), with only two of those listed (the Iranians and Israelis) limited to sample sizes in the hundreds. In addition, the table provides data on sex and age for each group, as well as the proportion of each group that is foreign born.

The data presented in Table 2 allow for an approximate rank ordering by size and median age of the largest national-origin groups within the first and second generations. As the data show, the Mexican-origin population clearly dwarfs all others in both the first and second generations. By the turn of the century, the first generation of Mexican immigrants totaled about 8.3 million persons – about 7 million more than the next sizable immigrant groups (the Filipinos, Chinese, Cubans, and Vietnamese) – and with a median age of 32 years they were one of the youngest immigrant populations in the United States as well. The Mexican-American second generation added another 7 million persons – over three times larger than the next largest second-generation group (the "old second generation" of Italian Americans, estimated at 2.1 million), but with a median age of only 12 years the Mexican-American second generation was far younger than Italian Americans of foreign parentage (whose median age was 66, mostly the children of Italian immigrants who had come to the United States in the early twentieth century). Both through immigration and natural increase, the Mexican-origin population of the United States is growing more rapidly than virtually any other group and is, as such, of central interest for the study of immigrant intergenerational mobility.

More than three out of every four immigrants in the United States today come from Latin America, the Caribbean and Asia; Mexico alone accounts for more than one fourth of the total. While only one fifth of the 31 million comprising the immigrant first generation hailed from Europe or Canada, nearly half of the 27 million comprising the second generation did so. Indeed, not only the Italian but also the Canadian, German, British, Irish, Polish, and Russian second generations are larger than any other except for the Mexican, but their median ages are much older, reflecting the fact that they consist largely of the surviving offspring of immigrants who had come to the United States before World War II.

The age data reveal sharp differences between the "old" and the "new" second generation. As Table 2 shows, the median age of the combined European and Canadian second generations was 57, compared to a much younger average of 12 to 13 years for the U.S.-born offspring of Latin American, Caribbean and Asian-origin immigrants. For the latter groups, the median age of the generation of their U.S.-born children is still very young – in fact, they mostly consist of children, with median ages ranging from 7 to 17 for almost all the groups, the principal exception being the Japanese second generation with a median age of 35 – a telling marker that reflects the recency of the immigration of the rest of the first-generation groups from Latin America and Asia.

In this table, a methodological caveat worth underscoring is the fact that the data on national origin for second-generation persons (defined as native born of foreign-born parents) are based on the parents' country of birth, as discussed earlier. The weighted estimates show that of the more than 27 million U.S.-born persons of foreign parentage, over 13 million have parents who were both born in the same foreign country, and nearly 12 million more have one parent born in the United States; for all of them, the national-origin classification of the U.S.-born child is straightforward. But in over 2 million cases (8% of the native-born second generation), the parents were born in different foreign countries, posing a problem in the allocation of ethnicity.

The data in Table 2 follow the mother-centric rule described above: *e.g.*, in cases where the mother is Mexican and the father is not, the child is assigned to the Mexican row. I carried out separate analyses (not shown) to ascertain the consequences for the size and ethnic composition of all the immigrant-origin populations using both mother-centric and father-centric rules in ethnic determinations. The results show which groups gain or lose in size by employing one rule or the other. For example, a mother-centric rule would yield an estimated 219,000 persons added to the "Mexican"

TABLE 2
THE IMMIGRANT FIRST AND SECOND GENERATIONS OF THE UNITED STATES, 1998–2002, BY REGION AND NATIONAL ORIGIN: WEIGHTED CPS ESTIMATES AND UNWEIGHTED CPS CASES

Region and National Origin	First Generation (Foreign-born)				Second Generation (U.S.-born)				Total (1st + 2nd)		
	Weighted Estimate	Sample Size	Median Age	Sex % (male)	Weighted Estimate	Sample Size	Median Age	Sex % (male)	Weighted Estimate	Sample Size	% Foreign Born
Latin America and Caribbean	15,006,700	50,315	35	52	10,422,919	36,079	12	50	25,429,619	86,394	59
Mexico	8,255,639	28,035	32	55	7,051,133	23,600	12	50	15,306,772	51,635	54
Cuba	928,831	3,229	52	49	436,143	1,551	17	48	1,364,974	4,780	68
Dominican Republic	669,359	2,434	37	40	446,122	1,627	10	51	1,115,481	4,061	60
El Salvador[a]	753,236	2,973	33	52	228,993	2,319	8	51	982,229	5,292	77
Guatemala	386,802	1,468	32	56	176,677	686	7	51	563,479	2,154	69
Other Central America	784,891	2,696	35	47	439,145	1,521	11	50	1,224,036	4,217	64
Colombia	486,272	1,719	39	46	236,848	850	12	47	723,120	2,569	67
Ecuador, Peru	552,521	1,949	37	50	263,477	967	10	51	815,998	2,916	68
Other South America	607,923	2,015	36	50	263,011	881	13	53	870,934	2,896	70
Haiti	472,444	1,090	38	51	241,569	555	11	48	714,013	1,645	66
Jamaica	441,896	1,026	40	47	250,275	574	13	51	692,171	1,600	64
Other West Indies	666,886	1,681	39	47	389,526	948	13	47	1,056,412	2,629	63
Asia and Middle East	8,015,700	18,807	38	48	3,884,143	9,616	13	50	11,899,843	28,423	67
Philippines	1,401,792	3,655	41	43	819,497	2,196	13	50	2,221,289	5,851	63
China	921,941	2,112	42	48	410,999	940	20	50	1,332,940	3,052	69
Hong Kong, Taiwan	510,773	1,141	37	47	195,997	444	13	48	706,770	1,585	72
Vietnam	894,880	1,819	37	51	306,718	627	8	57	1,201,598	2,446	74
Laos, Cambodia	259,436	647	36	46	213,762	511	10	48	473,198	1,158	55
India	991,647	2,256	35	55	332,436	773	11	51	1,324,083	3,029	75
Korea	764,097	1,850	38	41	274,146	667	12	50	1,038,243	2,517	74
Japan	428,232	1,146	37	44	335,253	1,138	35	48	763,485	2,284	56
Other SE Asia	821,489	1,873	34	49	368,338	825	7	50	1,189,827	2,698	69
Iran	286,976	600	43	55	125,722	276	12	51	412,698	876	70
Israel	91,448	225	36	56	68,570	172	16	44	160,018	397	57
Arab Middle East[b]	642,989	1,483	37	57	432,705	1,047	16	51	1,075,694	2,530	60

TABLE 2 (CONTINUED)

THE IMMIGRANT FIRST AND SECOND GENERATIONS OF THE UNITED STATES, 1998–2002, BY REGION AND NATIONAL ORIGIN: WEIGHTED CPS ESTIMATES AND UNWEIGHTED CPS CASES

Region and National Origin	First Generation (Foreign-born)				Second Generation (U.S.-born)				Total (1st + 2nd)		
	Weighted Estimate	Sample Size	Median Age	Sex % (male)	Weighted Estimate	Sample Size	Median Age	Sex % (male)	Weighted Estimate	Sample Size	% Foreign Born
Europe and Canada	6,199,879	15,562	45	47	11,839,018	31,059	57	48	18,038,897	46,621	34
Canada	928,037	2,553	45	47	1,698,139	5,113	48	50	2,626,176	7,666	35
Great Britain	755,340	1,901	43	48	1,136,724	3,067	46	49	1,892,064	4,968	40
Ireland	174,020	407	54	47	613,326	1,541	60	46	787,346	1,948	22
Germany	1,125,007	2,812	40	42	1,537,435	4,027	40	49	2,662,442	6,839	42
NW Europe	582,790	1,455	46	46	1,384,288	3,803	63	46	1,967,078	5,258	30
Italy	481,498	1,150	58	53	2,146,489	5,203	66	48	2,627,987	6,353	18
Poland	424,106	1,011	46	46	1,034,512	2,478	71	45	1,458,618	3,489	29
Russia, USSR	809,073	1,908	39	47	883,402	2,265	70	47	1,692,475	4,173	48
SE Europe	920,008	2,365	47	50	1,404,703	3,562	51	47	2,324,711	5,927	40
Sub-Saharan Africa	536,755	1,211	34	55	200,166	468	10	50	736,921	1,679	73
All Others	880,258	2,522	35	53	644,116	1,946	18	49	1,524,374	4,468	58
Total Immigrant Origin	30,639,292	88,417	37	50	26,990,362	79,168	23	49	57,629,654	167,585	53
Puerto Rico[c]	1,243,848	4,734	43	47	1,319,611	4,867	22	48	2,563,459	9,601	49
Other US Islanders[c]	212,266	666	36	51	179,639	548	19	44	391,905	1,214	54

Source: Merged Current Population Survey (CPS) annual demographic files (March), 1998 through 2002.

[a]The CPS estimate for the Salvadoran population has been adjusted based on data from the 2000 census.

[b]Includes North African Arab countries.

[c]Persons born in Puerto Rico or other U.S. island territories (Guam, American Samoa, U.S. Virgin Islands), or whose parents were born there, have birthright citizenship.

totals, while a father-centric approach would yield 158,000 – for a net differential of 61,000 persons added to the Mexican totals when a mother-centric rule is used (or an equivalent loss were a father-centric rule used).

Similarly, the Filipinos gain 34,000 to their second-generation totals via a mother-centric approach, the Canadians gain 46,000, while Dominicans lose 32,000 and the Italians and Russians lose about 40,000 each. For most other groups the plus/minus differentials are much smaller than those, and in any event they generally entail quite small percentages of their second-generation size estimates. Of course, in analyses of single nationalities as opposed to comparative studies, there would be no need to privilege the maternal or paternal country of birth in these allocations; rather, any instance in which a mother or a father is born in, say, Mexico, could be included in the analysis. (In the Mexican example given, a total of 219,000 + 158,000 = 377,000 persons could be tallied to the Mexican national-origin totals).

Table 3 switches lenses from the demography to the geography of the first and second generations in the United States. For each of the principal national-origin groups listed, Table 3 provides their top three primary areas of settlement, with a measure of their level of concentration in each as a proportion of their total national population. The results vividly document the huge significance of Southern California and the New York region; those two regions alone absorbed nearly one third of the national immigrant-stock population. In Los Angeles County alone, 5.9 million people, or 62 percent of its 9.6 million residents, were of immigrant origin; another 3.6 million persons of foreign birth or parentage lived in the adjacent counties of Orange, Riverside, San Bernardino and San Diego, so that the corridor stretching from San Diego to Los Angeles alone contained 16.4 percent of the country's foreign-stock population.

New York City and the adjacent New Jersey metropolitan areas on the other side of the Hudson River combined for another 16 percent of the country's first and second generations. The Bay Area in northern California – encompassing San Francisco, Oakland and San José – and the corridor stretching from Miami to Ft. Lauderdale and Palm Beach in South Florida each absorbed nearly 5 percent of the national immigrant-origin population. Nearly three fourths of greater Miami's population was either foreign born or of foreign parentage, the highest proportion in the United States.

Clearly, as Table 3 shows, some groups are far more densely concentrated than others. Nationally, four out of five Dominicans (78%) reside in the New York/New Jersey area or greater Miami – the most highly concentrated immigrant group in the country – while nearly two thirds (64%) of the Cubans are located in South Florida or the New Jersey areas on the other side of the Hudson. In general, Latin American and Caribbean groups are far more highly concentrated than are groups from Asia, Africa or Europe, which are much more dispersed by comparison – a reflection, in part, of socioeconomic and legal status factors: spatial mobility is linked to social mobility. But not on the whole. For example, CILS data from our recently completed third wave of surveys, with the respondents now in their mid-twenties, found that 60 percent of the Filipinos, one of the most successful groups in terms of socioeconomic status, were still residing at the home of their parents (Rumbaut, 2003).

Indeed, although not shown in Table 3, especially given the youthfulness of the U.S.-born second generation for most of the national-origin groups formed as a result of recent and sustained migration, the patterns of concentration for the first and second generations are largely in sync with one another. Put differently, there is no evidence at this point of large-scale spatial mobility in the new second generation outside of the areas of principal first-generation settlement.

DISTINGUISHING GENERATIONAL COHORTS: DOES IT MATTER?

Thus far I have sketched a demographic and geographic portrait of the immigrant-origin population of the United States without attempting to decompose the first and second generations, as earlier proposed. A more precise rendering of the generational composition of the foreign-born population (that is, of the first generation) is presented in Table 4; a breakdown of the native-born population of immigrant parentage (that is, of the second generation) follows in Table 5. Table 4 uses age at arrival (constructed from other variables in the CPS) to define and distinguish the foreign-born cohorts from one another;[6] Table 5 considers whether one or both parents

---

[6]Age at arrival is calculated from the year of entry into the United States and the year of birth of the respondent. It should be noted that the CPS question on year of arrival, which is also asked in the decennial census, assumes that immigrants are long-term settlers who enter the United States only once, but different types of migration may in fact entail multiple entries. There are no available national-level data sets at present that collect multiple-entry data.

TABLE 3

PRINCIPAL METROPOLITAN AREAS[a] OF SETTLEMENT FOR THE IMMIGRANT STOCK (FOREIGN-BORN AND U.S.-BORN) POPULATION OF THE UNITED STATES, 1998–2002, BY REGIONAL AND NATIONAL ORIGIN

National Origin	Total N	Primary MSA	Primary N	Primary %	Secondary MSA	Secondary N	Secondary %	Tertiary MSA	Tertiary N	Tertiary %	Top 3 Combined N	Top 3 Combined %
Latin America and Caribbean	27,993,079	Los Angeles	3,988,397	14	New York	3,126,339	11	San Diego/Orange	1,867,076	7	8,981,812	32
Mexico	15,036,774	Los Angeles	2,880,729	19	San Diego/Orange[b]	1,619,475	11	Chicago	804,633	5	5,304,837	35
Cuba	1,364,975	Miami	701,946	51	New Jersey suburbs	97,663	7	Ft. Lauderdale/Palm B.	81,174	6	880,783	65
Dominican Republic	1,115,480	New York	669,973	60	New Jersey suburbs	140,995	13	Miami	57,699	5	868,667	78
El Salvador	982,229	Los Angeles	316,455	32	Washington, DC	126,839	13	Houston	95,930	10	539,224	55
Guatemala	563,479	Los Angeles	241,719	43	New York	30,951	5	SF/Oakland/San Jose	30,346	5	303,016	54
Other Central America	1,224,035	Miami	176,224	14	Los Angeles	155,281	13	New York	108,331	9	439,836	36
Colombia	723,120	New York	139,894	19	New Jersey suburbs	113,145	16	Miami	106,617	15	359,656	50
Ecuador, Peru	815,998	New York	241,972	30	New Jersey suburbs	130,642	16	Los Angeles	62,647	8	435,261	53
Other South America	870,934	Miami	87,893	10	New Jersey suburbs	67,682	8	New York	65,911	8	221,486	25
Haiti	714,012	Ft. Lauderdale/Palm B.	158,133	22	New York	153,778	22	Miami	116,167	16	428,078	60
Jamaica	692,172	New York	248,475	36	Ft. Lauderdale/Palm B.	81,147	12	New Jersey suburbs	48,121	7	377,743	55
Other West Indies	1,056,412	New York	497,231	47	New Jersey suburbs	86,630	8	Los Angeles	43,952	4	627,813	59

TABLE 3 (CONTINUED)
PRINCIPAL METROPOLITAN AREAS[a] OF SETTLEMENT FOR THE IMMIGRANT STOCK (FOREIGN-BORN AND U.S.-BORN) POPULATION OF THE UNITED STATES, 1998–2002, BY REGIONAL AND NATIONAL ORIGIN

National Origin	Total N	Primary MSA	Primary N	Primary %	Secondary MSA	Secondary N	Secondary %	Tertiary MSA	Tertiary N	Tertiary %	Top 3 Combined N	Top 3 Combined %
Asia and Middle East	11,803,889	SF/Oakland/San Jose	1,290,912	11	Los Angeles	1,261,280	11	San Diego/Orange	1,019,533	9	3,571,725	30
Philippines	2,221,289	San Diego/Orange	360,172	16	Los Angeles	276,404	12	SF/Oakland/San Jose	268,969	12	905,545	41
China	1,332,940	SF/Oakland/San Jose	244,284	18	New York	176,792	13	Los Angeles	120,693	9	541,769	41
Hong Kong, Taiwan	706,769	Los Angeles	130,201	18	SF/Oakland/San Jose	129,714	18	New York	55,680	8	315,595	45
Vietnam	1,201,596	SF/Oakland/San Jose	211,807	18	San Diego/Orange	154,604	13	Los Angeles	106,067	9	472,478	39
Laos, Cambodia	473,199	San Diego/Orange	39,955	8	SF/Oakland/San Jose	23,681	5	Philadelphia	20,846	4	84,482	18
India	1,324,084	New Jersey suburbs	139,021	10	Chicago	115,200	9	New York	110,121	8	364,342	28
Korea	1,038,242	Los Angeles	196,708	19	New York	110,222	11	Washington, DC	83,189	8	390,119	38
Japan	763,487	Los Angeles	77,372	10	San Diego/Orange	53,435	7	San Diego/Orange	47,437	6	178,244	23
Other SE Asia	1,189,826	New York	155,138	13	SF/Oakland/San Jose	131,553	11	San Diego/Orange	77,424	7	364,115	31
Iran	412,701	Los Angeles	114,833	28	San Diego/Orange	44,408	11	Washington, DC	40,361	10	199,602	48
Israel	160,018	New York	29,808	19	Los Angeles	19,148	12	New Jersey suburbs	13,414	8	62,370	39
Arab Middle East	1,030,725	Detroit	120,770	12	New York	89,518	9	Los Angeles	89,041	9	299,329	29

TABLE 3 (CONTINUED)
PRINCIPAL METROPOLITAN AREAS[a] OF SETTLEMENT FOR THE IMMIGRANT STOCK (FOREIGN-BORN AND U.S.-BORN) POPULATION OF THE UNITED STATES, 1998–2002, BY REGIONAL AND NATIONAL ORIGIN

National Origin	Total N	Primary MSA	N	%	Secondary MSA	N	%	Tertiary MSA	N	%	Top 3 Combined N	%
Europe and Canada	18,038,893	New York	1,399,771	8	New Jersey suburbs	1,295,550	7	Chicago	841,844	5	3,537,165	20
Canada	2,626,177	Detroit	119,507	5	San Diego/Orange	116,712	4	Boston	107,057	4	343,276	13
Great Britain	1,892,063	New Jersey suburbs	94,214	5	San Diego/Orange	89,971	5	SF/Oakland/San Jose	84,616	4	268,801	14
Ireland	787,345	New Jersey suburbs	109,932	14	New York	95,631	12	Boston	78,428	10	283,991	36
Germany	2,662,439	New Jersey suburbs	118,549	4	New York	91,634	3	Washington, DC	84,958	3	295,141	11
NW Europe	1,967,077	New York	116,966	6	New York	83,492	4	San Diego/Orange	76,151	4	276,609	14
Italy	2,627,988	New Jersey suburbs	368,155	14	New York	317,372	12	Philadelphia	144,714	6	830,241	32
Poland	1,458,617	Chicago	206,473	14	New Jersey suburbs	176,648	12	New York	155,326	11	538,447	37
Russia, USSR	1,692,475	New York	321,325	19	Los Angeles	140,034	8	New Jersey suburbs	117,004	7	578,363	34
SE Europe	2,324,710	New Jersey suburbs	171,738	7	New York	171,628	7	Chicago	138,109	6	481,475	21
Sub-Saharan Africa	781,890	Washington, DC	87,737	11	New York	79,481	10	New Jersey suburbs	53,569	7	220,787	28
Total Immigrant Origin	57,886,202	Los Angeles	5,902,330	10	New York	4,959,890	9	San Diego/Orange	3,563,982	6	14,426,202	25
Puerto Rico	2,563,459	New York	608,466	24	New Jersey suburbs	257,603	10	Philadelphia	121,730	5	987,799	39
Other U.S. Islanders	391,906	Los Angeles	32,611	8	New York	26,538	7	SF/Oakland/San Jose	21,416	5	80,565	21

Source: Weighted estimates based on merged Current Population Survey (CPS) annual demographic files (March), 1998 through 2002.

[a] MSA = Metropolitan Statistical Area.

[b] Contiguous MSAs: San Diego/Orange = San Diego, Orange County, Riverside-San Bernardino; SF/Oakland/San Jose = San Francisco Bay area; Ft. Lauderdale/Palm B. = Ft. Lauderdale, West Palm Beach; New Jersey suburbs = Bergen-Passaic, Jersey City, Middlesex-Somerset-Hunterdon, Monmouth-Ocean, Nassau-Suffolk, Newark.

were foreign born. In both tables the data are broken down by national origin for the specific generational cohorts described above.[7]

Table 4 provides weighted CPS estimates of the size and proportion of foreign-born persons who arrived in the United States as adults or children, broken down by our proposed typology of "seven ages" or life stages: Early childhood (the 1.75 cohort who arrived as pre-school children, ages 0–5); middle childhood (the 1.5 generation, ages 6 to 12); adolescence (the 1.25 cohort, ages 13 to 17); adult transition (ages 18–24); early adulthood (ages 25–34); middle adulthood (ages 35–54); and late adulthood (ages 55 and older). As Table 4 shows, of the approximately 30 million foreign born (excluding Puerto Ricans and other U.S. islanders), an estimated 18 million (60%) arrived as adults and another 12 million (40%) as children under 18. Indeed, international migration is the province of the young. Among the adult cohorts, most came between the ages of 18 and 34 (44% of all immigrants), with the largest cohort composed of young immigrants 18 to 24 years old (about 6.9 million) and 25 to 34 years old (6.3 million). Very few (13%) immigrated in mid-adulthood (ages 35 to 54) and fewer still (3 percent) in late adulthood.

There are remarkable generational-cohort differences by national origin, suggesting both differences in migration histories as well as potentially significant implications for social and economic adaptation outcomes. For example, Mexico, El Salvador and Guatemala, the sending countries with the highest proportion of undocumented immigrants in the United States had the highest proportions of immigrants who arrived in their teens and early twenties, with the 13–17 and 18–24 age cohorts accounting for nearly half of their immigrant totals. More than a third (35%) of those born in India, however, came to the United States between ages 18 to 24 alone, a reflection of the large number of young Indian immigrants who have arrived in the United States with college degrees and preferred job skills and possibly of others who entered with H-1B work visas or as international students (and who may subsequently gain permanent residence).

By contrast, persons who came from Cuba, China and the former Soviet Union (all communist countries) were far more likely than other nationalities to have arrived in middle and late adulthood (with over one

---

[7]The construction of these distinctive cohorts further reduces the sample size for the smaller national-origin groups, shown earlier in Table 2, so that even with five years of merged CPS data the Ns for certain groups may become too small for reliable estimates, *e.g.,* for older-adult immigrants among the Laotians and Cambodians, Japanese, Iranians, Israelis, and the Irish.

TABLE 4

BREAKING DOWN THE IMMIGRANT FIRST GENERATION OF THE UNITED STATES POPULATION, 1998–2002, BY AGE/LIFE STAGE AT ARRIVAL AND NATIONAL ORIGIN

Region and National Origin	Total N	First Generation (foreign-born) by Age/Life Stage at Arrival												
		Ages 0–5 Early Childhood N	%	Ages 6–12 Middle Childhood N	%	Ages 13–17 Adolescence N	%	Ages 18–24 Adult Transition N	%	Ages 25–34 Early Adulthood N	%	Ages 35–54 Middle Adulthood N	%	Ages 55 and older Late Adulthood N	%
Latin America and Caribbean	14,845,274	1,976,265	13	1,887,070	13	2,413,614	16	3,729,898	25	2,863,994	19	1,679,849	11	294,584	2
Mexico	8,158,207	1,214,113	15	1,040,642	13	1,561,137	19	2,251,647	28	1,342,177	16	650,450	8	98,041	1
Cuba	910,189	105,862	12	102,673	11	76,281	8	98,982	11	217,109	24	244,343	27	64,939	7
Dominican Republic	663,278	82,119	12	101,308	15	93,027	14	133,232	20	136,970	21	97,743	15	18,879	3
El Salvador	753,236	59,498	8	86,418	11	131,684	17	248,828	33	146,186	19	66,242	9	14,380	2
Guatemala	385,372	39,271	10	49,485	13	69,563	18	105,058	27	73,261	19	46,804	12	1,930	1
Other Central/America	768,606	117,999	15	93,498	12	93,033	12	189,628	25	184,182	24	78,215	10	12,051	2
Colombia	485,661	56,992	12	51,858	11	49,580	10	107,215	22	122,430	25	81,138	17	16,448	3
Ecuador, Peru	551,605	58,599	11	67,432	12	71,546	13	133,712	24	127,782	23	76,208	14	16,326	3
Other South America	601,742	82,135	14	69,138	11	59,797	10	124,257	21	164,892	27	89,847	15	11,676	2
Haiti	471,715	44,666	9	68,897	15	52,802	11	104,151	22	112,267	24	75,695	16	13,237	3
Jamaica	437,835	34,389	8	69,093	16	62,973	14	84,906	19	99,863	23	78,779	18	7,832	2
Other West Indies	657,828	80,622	12	86,628	13	92,191	14	148,282	23	136,875	21	94,385	14	18,845	3
Asia and Middle East	7,941,695	1,105,156	14	778,366	10	736,020	9	1,824,985	23	1,943,557	24	1,181,246	15	372,365	5
Philippines	1,384,723	189,994	14	136,648	10	116,643	8	298,039	22	345,733	25	212,919	15	84,747	6
China	891,402	76,750	9	73,618	8	67,970	8	170,695	19	253,867	28	162,804	18	85,698	10
Hong Kong, Taiwan	510,294	66,649	13	73,981	14	60,870	12	124,622	24	106,973	21	63,634	12	13,565	3
Vietnam	894,879	100,289	11	119,319	13	107,707	12	178,784	20	158,607	18	181,217	20	48,956	5
Laos, Cambodia	250,436	34,684	13	35,790	14	38,754	15	57,957	22	49,580	19	33,714	13	8,957	3
India	989,481	85,988	9	57,585	6	56,345	6	342,715	35	273,926	28	127,976	13	44,946	5
Korea	762,645	168,368	22	64,688	8	55,170	7	131,765	17	201,026	26	114,226	15	27,402	4
Japan	422,058	129,473	31	24,650	6	24,636	6	79,974	19	107,028	25	50,134	12	6,163	1
Other SE Asia	819,742	118,944	15	84,266	10	86,631	11	205,206	25	199,385	24	101,970	12	21,340	3
Iran	286,306	21,336	7	31,142	11	44,458	16	57,447	20	69,337	24	43,793	15	18,793	7
Israel	90,677	22,253	25	11,794	13	10,289	11	22,882	25	21,064	23	2,395	3	0	0
Arab Middle East	630,052	90,428	14	64,885	10	64,547	10	154,899	25	157,031	25	86,464	14	11,798	2

TABLE 4 (CONTINUED)

BREAKING DOWN THE IMMIGRANT FIRST GENERATION OF THE UNITED STATES POPULATION, 1998–2002, BY AGE/LIFE STAGE AT ARRIVAL AND NATIONAL ORIGIN

| Region and National Origin | Total N | First Generation (foreign-born) by Age/Life Stage at Arrival | | | | | | | | | | | | | |
| | | Ages 0–5 Early Childhood | | Ages 6–12 Middle Childhood | | Ages 13–17 Adolescence | | Ages 18–24 Adult Transition | | Ages 25–34 Early Adulthood | | Ages 35–54 Middle Adulthood | | Ages 55 and older Late Adulthood | |
		N	%	N	%	N	%	N	%	N	%	N	%	N	%
Europe and Canada	5,500,303	1,367,132	5	596,576	11	448,436	8	981,809	18	1,183,116	22	765,428	14	157,806	3
Canada	775,014	209,516	27	96,033	12	69,428	9	137,757	18	155,390	20	96,918	13	9,972	1
Great Britain	666,672	173,840	26	65,973	10	51,335	8	118,548	18	163,846	25	83,828	13	9,302	1
Ireland	142,043	15,910	11	6,254	4	13,885	10	48,076	34	36,593	26	20,707	15	618	0
Germany	1,035,447	529,452	51	104,879	10	59,360	6	134,875	13	142,529	14	58,415	6	5,937	1
NW Europe	500,258	106,115	21	52,840	11	34,192	7	110,074	22	124,361	25	67,485	13	5,191	1
Italy	369,528	76,743	21	41,012	11	40,276	11	79,320	21	78,350	21	45,935	12	7,892	2
Poland	385,306	29,742	8	43,663	11	35,893	9	85,915	22	98,152	25	82,309	21	9,632	2
Russia, USSR	763,398	102,185	13	85,173	11	57,973	8	93,422	12	165,713	22	170,616	22	88,316	12
SE Europe	862,637	123,629	14	100,749	12	86,094	10	173,822	20	218,182	25	139,215	16	20,946	2
Sub-Saharan Africa	536,020	55,956	10	60,826	11	59,809	11	130,640	24	155,601	29	65,793	12	7,395	1
All Others	861,837	127,043	15	94,612	11	107,478	12	207,369	24	203,153	24	100,175	12	21,647	3
Total Immigrant Origin	29,685,129	4,631,912	16	3,417,450	12	3,765,357	13	6,874,701	23	6,349,421	21	3,792,491	13	853,797	3
Puerto Rico	1,155,060	290,737	25	178,584	14	169,440	15	242,623	21	146,896	13	103,069	9	23,711	2
Other US Islanders	204,768	65,282	32	25,870	13	25,175	12	41,119	20	29,412	14	13,968	7	3,942	2

Source: Merged Current Population Survey (CPS) annual demographic files (March), 1998 through 2002.

TABLE 5

BREAKING DOWN THE "IMMIGRANT SECOND GENERATION" OF THE UNITED STATES POPULATION,
1998–2002, BY PARENTAL NATIVITY AND NATIONAL ORIGIN

| Region and National Origin | Total N | Second Generation (U.S.-born) | | | |
| | | Both parents foreign-born (2.0) | | One parent foreign-born, one parent U.S.-born (2.5) | |
		N	%	N	%
Latin America and Caribbean	10,422,920	7,070,172	68	3,352,748	32
Mexico	7,051,133	4,821,870	68	2,229,263	32
Cuba	436,143	264,630	61	171,513	39
Dominican Republic	446,122	338,236	76	107,886	24
El Salvador	228,993	155,715	68	73,278	32
Guatemala	176,677	134,998	76	41,679	24
Other Central America	439,145	275,147	63	163,998	37
Colombia	236,849	164,804	70	72,045	30
Ecuador, Peru	263,477	171,816	65	91,661	35
Other South America	263,011	138,393	53	124,618	47
Haiti	241,569	206,686	86	34,883	14
Jamaica	250,275	152,247	61	98,028	39
Other West Indies	389,526	245,630	63	143,896	37
Asia and Middle East	3,884,141	2,660,039	68	1,224,102	32
Philippines	819,497	495,087	60	324,410	40
China	410,999	312,272	76	98,727	24
Hong Kong, Taiwan	195,997	146,617	75	49,380	25
Vietnam	306,717	263,885	86	42,832	14
Laos, Cambodia	213,762	186,206	87	27,556	13
India	332,436	289,268	87	43,168	13
Korea	274,146	174,327	64	99,819	36
Japan	335,253	139,169	42	196,084	58
Other SE Asia	368,338	243,923	66	124,415	34
Iran	125,721	83,395	66	42,326	34
Israel	68,570	39,879	58	28,691	42
Arab Middle East	432,705	286,011	66	146,694	34
Europe and Canada	11,839,017	5,106,917	43	6,732,100	57
Canada	1,698,139	374,031	22	1,324,108	78
Great Britain	1,136,724	266,046	23	870,678	77
Ireland	613,326	311,847	51	301,479	49
Germany	1,537,435	378,747	25	1,158,688	75
NW Europe	1,384,288	539,508	39	844,780	61
Italy	2,146,489	1,224,123	57	922,366	43
Poland	1,034,512	677,662	66	356,850	34
Russia, USSR	883,402	541,983	61	341,419	39
SE Europe	1,404,702	792,970	56	611,732	44
Sub-Saharan Africa	200,166	121,070	60	79,096	40
All Others	644,115	338,859	53	305,256	47
Total Immigrant Origin	26,990,359	15,297,057	57	11,693,302	43
Puerto Rico	1,319,611	858,799	65	460,812	35
Other U.S. Islanders	179,640	81,913	46	97,727	54

Source: Merged Current Population Survey (CPS) annual demographic files (March), 1998 through 2002.

third of the Cuban and Soviet/Russian totals coming in the 35–54 and 55-and-older arrival cohorts). Children under 6 years old predominated among those born in Germany, Japan, South Korea, Canada, and Great Britain (countries with large numbers of international marriages to U.S. citizens and of child adoptions in the case of South Korea).

Table 5 focuses on the approximately 27 million native-born persons of foreign parentage who form the second generation, and distinguishes between two groups: a 2.0 generation of persons who were born in the United States of two foreign-born parents and the 2.5 cohort of persons who were born in the United States of one foreign-born parent and one U.S.-born parent (approximating a more acculturated and intermarried population situated between the second and third generations). Overall, Table 5 shows that a high proportion (43%) of the second generation belongs to the 2.5 cohort, with one U.S.-born parent. But as would be expected, reflecting the relative recency of migration of different nationalities, there are very sharp differences by regional origin, with 68 percent of the Latin American and Asian-origin second generation having two foreign-born parents, in contrast to only 43 percent of those of European and Canadian parentage.

Theoretically, these generational cohorts may be hypothesized to differ significantly with regard to a variety of adaptation outcomes, from socioeconomic attainment and mobility to language and acculturation. But that is an open empirical question, the answer to which requires research that breaks down the first and second generations by nativity (of self and parents) and age/life stage at arrival into distinct generational segments, rather than lumping together, as is often the case, the 1.25, 1.5, 1.75, 2.0 and 2.5 cohorts into a de facto second generation. If there are no significant differences between these cohorts, and if they add little or nothing to our understanding of adaptive trajectories in the second generation broadly conceived, then it would make practical as well as theoretical sense to aggregate them. A similar logic would apply to the life-stage distinctions made among immigrants who arrive as adults. It is to that question that the remainder of this article is addressed.

EDUCATIONAL AND OCCUPATIONAL ATTAINMENT ACROSS GENERATIONAL COHORTS

Table 6 compares patterns of educational and occupational attainment across these generational cohorts for all adults who were 25 to 39 years old at the time of the survey – ages at which formal education can be expected

TABLE 6

EDUCATIONAL AND OCCUPATIONAL MOBILITY TRAJECTORIES OF IMMIGRANT-ORIGIN GROUPS IN THE UNITED STATES, 1998–2002, FOR PERSONS 25–39 YEARS OLD, BY GENERATIONAL COHORTS AND SOCIAL CLASS ORIGINS

Generational Cohorts[b]	Persons 25 to 39 Years Old		Educational Attainment			Occupational Attainment		
	N	%	% College Graduate	% Not High School Graduate	Ratio of College Graduates to H.S. Dropouts	% Upper White-Collar Workers[a]	% Lower Blue-Collar Workers[a]	Ratio of Upper-White Collar to Lower-Blue Collar Jobs
Mexico	6,932,883	30	6	53	0.12	7	29	0.25
1.0 Foreign-born, over 17 at arrival	3,280,758	14	5	65	0.08	3	32	0.10
1.25 Foreign-born, 13–17 at arrival	1,318,257	6	3	67	0.04	5	36	0.13
1.5 Foreign-born, 6–12 at arrival	615,100	3	6	47	0.13	8	28	0.27
1.75 Foreign-born, 0–5 at arrival	428,063	2	9	33	0.27	12	19	0.60
2.0 U.S.-born, 2 foreign-born parents	765,778	3	12	20	0.58	17	17	0.98
2.5 U.S.-born, 1 foreign-born parent	524,925	2	15	19	0.79	19	15	1.28
Low SES immigrant groups[c]	2,477,509	11	13	38	0.34	12	21	0.54
1.0 Foreign-born, over 17 at arrival	1,293,732	6	9	51	0.18	6	25	0.23
1.25 Foreign-born, 13–17 at arrival	429,204	2	9	41	0.21	9	25	0.35
1.5 Foreign-born, 6–12 at arrival	268,035	1	15	24	0.62	17	17	1.01
1.75 Foreign-born, 0–5 at arrival	131,082	1	24	15	1.61	24	13	1.94
2.0 U.S.-born, 2 foreign-born parents	191,296	1	30	9	3.33	30	11	2.83
2.5 U.S.-born, 1 foreign-born parent	164,160	1	25	10	2.66	23	13	1.80
Mid SES immigrant groups[c]	3,083,436	13	27	16	1.74	23	15	1.52
1.0 Foreign-born, over 17 at arrival	1,411,879	6	21	21	1.00	14	19	0.72
1.25 Foreign-born, 13–17 at arrival	444,218	2	19	19	1.00	18	18	1.02
1.5 Foreign-born, 6–12 at arrival	378,885	2	34	11	3.06	30	9	3.45
1.75 Foreign-born, 0–5 at arrival	256,467	1	33	8	4.36	31	9	3.50
2.0 U.S.-born, 2 foreign-born parents	374,249	2	42	6	7.01	38	7	5.87
2.5 U.S.-born, 1 foreign-born parent	217,737	1	38	3	10.93	37	12	3.04
High SES immigrant group[c]	10,418,159	45	49	5	9.20	37	7	4.90
1.0 Foreign-born, over 17 at arrival	4,469,516	20	56	6	9.01	34	8	4.11
1.25 Foreign-born, 13–17 at arrival	726,948	3	46	7	6.82	40	8	5.14
1.5 Foreign-born, 6–12 at arrival	696,761	3	48	4	11.31	38	6	5.80

TABLE 6 (CONTINUED)

EDUCATIONAL AND OCCUPATIONAL MOBILITY TRAJECTORIES OF IMMIGRANT-ORIGIN GROUPS IN THE UNITED STATES, 1998–2002, FOR PERSONS 25–39 YEARS OLD, BY GENERATIONAL COHORTS AND SOCIAL CLASS ORIGINS

Generational Cohorts[b]	Persons 25 to 39 Years Old		Educational Attainment			Occupational Attainment		
	N	%	% College Graduate	% Not High School Graduate	Ratio of College Graduates to H.S. Dropouts	% Upper White-Collar Workers[a]	% Lower Blue-Collar Workers[a]	Ratio of Upper White-Collar to Lower-Blue Collar Jobs
1.75 Foreign-born, 0–5 at arrival	1,178,492	5	40	6	7.00	36	7	5.44
2.0 U.S.-born, 2 foreign-born parents	1,365,127	6	52	4	14.73	42	6	7.47
2.5 U.S.-born, 1 foreign-born parent	1,981,315	9	41	4	9.14	37	7	4.92
Total Immigrant Origin	22,911,985	100	29	25	1.19	23	16	1.40
1.0 Foreign-born, over 17 at arrival	10,455,885	46	29	32	0.91	18	19	0.94
1.25 Foreign-born, 13–17 at arrival	2,918,628	13	17	41	0.42	16	24	0.65
1.5 Foreign-born, 6–12 at arrival	1,958,781	9	28	22	1.27	24	15	1.58
1.75 Foreign-born, 0–5 at arrival	1,994,104	9	32	12	2.53	29	10	2.94
2.0 U.S.-born, 2 foreign-born parents	2,696,450	12	37	9	4.14	34	9	3.55
2.5 U.S.-born, 1 foreign-born parent	2,888,137	13	35	7	4.79	33	9	3.47

Source: Merged Current Population Survey (CPS) annual demographic files (March), 1998 through 2002. Figures are weighted estimates, in percents except for ratios.

[a] Upper White-Collar = professionals, executives, and managers; Lower Blue-Collar = operators, fabricators, and laborers.

[b] Generational cohorts defined as follows: 1.0 = Foreign-born (F.B.), 18 years or older at U.S. arrival; 1.25 = F.B., 13–17 at U.S. arrival; 1.5 = F.B., 6–12 at U.S. arrival; 1.75 = F.B., 0–5 at U.S. arrival; 2.0 = U.S.-born, both parents born in foreign country; 2.5 = U.S.-born, one parent F.B., one parent U.S.-born.

[c] National-origin groups ranked by (educational and occupational) socioeconomic status (SES) as follows:
Low SES (well below U.S. norms): Dominican Republic, El Salvador, Guatemala, Honduras, Haiti, and Cambodia.
Mid SES (near U.S. norms): Cuba, Costa Rica, Nicaragua, Panama, Colombia, Ecuador, Peru, Guyana, Uruguay, Jamaica, Other West Indies, Vietnam, Armenia, Afghanistan, Iraq, and Jordan.
High SES (well above U.S. norms): Other South America (Argentina, Bolivia, Brazil, Chile, Venezuela), Philippines, China, Taiwan, India, Korea, Japan, Other Southeast Asia, Iran, Israel, Other Arab Middle East, Canada, Great Britain, Ireland, Germany, Italy, Poland, Russia/USSR, Other Europe, Africa, and Australia.

to have been completed. Limiting the data to persons currently 25 to 39 intentionally excludes from this analysis persons who immigrated at older ages (40 and older) and for the purpose of this analysis effectively controls for age within each generational cohort (the median age is 32 for each of the cohorts). For ease of presentation, those who arrived in the United States as younger adults (between 18 and 39) are considered in Table 6 as the 1.0 immigrant generation and compared against the 1.25, 1.5, 1.75, 2.0 and 2.5 cohorts, as shown in the table. The left-hand panels of Table 6 present a set of polar indicators of educational attainment – the percent of college graduates, the percent of those who did not graduate from high school – and the ratio of the two. The right-hand panels of the table present a set of polar indicators of occupational attainment – the percent of upper white-collar workers (professionals, executives, and managers) and the percent of lower blue-collar workers (operators, fabricators, and laborers) – as well as the ratio of those two.

These data are provided first for the largest of all the immigrant groups – those of Mexican origin – who not only account for fully 30 percent of all first- and second-generation persons aged 25 to 39, but also exhibit the lowest level of educational and occupational attainment among all immigrant nationalities in the United States, a legacy of their history as the largest and longest-running labor migration in the contemporary world. The table then provides the same generational-cohort breakdown for all other immigrant groups, now ranked by their human capital profiles into low-SES, mid-SES, and high-SES strata, as compared to U.S. norms.

The specific nationalities grouped in each of these three strata are listed at the bottom of Table 6, reflecting a mix of immigrant types and modes of incorporation – laborers, professionals, refugees (*cf.* Portes and Rumbaut, 1996). Low-SES immigrant groups (with attainment characteristics well below U.S. educational and occupational norms for adults 25–39) hail from the Dominican Republic, El Salvador, Guatemala, Honduras, Haiti, Laos and Cambodia. High-SES immigrant groups (with attainment characteristics well above U.S. norms) include most of the countries of Asia, Africa, and Europe, as well as Canada, Australia, and several South American countries. In the middle (with profiles closer to U.S. norms) are immigrant groups from Cuba, Costa Rica, Nicaragua, Panama, Colombia, Ecuador, Peru, Jamaica, Vietnam, Afghanistan, and Iraq. As a point of comparison, 28 percent of all 25-to-39 year olds in the United States were college graduates and 8 percent were high school dropouts (as estimated from the same merged 1998–2002 CPS data set). The rates for non-Hispanic whites of native parentage (third generation and beyond) were 32 and 7 percent, respectively. The patterns that emerge are revealing.

First, looking only at the patterns for the 1.0 generations, there is a huge gulf evident between high-SES immigrants as a whole – with college graduation rates of 56 percent and high school dropout rates of 6 percent – and those from Mexico, with only 5 percent of 25–39 year olds having college diplomas and 65 percent lacking high school diplomas. For the 1.0 Mexican immigrants, the ratio of college graduates to high school dropouts is 0.08, in sharp contrast to the 9.0 ratio for high-SES immigrants. In between are the mid-SES groups, with equivalent 21 percent rates of college graduates and high school dropouts (a ratio of 1.0), and the low-SES groups, with college graduation rates of 9 percent and high school dropout rates of 51 percent (a ratio of 0.18).

In most cases, these levels of education may be presumed to have been brought over from the home country – having arrived in the United States as adults, it is likely that their education was completed abroad – unlike the situation for those who arrived as children or who were born in the United States, whose education may be presumed to have been completed here. These data, especially when they are examined by country of origin for the 1.0 generation (not shown in the table), reveal extremely sharp differences in human capital from the top groups (the Indians and Chinese, Russian Jews, Koreans) to the bottom (the Mexicans, Salvadorans and Guatemalans, Cambodians and Laotians), with patterns of attainment that are virtually the polar opposites of each other.

How those initial advantages or disadvantages of the 1.0 generation of different immigrant nationalities play out across the other generational groupings is detailed in Table 6. One pattern that stands out is the fairly rapid advancement of the most disadvantaged groups from the 1.0 to the 1.5 and subsequent generational cohorts. Mexicans, as noted, start out at the 1.0 generation with only 5 percent college graduation rates and 65 percent having less than a high school diploma; those figures worsen to 3 and 67, respectively, among those who came as teenagers (the 1.25 generation). But by the 1.5 generation, the figures improve to 6 and 47 (a tiny increase in college graduation rates, but a nearly 20 point reduction in dropout rates), then to 9 and 33 (in the 1.75 generation), 12 and 20 (in the 2.0), and 15 and 19 (among the 2.5ers). Thus, by the second generation (2.0 and 2.5), Mexican adults in their late twenties and thirties had nearly tripled their college graduation rates and cut by more than a third the proportion of high school dropouts, relative to their 1.0 coethnics.

They were still lagging behind their counterparts by wide margins, to be sure, but had made substantial progress in the course of a generation. Low-SES and mid-SES immigrant groups also exhibit a similar pattern of upward educational "mobility" (to the extent that such an interpretation can be made with cross-sectional data). By contrast, high-SES immigrant groups tend to maintain the level of attainment from the 1.0 to the native-born second generation (in fact, there is a relative drop in the rate of college graduates). The top achiever by far – and the most highly educated ethnic group in the United States – is the population of Indian origin: 81 percent of young adults 25–39 years old in the 1.0 generation had college degrees while only 4 percent lacked a high school diploma; in the 2.0 generation, the commensurate figures were virtually identical: 82 and 4 percent, respectively.

The right-hand panels of Table 6 shift the focus to patterns of occupational attainment among employed young adults 25 to 39 (data on labor force participation and unemployment rates were examined separately but are not shown here; by and large they point to similar levels of labor force participation for most groups and generational cohorts at these ages). As a standard of comparison, for native-parentage non-Hispanic whites in this age group in the United States, the proportions employed in the top and bottom occupational categories were 29 and 12 percent, respectively.

The patterns and rankings are similar but not identical to those seen for education. As expected, looking first only at the data for the 1.0 generation, there are wide disparities between employed high-SES immigrants, a third of whom (34%) were employed as professionals, executives or managers while only 8 percent held jobs as operators, fabricators or laborers, and those from Mexico, with only 3 percent working in upper white-collar occupations while a third (32%) had lower blue-collar jobs. For the 1.0 Mexican immigrants, the top-to-bottom occupational ratio was 0.10, in contrast to the ratios for the high-SES (4.1), mid-SES (0.72), and low-SES (0.23) immigrant groups.

Looking next at the data across the generational cohorts, all groups show a general pattern of occupational advancement from the first to the second generation. Among Mexican and other low-SES immigrants aged 25–39, what had been a preponderant concentration at the bottom of the occupational structure in the 1.0 and 1.25 generations turns around by the second generation, as Table 6 shows, and the degree of occupational "mobility," as measured by the UWC/LWC ratios, is sharper still for the mid-SES groups. Even among high-SES immigrant groups, the data now show relative occupational gains from the 1.0 to the native-born 2.0 generation. In all cases except for the Mexicans, however, this trend is not linear; the gains peak with the U.S.-born 2.0 cohort (those with two foreign-born parents) and then dip among the 2.5ers (those with only one foreign-born parent). Why that is so is a complex and interesting question for future research (cf. Jensen, 2001; Oropesa and Landale, 1997).

Another nonlinear finding in Table 6 worth highlighting is that over-all, those who arrived in the United States in their teen years (13–17) – the 1.25 cohort – tend to do worse or no better than their 1.0 compatriots (and worse than all other cohorts, for that matter), both educationally and occu-pationally. Even among the high-achieving Indians, a notable slippage is seen among the 1.25ers, whose college graduation rates of 64 percent, al-though still well above the national average, represent a drop of nearly 20 points from the 1.0, 1.5, 1.75, and 2.0 averages. In general, the 1.25 cohort comes across as a distinctive and seemingly vulnerable one, all the more when compared to the patterns of their younger-at-arrival 1.5 and 1.75 compatriots. This evidence, added to other findings reviewed below, suggests that 1.25ers may undergo a comparatively more problematic adaptation, which should be taken into account in studies of the incorporation of the new second generation.

One last datum drawn from this comparative cross-generational analy-sis illustrates and underscores a key methodological point: namely, the need to place the data in the larger historical contexts of particular migration flows and the conditions of their reception. We already noted that among 25-to-39-year-old immigrants, certain nationalities in the 1.0 generation – notably Mexicans, Salvadorans and Guatemalans – labored preponderantly in the lowest rungs of the occupational ladder. Surprisingly, that defining charac-teristic of labor migrants was matched by 1.0-generation Cubans, with 6 percent in top occupations and 31 percent concentrated in lower blue-collar jobs. In the Cuban case, the 1.0 generation of persons who were 25 to 39 years old around the turn of the century is made up largely of those who came in the chaotic Mariel boatlift of 1980, and to a lesser extent the *balseros* of the early 1990s.

By contrast, the Cuban 2.0 generation of the same age group, who are preponderantly the children of more advantaged and better-received Cubans who came to the United States in the early 1960s, shows an occupational profile that is the exact opposite of their 1.0 counterparts: 37 percent are employed in top professions, while only 6 percent are at the bottom of the occupational structure. It is not the passage of time and generation alone that explains this about-face in their socioeconomic trajectories, but fundamental differences between these cohorts in their social class backgrounds, migration histories, and contexts of reception. The data presented in Table 6 do not control for such varying historical circumstances, but they need to be contextualized in any definitive interpretation of intergenerational difference and social mobility.

LANGUAGE ASSIMILATION ACROSS GENERATIONAL COHORTS

For immigrants who come to the United States from non-English-speaking countries, learning to speak the new language is a basic step to enable them to participate in the life of the larger community, get an education, find a job, obtain access to health or social services, and apply for citizenship. Instrumentally, language is often cited as the principal initial barrier confronting recent immigrants, from the least educated peasants to the most educated professionals. But language assimilation is expected of immigrants not only for instrumental reasons but for symbolic ones as well, since language also lies at the core of national identities and ethnic solidarities (Portes and Rumbaut, 1996, 2001; *cf.* Bean and Stevens, 2003:Ch. 7). This section focuses on patterns of linguistic assimilation among the generational cohorts composing the foreign-born population, using now the 5 percent Public Use Microdata Sample from the 2000 U.S. Census, since data on language are not collected by the CPS.

Table 7 presents cross-sectional census data on English language proficiency among all first-generation immigrants ages five or older from non-English-speaking countries, by age/life stage at arrival in the United States (*i.e.*, early and middle childhood and adolescence for those younger than 18 at arrival, and early, middle and late adulthood for those 18 and older at arrival). Excluded from this analysis are immigrants from English-speaking countries, 88 percent of whom speak English only, regardless of their age at arrival in the United States (those countries include the United Kingdom, Ireland, Canada, Bermuda, Jamaica and the anglophone West Indies, Guyana, Australia and New Zealand). The table focuses on three (self-reported) language measures: the proportion who speak English "not well or at all" versus those who speak English "very well" (among persons who report speaking a language other than English at home), and the proportion who speak English only.

Without exception, there are sharp linear differences in each of the language measures in the generational progression from those who arrived in

TABLE 7

ENGLISH LANGUAGE PROFICIENCY AMONG FIRST-GENERATION IMMIGRANTS FROM NON-ENGLISH SPEAKING COUNTRIES, BY AGE/LIFE STAGE AT ARRIVAL AND YEARS IN THE UNITED STATES, 2000 (IN PERCENTS)[a]

English Proficiency and English Monolingualism	First Generation (foreign-born) by Age/Life Stage at Arrival					
	Ages 0–5 Early Childhood	Ages 6–12 Middle Childhood	Ages 13–17 Adolescence	Ages 18–34 Early Adulthood	Ages 35–54 Middle Adulthood	Ages 55+ Late Adulthood
Speaks English not well or at all	11.2	14.4	33.6	37.3	53.9	73.5
Speaks English very well	68.9	61.4	37.2	34.1	21.6	12.7
Speaks English only	37.4	14.8	9.1	8.6	7.0	6.7
By time of arrival in the U.S.:						
Speaks English not well or at all						
Arrived after 1980	13.5	16.8	38.1	41.4	54.6	73.8
Arrived before 1980	6.9	9.1	21.2	26.6	51.8	71.0
Speaks English very well						
Arrived after 1980	62.8	56.6	33.2	31.2	21.2	12.5
Arrived before 1980	80.6	72.1	48.2	41.8	22.9	14.3
Speaks English only						
Arrived after 1980	25.4	9.7	7.1	6.9	6.3	6.5
Arrived before 1980	52.0	24.5	14.1	12.8	9.4	9.2

Source: 5% PUMS, 2000 U.S. Census.

[a]Excluded from this table are immigrants from English-speaking countries, 88% of whom speak English only, regardless of age at arrival in the United States. Those countries include: The United Kingdom, Ireland, Canada, Bermuda, Jamaica and the anglophone West Indies, Guyana, Australia and New Zealand.

early childhood (ages 5 or younger) through those who arrived in late adulthood (ages 55 or older), although the differences are not equivalent between the cohorts. Thus, among persons who use a language other than English at home, only 11.2 percent of early-childhood immigrants spoke English "not well or at all," as did 14.4 percent of those who came in middle childhood (ages 6–12). That figure jumps to 33.6 percent among those who came as adolescents (ages 13–17) and 37.3 percent of those who came in early adulthood (ages 18–34). More than half (53.9%) of those who came in mid-adulthood (ages 35–54) did not speak English well or at all, along with nearly three fourths (73.5%) of those who were 55 or older at arrival.

The proportions who speak English "very well" are reversed, ranging from over two thirds (68.9%) of early-childhood immigrants to only 12.7 percent of late-adulthood immigrants (subtracting from 100 percent the sum of those two indicators yields the proportion who reported speaking English "well"). Indeed, the data suggest that already among the foreign-born from non-English-speaking countries, a process of language extinction is under way, with over one third (37%) of those who came in early childhood speaking English only and 15 percent of those who came in middle childhood; the English-only proportions for the other cohorts fall below 10 percent.

To illustrate the effect of time in the United States on language competencies, the outcomes are shown in the bottom panel of Table 7 for immigrants who arrived in the United States before 1980 and those who came after 1980. The pronounced linear differences between generational cohorts persist, and indeed they are shown to be stronger than time in the United States, especially at the poles. For example, among those who arrived in the United States after 1980 and spoke English "not well or at all," the generational progression moves from 13.5 percent of those who came in early childhood to 73.8 percent of those who arrived in late adulthood; the corresponding figures for longer-established immigrants who arrived in the United States before 1980 range from only 6.9 percent of the early-childhood cohort to 71 percent of the late-adulthood cohort. The greatest improvement in this measure is observed among those who immigrated in their teens or early adulthood.

When the measure is the ability to speak English "very well," the increases are largest over time in the United States for the youngest arrival cohorts and miniscule for the oldest arrival cohorts, as Table 7 demonstrates. Finally, the shift to English-only is especially pronounced for those who arrived before their teen years and who have been in the United States for more than two decades: *e.g.*, in the middle-childhood cohort, only 9.7 percent of those who arrived after 1980 spoke English only, but the proportion jumped to 24.5 percent among those who arrived in the United States before 1980; the corresponding figures for the early-childhood cohort are 25.4 and 52 percent for those who arrived in the United States after and before 1980, respectively. Decomposing the foreign-born first generation into distinct generational cohorts thus clarifies the process of language acquisition and makes plain the importance of accounting for age and life stage at arrival in that central aspect of the process of immigrant incorporation.

ACCULTURATION AND IDENTITY IN THE NEW SECOND GENERATION

There are, of course, many other outcomes of theoretical interest in the study of the adaptation of the new second generation for which relevant data are not collected by the annual Current Population Surveys or by the decennial census. Given the lack of pertinent information in cross-sectional national data sets, this final section turns to recently collected data from our Children of Immigrants Longitudinal Study. Basic aspects of the CILS study were briefly summarized above (for details, *see* Portes and Rumbaut, 2001). In Table 8, selected longitudinal findings are presented for the sample originally drawn in San Diego, California, consisting principally of children of immigrants from Mexico, the Philippines, Vietnam, Laos, Cambodia, China, and other Asian and Latin American countries. They were first surveyed in 1992 when most were 14 or 15 years old, then again in 1995 as they neared the end of high school, and finally in 2001–2002, when most were 24 or 25 years old and were located not only in the San Diego area but throughout California and in 29 other states.

For our purposes here, the outcomes of interest across the decade from 1992 to 2002 – English versus foreign language proficiency, preference and use, ethnic identity, selected experiences with the criminal justice system – are presented by four generational cohorts: 1.5, 1.75, 2.0, and 2.5 (there are no 1.25ers in the CILS sample, since all respondents were younger than 12 at arrival or born in the United States). While the decennial census, as we have seen, collects data on English proficiency for persons who speak another language at home, no data are collected on their degree of proficiency in the foreign language or on their preferences and patterns of language use.

TABLE 8

LANGUAGE, ETHNIC IDENTITY, AND CRIMINAL JUSTICE EXPERIENCES AMONG YOUNG ADULT
CHILDREN OF IMMIGRANTS IN SAN DIEGO, 1992 TO 2002, BY GENERATIONAL COHORTS
(CILS LONGITUDINAL SAMPLE, SAN DIEGO)

Variable		Survey Year	Generational Cohorts[a]				Total	p
			1.5	1.75	2.0	2.5		
Language Proficiency		N =	355	390	534	224	1,503	
Speaks English very well		1992	39.4	69.5	85.6	91.5	71.4	b
		1995	51.8	71.1	83.6	87.1	73.3	b
		2002	71.3	83.6	88.0	92.3	83.6	b
Speaks foreign language very well		1992	51.0	32.1	22.5	9.4	29.7	b
		1995	50.3	29.4	22.4	11.0	29.1	b
		2002	55.9	33.6	27.8	13.1	33.7	b
Language Preference								
Prefers to speak English		1992	50.4	63.1	76.0	87.9	68.4	b
Prefers to speak English		1995	75.9	81.8	89.5	95.7	85.2	b
Prefers English or both languages the same		2002	95.4	96.9	98.5	98.6	97.4	d
Prefers to speak English *only*		2002	50.1	57.6	70.3	86.4	64.6	b
Language Use with		2002						
Parents	Foreign language		57.3	47.8	25.6	7.8	36.1	b
	Both the same		22.7	25.2	20.6	16.4	21.7	
	English		19.8	27.0	53.8	75.8	42.2	
Spouse	Foreign language		17.1	6.3	4.7	2.3	7.6	b
	Both the same		30.2	25.3	14.1	11.0	20.1	
	English		52.7	68.4	81.2	86.6	72.3	
Children	Foreign language		23.4	6.3	5.8	1.0	9.4	b
	Both the same		42.2	47.3	28.7	22.0	34.8	
	English		34.4	46.4	65.5	77.0	55.8	
Close friends	Foreign language		8.6	2.1	2.7	1.4	3.7	b
	Both the same		31.0	20.8	17.6	11.4	20.6	
	English		60.5	77.1	79.7	87.2	75.7	
Ethnic Identity								
Self-identifies by national origin		1992	43.7	45.1	20.8	6.7	30.4	b
(e.g., Mexican, Filipino, Vietnamese)		1995	63.4	59.4	39.2	11.4	46.1	b
		2002	45.5	40.1	25.5	8.8	31.3	b
Criminal Justice Experiences		2002						
Been arrested in past 6 years (males)			10.6	15.6	19.6	21.4	16.6	d
Family members have been arrested			13.8	13.8	20.1	28.1	17.8	b
Been incarcerated in past 6 years (males)			8.2	11.8	13.3	14.0	11.9	d
Family members have been incarcerated			9.1	10.4	16.8	21.9	14.0	b

Source: Children of Immigrants Longitudinal Survey (CILS), 1992–2002 (Rumbaut, 2003).
Notes: Mean age of respondents in 2002 was 24.2.
[a]Generational cohorts: 1.5 = Foreign-born, 6–12 years old at arrival in U.S. (middle childhood); 1.75 = Foreign born,
0–5 years at U.S. arrival (early childhood); 2.0 = U.S.-born, both parents born in foreign country; 2.5 = U.S.-born, one
parent foreign born, one parent U.S. born.
Statistical significance of mean differences between generational cohorts:
[b]p < .001,
[c]p < .01,
[d]p < .05,
NS = Not Significant.

First, looking at English language proficiency over time (from 1992 to
1995 to 2002), there are very clear and strong differences by generational
cohort. Over 90 percent of the 2.5ers (born in the United States, with one
U.S.-born parent and one foreign-born parent) reported speaking English
very well throughout the decade, and they overwhelmingly prefer English
and use it with their spouses and close friends. Three fourths also report

speaking only in English with their parents and (where applicable) their own children. The 2.0 generation (born in the United States but both parents are foreign born) come next in these rankings: about 85 percent reported speaking English very well at all three survey periods, but their preference for English increased from 76 percent in 1992, to 89 percent in 1995, and 98 percent by 2002, and their patterns of English use consistently fell behind the level reported by the 2.5ers, most notably with their parents (over 50% now speak with them in English only, even though in 1992 a foreign language was the principal language of their homes in the great majority of cases).

The 1.75ers (who came to the United States as children under 6) follow in their patterns of linguistic acculturation: 70 percent spoke English very well in 1992, and 84 percent did so by 2002; their preference for English increased from 63 to 82 to 97 percent across the three survey periods; and their patterns of language use with their parents, spouses, and children also show a significant distance from the patterns exhibited by their U.S.-born coethnics (indeed, half of them still speak with their parents in the mother tongue rather than in English). Finally, the 1.5 generation shows the lowest level of linguistic assimilation among the four cohorts, although the force of Anglicization clearly prevails over time: while only 39 percent spoke English very well in 1992, 71 percent did so in 2002; and while just under half said they preferred English in 1992, a decade later English was the overwhelming choice and used principally with spouses and close friends.

As Table 8 also shows, similar generational patterns obtained, in reverse, for their proficiency in the mother tongue (the non-English language spoken at home), except that there was basically no change over time in their ability to speak the foreign language very well (proficiency levels remained unchanged during adolescence from 1992 to 1995, followed by a slight increase from 1995 to 2002 for all cohorts in their transitions to adulthood). Even among the 1.5ers, only about half could speak the mother tongue very well, as did one third of the 1.75ers, around one fourth of the 2.0 cohort, and only about one tenth of the 2.5ers.

These patterned and strongly significant differences in language acculturation, not only over time but between the four generational cohorts, are also observed in their self-reports of ethnic identity (to an open-ended question about what they called themselves, asked in all three surveys from 1992 to 2002). The analysis of the determination of ethnic identity choices is complex, especially the boost registered in the proportion who identified by national origin in the 1995 survey, seen notably among Mexicans and Filipinos in the wake of Proposition 187 in California, an anti-immigrant referendum in a politically charged election (*see* Portes and Rumbaut, 2001:Ch. 7). Interestingly, that process of "reactive ethnicity" formation in the face of perceived discrimination and exclusion was observable for all four generational segments, although it was strongest for the 1.5 generation and weakest for the 2.5ers. It subsides for all cohorts by 2002, with levels of self-identification by national origin returning almost exactly to those reported in 1992.

For our purposes here, more to the point is the pattern observed between generational cohorts: by the latest survey (uncannily reflecting the responses given a decade earlier), close to half of the 1.5ers identified by national origin, as did 40 percent of the 1.75ers – the two cohorts born abroad – followed by 25 percent of the 2.0 and less than 9 percent of the 2.5ers – the two cohorts born in the United States. The widest difference between cohorts is actually that between the 2.0 and 2.5. For the latter, the fact that one parent is U.S.-born seems significantly to decrease the likelihood that the child will identify by the foreign national origin of the other parent, much as it also greatly decreases the likelihood that the child would become proficient in, prefer, or use the foreign language of the immigrant parent, whereas for the former (the 2.0), having two co-national parents (and the ethnic socialization that growing up in such immigrant families may imply) evidently continues to exert some influence in the respondent's self-identification into adulthood. It is, in any event, precisely because of such differences that the distinction between the 2.0 and 2.5 generational cohorts is proposed.

Table 8 provides additional evidence of significant differences among these generational cohorts in experiential domains quite unlike the educational, occupational, and acculturative dimensions considered thus far. One set of relevant data shown in Table 8 comes from questions asked at the latest CILS survey (when the respondents were in their mid twenties) about whether they or any family members had ever been arrested or incarcerated in the past six years. Again, linear patterns by generation are clear for each of the variables examined, and again they run counter to the direction in which they may have been expected to do so on the basis of the greater degree of acculturation and higher socioeconomic status of the 2.5ers (and the lower degree of both on the part of the 1.5ers). The 1.5ers were least likely to have been arrested (10.6%) or incarcerated (8.2%), whereas the 2.5ers were the most likely on both counts: 21.4 and 14 percent, respectively.

The 1.75 and 2.0 cohorts fell in between, as Table 8 spells out. Arrests of family members similarly were much lower among the 1.5ers (13.8%) than the 2.5ers (28.1%), as was the likelihood that family members were incarcerated: 9.1 percent (for the 1.5) to 21.9 percent (for the 2.5), again with the other two cohorts arrayed linearly in between. These seemingly paradoxical patterns – of outcomes worsening with increasing "Americanization," sociocultural assimilation and higher socioeconomic status – have been reported in the literature (for a review, *see* Rumbaut 1997b).

CONCLUSION

I have argued that the definition of the immigrant first and second generations can be made theoretically and empirically more precise, and avoid semantic confusion, by distinguishing among distinctive generational cohorts defined by age and life stage at arrival among the foreign born and by parental nativity among the U.S. born. Generational cohorts and their sociodevelopmental contexts matter in processes of adaptation and social mobility; they are not epiphenomena. Evidence has been presented that tends to support both the value and the validity of these calibrations, as well as the need for greater consensus in the conceptualization and operationalization of immigrant generations.

Intergenerational analyses of such multiple outcomes as explored here on a preliminary basis, however, need to take into account multiple other possible determinants and situate and interpret the data within larger social and historical contexts. Not all second generations are "new," for example, as are the Vietnamese or the Cambodians in the United States; others are only the latest second generation in a much longer history of sustained migration, as is the case of the Mexicans in the United States (*cf.* López and Stanton-Salazar, 2001). First waves and later waves of migrants from the same sending country may differ fundamentally in their class origins, ethnic composition, motives for migration, and reception in the United States – *i.e.,* there are different "vintages" in migration flows (*cf.* Kunz, 1973, 1981), not just waves, that need to be taken specifically into account in studies of intergenerational mobility to avoid confounding period and cohort effects.

At the same time, I have also pointed to a variety of methodological and definitional problems with such measures as age at arrival (*e.g.,* there may not be a single date of arrival but multiple entries), nativity (*e.g.,* definitions of foreign born and native born in U.S. official statistics have varied historically and are based on assignments of citizenship status, while immigrant status is not asked in the CPS or the decennial census; international migration statistics differ in the meanings of common terms and measures), and the determination and allocation of ethnicity for children of mixed marriages, where the ethnic and national origin of the mother and father differ. The continued reliance on one-size-fits-all racial categories in the United States (an "ethnoracial pentagon" of white, black, Asian, Hispanic/Latino, and American Indian/Alaska Native categories), in lieu of more refined classifications by national origin and ethnicity, is particularly pernicious to an understanding of the diversity and complexity of the new immigration and to the study of processes of acculturation, assimilation, and social mobility – indeed, to theory-building and policymaking. All of these considerations, in turn, underscore the need for better data and better measures that can help address those specific problems in comparative research.

Among urgent data needs, perhaps none is more important for the study of intergenerational mobility than the restoration of the parental nativity question in the decennial U.S. census and in the recently implemented American Community Survey (ACS), which is intended to replace the long-form questionnaire of the decennial census and, if funding is secured (although that is not certain at this writing), to collect long-form-type data annually between decennial censuses. As seen here, the data on parental nativity in the annual CPS yields much valuable information for the study of the new second generation, but the CPS is hampered by small sample sizes when the available data are broken down by national origin and generational cohort, let alone by other basic demographic variables, such as age and sex, reducing cell sizes to the point where it becomes impossible to carry out reliable analyses, even when merging multiple years of the CPS. In addition, data on English language use and ability (which is included in the census long-form) are not collected by the CPS, but should be, since the CPS remains at present the principal source of national-level information on second-generation populations.

The need for such data, from the national to the local level, is critical both for social science and for public policy. However, in the United States at present, there seem to be dark clouds on the data horizon for a variety of political, practical and budgetary reasons. Current plans call for dropping the long-form questionnaire (the one that asks questions about nativity, citizenship, year of entry, and language, among many other items) from the 2010 census, but there is no assurance that the U.S. Congress will fund its intended replacement, the ACS – a scenario that could precipitate a "data crisis" for the study of international migration and its consequences in the United States (*see* Grieco, 2003). Even if basic funding is ensured, the need to add critical items to the ACS questionnaire, and to the CPS and other relevant surveys, remains to be negotiated. Thus, clarifying and specifying our own definitions and methodological approaches in the study of the newest first and second (and soon to become third) generations has practical as well as theoretical value. It would not only help the field of immigration studies and expand our knowledge of a phenomenon of both national and international importance that is transforming both sending and receiving societies, but also make a compelling case for averting a potential data crisis and boost the likelihood that urgent data needs are met.

REFERENCES

Alba, R. D.
1990 *Ethnic Identity: The Transformation of White America*. New Haven: Yale University Press.

1985 *Italian Americans: Into the Twilight of Ethnicity*. Englewood Cliffs, NJ: Prentice-Hall.

Bean, F. D. and G. Stevens
2003 *America's Newcomers: Immigrant Incorporation and the Dynamics of Diversity*. New York: Russell Sage Foundation.

Berrol, S. C.
1995 *Growing Up American: Immigrant Children in America, Then and Now*. New York: Twayne Publishers.

Boyd, M. and E. M. Grieco
1998 "Triumphant Transitions: Socioeconomic Achievement of the Second Generation in Canada," *International Migration Review*, 32(4):853–876.

Bozorgmehr, M.
1997 "Internal Ethnicity: Iranians in Los Angeles," *Sociological Perspectives*, 40(3):387–408.

Caplan, N., M. H. Choy and J. K. Whitmore
1991 *Children of the Boat People: A Study of Educational Success*. Ann Arbor: University of Michigan Press.

Child, I. L.
1943 *Italian or American? The Second Generation in Conflict*. New Haven: Yale University Press.

Cropley, A. J.
1983 *The Education of Immigrant Children: A Social-Psychological Introduction*. London: Croom Helm.

Ebaugh, H. R. and J. S. Chafetz
2000 *Religion and the New Immigrants: Continuities and Adaptations in Immigrant Congregations*. Walnut Creek, CA: AltaMira Press.

Erikson, E. H.
1968 *Identity: Youth and Crisis*. New York: W.W. Norton.

1964 "Psychological Reality and Historical Actuality." In *Insight and Responsibility*. Ed. E. H. Erikson. New York: W. W. Norton.

Gans, H. J.
1992 "Second Generation Decline: Scenarios for the Economic and Ethnic Futures of the Post-1965 America Immigrants," *Ethnic and Racial Studies*, 15:173–192.

Gibson, C. J. and E. Lennon
1999 "Historical Census Statistics on the Foreign-Born Population of the United States: 1850–1990." Population Division Working Paper No. 29. Washington, DC: U.S. Bureau of the Census.

Grieco, E. M.
2003 "Census 2010 and the Foreign Born: Averting the Data Crisis," *MPI Policy Brief*, 1. Washington, DC: Migration Policy Institute.

2002 "Defining 'Foreign Born' and 'Foreigner' in International Migration Statistics." *Migration Information Source*. Washington, DC: Migration Policy Institute.

Harris, K. M.
1999 "The Health Status and Risk Behavior of Adolescents in Immigrant Families." In *Children of Immigrants: Health, Adjustment, and Public Assistance*. Ed. D. J. Hernández. Washington, DC: National Academy of Sciences Press

Hernández, D. J. and E. Charney, eds.
1998 *From Generation to Generation: The Health and Well-Being of Children in Immigrant Families*. Washington, DC: National Academy of Sciences Press.

Jensen, L.
2001 "The Demographic Diversity of Immigrants and Their Children." In *Ethnicities: Children of Immigrants in America*. Ed. R. G. Rumbaut and A. Portes. Berkeley and New York: University of California Press and Russell Sage Foundation.

Jensen, L. and Y. Chitose
1994 "Today's Second Generation: Evidence from the 1990 U.S. Census," *International Migration Review*, 28(4):714–735.

Kasinitz, P., J. Battle and I. Miyares
2001 "Fade to Black? The Children of West Indian Immigrants in South Florida." In *Ethnicities: Children of Immigrants in America*. Ed. R. G. Rumbaut and A. Portes. Berkeley and New York: University of California Press and Russell Sage Foundation.

Kunz, E.
1981 "Exile and Resettlement: Refugee Theory," *International Migration Review*, 15(1):42–51.

1973 "The Refugee in Flight: Kinetic Models and Forms of Displacement," *International Migration Review*, 7(1):125–146.

Levitt, P. and M. C. Waters, eds.
2002 *The Changing Face of Home: The Transnational Lives of the Second Generation*. New York: Russell Sage Foundation.

López, D. E. and R. D. Stanton-Salazar
2001 "Mexican Americans: A Second Generation at Risk." In *Ethnicities: Children of Im-*

migrants in America. Ed. R. G. Rumbaut and A. Portes. Berkeley and New York: University of California Press and Russell Sage Foundation.

Mannheim, K.
[1928]
1996   "The Problem of Generations." In *Theories of Ethnicity: A Classical Reader*. Ed. W. Sollors. New York: New York University Press.

Nahirny, V. C. and J. A. Fishman
[1965]
1996   "American Immigrant Groups: Ethnic Identification and the Problem of Generations." In *Theories of Ethnicity: A Classical Reader*. Ed. W. Sollors. New York: New York University Press.

Oropesa, R. S. and N. S. Landale
1997   "In Search of the New Second Generation: Alternative Strategies for Identifying Second Generation Children and Understanding Their Acquisition of English," *Sociological Perspectives*, 40(3):427–455.

Park, R. E. and E. W. Burgess
[1921]
1924   *Introduction to the Science of Sociology*. Chicago: University of Chicago Press.

Perlmann, J. and R. Waldinger
1997   "Second Generation Decline? Children of Immigrants, Past and Present – A Reconsideration," *International Migration Review*, 31(4):893–922.

Piore, M. J.
1979   *Birds of Passage: Migrant Labor and Industrial Societies*. Cambridge: Cambridge University Press.

Portes, A., ed.
1996   *The New Second Generation*. New York: Russell Sage Foundation.

Portes, A. and R. G. Rumbaut
2001   *Legacies: The Story of the Immigrant Second Generation*. Berkeley and New York: University of California Press and Russell Sage Foundation

1996   *Immigrant America: A Portrait*. 2nd Edition. Berkeley: University of California Press.

Portes, A. and M. Zhou
1993   "The New Second Generation: Segmented Assimilation and Its Variants," *Annals of the American Academy of Political and Social Sciences*, 530:74–96. November.

Riley, M. W.
1987   "The Significance of Age in Sociology," *American Sociological Review*, 52:1–14.

Rumbaut, R. G.
2003   "Legacies: The Story of the Immigrant Second Generation in Early Adulthood." The Sorokin Lecture, presented at the 74th annual meeting of the Pacific Sociological Association, Pasadena, California.

2002   "Severed or Sustained Attachments? Language, Identity, and Imagined Communities in the Post-Immigrant Generation." In *The Changing Face of Home: The Transnational Lives of the Second Generation*. Ed. P. Levitt and M. C. Waters. New York: Russell Sage Foundation.

1998a "Coming of Age in Immigrant America," *Research Perspectives on Migration*, 1(6):1–14.

1998b "Growing Up American in Cuban Miami: Ambition, Language, and Identity in the '1.5' and Second Generations." Paper presented at the XXI International Congress of the Latin American Studies Association, Chicago.

1997a "Ties That Bind: Immigration and Immigrant Families in the United States." In *Immigration and the Family: Research and Policy on U.S. Immigrants*. Ed. A. Booth, A. C. Crouter, and N. S. Landale. Mahwah, NJ: Lawrence Erlbaum.

1997b "Assimilation and Its Discontents: Between Rhetoric and Reality," *International Migration Review*, 31(4):923–960.

1994 "The Crucible Within: Ethnic Identity, Self-Esteem, and Segmented Assimilation among Children of Immigrants," *International Migration Review*, 28(4):748–794.

1991 "The Agony of Exile: A Study of the Migration and Adaptation of Indochinese Refugee Adults and Children." In *Refugee Children: Theory, Research, and Practice*. Ed. F. L. Ahearn, Jr. and J. Athey. Baltimore: Johns Hopkins University Press.

[1976] Forthcoming "The One-and-a-Half Generation: Crisis, Commitment, Identity." In *The Dispossessed: An Anatomy of Exile*. Ed. P. Rose. University of Massachusetts Press.

Rumbaut, R. G. and W. A. Cornelius, eds.
1995 *California's Immigrant Children: Theory, Research, and Implications for Educational Policy*. La Jolla, CA: Center for U.S.-Mexican Studies, University of California, San Diego.

Rumbaut, R. G. and K. Ima
1988 *The Adaptation of Southeast Asian Refugee Youth: A Comparative Study*. Washington, DC: U.S. Office of Refugee Resettlement.

Rumbaut, R. G. and A. Portes, eds.
2001 *Ethnicities: Children of Immigrants in America*. Berkeley and New York: University of California Press and Russell Sage Foundation.

Ryder, N. B.
1965 "The Cohort as a Concept in the Study of Social Change," *American Sociological Review*, 30:843–861.

Schmidley, A. D.
2001 *Profile of the Foreign-Born Population in the United States: 2000*. Series P23–206, Current Population Reports, U.S. Census Bureau. Washington, DC: U.S. Government Printing Office.

Schmidley, A. D. and J. G. Robinson
1998 "How Well Does the Current Population Survey Measure the Foreign Born Population in the United States?" Population Division Working Paper No. 22. Washington, DC: U.S. Bureau of the Census.

Suárez-Orozco, C. and M. M. Suárez-Orozco
2002 *Children of Immigration*. Cambridge: Harvard University Press.

Sung, B. L.
1987 *The Adjustment Experience of Chinese Immigrant Children in New York City.* New York: Center for Migration Studies.

Thomas, W. I. and F. Z.
[1918–20]
1958 *The Polish Peasant in Europe and America.* New York: Dover.

Warner, W. L. and L. Srole
1945 *The Social Systems of American Ethnic Groups.* New Haven, CT: Yale University Press.

Waters, M. C.
1999 *Black Identities: West Indian Immigrant Dreams and American Realities.* Cambridge and New York: Harvard University Press and Russell Sage Foundation.

1990 *Ethnic Options: Choosing Identities in America.* Berkeley: University of California Press.

Zhou, M.
1997 "Growing Up American: The Challenge Confronting Immigrant Children and Children of Immigrants," *Annual Review of Sociology,* 23:63–95.

Zhou, M. and C. L. Bankston III
1998 *Growing Up American: How Vietnamese Children Adapt to Life in the United States.* New York: Russell Sage Foundation.

Part V

RELIGION AND MIGRANT INCORPORATION

Chapter 13

THE ROLE OF RELIGION IN THE ORIGINS AND ADAPTATION OF IMMIGRANT GROUPS IN THE UNITED STATES[1]

Charles Hirschman

The wave of post-1965 immigration has brought a new religious diversity to the United States. Over the last few decades, Islamic mosques and Buddhist and Hindu temples have appeared in most major cities and in quite a few smaller cities and towns. New places of worship have been constructed, but many new churches or temples begin simply in storefronts, the "borrowed" quarters of other churches, or in the homes of members. New immigrants are also bringing new forms of Christianity and Judaism that have shaped the content and the language of services in many existing churches and synagogues. There were more than 800 Chinese Protestant churches in the United States in 2000, and by the late 1980s, there were 250 Korean ethnic

[1]Revision of a paper presented at the conference on "Conceptual and Methodological Developments in the Study of International Migration" at Princeton University, May 23–25, 2003 sponsored by the Center for Migration and Development, Princeton University and the Social Science Research Council Committee on International Migration. I am grateful to Josh DeWind, Calvin Goldscheider, Alejandro Portes, and Lydio Tomasi for their insightful and constructive comments on an earlier draft of this paper. My reading and review of the literature benefited from the excellent assistance of Duc Ngo.

churches in the New York City metropolitan area alone (Min, 1992:1375; Yang, 2002:88).

Although these new forms of religious practice may appear to be "foreign," they represent the characteristic path of adaptation of newcomers to American society. Just as many immigrants come to learn that they are ethnics in the United States, a significant share of immigrants also "become American" through participation in the religious and community activities of churches and temples. There is not one monolithic interpretation of the role of religion on immigrant adaptation, just as there is no single path to assimilation in American society. Many old and new immigrants are indifferent, if not hostile, to organized religion. But many immigrants, historical and contemporary, joined or founded religious organizations as an expression of their historical identity as well as their commitment to building a local community in their new country.

Although the obituary for religion in modern societies has been written many times, there is very little support for the secularization hypothesis that religion will disappear with modernity (Stark and Bainbridge, 1996). Institutional religion has withdrawn from its paramount position and ubiquitous influence in traditional societies to a more circumscribed role in modern industrial societies. However, religious faith and religious organizations remain vital to many, if not most, persons in the modern world. It is only through religion, or other spiritual beliefs, that many people are able to find solace for the inevitable human experiences of death, suffering, and loss. With the expansion of knowledge and the heightened sense of control that accompany modernity, the inexplicability of death may be even more poignant in the contemporary world than in traditional societies where death is an everyday experience.

Churches and other religious organizations also play an important role in the creation of community and as a major source of social and economic assistance for those in need. In past times, individuals could turn to the extended family (and the larger community) for social and spiritual comfort as well as for material assistance. With smaller and less proximate families in present times, churches and temples can sometimes fill the void. Members in many religious bodies, similar to members of a family, do not expect immediate reciprocity as a basis for friendship and social exchange. The idea of community – of shared values and enduring association – is often sufficient to motivate persons to trust and help one another, even in the absence of long personal relationships.

Immigrants, like the native born, have spiritual needs, which are most meaningful when packaged in a familiar linguistic and cultural context. In particular, immigrants are drawn to the fellowship of ethnic churches and temples, where primary relationships among congregants are reinforced with traditional foods and customs. Immigrants also have many economic and social needs, and American churches, temples, and synagogues have a long tradition of community service, particularly directed at those most in need of assistance. The combination of culturally attuned spiritual comfort and material assistance heightens the attractions of membership and participation in churches for new immigrants to the United States.

In this essay, I begin with a review of the classical thesis of Will Herberg that new immigrants become more religious after arrival in the United States in order to maintain cultural continuity following the trauma of international migration. Although religious faith provides continuity with experiences prior to immigration, the commitment, observance, and participation are generally higher in the American setting after immigration than in the origin country. The argument is supported with the frequent observation that one of the first acts of new immigrants is to found their own church, temple, or mosque. Many supportive examples can be cited from European immigrants in the early twentieth century and for contemporary immigrants from Asia and Latin America.

Many important issues, however, are not addressed in the classical model. Even though every immigrant community may found a church, there were significant variations in the religiosity of immigrants, as measured by the frequency of church attendance. The classical model assumes a high level of religious participation to be a characteristic American practice, but there appears to have been a secular increase in American religiosity over the nineteenth and twentieth centuries, both among natives and immigrants. An important element in the increasing religious observance in American society was the importance of churches as a means of collective and individual socioeconomic mobility for immigrants and second-generation ethnic communities. These themes are explored in this essay after an elaboration of the classical model.

THE CLASSICAL MODEL OF HERBERG AND HANDLIN

The classic account of immigration and religion in the United States was written by Will Herberg over 40 years ago in his book *Protestant, Catholic, Jew* (1960). Drawing upon the research of Ruby Jo Reeves Kennedy (1944, 1952), Herberg argued that twentieth century America was not one big melting pot, but three, and that the three major religious faiths provide enduring ethnic identities that persist along generations. Herberg's account extended the interpretation of Oscar Handlin (1973), who claimed that immigrants become Americans by first becoming ethnic Americans. For example, an immigrant from Sicily learns after arrival in the United States that he is an Italian American. The development of national-origin attachments is more than just a symbolic expansion of local or regional identities, but reflects the communal life in the neighborhoods and cities in which immigrants live, work, attend church, and develop personal ties. In the Handlin framework, these new affinities and ethnic identities are not substitutes for a broader American identity, but represent the typical way most Americans see themselves. An American identity, as with American society and culture, is not a monolithic historical memory, but rather a variable mosaic of regional, national origin, social class, and religious beliefs, customs, and attachments.

Joining the logic of Handlin with the empirical findings of Kennedy, Herberg claimed that first generation national origin identities blend into religious identities in subsequent generations. Intermarriage in second and third generations weakened the solidarity of national-origin groups, but rarely bridged the strong divides between Protestants, Catholics, and Jews. Simply put, immigrants and their children became Americans over time by settling in neighborhoods, joining associations, and acquiring identities of ethnic Americans defined more by religion than by country of origin.

To "become American," according to the Handlin and Herberg model, does not require complete assimilation. New immigrants must acquire a new language, develop new loyalties, and learn the basic tenets of political culture, but they are not required to change their religion (Herberg, 1960:22). This easy acceptance of varied faith communities as fully American has emerged over time. Although Protestant dominance and prejudice toward other religions has never completely disappeared, it has receded with the growing diversity of the American population.

As the country grew during the nineteenth century, the definition of American identity had to be sufficiently broad to include the wide cultural variations between town and farm, the north and the south, and the frontier and the more established regions of the country. Gradually, it was accepted that new immigrants and their descendants could find their place in the American mainstream by joining one of the already existing subcultures or by creating their own. This could be by adherence to one of the major European religious traditions, perhaps combined with a national origin culture. American society expands, not by adding completely assimilated persons into the old culture, but by broadening the definition of American culture. For example, the ever-expansive American culture could include German beer, Italian pizza, and Greek salad as a typically American dinner.

The classic thesis of Handlin and Herberg – of immigrants becoming American through their affiliation with an immigrant/ethnic church – can be illustrated from a number of examples from the past and the present. However, the thesis does not fully describe or explain the variable role of religion and religious organizations across different immigrant communities and historical periods. The primary limitation of the Handlin and Heberg thesis is that it is ahistorical – it does not allow for the changing receptivity of American society and the changing composition and structure of religious groups over the last two centuries. Moreover, the primary focus of the Handlin and Herberg thesis is on the psychosocial benefits of religious participation, which neglects the important role of churches and temples as information-sharing communities that enhance the socioeconomic opportunities of immigrants and their children. These issues are explored at length below, but I begin with a review of the classical idea that immigration is a "theologizing experience" (Smith, 1978:1175).

WHY RELIGION MATTERS TO IMMIGRANTS

International migration, even in this age of instant communications and inexpensive travel, can be a traumatizing experience. Immigrants become strangers in a new land with the loss of familiar sounds, sights, and smells. The expectations of customary behavior, hearing one's native language, and support from family and friends can no longer be taken for granted. Even the most routine activities of everyday life – shopping for food, working, and leisure time pursuits – can be alienating experiences for many new immigrants who find themselves in strange settings that require constant mental strain to navigate and to be understood. Smith (1978:1174) cites the enduring contribution of Handlin in "his evocation of the anxieties. . .that resulted from the forsaking of an old home and searching for a new community."

It is no wonder that most immigrants gravitate to the familiar – residence in ethnic neighborhoods, employment in ethnic enclave firms, and social pursuits in the company of family and friends with similar backgrounds. Although national authorities worry about the reluctance of many immigrants to immediately join the mainstream of American society, assimilation is inevitably a slow process. For immigrants who were socialized in another country and arrived in the United States as adults, acculturation may take decades, and assimilation will always be partial. In most cases, assimilation to a new society, however defined, is typically a multigenerational process that requires education and childhood socialization in the new setting (Alba and Nee, 2003:215).

Religious beliefs and practices can serve as ballast for immigrants as they struggle to adapt to their new homeland. Herberg (1960:12) claims the immigrants must confront the existential question of "Who am I?" In a new social context, immigrants could often find meaning and identity by reaffirming traditional beliefs, including the structures of religious faith that may have been taken for granted before. The certainty of religious precepts can provide an anchor as immigrants must adapt and change many other aspects of their lives and habits. Religious values can also provide support for many other traditional beliefs and patterns – intergenerational obligations, gender hierarchy, and customary familial practices – that are threatened with adaptation to the seemingly amoral American culture.

These sentiments were expressed by a member of the Korean-American community:

> We came here, of course, for our own personal and very human reasons – for a better education, for financial well being, for greater career opportunities and the like. But we now find that we do not wholly control our circumstances by ourselves. We find ourselves in a wilderness, living as aliens and strangers. And the inescapable question arises from the depth of our being: What is the real meaning of our immigrant existence in America? What is the spiritual meaning of our alien status? (Sang Hyun Lee (1980) quoted in Hurh and Kim 1984:134).

Customary religious practices, such as attending weekly services, lighting candles, burning incense in front of a family altar, and reciting prayers are examples of communal and family rituals that were brought from the old country to the new. However, these activities often take on new meanings after migration. The normal feeling of loss experienced by immigrants means that familiar religious rituals learned in childhood, such as hearing prayers in one's native tongue, provide an emotional connection, especially when shared with others. These feelings are accentuated from time to time with the death of a family member or some other tragedy. For these reasons, Herberg and others believe that religious beliefs and attachments have stronger roots after immigration than before.

In addition to the psychological benefits of religious practices for immigrants, the social organization of churches, synagogues, and temples also serves the material needs of immigrants (Ebaugh and Chafetz, 2000:8). Upon arrival, immigrants need to find housing and employment, enroll their children in schools, learn (or improve) their language skills, and begin to create a "new" social life. Churches and other religious institutions are one of the most important sources of support for the practical problems faced by immigrants. Helping others in need, including new immigrants and the poor, is considered as one of the missions of many churches and temples, and many of these charitable works are directed to fellow congregants.

RELIGIOUS CHANGE AND CONTINUITY IN AMERICAN HISTORY

According to the model described above, most immigrants seek to maintain, or renew, their religious faith after arrival. If immigrants cannot find a church or temple with their religious traditions, and preferably in their mother tongue, the American custom is to start one of their own. Handlin (1973:Ch. 5) argues that religion was a bridge that connected the old world with the new. Faced with changes and challenges in every other aspect of their lives, immigrants sought to recreate the church and faith of their homeland in their place of settlement.

There are many examples to illustrate this model. Vietnamese Catholics began to settle in poor neighborhoods in New Orleans in the late 1970s, and by the early 1980s they applied to the local Catholic Archdiocese to erect a church. In 1985, less than two years after approval, the Mary Queen of Vietnam Church was completed, largely by the efforts of lay participants (Bankston and Zhou, 2000). Many new Indian immigrant families to the United States meet regularly for Hindu religious services in private homes, even though group religious activities are not a typical practice of Hinduism in India (Kurien, 2002). Based on their study of religious behavior of Southern and Eastern European communities in "Yankee City" in the early decades of the twentieth century, Warner and Srole (1945:166) posit a general sequence of steps in the institutionalization of local religious traditions, beginning with the holding of religious gatherings in private homes, followed by the rental of temporary quarters and finally the construction of a permanent church, temple, or synagogue.

This model – immigrants starting their own churches or temples – is a reflection of the American context as well as the desires of new immigrants. The American context or tradition is thought to consist of two fundamental characteristics. The first attribute is of a historically religious nation, with high proportions of Americans who are members of churches or synagogues and who participate through regular attendance at religious services. The second attribute is "freedom of religion," with the absence of an establishment religion that compels conformity. The first amendment to the constitution provided the basis for freedom of worship by erecting a barrier between government and religion.

This American tradition – pluralist yet religiously observant – is distinctly different from most European countries of origin and is often thought to be reflective of the desires for religious freedom of the early seventeenth and eighteenth century English settlers. According to the often-retold stories of America's founding, the early colonists were fleeing religious intolerance in the Old World, and they wanted freedom to express their deeply felt religious beliefs. Their own experience with religious persecution was thought to have created a social and cultural environment in which freedom of religion would eventually flourish.

The reality, however, was that colonial America was not particularly religious and quite intolerant. The creation of an American society that was highly religious – in terms of the proportion of adherents and high levels of participation – and pluralist happened slowly over the course of the nineteenth and twentieth centuries. Based on careful study of the number of churches in the eighteenth century, Finke and Stark (1992:15–16) conclude that less than one in five persons – only 17 percent – in colonial America on the eve of the revolution were members of a church. Although the story of the highly religious Puritans as the first English settlers is part of American nostalgia, most of the new settlers, even in New England, were not affiliated with any church (Finke and Stark, 1992:Ch. 2).

Well into the eighteenth century, colonial America remained a frontier society that was shaped by the character of migrants who left settled traditional European societies to find their fortune and adventure in the New World. The attributes of a frontier society, including a youthful age structure and a surplus of men to women, usually reduce adherence to traditional conventions, including routine religious practice. Beyond the middle class of the settled populations in the large cities, most Americans, at the time of the founding of the nation, were probably "unchurched."

There were, of course, well established churches in many parts of colonial America, but the majority were distinctive for their religious intolerance. In the mid-1600s, Puritans in Massachusetts hanged two Quakers who refused to quit their province. Although Catholics made up less than one percent of the population, most of whom lived in Maryland, they were forbidden to practice their faith in every colony except Rhode Island and Pennsylvania in the seventeenth century. Massachusetts threatened to execute priests who were caught in the colony twice, and Virginia banned Catholics from public office (Archdeacon, 1983:11, 21). The small number of Jews in colonial America, perhaps only 1,000, made them less of an object of fear and hatred than Catholics, but derogatory comments about Jews were commonly expressed by most leaders of colonial society (Dinnerstein, 1994: 3–12). The degree of religious intolerance in colonial society was only exceeded by the prejudicial attitudes towards the one in five Americans who were of African ancestry and the American Indian population whose lands were coveted. "Indian wars" – an early and popular American tradition – were organized to wrest land from the Native American inhabitants for the expanding European-origin settlers.

Freedom of religion (or of no religion) as mandated by the First Amendment does not appear to be a sign of tolerance among religious people, but perhaps the compromise that emerged from the rivalries among the many Protestant denominations and the majority of colonialists who were not adherents to any religion. If Americans did not begin as an especially religious people, they seem to have become so over the course of the nineteenth and twentieth centuries. Tolerance of different religious traditions was much slower to develop.

The American religious tradition was "created" slowly over the nineteenth and twentieth centuries as the proportion of the population who were affiliated with churches increased. By the middle of the twentieth century, this upward trend crested, with about 60 percent of the total population affiliated with churches or formal religious bodies (Finke and Stark, 1992: 15–16). The increase in American religiosity over the past two centuries appears to be due to two primary sources. The first was the competition for church membership created by the "upstart sects," most notably Baptists and Methodists, on the American frontier. Finke and Stark (1992) argue, convincingly in my opinion, that competition among churches for support and members increased the fraction of the total population that were churchgoers.

The other major factor was the ability of the American Catholic Church, especially after 1850, to retain a high degree of religious identification and practice among the descendants of immigrants from Catholic nations and regions in Europe. Since most of these immigrants were nominal Catholics in their homelands, the question is how the American Catholic

Church was able to convert them (or their children or grandchildren) into practicing Catholics in the United States.

The upward trend in religious adherence was buoyed by demographic and socioeconomic changes in the American population. Over the course of the nineteenth century, the European population of colonial America spread across the country. Frontier areas gradually became settled areas with several generations of local history. Among the cultural changes that followed from the ending of the frontier are communities with children, schools, and churches. People who live near relatives, and who expect to live in communities for their entire lives, are more likely to sink organizational roots and to join churches.

The other change in American society was an increase in the middle class or people with some claim to social status. A recurrent finding in research on religiosity is that persons with above average socioeconomic status are more likely to join churches and attend services regularly (Lenski, 1963:48; Roof and McKinney, 1987:115). As more and more Americans experienced upward mobility and joined the "respectable" middle class (most of their early immigrant ancestors were probably not respectable in their countries of origin and probably not in the early years after arrival in the United States), church membership and participation became more of a part of everyday life.

Although much is made over the inevitable conflict between religion and modern scientific rationality, there is little evidence in support of a trend in secularism or a decline in religiosity in late twentieth century America. In their study of church attendance over the middle decades of the twentieth century, Hout and Greeley (1987) find only a modest decline for Catholics in the late 1960s following the ban on birth control, but no further decline among Catholics after the mid-1970s. There was no decline in church attendance among Protestants from 1940 to the mid-1980s.

Another aspect of the American religious tradition is the gradual "Americanization" of immigrant churches and religious practices in the United States. Although different religious rituals have not disappeared entirely, there is a trend to conformity, including features such as the use of the English language, holding weekly services, having a sermon as a focal point of the service, and an increasing role of the laity in managing the affairs of church activities. This process has recently been labeled "de facto congregationalism," which means a shift from traditional hierarchical religious organization to a model along the lines of a reformed Protestant congregation (Warner 1998; Bankston and Zhou, 2000). Although many differences persist, there are striking examples of the change in the structure and form of immigrant churches, temples, and synagogues in the American context.

In the predominately Buddhist countries of Asia, most young men enter the monastery to serve as monks, typically for a few months, before becoming adult members of the community. Among Buddhist communities in the United States, this custom has died, and the role of a monk has become a specialized and professional role, closer to that of a minister. In the American context, authority in the Buddhist community has generally shifted from the *sangha* (the order of the monks) to the laity along the lines of Christian congregations (Zhou, Bankston and Kim, 2002).

These features, and other aspects of traditional religious practices, are shaped by the many practical demands in the course of adaptation to American society by various immigrant communities. Warner and Srole (1945: 200–204) note that many second-generation Jewish immigrants found it impractical to observe the Sabbath as strictly as Orthodox Judaism requires. Many Jewish families were merchants, and Saturday was an important business day. Even elder first-generation Jewish immigrants who strictly observed the Sabbath themselves accepted the reality that their American-born children had to keep their stores open. One informant in the Warner and Srole study, an elderly Jewish immigrant, noted that men now take off their hats in temples and that some reform temples have organs just like in churches and says "We are imitating someone else and forgetting that we are Jews" (Warner and Srole, 1945:204).

Even with these adaptations, however, there is no sign that Jewish identity or even religious adherence was declining in "Yankee City" in the 1930s. Even with low attendance at religious services, there was strong Jewish support for a campaign to create a more modern synagogue in a better part of the city. In the depth of the Depression, almost every Jewish family in the city provided financial support to create a new synagogue that would cater to social needs (youth activities) as well as the religious traditions of the community (Warner and Srole, 1945:211–217).

HOW RELIGIOUS ARE NEW IMMIGRANTS?

The founding of a church or temple by an immigrant community is one of the most common features of the "Americanization" process. As native-born Americans were becoming more religiously observant over the course of the nineteenth and twentieth centuries, immigrants were probably more motivated to follow suit. There were also internal motivations for new immigrant communities to start their own churches or temples soon after arrival. As noted earlier, participation in religious rituals reinforces traditional cultural identities and provides comfort to those enduring the hardships of adjusting to a new life in a strange environment. However, it is important to distinguish between the creation of new ethnic churches and temples and the question of whether most immigrants are religiously observant. The evidence on the latter question is mixed.

There are examples of a very high level of religious participation among immigrant groups, of which the Korean-American Christian community is the most widely cited. Korean immigrants to the United States were drawn disproportionately from the minority of Christians in Korea. Less than one fifth of Koreans (in Korea) are Christian, but over half of Korean immigrants were affiliated with Christian churches in Korea prior to immigration (Hurh and Kim, 1984:129–130; Min, 1992:1375–1376). There is also a very high degree of conversion to Christianity among Koreans after immigration. About 70 percent of first-generation Koreans in Los Angeles reported affiliation with Korean ethnic churches in the United States (Hurh and Kim, 1984:130). There was also an extraordinarily high level of religious participation among Korean-American Christians, with 83 percent of the church-affiliated attending church once a week or more (*see also* Min 1992:1371).

On the other hand, there are many examples of immigrant groups that were not very religious, at least not at the outset. The most frequently cited example at this end of the continuum was the so-called "Italian problem," as it was labeled by Catholic bishops in the early decades of the twentieth century. Vecoli (1964) reports that Italian Americans showed little interest or enthusiasm in Catholic practice, and the standard refrain was that Italian Americans only entered churches to be christened, married, and buried (*see also* Cinel, 1982:209). Although estimates of religiosity are hard to come by, it appears that upwards of half to two thirds of Italian immigrants in the early decades of the twentieth century were not practicing Catholics (Vecoli, 1969:268–269). Italian peasants from Southern Italy brought with them a strong anti-clerical tradition, often viewing the Church as an oppressive landlord at home and a strong opponent of Italian nationalism.

There have been many other *ad hoc* reasons offered for the apparently exceptional case of Italian Americans. Many Italian immigrants were men who came as sojourning laborers, to earn money and to return home. Joining a church, which probably required contributing time and money, may not have been considered a terribly attractive "investment" for men who did not expect to continue their careers and begin family life in the United States.

Another reason frequently mentioned in the literature is that Italians did not resonate with the Irish-dominated Catholic Church, which the Italians found to be cold, remote, and Puritanical (Nelli, 1980).

The Italian case, however, may not have been all that exceptional. Although there were sufficient numbers of religiously motivated immigrants to found ethnic churches in every city, many new immigrant groups appeared to be closer to the Italian model than that of the Koreans. Upwards of 80 percent of Mexican Americans in Los Angeles remained nominally Catholic, but only about 40 percent were observant, as measured by regularly attending Mass (Sanchez, 1993:165; *see also* Camarillo, 1979). Finke and Stark (1992:115) report that most immigrants from Germany, Italy, and Poland were nominal Catholics in their homelands. In spite of major efforts by several Protestant denominations to convert immigrant Chinese in the early twentieth century, only 2 to 3 percent of Chinese immigrants ever became practicing Christians (Woo, 1991:216–217).

The question of how religious were the new immigrants depends, in part, on the definition of religiosity. In the American context, religious practice usually means attending weekly services on a regular basis. In most rural areas of Europe, as well as in Asia and Latin America, religion and folk beliefs were intertwined into a way of life. Spirits of nature and the souls of the departed were nearby, and the daily life of villagers included many rituals to bring good fortune, to cure illness, and to avoid dangers. Many of these ideas were intertwined with formal religious beliefs in ways that religious purists criticized. For example, Polish immigrants are described as having a Polish version of Catholicism that was infused with animism and magical beliefs (Lopata, 1976:48). The characterization of Italians was that their Catholicism was "a folk religion, a fusion of Christian and pre-Christian elements, of animism, polytheism, and sorcery in the sacraments of the Church" (Vecoli, 1969:228). The Italian religious tradition of the *festa*, when the statue of a saint was paraded throughout the local community with the community following in a procession, was considered by the established Catholic Church to be a pagan ritual. Similar descriptions have been made about the religious beliefs and traditions of nominally Catholic immigrants from the Philippines and Mexico.

In spite of these tensions in the first generation, Russo (1969) reports that, over generations, Italian Americans were gradually acculturated and assimilated into the American Catholic Church. The first generation – labeled the "Italian problem" by the Church – was anti-clerical and encountered an Irish-dominated Church that was conservative, preoccupied with fundraising, and unsympathetic and often hostile to poor Italians. As the second and third generations left the cities for suburbs, they often joined mainstream Catholic churches. Other measures of religiosity, such as weekly attendance at Mass and frequent communion, increased among the second- and higher-generation Italian Americans. This is due, Russo argues, to intermarriage, suburbanization, and increased exposure to American Catholic norms and practices

More recent evidence on religious conformity to Catholic strictures comes from a study of Hispanic migrants to New York. Fitzpatrick and Gurak (1979:60–63) report that second generation Hispanics are more likely to have Catholic wedding ceremonies than first generation Hispanics – consistent with the thesis that religiosity (or religious practice) increases with exposure to American society.

One Catholic immigrant group, however, was very different from all the others. Upwards of 90 percent of the Irish in Ireland and the Irish in the United States populations attended weekly Mass circa 1900. The case of the Irish is of particular significance because the Irish clergy dominated the hierarchy of the American Catholic Church and defined the culture of the Church. This is not just an American phenomenon. Irish priests and nuns have played a significant role in the development of the Catholic Church throughout the English-speaking world:

> Not only did Roman Catholic Churches in England and Scotland become essentially Irish, but the Churches in the United States, English speaking Canada, South Africa, Australia, and New Zealand were all strongly influenced by the developing values and mores of Irish Roman Catholicism (Larkin, 1984:9).

There are frequent observations about the negative reaction of many Catholic immigrant groups to the Irish-dominated American Catholic Church, which created a very formal set of obligations and was not particularly receptive to the folk versions of Catholicism from other lands. Nonetheless, the American Catholic Church gained ground in the competitive American religious market and eventually captured the children of most Catholic immigrants, even if the first generation rejected the Irish model of the American Church. By the middle of the twentieth century, about one third of all Americans identified as Catholics.

Why were the Irish different? What made them so much more religious than other groups? To address these questions requires a digression into Irish religious history and Irish immigration the United States. The first point is that the late nineteenth century version of Irish Catholicism – which created American Catholicism – was a reversal of the trend in Irish Catholicism prior to the Great Famine of the 1840s. According to Emmet Larkin (1984), the formal practice of Catholicism was actually on the decline in Ireland for the first four decades of the nineteenth century. The number of priests could not keep up with the rapidly growing population, and less than 40 percent of Irish Catholics regularly attended Mass (Larkin, 1984:68, 87). Widespread poverty and the growing immiserization of the Irish population contributed to a weak Church establishment. There were also accounts of lax discipline, with avarice, lust, and drunkenness among some priests. These Irish examples were not too dissimilar to reports about some members of the Italian clergy who came to the United States after having been expelled from Italy because of sexual misconduct (Vecoli, 1969:240).

This account of nominal Catholicism in Ireland in the early part of the nineteenth century corresponds to reports of nonreligious Irish immigrant communities at the same time period (Bodnar, 1985:151). The pre-famine Irish immigrants were not avid churchgoers and the "great body" of people received communion only once or twice a year (Dolan, 1975:55–56). At the Church of the Transfiguration – the largest Irish parish in New York City – only 10 to 25 percent of the 10,000 members rented pews, which might be interpreted as a sign of irregular attendance (Dolan, 1975:51). The problem was not just the Irish. A similar attitude prevailed among German Catholics in mid-nineteenth century New York, where only about 50 percent of the parish community of the Most Holy Redeemer Church regularly attended Sunday services (Dolan, 1975:85).

In the second half of the nineteenth century, however, nominal Irish Catholics were transformed into practicing Catholics, as were most Irish-American Catholics. Following the famine of the late 1840s, the Catholic Church in Ireland changed dramatically with the "Devotional Revolution." The Irish famine had a devastating impact on the Irish population, which declined by more than 2 million, or by almost one third, because of death and emigration in the space of four years from 1846 to 1850 (Larkin, 1984:59). The depopulation of Ireland continued for the balance of the century, with annual emigration averaging from 50,000 to 100,000 per year. Although the psychological effect of the famine is generally thought to be a key reason for the increasing religiosity of Irish Catholics, there were a number of other contributing factors.

The demographic losses among the Irish population were not random, but were primarily among the poorest and least religious of the Irish population. The first order effect of depopulation in Ireland was a sharp shift in the ratio of clergy to the lay population. This meant more churches had regular priests. The change in the class composition of the Irish population following the Famine also left more middle-class Catholics that had been the historical bulwark of the Church.

There was a gradual improvement in the incomes of middle-class Irish Catholics in the decades following the Famine. Because of their strong religious convictions and a lack of investment opportunities in the nineteenth century, the Irish middle class contributed a very large share of their discretionary income and their lifetime savings to the Catholic Church (Larkin, 1984). These contributions enhanced the wealth and status of the Irish Church, which led to an ambitious building program of cathedrals, churches, chapels, monasteries, convents, schools, and hospitals in every part of Ireland in the later decades of the nineteenth century (Larkin, 1984:26–27). The number of Irish priests, monks and nuns almost tripled from 1850 to 1900 as the Irish Catholic population decreased by one third. At the same time, Ireland began to export clergy (and capital) in service of Catholicism around the world.

The Devotional Revolution – which began with the reform of the Church and led to the transformation of nominal Catholics into practicing Catholics within a generation – was larger than just a psychological response to the Great Famine (Larkin, 1984:82–85). Larkin's interpretation is that Catholicism became the primary component of Irish identity as they lost their "language, culture, and way of life" under British domination. Although the trend toward the Anglicization of Ireland had been underway for more than 100 years, the Devotional Revolution of the second half of the nineteenth century crystallized Catholicism as the "symbolic language and cultural heritage" of Irish at home and abroad.

This historical evidence points to two reasons for the vigor of the Catholic Church in late nineteenth century America, both stemming from the Devotional Revolution in Ireland. The first is simply the export of Irish clergy. The American Catholic Church became Irish in character not just because the Irish were the first major wave of Catholic immigration, but also because Irish priests and nuns staffed the American Catholic Church. The savings of the Irish middle class led to the expansion of seminaries in Ireland, producing far more priests and nuns than were needed in Ireland. Religious careers were one of the few growth sectors of the Irish economy that lagged far behind the rest of Europe. One seminary alone, the College of All Hallows in Dublin sent 1,500 priests to the New World in the 60 years after its founding in 1842 (Blessing, 1980:534).

The second issue is the one of identity. Larkin's thesis is that after 300 years of English domination, the Irish had few cultural props left to define themselves. Catholicism and clerical vocations became cherished ideals. This question of identity was especially important in the American context because of the growth of the Irish population in the United States and the hostile reception that most Irish Americans encountered. Catholic Americans rose from less than one percent of the population in 1790 to 7.5 percent of the 23 million Americans in 1850 (Archdeacon, 1983:74). Over the course of the nineteenth century, Irish immigrants, and to a lesser extent German immigrants, made Catholicism the majority religion in most large cities. Although the growing American Catholic population had the constitutional freedom to establish churches, there was not an increase in tolerance for Catholics in Protestant America.

Fear of Catholic immigrants and Catholicism dominated much of nineteenth century political life. From the xenophobic Know-Nothing movement of the 1840s and 1850s to the anti-Catholic, nativist American Protective Association of the 1890s, Catholics were under attack, both rhetorically and physically (Archdeacon, 1983:74–84; Higham 1988:77–87). The great American inventor, Samuel Morse, was one of many nineteenth century voices that claimed Catholics were preparing to overthrow the government. In May 1844, there were three days of rioting in Kensington, a working-class Irish suburb of Philadelphia, which culminated in the burning of two Catholic churches and other property (Archdeacon, 1983:81). This case was one incident of many during the 1840s and 1850s when Catholic churches and convents were destroyed and priests were attacked by Protestant mobs (Daniels, 1991:267–268).

These attacks provide another reason why new immigrants were highly motivated to start and join churches in the United States, namely self-protection from the hostility of the native-born population. Although there may have been occasions when numbers may have been important to provide protection against mob violence, the primary advantage of religious affiliation was to create a sheltered community where immigrants and their families did not have to endure the daily insults. Finke and Stark (1992:115) conclude that "a major achievement of the American Catholic Church was to appeal to a broad spectrum of ethnic backgrounds and to prevent ethnic differences from producing major schisms . . . (and to have) . . . created a social structure that protected Catholics from the dominant and hostile Protestant environment."

Periods of wars, perhaps unexpectedly, may have contributed to a reduction in religious intolerance. John Higham (1988:12–14) reports that

the service of foreign-born Americans, especially Irish Catholics, on the
Union side of the Civil War led to the erosion of the Know-Nothing Party
in the North. It was much more difficult to demonize the new Irish immigrants as heathen and un-American when they were fighting and dying to
preserve the American republic. This argument is consistent with the claim
of Klinkner and Smith (1999) that the major political and economic gains
for African Americans have occurred in the Revolutionary War, the Civil
War, and in subsequent twentieth-century wars when African-American
soldiers were an essential resource needed for victory. These gains were,
however, often temporary as racial and religious prejudices generally returned as the memories of common alliances during wartime faded.

Churches were social communities as well as places of worship, with a
variety of associations and groups for men, women, and children. In addition
to their educational value and leisure time pursuits, church associations
created opportunities for leadership and civic contributions that would not
have been possible in the broader community. For many immigrant groups,
starting with the Irish, identity as Catholics provided a sense of internal
cohesion and status as they encountered prejudice and discrimination in the
United States. In an odd way, generalized hostility from the majority population may have contributed to the American tradition of new immigrant
communities founding their own ethnic churches.

Over the course of the nineteenth century and the early decades of the
twentieth century, the Catholic Church grew by continued immigration of
Catholics from eastern and southern Europe. But the creation of a practicing
Catholic population in the United States in the twentieth century was
created by the infusion of Irish priests, nuns, and resources. The example of
an Irish Church that defined national identity became the model for other
nationalities. For many European ethnic groups, identification with a religious tradition was also a form of nationalism, especially if there was no
contemporary state with which they identified. "There were national
churches, including the Irish Catholic, the Armenian Apostolic, the Polish
Catholic, the Greek Orthodox, at a time when there were no Ireland, Armenia, Poland and Greece in the political sense" (Warner and Srole, 1945:
159).

A major means of creating immigrant/ethnic churches was the promotion of national languages. The Catholic Church permitted two types of
parishes: neighborhood and national. National parishes could be attended by
members of a specific nationality from across a city. Between 1880 and
1930, 30 percent of new parishes in the Northeast were "national" (Finke

and Stark, 1992:130). In 1916, approximately half of Catholics attended parishes where a language other than English was used in religious services. Mass was said in Latin in all Catholic Churches, but the sermon was given in the local language in national parishes (Finke and Stark, 1992:126–127). For many decades, the Italian-American community was served primarily by national Catholic churches (Tomasi, 1975).

Although the American Catholic Church allowed variations in language, the high standards for religious observance were set by the Irish Devotional Revolution. In doing so, they strengthened the Catholic Church and contributed to a more "churched" American society – a topic that will be reconsidered in the concluding discussion.

THE VALUE OF RELIGIOUS AFFILIATION AND COMMUNITIES TO NEW IMMIGRANTS

Although the value of religion is usually considered in spiritual terms, there are many social and economic benefits derived from participation in religious organizations. These aspects of religious participation are particularly salient to immigrants because they have many needs and few resources. Many evangelical efforts to win religious converts among immigrants begin with the provision of needed services. For example, Protestant missions offered English classes and medical and social services in their efforts to convert Chinese on the Pacific Coast in the early twentieth century (Woo, 1991:214–215). Protestant missionaries offered clothing, food, jobs and even candy to lure Italian families and their children to Protestant churches (Vecoli, 1969:252). There was a counter-effort to teach the catechism and offer social activities to children in Little Italy by the Catholic Church.

Almost all immigrant/ethnic churches make major efforts to serve the social and economic needs of their congregants, including information about housing, social, and economic opportunities that facilitate their adaptation to American society (Bodnar, 1985:148–150). Min (1992:1379) reports that some Korean ethnic churches in New York City offer language classes (both Korean and English), a full Korean lunch after services, and seminars on practical as well as spiritual topics.

Churches also provide opportunities for fellowship with coethnics. Korean churches in New York City tend to be small (less than 100 members) and allow for extensive social interaction after services as well as celebrations for holidays and birthday parties for children and the elderly – operating as an extended family for many Korean immigrants (Min, 1992:1382).

Churches provide a means of continuity with the past through reaffirmation of traditional values as well as coping with the problems of the present.

Churches assist new immigrants with finding housing and jobs as well as offering language assistance and navigating the American bureaucracy. Churches are particularly helpful for parents who need counseling on how to handle their American-born children and also provide special religious and education programs for children (Min, 1992). The Korean Catholic Apostolate Church of Queens, with more than 2,500 members, runs a credit union that serves members of five other Korean Catholic churches in the New York City region. Bankston and Zhou (2000) note that while the manifest purpose of the Vietnamese Catholic Church in New Orleans is to provide a place of worship, the latent purpose is to bring people together so they can find out what opportunities are available, especially jobs and other economic opportunities. Religious participation in the Vietnamese community is also a means to ease the social adjustment of children and adolescents into American society (Bankston and Zhou, 1995).

Several thousand Laotian Americans live in a rural area of Louisiana, initially drawn there by a government training program in pipefitting, welding, and other skills needed in the Gulf Coast region in the early 1980s (Zhou, Bankston and Kim, 2002). They first lived in public housing, but over time they began to settle in clusters in middle-class neighborhoods. By 1986, the leaders of the community formed an association to build a Lao-style Buddhist temple in a rural area of the county, which became a place of residential settlement for many Lao families. In addition to providing cultural and spiritual continuality with their past, the temple served as a communication hub for economic opportunities.

As part of their research on the Lao community, Zhou, Bankston and Kim (2002:57) report an interview with a non-Lao director of a firm that employed about 75 Lao as welders, fitters and other skilled craftsmen in constructing offshore oil structures and asked him how the firm got so many Lao workers. The director replied, "One of our foremen is the financial manager at the Buddhist 'whatchmacallit'. . . . People go to him for a job and he just refers them here." Another member of the temple community provides assistance for housing through her position as a loan officer in a local bank.

Although the Catholic Church is usually not credited with providing the same array of social services as other churches, this perspective neglects the historical role of the Church in providing educational opportunities through parochial schools. With the advent of the public common schools in the mid-nineteenth century, Catholics faced a crisis. In addition to the general anti-Catholic bias of nativist America, public schools communicated a distinctly Protestant culture that many Catholics considered demeaning (Dolan 1975:101–102). The response was to create an alternative Catholic educational system. Although many (perhaps most) Catholic parents did not send their children to parochial schools, Catholic education was particularly attractive to the emerging middle class. In particular, Catholic secondary education and colleges provided an upper-class educational system, with students from all ethnic groups (Dolan, 1975:111).

There was also a tradition of Catholic charities, including orphanages and hospitals that aided immigrants and the poor (Dolan, 1975:128). These institutions, as well as Catholic schools, were staffed primarily by nuns. Because nuns served for wages much lower than other workers, Catholic institutions were able to provide high quality services for a fraction of the costs of the market economy. Many of these nuns were immigrants, particularly from Ireland. From 1850 to 1900, the number of Catholic priests in the United States grew a bit more than ten-fold, while the number of nuns grew 25-fold (Finke and Stark, 1992:135). The ratio of nuns to the Catholic population more than tripled during this period. Church mutual benefit associations, such as the "Sons of Italy," provided insurance for sickness and death, which was a much needed service for immigrants and the poor (Finke and Stark, 1992:132).

It is difficult to evaluate the long-term impact of Catholic schools, but they may have been critical for the upward mobility for the children and grandchildren of immigrants. James Coleman and his colleagues claim that Catholic schools provide stronger academic environments than some public schools (Coleman, Hoffer and Kilgore, 1982). Because private schools have fewer discipline problems, it is possible for students to concentrate on academic studies.

CONCLUSIONS

The growing numbers of new immigrants in the United States in the latter decades of the twentieth century have sparked a religious resurgence, which has become the subject of popular and scholarly attention (Ebaugh and Chafetz, 2000; Min and Kim, 2001; Warner and Wittner, 1998). This phenomenon does not mean that all, or even a majority, of new immigrants are very religious or regularly attend formal services. But the creation of new immigrant churches and temples, as well as the presence of immigrants in established American churches, is leading to major changes in the American religious landscape. For example, in many small towns in the American South – a region of the country that is experiencing its first wave of immigration since the 1700s – some Catholic churches have begun to offer Mass in Spanish.

The most visible manifestation of the impact of new immigrants on American religion has been the establishment of thousands of new churches and temples that serve the particular needs of immigrant communities. Some immigrant churches are in newly constructed buildings, which are financed by the hard-earned savings of immigrants. More often, immigrants hold their services in rented quarters in the basements of established churches or in storefronts that have lost their commercial tenants. Many immigrants simply gather to pray, sing, and socialize in each other's homes. These patterns are quintessentially American. One of the first projects of most early twentieth century American immigrant communities was to start their own churches and synagogues. Indeed, the development of American religious traditions is closely intertwined with the history of immigration (Herberg, 1960).

On many dimensions, the classic Handlin and Herberg model of reinvigorated religious beliefs and practices after immigration captures many features of the contemporary revival of religion among new immigrants to the United States. Just as religion played an important role in maintaining community and continuity in the lives of early twentieth century European immigrants, many new immigrants find comfort, security, and fellowship through participation in religious activities. There are many historical parallels to the present. The diversity of different sects of Islam and Buddhism, which often appear to be incomprehensible to outsiders, resembles the myriad versions of folk Catholicism brought by earlier waves of immigrants. Another feature stressed by Herberg was the tension between the first generation's need for a church with services in the mother tongue and the second generation's preference for a "less ethnic church" with services in English. This historical pattern offers a template for comparisons with the growing diversity among contemporary Chinese and Korean Christian Churches.

The Handlin and Herberg account, however, does not really provide a clear sociological explanation for the nontheological appeals of religious participation for immigrants. Moreover, the Handlin and Herberg model, in my judgment, falls short as an explanation for some puzzles in the changing historical context of American religious institutions. By assuming a constant presence of religion in American society, Handlin and Herberg do not come to grips with how the United States became a more religious society over the course of the nineteenth and twentieth centuries. One of the central elements in the "churching of America" has been the ability of the American Catholic Church to incorporate a large fraction of the children and grandchildren of southern and eastern European immigrants as practicing Catholics.

According to many accounts, the first generation was largely indifferent, if not hostile, to organized Catholicism. Moreover, the Irish-American Church appeared cold, unsympathetic, and puritanical to many new immigrants, whose traditional forms of folk Catholicism did not require following Church strictures for regular attendance and receiving the sacraments. The Catholic Church was successful in the long run by allowing the first generation to go their own way with national churches that allowed for variations in language and cultural forms. By the time the second generation was ready to make religious choices, the Catholic Church offered an incredibly good package – a respectable church that was free of Protestant prejudices; schools, hospitals and other social services staffed by caring and dedicated nuns and demanding religious obligations that appealed to many people. Although intuition may suggest that lax and undemanding religions will be the most popular, recent research in the sociology of religion suggests the opposite (Finke and Stark, 1992). Religious commitments are stronger if a faith expects conformity to principles and enforces obligations by creating a strong sense of community.

The centrality of religion to immigrant communities can be summarized as the search for refuge, respectability, and resources.[2] The immigrant's need for refuge from the trauma of loss and separation was a central theme in the classical writings of Oscar Handlin and Will Herberg. The process of adjustment following international migration varies across national origin groups over time and from person to person. For many immigrants, the separation from family, language, and community often leads to a search for meaning and stability in their new homeland. Religious participation and rituals can often fill the psychological void and create a sense of belonging and community for newcomers. American religious pluralism allows (and encourages) immigrants to form their own churches or temples that fit with their unique sociocultural and linguistic needs.

---

[2] I am grateful to Alejandro Portes for suggesting this formulation.

At various times in American history, the search for refuge by immigrants has been for physical safety as well as for psychological comfort. American nativism occasionally turned violent, especially against Catholics in nineteenth century cities. Communities and neighborhoods that shared a common religious identity centered on church or temple could provide a sense of local protection against toughs from the outside. In the late 1980s and early 1990s, some liberal American churches created the sanctuary movement to protect illegal immigrants who had fled warfare in Central America. Churches are often symbolized as places of refuge from unjust secular power.

Churches can also provide respectability or opportunities for status recognition and social mobility that is denied in the broader society. Even though many immigrants (and their children) may be granted formal access to education and employment in the United States, they may still encounter informal barriers to intimate circles of friendship, clubs, and other social groups. Milton Gordon (1964) observed the persistence of "ethclasses" in the face of continuing discrimination by older stock Americans that blocked structural assimilation for the second and third generation descendents of immigrants. By creating a parallel set of social institutions, immigrants were able to find avenues for social advancement, leadership, community service, and respect than may have been possible in the broader community. Many of these institutions were centered in ethnic churches and religiously affiliated associations, such as the Knights of Columbus, the Sons of Italy, B'nai Brith, and comparable organizations for women and adolescents.

Churches and temples also become central to the lives of immigrants by catering to their needs through the provision of resources and services. The bonds of faith are reinforced when a religious community can provide nonspiritual fellowship and practical assistance for the many problems that immigrants face. Almost all studies of contemporary immigrant churches and temples describe the multiple services provided to newcomers. Immigrants and their families go to church to acquire information about housing, employment opportunities, and other problems. Churches sponsor classes to help immigrants to learn English, deal with their Americanized children, and acquire benefits for their aging parents. Young immigrants or the second generation can go to church for help with their homework, for social activities, and to meet prospective marriage partners who will likely meet with parental approval.

The social, cultural, and socioeconomic roles of American churches, from potluck dinners to job referrals, are not limited to immigrant churches and temples. Most American churches, synagogues, temples, and mosques respond to religious and spiritual needs while also catering to the everyday practical needs of their members. This model of religious organization has helped successive generations of immigrants and their children to become American. And, in turn, the long history and diversity of immigrants to the United States have played a major role in creating a unique American religious landscape that is pluralist, generally observant, and very responsive to the cultural and socioeconomic needs of adherents.

REFERENCES

Alba, R. and V. Nee
2003 *Remaking the American Mainstream: Assimilation and Contemporary Immigration.* Cambridge, MA: Harvard University Press.

Archdeacon, T. J.
1983 *Becoming American: An Ethnic History.* New York: Free Press.

Bankston, C. L. and M. Zhou
2000 "De Facto Congregationalism and Socioeconomic Mobility in Laotian and Vietnamese Immigrant Communities: A Study of Religious Institutions and Social Change," *Review of Religious Research,* 41:453–470.

1995 "Religious Participation, Ethnic Identification, and Adaptation of Vietnamese Adolescents in an Immigrant Community," *The Sociological Quarterly,* 36:523–534.

Barton, J.
1975 *Peasants and Strangers: Italians, Rumanians, and Slovaks in an American City, 1890–1950.* Cambridge, MA: Harvard University Press.

Blessing, P. J.
1980 "Irish." In *Harvard Encyclopedia of American Ethnic Groups.* Ed. S. Thernstrom, A. Orlov and O. Handlin. Cambridge: Harvard University Press.

Bodnar, J.
1985 *The Transplanted: A History of Immigrants in Urban America.* Bloomington, IN: Indiana University Press.

Buczek, D. S.
1976 "Polish American Priests and the American Catholic Hierarchy: A View from the 1920s," *Polish American Studies,* 33:34–43.

Camarillo, A.
1979 *Chicanos in a Changing Society: From Mexican Pueblos to American Barrios in Santa Barbara and Southern California, 1848–1930.* Cambridge, MA: Harvard University Press.

Cinel, D.
1982 *From Italy to San Francisco: The Immigrant Experience.* Stanford, CA: Stanford University Press.

Coleman, J., T. Hoffer, and S. Kilgore
1982 *High School Achievement: Public, Catholic, and Private Schools Compared.* New York: Basic Books.

Daniels, R.
1991 *Coming to America: A History of Immigration and Ethnicity in American Life.* New York: HarperPerennial.

Dinnerstein, L.
1994 *Anti-Semitism in America.* New York: Oxford.

Dolan, J. P.
1975 *The Immigrant Church: New York's Irish and German Catholics.* Baltimore, MD: Johns Hopkins University Press.

Ebaugh, H. R, and J. S. Chafetz
2000 *Religion and the New Immigrants: Continuities and Adaptations in Immigrant Congregations.* New York: AltaMira Press.

————, eds.
2002 *Religion across Borders: Transnational Immigrant Networks.* New York: AltaMira Press.

Finke, R. and R. Stark
1992 *The Churching of America: Winners and Losers in the Religious Economy.* New Brunswick, NJ: Rutgers University Press.

Fischer, D. H.
1989 *Albion's Seed: Four British Folkways in America.* New York: Oxford University Press.

Fitzpatrick, J. P. and D. T. Gurak
1979 *Hispanic Intermarriage in New York City: 1975.* New York: Hispanic Research Center, Fordham University.

Gordan, M.
1964 *Assimilation in American Life: The Role of Race, Religion, and National Origins.* New York: Oxford University Press.

Handlin, O.
1973 *The Uprooted.* Second Edition. Boston: Little, Brown and Company.

Herberg, W.
1960 *Protestant, Catholic, Jew: An Essay in American Religious Sociology.* Revised edition. Garden City, NY: Anchor Books.

Higham, J.
1988 *Strangers in the Land: Patterns of American Nativism, 1860–1925.* Second Edition. New Brunswick, NJ: Rutgers University Press.

Hout, M. and A. M. Greeley
1987 "The Center Doesn't Hold: Church Attendance in the United States, 1940–1984," *American Sociological Review,* 52:325–345.

Hurh, W. M. and K. C. Kim
1984 *Korean Immigrants in the United States: A Structural Analysis of Ethnic Confinement and Adhesive Adaptation.* Cranbury, NJ: Associated University Presses.

Kennedy, R. J. R.
1952 "Single or Triple Melting Pot? Intermarriage Trends in New Haven, 1870–1950," *American Journal of Sociology,* 58:56–59.

————
1944 "Single or Triple Melting Pot? Intermarriage Trends in New Haven, 1870–1940," *American Journal of Sociology,* 49:331–339.

Klinkner, P. A. and R. M. Smith
1999   *The Unsteady March: The Rise and Decline of Racial Equality in the United States.*
Chicago: University of Chicago Press.

Kurien, P.
2002   "'We Are Better Hindus Here': Religion and Ethnicity among Indian Americans." In
Religions in Asian America: Building Faith Communities. Ed. P. G. Min and J. H. Kim.
Walnut Creek, CA: AltaMira Press.

Larkin, E.
1984   *The Historical Dimensions of Irish Catholicism.* Washington, DC: The Catholic University of America Press.

Lenski, G.
1963   *The Religious Factor: A Sociologist's Inquiry.* Garden City, NY: Doubleday and Company.

Lopata, H. Z.
1976   *Polish Americans: Status Competition in an Ethnic Community.* Englewood Cliffs, NJ:
Prentice-Hall.

Min, P. G.
1992   "The Structure and Social Functions of Korean Churches in the United States,"
International Migration Review, 26(4):1370–1394.

Min, P. G. and J. H. Kim, eds.
2001   *Religions in Asian America: Building Faith Communities.* Walnut Creek: AltaMira Press.

Morawska, E.
1996   *Insecure Prosperity: Small Town Jews in Industrial America, 1890–1940.* Princeton, NJ:
Princeton University Press.

Nelli, H. S.
1980   "Italians." In *Harvard Encyclopedia of American Ethnic Groups.* Ed. S. Thernstrom, A.
Orlov and O. Handlin. Cambridge, MA: Harvard University Press.

Roof, W. C. and W. McKinney
1987   *America's Mainline Religion: Its Changing Shape and Future.* New Brunswick, NJ:
Rutgers University Press.

Russo, N. J.
1968   "Three Generations of Italians in New York City: Their Religious Acculturation,"
International Migration Review, 3(2):3–17.

Sánchez, G. J.
1993   *Becoming Mexican American: Ethnicity, Culture and Identity in Chicano Los Angeles,
1900–1945.* New York: Oxford University Press.

Smith, T.
1978   "Religion and Ethnicity in America," *The American Historical Review,* 83:1155–1185.

Stark, R. and W. Bainbridge
1996   *A Theory of Religion.* Republished edition. New Brunswick, NJ: Rutgers University
Press.

Tomasi, S.
1975   *Piety and Power: The Role of Italian Parishes in the New York Metropolitan Area,
1880–1930.* New York: Center for Migration Studies.

Vecoli, R.
1969 "Prelates and Peasants: Italian Immigrants and the Catholic Church," *Journal of Social History*, 2:217–268.

———
1964 "Contadini in Chicago: A Critique of The Uprooted," *The Journal of American History*, 51:404–417.

Warner, S.
1998 "Introduction: Immigration and Religious Communities in the United States." In *Gatherings in Diaspora: Religious Communities and the New Immigration*. Ed. S. Warner and J. G. Witter. Philadelphia: Temple University Press.

Warner, S. and J. G. Wittner, eds.
1998 *Gatherings in Diaspora: Religious Communities and the New Immigration*. Philadelphia: Temple University Press.

Warner, W. L. and L. Srole
1945 *The Social Systems of American Ethnic Groups*. New Haven, CT: Yale University Press.

Woo, W.
1991 "Chinese Protestants in the San Francisco Bay Area." In *Entry Denied: Exclusion and the Chinese Community in America, 1882–1943*. Ed. S. Chan. Philadelphia, PA: Temple University Press.

Yang, F.
2002 "Religious Diversity among the Chinese in America." In *Religions in Asian America: Building Faith Communities*. Ed. P. G. Min and J. H. Kim. Walnut Creek, CA: AltaMira Press.

Zhou, M., C. Bankston and R. Kim
2002 "Rebuilding Spiritual Lives in the New Land: Religious Practices among Southeast Asian Refugees in the United States." In *Religions in Asian America: Building Faith Communities*. Ed. P. G. Min and J. H. Kim. Walnut Creek, CA: AltaMira Press.

Chapter 14

RELIGION AND INCORPORATION[1]
Islam in France and Germany

Riva Kastoryano

Religion, like language, is closely related to national history. The same can be said about secularism. The philosophy of Enlightenment, the foundation of secular politics in Europe, specifically in France, has placed religion in the private domain of individual believers and opposed it to "public reason." The movement of emancipation that followed the Enlightenment extracted the individual from religious and communal constraints and promoted integration into the political community comprised of individual citizens. In Germany, as a result of the long term influence of the reformation and religious wars, religious communities took a corporate character. Today the "return" of religion to public debate in Europe is associated with the settlement of post-colonial migrants, Muslims comprising a large majority.[1]

---

[1]They are mainly North Africans (820,000 Algerians, 516,000 Moroccans, 200,000 Tunisians), in France, migrants from India (689,000), the West Indies (547,000), and Pakistan (406,000) in Great Britain. The economic reconstruction of European countries also brought Turks to Germany (almost 2 million), to the Netherlands, Belgium, Sweden, Denmark and other European countries. Today, the post-colonial trajectories have been replaced by economic opportunities, and family networks and have led immigrants, whatever their historical relation to the country of immigration, throughout the European continent.

Those Muslims who have become citizens in the West today, but who have been outside the history of the relationship between church and state that shaped Western national character, are now demanding recognition and representation for Islam within national societies. This confrontation of populations having a collective identification with Islam with established European political traditions is one that blurs the accepted boundaries between private and public.

Further, the emergence of Islam as a transnational political force has become a source of tension and suspicion with regard to citizenship and loyalty. Some Europeans question Islam's compatibility with the West and the ability of its adherents to adopt Western "universal" values. A survey of French citizens reveals that the disquiet is not about immigrants, but rather Islam itself. In 1985, 42 percent of those questioned thought most immigrants (synonymous with North Africans) "will not be able to integrate into French society," an opinion that excludes Muslim migrants from national identification. But two "affairs" – the Rushdie affair in Great Britain and the headscarf affair in France – suggest that the issue is no longer the assimilation of immigrants but the recognition of a religion – Islam – and of a new emerging minority in individual European countries and the European Union as a whole.

Studies of immigrant integration have focused mainly on modes of integration in relation to principles of citizenship (Brubaker, 1992). Debates on religion, however, need to focus on the relationship between church and state in order to interpret and acknowledge diversity resulting from the immigration of Muslims. Their settlement tests the principle of secularism in the context of the emergence of multiculturalism and identity politics in different Europeans countries. Public recognition and representation of Islam challenges democratic states' approach to diversity and multiculturalism and counters a dichotomist view opposing assimilation and multiculturalism (Freeman, 2004). In this age of the "politics of recognition," I argue that it is impossible for democracies to dissociate multiculturalism from assimilation and to maintain boundaries between social, cultural and political domains.

In order to resolve the conflicts that Islam brings to secularisms that have emerged in the public space and the political community, leading liberal democratic societies need to respond to two complementary pressures: one institutional and the other political. Institutionally, the secular state is under pressure either to reshape its institutions so as to provide for the general recognition of Islam or, as Biku Parekh suggests, to extend these institutions to include the newly emerging Islam in European societies. At stake here is the institutional assimilation of diversity. Politically, states must find the means by which equal institutional representation and individual national citizenship can be reconciled. How can Muslims be integrated into the political community? How can common membership be promoted and a common civic culture defined that allows citizens to find adequate identification? What is at stake is the contemporary acceptance of Islam as part of Europe's historical continuity. The political approach strongly rejects the oft-stated argument that Islam and Western democracies are by definition "incompatible."

Both approaches suggest the necessity of a contextual analysis that focuses on how state institutions accommodate change in order to clarify the dynamics of citizenship in plural democratic societies. This article attempts to examine religion, particularly Islam, as an emergent type of corporate ethnicity in France and Germany. It seeks to address how Islam is represented and recognized in relation to the established principles that govern the interaction of church and state in the history of both countries, with an eye towards a comparison with the United States.

ETHNICIZATION OF RELIGION IN FRANCE AND GERMANY

Several studies of new immigrant groups in the United States indicate that religion has been a basis for shaping their communities in their new land. Often divided by nationality, churches comprised the center of efforts to maintain and transmit the values of the old country. Charles Hirschman (2004) claims that historically "immigrants become Americans by joining a church and participating in its religious and community life." A recent study shows how America succeeded in dealing with religious diversity because "the mills of ideological and definitional change grind slowly and that, consequently, the Americans and America-watchers of any given era, employing time-honored definitions, could easily refer to the United States as the showcase for religious pluralism" (Hutchison, 2003). Peter Schuck (2003) wonders "why is protection of religious diversity a constitutional value" and argues that religious diversity emerged in 1965 as a political ideal linked to immigrants' assimilation. He shows that historically "religious identities have played important, often decisive roles in orienting them to American civil society, effecting their integration into it, and eventually incorporating them into the polity."

One aspect of such an assimilation in France has been the acceptance and internalization by immigrants of the separation between religion and public life. Historical studies have pointed out that the "cult of assimilation," as the basis of national unity, produced in citizens an "indifference" to their separate linguistic or religious origins, which became obscured or suppressed in private life once they passed through the "mill of institutions" (Noiriel, 1987). The same was true in early twentieth century Germany, where "Germanization" meant forced assimilation with reference not to religion but to language.

However, as Georges Balandier (1988) correctly emphasized, "it is in religion, especially its cultural or ecclesiastical institution, that tradition finds its most solid anchor." When newcomers arrive in a new society, religion responds to the loss of past common references and establishes social bonds. In the early days of immigration, immigrants, especially those from rural areas, structured their communities around religion. They were trying to maintain close relations with their homelands and extended families for as long as possible in order to ensure respect for their cultural traditions. Religion provided the most important components of moral and social order, ethnic pride, and "self-enhancement." Such feelings led to a "defensive traditionalism," which sheltered them from the "danger" of assimilation even when the religion of the immigrants was not different from that of the larger society. Using Polish immigration in France as an example, Janine Ponty has shown that the Church constituted "the soul of resistance." The merging of Polish national and religious sentiment caused immigrant families in Pas-de-Calais to bring a priest from Poland to organize the local community (Ponty, 1988). Similarly, in the early 1970s, at the very beginning of their settlement, Muslim immigrants in France and Germany brought imams (Muslim religious leaders) from their homelands to manage the prayer halls in concert with municipal authorities. Those imams were to help the immigrants transmit moral values and identity by teaching extracurricular courses on the Koran to the children, usually on Saturday afternoon or Sunday. Moreover, the imams stayed long enough to become central figures of the community, particularly when it was necessary to pray following the death of relatives, prepare their coffins, and send their bodies back to the homeland.

Religion in this context is limited to the private spheres of the family and local community. Even though Islam is defined by immigrants themselves in terms of practice, tradition and moral values, its perception as a "permanent difference" both by immigrants and public authorities constitutes a step toward the construction and recognition of an ethnic group, generating an "awareness of belonging." This awareness found an institutional basis with the "right to difference" promoted by the socialist government in 1981. Promotion of this right was followed by the liberalization of the law allowing foreigners to create their own voluntary associations and therefore "institutionalize" such difference. Spontaneous gatherings of immigrants based on interpersonal relations in areas of concentrated settlement therefore found an institutional and formal structure in associations and have become true identity organizations. Ever since, foreigners acting in labor unions, political organizations, or parties (particularly the French Communist Party) have organized around special cultural traits that have been invented and reaffirmed through their relationship to politics. While in the 1960s or 1970s immigrants expressed their interests in terms of class, today the younger generation expresses such concerns in terms of cultural or religious "identities of origin," which have been reinterpreted within the framework of new collective actions. These associations were a refuge, sometimes even a sanctuary, where culture, religion, ethnicity, and nation of origin were interpreted, became manifest, and took root.

Public resources legitimized the organization of immigrant associations. The declared objective of public authorities has been to make public opinion accept differences and counter racism. By encouraging the institutionalization of collective identities through associations, the republican state intended to instruct the accommodation of differences into its ideological framework and structures. In this way, rhetoric converged with policy. From the point of view of association activists, identities are now the element structuring their communities in order to compete for state resources.

With the proliferation of associations in the 1980s, Islam became an agent in the discourse of action or reaction. Even the so-called secular associations integrated into their activities the celebration of Islamic holidays, like Ramadan, and animal sacrifice. Although the state officially does not support religious organizations, state funding for public service and community groups that incorporated Islamic identity and culture into their activities indirectly gave greater public value to religious organizations in the eyes of the Muslim population. From comprising only one component of culture in early secular associations, Islam has now come to signify culture in its entirety and has become another way of reappropriating identity.

Such an appropriation has crystallized around the so-called "headscarf affair." The issue shook French society for the first time in November 1989, when three teenage girls arrived at their public school wearing Islamic headscarves. The event unleashed a flood of commentary on identity: the identity of the latest wave of immigrants and of the nation. The emphasis lay on Islam and its compatibility with the secular principles of French society. Moreover, the issue used *laïcité* to illustrate French differences from the secularism of other Western states.[2] Public opinion and public authorities were torn between defensive republicanism and a pluralistic liberalism. The political class and certain intellectuals took it upon themselves to remind society of the basic principles of the Republic, principles that constitute the "core of a national identity" and the "way of life" for immigrants in a *laïc* (secular) country.

Nevertheless, secularism, or *laïcité*, remains ambiguous about the boundary between culture and religion. Culture includes religious identity, while religion refers to beliefs or practices that may be culturally specific. Studies on French religious expression show a constant decline in practice, a statistic much easier to measure than more abstract cultural references. Since the principle of *laïcité* was established, such a decline has occurred for all religions that, like Islam today, have been outside the pubic sphere. In reaction to issues raised by the headscarf affair in 1989, the principle of *laïcité* has undergone several interpretations and has emerged as the "official religion" of France. Today, Islam is at the core of the redefinition of *laïcité* and serves as its mirror. The headscarf was perceived as challenging the long historical process of national assimilation and the transformation not just of "the peasant," but also of the foreigner or the immigrant "into Frenchmen" (Weber, 1979).

The headscarf affair has situated Islam at the core of negotiations challenging the relationship between state and religion (Kastoryano, 2002). The case of the headscarf has made an issue of the balance of power between French perception of a national identity on the one hand, and the identity of the last waves of immigrants on the other. In this dichotomy, the former is remolded around *laïcité* and the latter around Islam, as if the law of the Republic were being challenged by the "law of the Koran," as it is being spread and practiced by the local Muslim institutions in the suburbs (*banlieues*). Even though politicians rallied around the case of the headscarf in the name of *laïcité*, this mobilization reinforced Islam as the core of a collective identity of North African immigrants and their descendants, making religious identity paramount over that of national origins. As Hirschman (2004) mentions in reference to Oscar Handlin's view of immigrant assimilation in

---

[2]In the remainder of the text I will use the word *laïcité* as a French form of secularism that has no exact translation in English.

America, "national origins blend into religious identities by the second or third generation." But in the French case, the same religious identification is a consequence of the interactions between public opinion, public authorities and immigrant groups, rather than the result of a generational process of assimilation as in the United States.

At the same time, the state's refusal to acknowledge associations of a strictly religious nature reinforced Islam as the locus of identity. Islam is perceived as a source of pride for action independent from supposedly secular, cultural associations subsidized by public agencies. Muslim religious institutions position themselves as an alternative to cultural associations and contribute to a withdrawal into their own circle, but in most cases they work alongside cultural associations when it is a question of their social utility. A "social division of labor" has been established between cultural and religious associations in immigrant neighborhoods: whereas the so-called secular associations are content dealing with social action, the religious ones address the issue of identity.

Mobilizations around the headscarf issue have strengthened the leadership of Islamic associations as representatives of a community taking shape around Islam. The imams, who have been sent by their countries of origin within bilateral accords giving them official status or who represent political parties such as the Islamic Salvation Front (FIS) in Algeria or the religious party (Fazilet at that time) in Turkey, have ordained themselves spokesmen for their "community." But the French state, by selecting imams of all ideologies as interlocutors in order to calm tensions, has inadvertently increased the negotiating power of the religious associations by excluding others or forcing them into the Islamic sphere. This emphasis on Islam as a new subject or object of French society and on Muslim populations within a cultural and ideological public discourse has facilitated Muslim families' choice of situating religious identity at the center of their political interests. The emergence of Islam in the public space corresponds with that of ethnic groups in the United States. The efforts to shape a religious community with its institutions claiming public recognition have engendered disputes over boundaries between political and ethnic community in France.

As France was suffering from an existential crisis caused by the challenge to secularism raised by the Islamic headscarf, the German political class regarded French concerns as an exaggeration. The German press often reported that, whereas the daily sight of girls dressed in headscarves caused unease among the French because it was seen as a threat to the republican tradition, the wearing of headscarves was considered completely natural to people in Germany.

The surprise expressed by German public opinion to the scale of the headscarf debate in France affords us two interpretations. The first rests on a different conception of separation between church and state and on a more distinct internalization of religious pluralism in Germany. The second posits a general indifference about the dress codes of foreigners who are not regarded as part of the nation but as a separate population set. If Germany is not a country of immigration, as official discourse stated clearly for quite some time, there was little interest in the religious customs of the "guests" so long as they did not affect public order and remained within civil society.

During the 1980s, militants of Turkish immigrant origin appeared on the German public scene and demanded recognition of a collective identity. In 1981, the government created the Committee for Foreigners (*Ausländerbeauftragte der Bundesregierung*) in Berlin. This federal institution enjoyed freedom of action in all local decisions, principally in helping foreigners to create their own organizations (*Selbshilfe*). The equivalent of the Social Action Fund (FAS) in France, this committee finances immigrant association projects judged to be of social benefit, *i.e.*, designed to unite young foreigners of every nationality with Germans in common activities. Social benefit includes the salvaging of deviants, unemployed persons, delinquents, or young members of violent gangs. The idea is akin to community organizations in the United States that unite migrants by national or religious origin (or both) as a means of integrating them into the community structure. But in the German case, nationality became the primary source for (Turkish) ethnicity whereas in France religion became the basis of ethnicity. In 1998, when the laws concerning access to German nationality were debated, not coincidentally, the case of a naturalized German teacher of Afghan origin, who wore a headscarf at work as a civil servant in the *Land* of Baden-Württemberg, upset German public authorities just as much as the wearing of headscarves by students had in France. As a result of a federal court ruling in Karlsruhe, the teacher was banned from the school and excluded from public office.

Since then, there have been many public debates in Germany about the function of civil servants and the wearing of the headscarf, mainly by teachers. Whereas French authorities first encouraged negotiations between students' parents and teachers or school administrators, cases in Germany have been brought to the courts, whose decisions can vary from one *Land* to another. In some cases the arguments are focused on the competence and skill of the teachers and in other cases on public education and the diffusion of Western education and norms (in Baden Württemberg and Leipzig) (Tietze, forthcoming). This debate must be seen as related to debates over citizenship and the inclusion of the foreign minority into the political community and civil society and whether they ought to remain *Auslandische Mitburgeren,* foreign co-citizens, or become full citizens, with equal rights and duties.

Thus, in both countries the creation of a community became an "option" (Goulbourne, 1995) to define an identity that would be a basis for collective action and self-assertion. The preference of religion in France and the preference of nationality in Germany correspond to these states' understandings of difference and ethnicity. From the perspective of migrant populations, their identities as minorities within Europe appear to be contiguous with their collective identities with their home countries. In North Africa, nationality and religion have been officially linked. In Turkey, secularization has been officially enforced and, ironically, Islam has become liberated from its national and political taboo among Turkish Muslims who have migrated to Europe. Nevertheless, the legitimacy of collective demands in both France and Germany relies on normative affirmation of multiculturalism and cultural diversity in liberal Western societies. The question they face is how to insure a historical continuity between the principles and ideals of secularism and at the same time integrate the religious diversity created by Islam.

Laïcité, Secularism and Islam

According to Article 2 of the French Constitution (1958), "France is an indivisible, secular (*laïc*), democratic, and social Republic. It insures equality to all of its citizens before the law without distinction of origin, race and religion. It respects all beliefs." In this respect it is not different from the American Constitution, which emphasizes the "protection of religious diversity as a value" (Schuck, 2003). What is different between these countries is the organization of religious diversity, its relationship to the state, and the interpretation – not its juridicial definition – of the principle of separation of church and state.

Interpretations and practices diverge according to national context – the dominant national, religious, cultural, and political projects of nation-state building. Established and internalized as a "reasonable" approach to religion, the concept, principle, and practice of secularism have come into public debate over the past twenty years as Western societies have been faced with Islam within their national territories and societies. Although secularism has been represented as a fundamental value of Western societies, debate has made manifest an unresolved ambiguity in the concept and its establishment in the formation of liberal states. The ambiguity stems from the concept's loose definition and its lack of coincidence with social realities. In other words, there is a gap between the principle and its application when dealing with religions such as Islam that until now have been outside the history of the relationship between church and state.

Since the legal separation of church and state in 1905, the principle of *laïcité* has been taken for granted in debates over church and state relations. This separation began with the Enlightenment, when *laïcité* was first defined as both an "exit from religion" and the "public use of individual reason." In republican France, secularism has become a dogma expressed as the very definition of republican culture, in opposition to clericalism and to "Catholic culture." *Laïcité* was established after a century of struggle between church and state. For the French republic, it has been considered as progress, a step towards modernity, and a passage from community ruled by the church to society ruled by law. The new structure of secular power replaced the religious community with a political community, excluded religion from public political life, and gave rise to a still-present anti-religious and anti-clerical discourse which renders *laïcité* a "particular" experience.

In France, the separation of church and state confers institutional legal status on the Catholic clergy, the Protestants of the National Federation of Protestant Churches of France, and to the Jews governed by the Consistory created under Napoleon. The "universality" of secularism, however, relies on the principle of equality according to which there is no domination of one religion of the national majority over other religions in a *de facto* minority situation. Thus, the neutrality of the state towards religion shies away from religion but ensures that individuals can practice "freedom of conscience." The principle of a dichotomous separation of the private and religious from the public and political generated a significant amount of controversy from the outset because it questions the moral support of religion in public life and its replacement with "civic virtues" that are necessary to define a shared public space. Counter to the American "notion that social and civic integration is obtained through religious participation in ethnic churches," as underlined by Hirschman (2004), the principle of *laïcité* in France implies the participation of the individual in politics as a citizen, free of community and ethnic ties and equal before the law. Representative institutions have been adapted to the principle, and special status has been assigned to the majority church and to the clergy as well as to "minority" religions existing in civil society.

In Germany, the philosophy of Enlightenment (*Aufklärung*) was not against religion, just as rationality was not against Protestant piety. The concern for equality consisted mainly of destroying the barriers between the clergy, the nobility, the middle class, and the peasantry. In this sense, *Aufklärung* refers to both secularization and modernization (Müller, 1995). After the formation of the federal state, the *Kulturkampf* was characterized by an effort to guarantee social cohesion by minimizing the role of the Catholic Church while also limiting Protestant influence on politics.

Traces of German secularism date back to the Treaties of Westphalia in 1648, which not only put an end to the religious wars, but also asserted the superiority of territorial allegiances based on the principle of *cujus regio, ejus religio* (whose realm, their religion) and the decline of religion relative to secular power. German secularism expressed itself in terms of a religious pluralism, recognizing the denominational duality of Protestants and Catholics in the public space. This recognition resulted in the interpenetration of ecclesiastical, social, and political structures that perpetuate the two churches' denominational character to the present day. The Basic Law reinforces the article of the Weimar Constitution regarding "the freedom of conscience and religion" (art.137.4). In addition, the law integrates the principle of the separation between church and state and does not recognize an established church (Oédraogo, 1994). The religious freedom of Catholics and Lutherans assumed a corporative nature, "granting equal rights only to communities formed as corporations" and recognized by the public law (François, 1993). The historian Etienne François emphasizes the permanence of identities in the mentality of denominational behavior, giving them anthropological, social, and cultural dimensions which surpass the strictly religious sphere.

The difference between French and German secularism originates from their relation to public space and to civil society. Contrary to *laïcité* in France, which excludes religion from public life, secularization in Germany constitutes Catholic and Protestant churches as corporate bodies in public law. In Germany, the churches are recognized in legal terms by their social and moral functions, and the state levies a tax on their behalf which is paid by all citizens who are members of these congregations. Churches therefore constitute semi-public, "semi sovereign" institutions according to Peter Katzenstein (1988), and they enjoy an important role in the stability of German society. Relevant to this role, German churches and religious organizations assisted foreigners during the 1960s, when the needs of workers from the entire Mediterranean basin were handled by denominational charities. The Catholic *Caritas* was mainly concerned with Catholic immigrants from Spain and Italy, while the Protestant *Diakonisches Werk* dealt with Orthodox Greeks and Serbs. The *Arbeiterwohlfahrt,* which was created in 1919 by the Social Democratic Party, introduced Turkish Muslims to the German welfare state.

Different national histories, interpretations, and definitions of social cohesion led to different institutional settings in France and Germany with regard to religion. But in both national contexts, the distinctions between private and public and the neutrality of the state regarding religion are sources of contradictions when the state confronts Islam. Although Islam constitutes one element of pluralism and diversity among ethnic groups in the United States, Islam emerges as a "minority religion" in European nation-states. Such a conceptual difference is reflected in the different understandings and applications of multiculturalism and the recognition of diversity in European countries and the United States.

RECOGNITION AND "INSTITUTIONAL ASSIMILATION"

Multiculturalist promotion of diversity in the public sphere is expressed in France and Germany in terms of recognition. If secularism is the exclusion of religion from the public sphere in the name of neutrality of the state and equality among all religions in the civil society, recognition brings religion – like cultural and ethnic identity in the United States – back to the public sphere for equal representation. As a result, there is no clear boundary between private and public since, as through identity politics, states penetrate into the private sphere and make a public affair out of the social reality of religious difference. This evolution leads to a reinterpretation of the notion of neutrality in light of multiculturalism, particularly when the politics of recognition positions the group to be "recognized" specifically by its religion. The question is not how to promote differences, but rather how to assimilate them institutionally. The task becomes integrating these differences into state institutions for equal representation along with other religions, preserving the public sphere from private expressions of belonging, and promoting a common civic culture internalized precisely through institutional assimilation.

Secularism is an element of national history that is related to the institutional setting of religion and its contextual accommodations. In

France, although the fight between church and state in 1905 never addressed the question of minorities, Islam today raises a double challenge: that of a minority in a republican state that rhetorically rejects the very concept of minority, and that of a religion in the public space. For the political class, the headscarf affair revealed that a minority religion has become established in society and its institutions, especially public schools. For the proponents of Islamist associations, the headscarf has become an affirmation of identity for a part of the immigrant population. It is nonetheless an issue that necessitates negotiation with the public authorities: the negotiation of the permanent cultural and structural presence of Islam and its cultural expression (Kastoryano, 2002).

Since 1990, following the passionate debates concerning the place of religion in French society aroused by the headscarf affair, successive Interior Ministers from both the Left and the Right tried to create representative Islamic institutions. In 1991, Pierre Joxe created a Council of Thought on Islam in France, the CORIF, in order to explore different means of adapting the requirements of Islam to the norms of society (or vice-versa). "Unable to represent Islam, I have withheld the suggestion of Jacque Berque, who stated that it was possible to symbolize Islam," he explained in an interview in *Débat* (Joxe, 1990). Subsequently, the next Minister, Pasqua, of the Rally for the Republic (RPR), created a Representative Council of Muslims, with the idea that "the issue of Islam must be treated as a French issue." He declared in *Le Monde* of January 11, 1995: "I have always wanted Islam to progress from the status of a tolerated religion in France to that of a religion accepted by all, and one that forms part of the French spiritual landscape." His successor, Jean-Pierre Chevènement (Socialist Party), recalled that the recognition of Islam was "not a question of Left or Right but a national question which affects the Republican state" and set up a commission called a "Consultation" that also gave its name to a journal. He declares in the first issue that his goal is to "help Muslims to form themselves into a religious minority in France." Finally, on April 16, 2003, Interior Minister Nicolas Sarkozy succeeded in creating a French Council of the Muslim Faith (Conseil Français du Culte Musulman), which elected its first national representative.

Thus, Islam has been integrated according to a logic that Danièle Lochak (1989) refers to as a "pragmatic management of differences." It is a logic that consists of "gradually introducing the minimum amount of institutionalization necessary to resolve in concrete terms the practical problems resulting from the existence of minority groups" with the objective of eventually achieving "an official recognition which in its turn would lead to the institutionalization of differences."

This process clearly aims to organize a transition from Islam in France to an Islam of France; from the simple presence of Muslims and their visible practices in French space to an Islam that will express itself and grow within the framework of national institutions. The latter assumes its liberation from foreign influences, especially those of the homeland. But the discussion is far from over. "Nationalizing" Islam and making it a "French Islam" might introduce a liberating process. This was how the shift of the Jews of France to "French Judaism" took place, if only in terminology. In both cases, representation implies a legal protection more broadly guaranteed by all representative organizations initiated by the state. In this case, the state intervenes both as arbiter and as dispenser of official recognition. This experience makes existing representative organizations, particularly Jewish institutions, which are older and which were produced and developed with respect to secularism, the reference point for associations of Islamic immigrants. France-Plus, for example, proposes the creation of a Muslim Consistory, with one of its advocates arguing that "secular Islam is completely compatible with life in France." The chairman of the Federation of the Muslims of France, on the other hand, rejects this plan precisely because of the argument advanced by France-Plus: "They want us to copy the model of the Consistory made up of people who are Jews but not religious." Note that the same quarrel divided observant or believing Jews from secular Jews when the centralized Consistory was established and its leaders insisted on secularizing it by removing all religious content (Cohen, 1977).

It is interesting to note that while Muslims now refer to the legal status of Jewish institutions, some Jews increasingly draw on Muslims' claims for recognition to express their sense of belonging to a "Jewish community" and signaling their rejection of the concept of "Jews of France." Inspired by Muslim aspirations for a permanent redefinition of secularity, even the Catholic Church of France has revived the discussion of its relations with the state. Contesting the creation of the French Council of the Muslim Faith, Cardinal Lustiger criticized the initiative by declaring in *Le Monde* of April 14, 2003 that a "state religion is being created."

Recognition of Islam has thus spawned a general revision of the place of religions in the public sphere, challenging not only the concept of republican secularity, its universalism, and its practices, but also the connection between church and state in France. As if to assert historic continuity, the state has taken refuge behind an "inclusionist" strategy and discourse that encourages representative institutions to make their chairmen its collective spokespersons and to consider their members full partners in the political community. The greatest change, however, is the explicit reference to religion and its representation leading to the recognition of an implicit ethnicity in France even if its recognition remains taboo.

In Germany, the same question regarding the public recognition of Islam affects in a more complex way the status of Turks as an ethnic minority, based on both a Turkish national identity and a Muslim religious identity. As early as the 1980s, the German Commission on Foreigners had debated ways of including Islam in religious pluralism. The debate relied on the definition of a community given by the Commission as "a grouping of people who feel that they are linked to one or several deities and which eventually give rise to a faith." Such a definition refers to a religious conception of community and dates back to the nineteenth century when the religious freedom granted to both Catholics and Lutherans took on the corporate character of "granting equal rights to communities constituted into organized bodies" (François, 1993). Therefore, recognition by public authorities of a "Muslim community" was broadly proclaimed as a means of integrating Turkish immigrants into German society. The argument was firmly based on the official place of religion in German public space and the role of churches in taking care of foreigners in the manner of a "religious society" (*Religionsgesellschaft*). On March 1, 1979, the Confederation of Islamic Cultural Centers presented a request for recognition along these lines within the legal framework of the corporate body of public law (*Körperschaft des öffentlichen Rechts*) from which other religions in Germany benefit. The Islamic Federation of Berlin, hoping to gather all Muslim associations in the *Land* of Berlin, asked for recognition as *Religionsgemeischaft* in 1980, and this status was finally given to them in 2000 (*see Deutsches Verwlatungsblatt*, July 1, 2000). After twenty years of fighting for representation, the federation obtained the authorization for Islamic instruction in Berlin in 2001 (*Süddetsche Zeitung*, October 26, 2001). So far, this is the only such case in Germany, but it affected the organization of other Muslim associations in Berlin and other *Länder* (de Galembert and Tietze, 2002). Recognition, however, has raised questions about the place of Islam in public instruction, just as with the Christian faiths.

In both France and Germany the central or regional public authorities who have attempted to integrate Islam into an institutional, historical continuity have run into difficulties with the Muslim populations. The question of their representation has led to internal organizational negotiations over ideological, ethnic, national, regional, and religious components of collective identity in order to reach a consensus on terms of representation. This has caused heads of associations in both countries to organize, go beyond internal divisions, and seek a legitimate collective representation among Muslims. The institutional structures in each country are different, but the issue is the same – that of democratic equality in societies that are *de facto* pluralist. The question of recognition is all the more important, as it is closely related to that of incorporation on the basis of equal citizenship. The negotiations around collective recognition are, in fact, related to negotiations of the terms of individual citizenship and of the new methods for including immigrant populations in the political community (Kastoryano, 2002).

An institutional approach maintains the role of the state as both a legitimate source of power and as a legal and democratic guarantor of equal representation and citizenship. This approach therefore emphasizes historical continuity and the importance of context in either a descriptive or normative analysis of identities. Asking for recognition as a minority allows a group that declares a specific identity to emerge from their political marginality and thus express a struggle for liberation. But unlike the liberation of the Enlightenment, which separated religion from public life and the individual from his community to guarantee his essential identification with the national community, the demand for recognition in this case is spawned by a desire for participation with equal rights for religious community identities within the structures of both the state and society.

While the political and normative issues remain justice and equality, the social issue is the ethnicization of a religious minority, with Islam as the main identity element, thus cementing a "legitimate" community. Although not all Muslims necessarily recognize themselves within such an institutional representation, they express their need for social and cultural inclusion and mobilize against racism, discrimination, or any other form of exclusion. The question is then: does institutional justice compensate for social injustice? Can the demand for recognition be limited to official representation when other institutions, such as schools, are not fulfilling their function in integrating and promoting "civic values" as a basis for social, cultural and religious equality? Religious diversity and its expression in the public sphere has imposed new realities on Western Europe and will require a continued redefinition of the relationship between religion and state in order to calm the tensions within society and the political community: a new social contract combining reason and religion.

Obviously, if religion appears empirically as the main cleavage, its recognition in France or Germany can be seen as the means for incorporating Muslims. But this will require going beyond a solely institutional approach and developing tools for Muslims' identification within national institutions. Nevertheless, institutional assimilation constitutes an important step toward the acceptance of the "other," which is possible if mentalities open up along with the institutional changes. For this to occur, social and political discourse, along with discourse in the media, must help immigrants – the new citizens – to identify with the state and its institutions.

For Muslims, German or French national identification can help to liberate them from external political forces of the home country and transnational networks and to push them to participate fully in the political community. Through this perspective of liberation, the law banning "all conspicuous signs of religion in public school" should be understood. Law alone cannot help to liberate the individual – especially when the individual is a woman – from community pressures in concentrated areas like the *banlieues* in France. Still, such a law is important for liberating Muslims from Islam as a political force that weighs on Muslim migrant communities wherever they are settled.

SYMBOLIC ETHNICITY OR A TRANSNATIONAL ISLAM IN EUROPE

The international dimension of ethno-religious identification has been analyzed by Herbert Gans (1979) as a component of what he calls "symbolic ethnicity," defined as an ethnicity of last resort. In politics, such ethnic identification is expressed through international preoccupations, especially concerning the country of origin. This is true, for example, among Catholics in the United States, who consider Ireland an identity symbol, just as Israel is for the Jews. In American political life, Congressional lobbyists cite these symbolic ties to justify interest groups' influence on international policy decisions. In France or Germany, more broadly in Europe, even though the political identity of Muslim immigrants has been shaped and developed primarily according to their specific relations with each state, the international agenda for Muslims is expressed through transnational networks throughout Europe and beyond. Their scope is broad and expansive with regard to nationality of origin, regional identity, and even denominations. Sometimes, their agendas call for collective identification with the Muslim world in general.

The Muslim population settled in Western Europe participates actively in the elaboration of transnational solidarity like other transborder professional, social or political networks covering the European space like a spider's web. They fit within Europe, defined by the Single European Act of 1986 as a "space without internal frontiers" in which the "free movement of goods, property, and capital is safeguarded." Some of the existing networks are formal, some informal; some are based on identity, some on interest; and some are based on both identity and interest. Some arise from local initiatives in countries of immigration, while others begin in the country of origin and extend through formal or informal international organizations – such as religious ones. Immigrants' networks have been initiated by European supranational institutions, such as the European Parliament or the European Commission (Kastoryano, 2003).

Such networks, built on common interests defined and formulated at the European level in terms of equality of rights, were intended to "liberate" immigrants from the politics of both their home and host countries and to express claims beyond nation states. According to the logic of the European harmonization of institutions, these networks were intended to define a common denominator for claims beyond their relationships with nation states. From this perspective, Islam has provided a basis for transstate and transnational organization, with the common identification and experience of being Muslim in Europe. Islamic associations use the European space in the same way as do cultural and social associations, but Muslims receive no support in the name of secularism, either by national or supranational institutions. Representatives of Islamic associations work mainly in connection with the home countries, with international organizations, or both. The home countries try to rally their nationals to achieve recognition from the European authorities, and they reactivate migrants' home country loyalties through religion and contributions to the creation of a transnational community. International organizations interested in Islam in Europe mobilize resources to allow Muslims to go beyond the national diversity in the various countries of the European Union and to create a single religious identification and a transnational solidarity based on this diversity. Because of this policy, international and denominational networks have fit into the European system and rival the sociocultural associations on a local level.

Although Islamic associations are autonomous with respect to European welfare states, they do interact with the public authorities of the countries where Muslims reside in a manner similar to so-called cultural associations. Although these Islamic associations are fragmented from within by various home and host national identities and denominations, more and more, Islam represents a unifying identity among Muslim immigrants for asserting collective interest and structuring a transnational community that transcends the boundaries of member-states. The internal diversity to the transnational community is "recentered" demands for Islam's representation and recognition within the institutional framework of the European Union. The objective is to promote a common identification: to be Muslim in Europe.

An obstacle to Muslim unity arises from the diversity of the nationalities, sects, and ethnocultural groups among the Muslims in Europe. But some association groups, like the *Jamaat-Tabligh* (Faith and Practice) organization, are concerned with European representation and present themselves as "multinationals," collecting several nationalities of origin while branching out in the various countries of the Union. Indian in origin and first established in Great Britain in the 1960s, this Islamic movement has extended its networks into France and Belgium, and more recently into Germany and the Netherlands, and sent missionaries into local communities to promote the faith and organizational support of Muslims (Kepel, 1987). The movement "transcends not only material boundaries, but also sects, legal schools, and Sufi orders in their ideological conception," and its activists express the desire "to be good citizens" but avoid political positions because they believe, "politics divides Islam" (Diop, 1994).

Other Islamic associations openly express the political position of their home countries and represent associations of political parties organized in Europe where they serve as representatives. One example is National Vision, which has been an affiliate of successive religious parties in Turkey and which operates 28 foreign offices in Europe, ten of them in Germany. Algerian networks associated with the Islamic Front of Salvation and its armed branch (GIA) pursue political legitimization with Muslims abroad. If these networks are necessarily transformed into structures of absorption on behalf of the religious or political identification they share with Muslims of other countries, their presence affects both Europe and the home countries, especially the overall relations between Europe and a "Muslim bloc."

In short, Islam in Europe is seeking a unity in its diversity through a transnational solidarity based on religion. Yet, as with social and cultural networks, the strategy aims at the recognition of identities that are primarily national and ethnic. Despite the influence of the home countries or international organizations that endow them with political importance, their claims are adapted to the European context. But they also raise a question of representation in European institutions, especially since the European Convention of Human Rights recognizes freedom of religion. Article 9 of the ECHR states that "every person has the right to freedom of thought, conscience, and religion. This right implies the freedom to have or adopt a religion or conviction of one's choice, as well as the freedom to demonstrate one's religion or conviction, individually or collectively, in public or in private, through worship and instruction, including the practice and performance of rituals" (Leveau, 1994).

The elaboration of transnational structures clearly reveals multiple references and allegiances: to the host country, to the home country, and to Europe through a constructed transnational community. Whether or not immigrants are citizens, their loyalty to the host country comes from sharing in its social and political institutions. The home country, despite its cultural and ethnic heterogeneity, provides emotional support and identity resources. A transnational community combining both host and home country ties represents a new reference of involvement that gives rise to the formation of a transnational identity as inspiration for political action and as an instrument for cultural and religious purposes beyond national borders.

Transnationality is, however, paradoxical. The consolidation of a transnational solidarity generally aims to influence the state from outside. Even if it contributes to the formation of "external communities," transnational networks today are imposed on the states and their national public authorities, who define the limits of their legitimacy as indispensable structures for negotiation of collective identities and interest. Clearly, the objective of transnational networks is to reinforce their representation at the European level, but their practical goal is recognition at the national level. Shall we add that Islamic activists, even the most active ones at the European level, ultimately see the states as their "adversary"? The states' predominance is visible in the difficulties that voluntary associations have in coordinating actions and claims that spring from their own initiative without the intervention of supranational institutions.

In other words, the ultimate goal is to reach a political representation that can only be defined at the national level. Rights and interests for non-European residents and citizens – for housing, employment, family reunification, mobilization against expulsion and other government programs and policies related to identity – can only be claimed from the state. But all claims at the national level imply a parallel pressure at the European level and, conversely, all claims on the European level aim to have an impact on decisions taken at the national level within each of the member states. For the Muslim populations in Europe, a transnational organization of interests that employs identity in order to win recognition at the European level reflects the Europeanization of political action, but it does not involve the Europeanization of demands. The latter remain linked to the state, the body which remains the only solid framework of reference for mobilization and negotiations.

REFERENCES

Balandier, G.
1988 *Le Désorde. L'Éloge du Mouvement,* Paris, Fayard.

Brubaker, R.
1992 *Citizenship and Nationhood in France and Germany,* Cambridge, MA: Harvard University Press.

Cohen, Albert P.
1977 *The Modernization of French Jewry: Consistory and Community in the Nineteenth Century.* Hanover, NH: Brandeis University Press.

de Galembert, C. and N. Tietze
2002 "Institutionalisierung des Islam in Deutschland. Pluralisierung der Weltanschauugen," *Mittelweg,* 36(11/1):43–62.

Déloye, Y.
1994 *Ecole et Citoyenneté. L'Individualisme Républicain de Jules Ferry à Vichy: Controverses,* Paris: Presses de Sciences-po.

Diop, M.
1994 "Structuration d'un Réseau: la Jamaat-Tabligh Société pour le Propagation de la Foi," *Revue Europeéene des Migrations Internationales,* 10(1):145–157.

François, E.
1993 *Protestants et Catholiques en Allemagne. Identités et Pluralisme, Augsbourg 1648–1806.* Paris: Albin Miche. P. 239.

Freeman, G. P.
2004 "Immigrant Incorporation in Western Democracies," *International Migration Review,* 38(3):945–969.

Gans, H.
1979 "Symbolic Ethnicity. The Future of Ethnic Groups and Cultures in America," *Ethnic and Racial Studies,* 2(1):1–21.

Goulbourne, H.
1995 *Ethnicity and Nationalism in Post Imperial Britain.* London: Cambridge University Press.

Hirschman, C.
2004 "The Role of Religion in the Origins and Adaptation of Immigrant Groups in the United States," *International Migration Review,* 38(3):1206–1233.

Hutchison, W. R.
2003 *Religious Pluralism in America, The Contentious History of a Founding Ideal.* New Haven, CT: Yale University Press.

Joxe, P.
1990 "La France vue de l'Intérieur," *Débat,* 61:15, September-October.

Kastoryano, R.

2003 "Transnational Networks and Political Participation. The Place of Immigrants in the European Union." In *Europe without Borders. Remapping Territory, Citizenship and Identity in a Transnational Age.* Ed. M. Berezin and M. Schain. Baltimore, MD: John Hopkins University Press. Pp. 64–89.

2002 *Negotiating Identities. States and Immigrants in France and Germany.* Princeton, NJ: Princeton University Press. (English translation).

Katzenstein, P.

1988 *Policy and Politics in West Germany. The Growth of a Semi-Sovereign State.* Philadelphia, PA: Temple University Press.

Kepel, G.

1987 *Les Banlieues de l'Islam.* Éd. Du Seuil.

Leveau, R.

1994 "Élements de Réflexion sur l'Islam en Europe," *Revue Européenne des Migrations Internationales,* 10(1).

Lochak, D.

1989 "Les Minorités dans le Droit Public Français: du Refus des Différences à la Gestion des Différences." In *Les Minorités et Leur Droit Depuis 1789.* CRISPA-GDM. Paris: L'Harmattan.

Müller, H.

1995 "Der Aufklärung á Weimar. Mouvement des Idées et Mutations Politiques." In *lé etat de l'Allmagne.* Ed. A. M. LeGloannec. Paris: La Découverte. Pp. 35–37.

Noiriel, G.

1987 *Le Creuset Français,* Paris: Éd. du Seuil.

Ouédraogo, M.

1994 "Eglises et Etat en Allemagne: La Difficile Laïcisation d'une Société Sécularisée." In *Religions et Laïcité dans l'Europe des Douze.* Ed. J. Baubérot. Éd. Syros. Pp. 19–21.

Ponty, J.

1988 *Polonais Méconnus. Histoire des Travailleurs Immigrés en France dans l'Entre-deux-Guerres.* Paris: Éd. de la Sorbonne.

Schuck, P.

2003 *Diversity in America. Keeping Government at a Safe Distance.* Cambridge, MA: Harvard University Press. Pp. 272–273.

Tietze, N.

Forthcoming L'Institutionalization de l'Islam en Allemagne: Les Défies pour l'Intégration Nationale.

Weber, E.

1979 *From Peasant into Frenchmen; Modernization of the Rural France, 1870–1914.* Stanford, CA: Stanford University Press.

Index

Printed in the United States
116316LV00001B/261/P